AMERICAN OUTLAW
~PRICE OF PRIDE~

JIMMY MAXWELL

This is a work of non-fiction. However, some of the
names and locations have been changed to protect the
innocent as well as the guilty.

Published by Arkmast Books.

First published in Great Britain by Arkmast Books.

First Edition

ISBN-10: 0992831180
ISBN-13: 978-0992831189

Jimmymaxwell.net

CONTENTS

DEDICATION

This book is dedicated to Mr. Big - my partner in crime.

ACKNOWLEDGMENTS

A special thanks to my fiancée, Karyn, who has let me read the same page of a book to her twenty times. Always loving and always supportive, without whom I couldn't breathe. Also, I want to thank my friend and editor Mark Parham, without your help and expertise I would still be crayoning in a coloring book. Thanks to all my friends and family that have proof-read, fact-checked and have just down right been there for me. People like you inspire me to hope for a better world.

PROLOGUE
THE END OF THE ROAD

"**P**assenger! Passenger! Put your hands up!" an officer from the Violent Crimes Fugitive Task Force yelled. They'd been sent out, along with a dozen members from other law enforcement agencies, including the F.B.I., to find and apprehend me.

Twelve hours before, I'd escaped from the Northeastern Oklahoma Correctional Center, N.O.C.C., which is part of the Oklahoma Department of Corrections. During the break-out, I had dislocated my shoulder after falling from a fence and had been forced to reset it myself whilst hiding in a ditch.

With my shoulder still hurting, I grimaced and growled under my breath, directing my angst at the men aiming their guns at me from behind the safety of their cars.

"Passenger, comply or we will shoot!" another of the officers repeated. They had just pulled us over by blocking off a six-lane highway ahead and behind us.

The driver of the truck I was in had already thrown his keys out. He'd exited the red pickup and was laying face down on the roadway where the officers had directed him. Stephanie, my outlaw-hearted oldest daughter, was sitting beside me in the middle of the pickup's seat. Through her tears she begged for me to raise my hands and comply with the officer's demands before I was killed.

Sitting there angry and disgusted, stunned at the sudden change of fortune, I finally shook myself. I slammed my phone against the dashboard, not wanting the police to retrieve any incriminating evidence against those who may have aided me in my escape. I stuck my address book in Stephanie's purse and exited the vehicle, where I defiantly stood and challenged the small militia that was gathered and threatening me with their guns, locked and loaded, all aimed in my direction.

I have no death wish, but my life's been one jail and prison cell after another and I have become completely worn out and disabused with crime and doing prison time. I did not want to be caught. I'd put a year of planning into this escape. To say that I was extremely angry and disappointed would not even begin to describe how I was feeling as I faced the men and the open bores of their guns. I flipped them off and yelled at them, to "just shoot me!" Then one of the officers who had chased me for so long a couple of years before ran up, pointing a shotgun at me. I turned and ran.

I heard the Boom as the firing pin struck the cap of the shell that was loaded in the officer's shotgun, causing the load to explode from the barrel as he fired the gun. I was immediately slammed from behind as if I'd been kicked in the back by a mule. I was hit hard enough to knock me to my knees. It surprised me how calm I felt as I realized the end had come. My mind seemed accepting and almost relieved that my struggles were finally over.

A fog blanketed my mind and my world went black. Then I saw myself through the murk as fragments of my life danced before my eyes.

AMERICAN OUTLAW
~PRICE OF PRIDE~

JIMMY MAXWELL

PART I

CHAPTER ONE
THE INTERVIEW

I was sitting in an isolation cell full of anger and despair... in the same jail as my nineteen year-old son, Brandon, whom I had not seen in years. He was having trouble dealing with his tragic situation and was in isolation, himself. However, he was at the other end of the long, sprawled out facility. He needed me more than he ever had and somehow I was here...

The television show 'Lock-Up' had picked up on us due to my status as a leader of the Aryan Brotherhood in Oklahoma and my son's high profile murder case. They were going to come get me out of my cell soon for an interview. Hopefully, it would include my son, giving us a chance to see one another after so long; my only reason for agreeing to be interviewed in the first place.

I was sitting there contemplating how our lives had got to this point when the guard yelled at me to come up to the door and: "Cuff-up." It was time. I looked out the window and saw Sara, Brad and the rest of the film crew standing out there waiting to catch the shot of the big, Universal A.B. ramrod emerging from his cell. Glancing in my mirror, I saw the reflection of a tall, heavily-muscled, tattooed, aging man staring back at me through tired and hard-traveled brown eyes. Flattening my short, dark, shaggy hair I walked over and stuck my arms out of the bean-hole to be cuffed.

As I was being led down the hall, I wondered how I'd made such a mess of things? It was just a few years before that I was getting out of prison, after almost two decades, sure I was never going back... full of hopes and dreams of a promising future for me and my family. I've been in trouble all my life… and now… my son was following right behind me!

They took me and seated me in a small, fifteen by fifteen foot, concrete interview room. Sara O'Conner the producer, stared at me through her sparkling, and slightly mischievous blue eyes. She brushed her frizzy, shoulder length light-brown hair out of her face, while Tim, a tall, lanky light technician tried to move the chains that encircled my waist and wrists so that his lights wouldn't glare off of them. He looked at the three burly guards standing to the side, "Isn't there any way we can get these handcuffs removed?" He waved at the big, 'locked', steel door, "It's not as if he has anywhere he can go."

"Not a chance," the crew-cut wearing sergeant said flatly. Tim shrugged and backed off.

Tracy, the young, dark-haired assistant circled around looking me over and powdering my forehead, I notice how good she smelled after the dank odor of the grime-covered walls of my cell. "It's just to keep the glare down," she said with a nervous smile in her brown eyes. She looked at Brad who was peering through the view finder of his T.V. camera.

"There is still a little glare on his cheek bone," he told her. Tracy dabbed at the spot and Brad held his thumb up confirming that it was fixed, with that she moved away.

Sara looked at the stocky, blond-headed cameraman one more time, to make sure he was ready. Brad leant forward putting his eye back to the lens, and nodded, "We're all good," he said. Sam, the sound guy stepped forward and slapped the black and white striped, clapperboard together. Brad waved his hand at Sara. "We're rolling."

"So," she said. "As you know, we are planning to get you and your son together for an interview later, but for now we're curious about *you*."

"What do you want to know? My name is Jimmy Maxwell, I was born in Guymon, Oklahoma, U.S.A.. I had an abusive degrading childhood, I moved around the country a lot never having any real roots, ending up in El Paso, Texas, where I grew up. Eventually returning to Oklahoma. But I'm not going to blame my life on that, if that's what you want, mine sucked but I know of a lot of people who had it worse, and made good on their lives."

"Well, what do you think *did*, lead you to where you are at now," Sara asked as she moved in the hard plastic chair.

"I don't know, I pretty much raised myself and obviously didn't do a very good job of it. I've been on my own since I was thirteen, found myself in a juvy at fifteen, and after a few harrowing escapes, I finally aged out at eighteen."

Tracy stopped us, then came back over and powdered another spot on my forehead.

When she'd stepped back Sara went on, "What juvenile detention facility was that, and is that where you got started in the Aryan Brotherhood?"

"It was, Helena Boys Home, 'Hell' for short. The roughest juvenile facility in the State, at the time; and it definitely was what started my education, reputation and the never-ending cycle of recidivism. The A.B. came later, though, however, my detention center days is where I *learned* about racism. I never knew how much black people didn't like whites, until then. In El Paso everyone was down on the illegal Mexicans because they'd come across the border and work cheap, taking jobs from Americans. Personally, I didn't have a problem with anybody until they had one with me. But it was from there that I graduated to prison, where I spent a lifetime immersed in drugs, violence, and gang life, along with the never ending pursuit to regain my liberty."

"Okay, well tell us about that, you seem to be a smart guy, why is it that you keep coming back; what brought you back this time? What made you want to be A.B.? How did you get such a reputation, we've walked up and down these quarter mile long hallways of this jail and cannot hardly find anyone who doesn't know 'of you', or has a violent prison story to tell about you?"

"The best advice I can give you, is not to believe everything you hear." I waved my hand dismissively, at what I could only imagine they'd been told.

Sara leant forward, "Well what is the real deal then, Jimmy Maxwell?"

I looked at Sara then at Brad. "You don't really want to hear shit like that, and I'm not all that big on telling war stories, anyway," I said.

"Well if you don't tell us something that's true, then we'll be left having to go with one of these stories that we hear down the hall."

"Whatever," I shrugged. Then I gazed with determination at the pretty Irish girl. "Do you promise I'm going to get to see my son, because I'm not going to waste my breath if not."

3

"We promise," she said, crossing her legs and sitting a little straighter with a triumphant little smile on her face.

"Okay then, you asked for it. It was 1996 and I was being housed in a private high-medium prison…"

~ ❑ ❑ ❑ ❑ ❑ ❑ ❑ ❑ ❑ ~

Dink, dink, dink came the audible chime of the aluminum baseball bat as I was bringing it down – breaking one of Randy's bones with every ringing swing!

Just thirty minutes earlier I had been casually on my way to lunch when I'd spotted Ace Haley outside the mess hall. "Where's my money, Ace?" I demanded.

"Man, bro, my people are broke and they are cutting me off, I don't know what I'm going to do," the ex semi-pro boxer told me shaking his head in mock dismay.

I felt like knocking the white baseball cap off of his shaggy, brown-hair. "You're *going* to get my fucking money is what you're going to do. You came and got my shit and you're going to pay for it. I'm not the one to be jacking with." I paused to sniff his attitude. "If your people want you to make it home in one piece they will cut you off *after* you pay me!"

I left him standing there looking at the ground; no doubt wondering just how tough he was. Sure he was a boxer, quite-possibly better than me in the ring, but where we were at that moment, there were no referees and the only place where anyone could find the Queensbury Rules was in a dictionary. Ace was *far* out of his depth, whether he knew it yet, or not.

I had no sympathy and I was in the right. Money, after all, keeps the globe spinning. I hustled and, yes, that means I was the go to guy for pot, pills and powder, which had survived the perilous journey past the double-rowed fences and triple-stranded concertina wire of our concrete compound. We're all adults here and I'm not going to apologize for it. It's commerce, I bought something at a lower price and sold it at a higher price, the same as every other business man on the freaking planet. And… with that money; I sent it out of the prison to help support Maryjo, my long dark haired, half-Korean, first wife and our kids. As well as, pay her way to be able to bring them to see me.

So, yeah, I took it personal when a junky came and bought my shit on false pretenses. Let me tell you: when you knock on my door, it won't be *my* family who suffers for your weak-ass, dope-fiend greed. After all, I could have sold what I had to someone else who had the money and all involved would have walked away with a spring in their step and a whistle at their lips. My word is good and I expect no less from anyone else. Short of that... well, I built a whole reputation around the corollary, that's just the way you do business around here.

I grumbled to myself on my way into the mess hall. I was thinking I was probably going to have to make an example out of that one. I let it go for the moment it was nothing to keep me preoccupied, I dealt with that B.S. everyday and I dealt out the consequences for testing my patience, just as nonchalantly. Storing my conversation with Ace in the back of my mind for a later date, I got my tray and sat down at one of the white boy tables.

I'm sorry if that offends your Liberal sensibilities, like it or not, *every* prison is segregated by color. Blacks choose to eat on one side and whites on the other and everyone in-between sits in-between. It's almost like looking at colored pencils that have been laid out by an artist with O.C.D.. It doesn't mean we hate each other, well not much; that's just the way it is.

Holdenville's mess hall is a cavernous building with rows upon rows of twenty-foot long, white acrylic-painted tables lined up along its length like teeth in a giant jaw.

I sat where I normally sat in white-boy central, where I could see most of the expansive interior. I parked my ass across from Junior Simmons. He was dressed in his navy blue khakis and staring mournfully at his chopped carrots and chicken patty. The chicken patties looked, and tasted, like hockey pucks and Junior was in no mood for sport. I'd known the stocky ball-headed convict a long time. "Hey, bro, you want this shit?" he asked when I flopped my sectional plate down opposite his.

"Why not," I said. "You've got to grow a thicker skin Junior. I quit eating for taste a long time ago." I was just reaching for his tray when he inquired if I knew Randy Staggs.

"What?"

"I said: do you know Randy Staggs?" he asked again. Junior was looking at me oddly. I must have had a funny look on my face as well. I damn-sure did know Randy, although I hadn't heard his name in a long time and hadn't really expected to.

The Davis Correctional Facility in Holdenville, Oklahoma, was a private prison and they generally didn't accept sex offenders and Randy Staggs was all of that. He and his brother had taken Maryjo's cousin out in the woods and repeatedly raped and sodomized her. Among other things, they beat her with sticks and mashed her face down into the mud making her eat it. Eventually, after discussing whether to kill her or not, Randy and his brother kicked Michelle out naked on the side of the road, where she was eventually found and taken to the emergency room. She told me that Randy had said he was a good friend of mine, so she'd assumed it would be alright to get a ride from them. It never occurred to her that someone who knew me would ever hurt her. Those words, and the way the simple, trusting look faded from her eyes when she said them to me, had haunted me for a long time. "Yeah – I know him," my voice dropped to a deadly calm. "Why?"

"He just got here last night," Junior mumbled, pushing his peas around his plate disgustedly with his spork. He was not perceiving that there was a problem, because Randy had always been one of the *'fellas'*. He'd been in and out of prison several times and had earned himself a little reputation as a pretty successful southpaw style fighter.

The hollowness of my voice matched the hollowness I suddenly felt in my soul. "Where?" I asked, looking intently at my friend.

"Hell, right there in line. Don't you see him?" I looked where Junior was pointing with his crooked index finger and sure enough there stood a six foot one inch, two-hundred pound, brown-headed, hazel-eyed pile of rapist shit. My blood suddenly turned cold, as if my heart was pumping out ice cubes. Honestly, I had no idea how strongly I had felt about this guy, until I saw him at that moment and it was pure, focused, mind-numbing cold rage.

After Randy and his brother had gotten sent back to prison, Michael, Michelle's husband, had asked if he could pay me to have them dealt with. He knew that I had many friends and connections on the inside. He and my wife's cousin, would get regular victims reports of where Randy and his brother were housed at any given time. However, I was free at the time the crime occurred, and I had Maryjo call every Staggs in the phone book until she got someone on the line that said Randy wasn't there at the moment. With that information I found the address and looked the house over for signs of Randy, his brother or the vehicle that Michelle had described. They weren't there, but *someone* was. It was three in the morning, and I was packing a snub-nose .38. I told Maryjo what I wanted to do, but she convinced me that Michael deserved to be in on the retribution since it was *his* wife. I couldn't argue with logic like that, so I drove to Michael's house and told him what I'd found. I told him, if it were me, I would go in and take whoever was in that house and make them take me to wherever they were, or make the brothers come to me. I showed him my pistol and assured him that I'd lead the way to right the wrong, with pure, prison-yard brutality!

Michael, however, just looked at me through his watered-down, pale blue eyes and informed me that he didn't want any more trouble. I was shocked and taken aback! At that time, I couldn't even imagine taking such a passive attitude – not for something like that! I didn't even know what to say. It caught me as if I'd been poleaxed. I stumbled out of his house in disbelief. So… when he asked me to have one of my friends put their life in jeopardy to take the life of the Staggs' brothers, I was torn. I liked Michelle and after a year of watching her try to deal with what they had done to her I *wanted* to help. I even told her that if she would drop the charges on the brothers, that I would wait for them at the bottom of the courthouse steps to avenge her. However, the brothers pled out for twenty-five years before she could make up her mind. Anyway, I couldn't bring myself to ask my friends to do something for Michael that Michael had the chance to do himself, and wouldn't.

But now… there Randy was, right in front of me.

I stood up, with Junior's tray completely forgotten about. Walking on autopilot, I turned to put mine up. "Where are you going bro?" Junior was saying over my shoulder. I ignored him; my mind was consumed with a single-minded purpose as I threw my untouched plate in the slop window, my eyes still staring across the dining hall at the man who had hurt my cousin-in-law. I didn't have to consciously think about what I was going to do; every cell in my body was of one accord as I headed out the door to the cell house to get a weapon.

When I came busting out of the messhall exit there stood Ace, waiting to plead his case, with more lame excuses. Before he could even say anything I held my hand up and stopped him. "You and I would *already* be fighting if I didn't have some other pressing business," I told him.

"But… but…" he stammered, wanting to get his new excuse out.

"Hopefully, I'll have time to see you when this is done – so don't go far," I finished; my meaning multi-layered and venomous. I passed him while he was trying to sort it all out.

I don't even remember the rest of the walk back to the cellblock. Ace was already forgotten. My mind had a single thought in it – to get a knife. I'm not one to usually grab a weapon. I've even had to take a few away from people when I probably should have had one. But, in my opinion, most things are not stabbing, maiming or killing offenses. Most altercations stem from some punk-ass dope-fiend move or delinquent bills. I usually save the artillery for gang fights or opponents that I *know* are going to be armed. I didn't even own a shank at that time, but relied on those around me that I knew did, if I really needed one.

As I came up the stairs I ran into Dickie Mitchell, my oldest friend; and when I say *oldest* that's what I mean. He was around sixty, what I thought was old at the time. He had so many wrinkles that when he smiled he looked like the Grinch that stole Christmas. He was short and thin - and loyal as any friend that I've ever had. So when he saw the look on my face as I was coming up the steps to my tier, he ran to meet me at the top of them.

"What's going on?" he asked in an urgent whisper whilst staring at me from under his bushy, grey eyebrows.

"Get me a knife," I snarled as I met his green eyes with a dead, black stare. He knew what that look meant and that I was in a take-no-prisoners, take-no-precautions state of mind.

He instantly started jumping from foot to foot in nervous agitation. "No, Jimmy… no! Whatever this is, we can do this differently," he said, trying to be the voice of reason.

"No, Dickie, this isn't one of those kind of things. Either help me or get the fuck out of my way," I scowled as I pushed past him. Like I said, he was a good friend and he wouldn't let it go. He ran up beside me as I stuck my head into a cell. "Fat Jack, give me your steel," I said to the fat, bald-headed guy who was sitting there. Jack looked up and saw the sheer intensity on my face, making the blood drain from his own.

"I - I - I'm sorry, bro, they got mine in a shakedown..." he was saying when Dickie jumped in.

"You don't need one anyway, Jimmy. Think of your kids. Think of Maryjo!" he sputtered. I shoved him out of my way and glared at him. I did not need to be hearing shit like that... *this* was not negotiable. So, there was no room for sentiment, *none*.

"Get out of my face," I growled at my friend as I stopped at Big Nick's cell. Big Nick looked like an overweight Hulk Hogan; blond mustache and all. He was my friend although I'd knocked him out over at Granite the year before. "Give me your knife, Nick," I grated.

"Don't do it, Nick," Dickie threw over my shoulder. "He won't even tell me why!"

"You're my friend, Dickie, but you'd better get out of my way. A man that raped someone close to me just showed up. Now get out... of... my... face!"

"Oh my God – no! Jimmy, you can't go out there like this. You will kill that guy right in front of everyone! Think of your kids! Your future!" Dick pled with me.

Nick raised his hands in surrender. "I'm sorry, Jimmy. Jerry's got my knife over on D-block..."

I couldn't even hear the rest of what he said, because what Dickie was saying was trying to squeeze past the steel door in my mind that I'd shut on it. It was too sensible and too true to hold off forever, some would get past and as soon as that happened, it would break like a cracked dam. I *needed* to do this. I don't think I ever realized what a rape victim went through, until I saw the change in Michelle first hand. My unwillingness to help Michael by having my friends go after the brothers when he asked had bothered me. I was right not to, but now – I could right the wrong that I felt a weird, abstract, sense of responsibility for... myself. Those feelings sparked an anger that simply put, overwhelmed me. I could not wait any longer – I shoved past Dickey and went to my cell. I pulled the combination locks off my lockers and I jerked a belt off the back hook. I was stringing it through the hasps on my way down the stairs. I had to get away from Dickie. He'd finally relented after I'd threatened him again, but he was dogging my every step, trying to think of something, anything, to break my intensity.

9

I was irritated – *locks on a belt? Chump ass shit… I will have to find something on my way through the gym*, I thought to myself. The gym and the ball–field were common areas and, chances were, that's where I would find Randy.

I vaguely noticed that we were picking up followers as I made my way. People could see that I was in a state and with Dickie running behind trying to dissuade me from something, it could only mean something exciting was about to happen. I was charging through the indoor basketball court of the gym, when it occurred to me that with all the people gathering, that whatever I did I wouldn't be getting away with it. So, if I wanted to settle up with Ace before I went to lockup, I'd better get him while I was at it.

About that time I came out of the wide, overhead door that accessed the ball-field from the gym. I saw there was a softball game going on and my eyes fell on the baseball bats, which were lent up against the backstop. *Aaaah there we go,* I thought. I hoped both men were out there as I scanned the field with a sweeping glance never even missing a step. No sign of Ace, which was disappointing, but I saw Randy standing against the back of 'C' building with four or five guys who were obviously clueless as to what a maggot he was. As well as, completely oblivious to the ensuing storm that was about to blow in.

I reached the bats. I spared one more glance for Ace, so I could move seamlessly from one to the other, still no sign of him. Oh well… I slung the bat up on my shoulder and walked straight to where Randy was gathered with the guys. He was facing me as I strode up. I barely noticed Junior was out there talking to him. He'd had his back to me and was just turning when Randy looked up and said: "Hey Ji-". I brought the bat down across Randy's collarbone breaking it in the first strike. Junior was in my path and I hit him also in my rage, knocking them both to the ground.

"Whaaa nooo," Randy screamed as I hit him again and again. Dink! Dink! Dink! The aluminum ball-bat sang out as I chased him around on the ground while he rolled and tried to dodge the onslaught. Dink, dink, dink was the simple sound the bat made as it was accompanied by the crunching of breaking bones from almost every crushing strike. I was going for his skull, but his survival instinct caused him to block my blows even with broken limbs. "It wasn't me! It wasn't me, I swear!" he was screaming; pleading for his life.

"Yes it was, you rapist piece of shit. How do you like it now mother-suckin-bastard? It was all good when you were beating Michelle with sticks and sticking them up her ass, how do you like it now!!" I snarled, lost in a total justice serving fury. I raged as I brought the bat down again, I could see the leg break as it jutted out at an odd angle. I wanted his head – I wanted to see his brains spread across the dirt. It's funny that I wasn't consciously thinking about killing him, but that's what I was doing... without a seconds thought.

"It wasn't me! It wasn't me," Randy cried as he crab-crawled through the dirt; backing away the best he could with me looming over him looking for any opening. I could hear Dickie in my periphery, giving me a play by play, of where the perimeter truck was on the outside of the fence, and the proximity of the guard on the ball-field.

"Oh fuck! He just saw you... You might as well just finish him now, Jimmy," Dickie said with defeat entrenched deep in his voice. Then, suddenly, he recanted: "No – no – wait! I don't think he did! If you *stop now!*"

I was hearing him through my madness and it was beginning to sink in that maybe if I didn't kill this maggot, I could get away with this. I was surprised the thought hadn't occurred to me until that moment. I was still swinging as my mind was throwing grappling hooks out to rein itself in.

I stopped.

I was surrounded by guys ringing me trying to block the officers' view.

"They *still* haven't seen me?" I asked, totally astounded; the bat drawn back, for yet another swing.

"No... well, yes and no. The old guard looked up and I'm sure he saw what you were doing, but as soon as he did, he went back to looking at cigarette butts on the ground pretending he didn't. I think you're good, if... you... *stop!*"

Hmmm, I thought, but I was still out of control – dink – dink – dink, I hit Randy some more. I could see the pleading anguish in Randy's eyes, as he was forced to raise his broken arms in front of him to block the bat from hitting his head. I watched as his fingers shattered – suddenly all pointing in different directions from the bat's destructive pass through his hands. I heard a voice in my head say, *"If you don't kill him you might get away with this. Look at him... You've destroyed him, he will never be the same.. no need to kill - he's done. Vengeance has been had,"* the voice was as clear as if someone else was talking.

I stopped again.

"How about now?" I asked looking at Dickie.

"Yeah – yeah, you're good!" he said, followed by a couple of others who agreed. "They still haven't seen you or at least they are acting like they haven't."

I looked down at the pitiful sack of broken bones that was now weeping; begging me to stop. I could see the wet spot spreading across the front of Randy's trousers and smelled the pungent stink of urine from where he was pissing himself. *Yes – vengeance was paid,* the inner voice said. *He knows how it feels to be on the receiving end now.* Out loud I said: "You're lucky I couldn't find a knife, because it would be hanging out of the middle of your chest right now. You raped the wrong man's friend, Randy."

I held the bat out to Dickie, and as I walked off I saw Randy from the corner of my eye attempt to rise only to collapse back into the dirt.

Dickie handed the bat off to someone else and followed me. Everyone else just stood still as if stunned by the level of violence I had reaped in the few minutes I'd been out there. As I went back through the rolled up metal gym door, I heard a big Indian name Harjo say: "I guess that guy ran into the wrong motherfucker today."

Amazingly, I made it back to my housing unit unscathed. I was just in my cell washing up, with Dickie still by my side. There were four or five others standing out in front of my cell keeping the gawker's at bay. I was just thinking that I might as well go get Ace as well before the law came and got me for what I had done, when I heard a commotion. I looked up as Ace was trying to push his way through the blockade. "I *need* to talk to Jimmy," he was saying.

I stepped out of the cell. "I was just fixing to come see you," I scowled.

"I know, I know. I just got off the phone," he gasped, breathing hard, as if he'd run all the way over to my unit. "Your money is on the way as we speak!"

~ロロロロロロロロロ~

I leaned back in my chair and looked around the interview room, which had gotten very quiet. "This is who I was. Randy lived through the attack, although he's crippled and now bears permanent reminders of the consequences awaiting a rapist. If you are looking for an apology you'll find none. I am a different man now; a redeemed, reformed character, but even though I hope for forgiveness for my past I do not demand nor expect it." I looked at Sara and the film crews' shocked faces. "All I can say is if you don't believe in, or can't empathize with my sense of justice in this case then you may as well stop filming now, because I stand on it. The man had it coming."

"Did you ever get caught for that?" Sara asked.

"No. And if you think I'm a terrible person we can end this interview here. I'm not going to sit here and tell you stories just to be painted as a psychopath. I'm a good kind hearted man, but I've lived my life around the worst of the worst and I've learned to be hard. That man hurt someone close to me in a way that truly effected everything about her, forever to come. The way she described how Randy handled her, I could only wonder about the others he and his brother had done similar things to." I eyed her trying to discern the level of judgment that was being weighed against me. "I stand on my actions," I repeated.

"Thank you for telling us that story, no one is here to judge, there are a lot of people in this world that wish they had a friend like you in there corner," Sara said. Brad, the 'Lock-Up' cameraman was nodding in agreement.

"So do you want to continue?" I asked.

"Yes, I think you've adequately described how you have acquired such a violent reputation. What about the Aryan Brotherhood, would it be alright to ask you what made you want to become A.B., how did you get so far up?"

"Well I can tell you what I can tell you, no more than that," I said. I struggled with the shackles, which were wrapped around my wrist and waist, to get a drink from the bottle of water that Tracy, the production assistant had given me. My thirst quenched, I looked at Sara and relaxed the best I could in my seat, "Why I came to be A.B...."

CHAPTER TWO
PRISON

The first time I went to prison was in 1982. Since then I've been in and out five times and have lived through three full-blown riots, a couple of small ones and just as many major gang fights. This window I'm sharing with you into my life isn't so much about that, because you don't need to hear one more Grub Street penny-dreadful that either lionizes or vilifies such a lifestyle? You can turn on cable television and find countless documentaries doing just that. So, rather than focusing on titillating prison voyeurs, let me tell you about the evolution of a man. The good, bad, and the ugly.

As I've said, I have been locked up in one jail or another since I was a kid. Honestly, it was a natural progression for me to become part of the Aryan Brotherhood. I'd been representing strength in whites, long before there was even a Brotherhood in Oklahoma. Not that I was a "hater" of people of other races, because I wasn't then, and I'm not now. However, I've had to stand up for myself and my kind since the boy's home and juvenile center days. That's where I discovered there was a misguided mentality among many other races, suggesting that they were better, or stronger, or tougher than me; based solely on the fact that I was white. I fought hard to defend myself and prove those egotistical and uneducated individuals wrong. I'd walked that path for many years and by the time the Brotherhood moved into Oklahoma I was already high in the ranking of the prison hierarchy. It started out as simply the Oklahoma Prison Brotherhood, but eventually evolved into the Universal Aryan Brotherhood (U.A.B.).

People get the A.B. confused with hate groups like the K.K.K. and Skinheads. The word 'Aryan' may be a term made known by the German Nazis in the early 1900's, 'Hail Hitler' and all that crap, but most A.B. members, from whatever State they are from don't give a damn about Adolf and his twisted political ambitions. Notice I used the word 'most'. The majority are just trying to stand strong and proud of who they are in a world that has become brainwashed with the ideology that if you are white and proud of it then there is something wrong with you. Not to say that any and all societal travesties committed against whoever, wherever, whenever are not tragic. They were all absolutely horrific and should never be repeated. But, people forget that a lot of whites died fighting the British, Indians, Spanish, then each other, to free the slaves too; with very little recognition for it. We all paid a heavy price to be Americans in the end.

Anyway, for many A.B. gang members it's not even a matter of being proud of one's own race. It's simply to combat the reverse racist environment that most prisons are comprised of; since they are often predominantly filled with Blacks, Mexicans, Indians and Asian people who all tend to hate on the Whites. For the most part, Caucasians in general, whether in or out, are weakened because any understanding of unity and pride for who they are has been lost out of fear of being termed a racist. Every other race has events, marches, T.V. channels and days of the year dedicated to the purpose of instilling the unified traits in their people, which they are simultaneously trying to stamp out of mine. This leaves white Americans, especially in prisons or low income environments, vulnerable to those who have learned to stand together.

Whatever the reason, the bottom line is: in prison, you're either a lion, a gazelle or a hyena; and even if you are a lion and don't have a pride, a pack of much smaller hyenas can eventually take you down. The Aryan Brotherhood appeals to the whites in prison who don't want to be a lone lion, or prefer not to be a gazelle. In the beginning it has very little to do with hate or feelings of superiority.

What propelled me to the top of our Hood was the war between us and the Oklahoma Aryan Brotherhood, or O.A.B. for short. They were an offshoot faction whom we had barely tolerated for years; comprised mostly of men who had either been rejected from the U.A.B. or outright kicked out. That's not to say there weren't a few who were of the right caliber to carry our brand, but not near enough.

The O.A.B. had dropped the proverbial ball of carrying an Aryan patch many times, but the last straw came in '98 when a bunch of us were being housed at the Lawton Correctional Facility. A couple of O.A.B. members were robbed by a black gang on the other side of the prison. L.C.F. was, and still is, a wicked, rough prison located in the southwest part of the State right outside of Lawton, Oklahoma. The prison itself was built like a pinwheel, where each spoke of the six spokes of the wheel were numbered one through six and had several locked crash gates along their hallways, which separated one cell block from another. Even with its restricted movements, the word spread quickly enough. When the news reached me and the rest of my crew of U.A.B.'s, though some were angry, most just laughed at the misfortune of the rival gang, but we all watched to see what would happen.

I didn't laugh at all.

I know that people from other races, even regular white people reading this, do not understand the difference between an O.A.B. and a U.A.B.. To most people, an A.B. is an A.B., so consequently it would appear to the uninformed that some gangbangers had just robbed an A.B. down on cellblock one and, so far, the white boys had done nothing about it. This was unacceptable, not just for pride's sake, although that was a factor, but the loss of respect in such a violent, predatory environment would affect every white resident there for years to come. With that in mind, I told my guys we would give the O-abs, which is slang for O.A.B.s, the opportunity to respond. If they stepped up the way they should, the U.A.B.s would stand at the ready to aid them. However, if they did not, then we would simply do it ourselves. Something like that could not go unanswered... but afterwards we would deal with the O.A.B.s, as well.

Knowing that they were under the gun, the O-abs put word out that they were making plans. One of their young prospects who I'd been counseling, because he was getting ready to go home and was nervous about it, was sitting in my cell. I realize that you probably would need to have done some time before to understand that last statement. But for a lot of inmates fear of failure starts long before release. Anyway, he told me that since he couldn't get through the crash-gates he needed to go put the shank he had down his pants somewhere until he could.

"What are you doing with a knife?" I asked. "I thought you said you were going home in a few months?"

"Four months to be exact," he replied. "But they told me I had to stab that black guy."

I stared hard at the dark headed, twenty-one year old, thinking about the family he'd just told me about. "By yourself? Where's... what's his name? The guy who was robbed? Why isn't he doing it?" I asked, assuming that there must be some sensible and reasonable answer behind the orders given to this kid by his so-called 'shot-callers', but scratching my head to find it.

"Yeah, they sent me by myself. Said if I want to get my patch before I go home that I'll do it. Joker is the one who got the dope taken. He's doing twenty-five to life." Then, after going over the whole story once again he concluded with: "I don't know why he's not at least going with me. I'm scared, but I'll do it when the gates open."

I got up looming over the kid, irritation sparking off of me like a downed power line. "No, you won't! First of all... you don't send a guy who is going home in a few days on a suicide mission. Second... whatever you do, you make sure there is enough support to make your strike effective and ensure you walk away from the attack a winner. If you went down there and three or four of them got your knife away from you and stabbed you up with your own shank, you and every other A.B. here would be the laughing stock of the system! Who's the genius that came up with this plan?" I asked sarcastically.

"Big Dave," the youngster responded, a nervous and fearful look on his face.

Big David Phelps... The O.A.B.'s head honcho. He was a huge son of a bitch; three hundred and fifty pounds spread over a six foot and six inch frame; shoulders like an outhouse door, but, in my opinion, coming up a little short on intellect.

I am all for people putting in work to earn their patches, but... if I'm going to call that man a Brother, I'm going to protect him in the process. I'm going to make sure that in a political battle he has all the resources available to him to be victorious, not to mention survive. I didn't know Dave, but I already didn't like him.

"Son, you're prospecting for the wrong bunch," I said. "Go give that piece of steel to Goose down the hall and stay out of the way. Go home to your wife and daughter like we have been talking about." He started to protest, but I held my hand up, shutting him off before he could speak. "Just do what I say and I'll deal with Dave."

Word got back to Dave that I was unhappy with his handling of the situation. He tried to rally something together to save face, but it was too late. We'd already had our guys on the other end of the prison handle the gangbangers who had made the move.

I went to see Dave.

The unit he lived on was on the south end of the prison, cellblock four. I had to slip through several gates. Well, '*slip through*' is a bit of an exaggeration; the guards didn't pay that much attention. I just sat in the mess hall taking my time eating and waited for Dave's unit to be called for chow, whereupon I went back to their cellblock with them. The wing he lived on housed more Brotherhood members from both sects than almost all the others put together, so it wasn't very hard to blend in with them on the way back.

My intention was to cut the head off of the snake. Take the big one out and disband the rest. I walked in with one of my bros who lived on that block. Not seeing any reason to put off what needed to be done, I walked up to Dave, who already knew I had issues with him, pulling off my watch and necklace as I did. After I tossed them on the day room table, I said simply: "Well, let's just get this party started," and hit him in the jaw with a left hook that would have torn an average man's head off.

He was big and I poured it all into him. Dave went to his knees as I pounded him, while he did his best to throw a few feeble blows back and grab on to me on his way to the floor. Before I had him all the way down, I heard, or more or less sensed, several other eruptions around me. When I had David dazed enough for me to safely look around I saw the whole day room was fighting. My poor choice of words right before lighting into Dave, about '*starting the party*' implied that the light was green on the whole bunch. Every U.A.B. in the room attacked.

With the rest of the Brothers on the other side of the prison, we were slightly outnumbered. As we traveled the room fighting I found myself momentarily pulling off of David every now and again to aid one Brother or another who had found himself facing two or more of the opposition. For the most part, my bros were wiping the floor with them. Within minutes, my guys had loaded several pillow cases with canned goods and grabbed a couple of knives and the fight quickly came to a bloody end. The

O.A.B.s who couldn't get away from us were life-flighted out to the nearest hospital. Big Dave made it, minus all his top right side teeth, only because I refused to let anyone interfere with us. I had a point to make and didn't want him to be able to claim it took more than me to take him down.

My declaration that day was that there would be no more phony A.B. in our State. With that, the fight spread from prison yard to prison yard and the O.A.B.s were eradicated over the next six years. David Phelps was killed by his own people as soon as he was released from the medical lock-up for starting the trouble between us.

Later, I learned from an Oklahoma State Bureau of Investigations agent who had come to interrogate me about Dave's death, that Dave's guys thought his death would appease us and stop the onslaught. They thought that I had put a *'green light'* on him, which is a directive to kill on sight, but it was an order that I did not give.

Needless to say, with that and everything else going on, I ended up back in high max. There it was decided by the Brotherhood's governing council that it was time to structure our brotherhood with a President and Vice President for the first time. After a State-wide vote I was elected to our State's top spot, with Big John as my second in command closely followed by a counsel of five. I didn't necessarily have much more power than the rest, but, with seven of us, I would be the deciding factor.

Over the course of my several year stay in the supermax at McAlester, my marriage to Maryjo, ended, she met and married someone else. To her, it seemed as if I would never come home. I have to admit it seemed that way to me also at times, it broke my heart to watch my kids grow up through the cold bars of a prison window.

Not long after my break up with Maryjo, I received a time cut I'd been working on since the day Judge Jennings slammed me with a forty-five year sentence for five grams of meth; getting it reduced to twenty-five. Now, with the possibility of freedom in sight, me and a few of the other council members decided I was needed on the streets, where I could coordinate and unite the hundreds of free U.A.B.s into a fully functioning organization, bridging the gap between the Brothers on the inside and the Brothers on the bricks. This would take our Hood onto the next rung of the evolutionary ladder; making what we were stand for more than just what was going on in prison. My personal goal was to give Brothers a hand up and a place to go when they got out. It was agreed and we rescinded the title of President. I went underground, knowing that, as a known and active A.B. leader, I would never be freed. It was around that time I met and married Jenna, a pretty, dark headed girl, who just seemed to appear in my life.

A few years later I made parole and was sent to a Federal Corrections Institution (F.C.I.) in Oklahoma to finish up my last five year bit for possessing a firearm in the commission… There I found representatives from every other State's Aryan Brotherhood, as well as national brotherhoods, such as the Dirty White Boys (D.W.B.) and the Aryan Circle (A.C.), running the internal prison politics of our State and holding court on my Okies. 'Court' meaning that those families determined whether a 'convict rule' had been violated and dealt out the punishment in the form of violence for any such infractions.

This was happening due to the fact that there was no one else governing the white residents when I got there and, in Federal prison, everyone is accountable to someone… patched or not.

The circumstances being what they were, I could no longer stay in the shadows and allow that to go on in my State while I was present. I stepped up and pulled the few Brothers who were there together, restructuring the Hood to adapt to a national system. I squeezed them into shape along with taking responsibility for our State's people and pushing the rest of the families out of Oklahoman affairs. We eventually won over the hearts and respect of those around us by the way I, and the rest of us, carried ourselves; making what we had a solid, unified white community with the U.A.B. sitting at the helm, where it should have been all along, in Oklahoma anyway…

~❑❑❑❑❑❑❑❑❑❑~

The chair I was sitting in was hard, I shifted my weight, the guards by the door shifted theirs. I glanced at them, then finished my line of thought, "I spent over four more years in prison before it was over. By then Stephanie and Eric my step-kids, through Maryjo were grown, and my two youngest Echo and Brandon, who you already know, were teenagers."

Brad held his hand up, "Hold up, this is good stuff, let me change tapes." He hurriedly went about unloading the full cartridge from his camera…

While we waited, for him to put another one in, the rest of the crew scrambled like ants to do their jobs. Tim adjusted his lights in coordination with Tracy powdering my shiny spots again, and Sam, the tall, lanky soundman checked my mic.

Sara was looking at me, "Yes this is good stuff. I don't want to get you started talking until we get rolling again, but when we do, can you tell us how long you did... and how it felt to get out and adjust after so many years disconnected from society?" She took a drink from her water bottle and directed Tracy to give me another one.

Brad indicated that he was ready, and the crew attended to their last second preparations, they pulled back and Sam clicked his sound marker. I struggled to take a sip from my water bottle, then sat up, "Ready when you are," I said.

"We're rolling..."

CHAPTER THREE
GETTING OUT

It was June 2009, the day I was finally getting out! It had taken over sixteen years, but here it was the day I was walking out the door. What a long haul it had been, but at least I'd made it out alive and without catching a life sentence. This prison term had already taken a third of my life from me and, still, every few months or so, some incident would threaten to push back my release date even more. Nevertheless, here it was... finally.

Actually, I wasn't completely done with my time. I was just being released from the high-medium F.C.I. in El Reno, Oklahoma. Also known as the '*Red Roof Inn*,' because of the red tin, gabled rooftops of its four huge cell houses, administration, chow hall and recreation buildings that can be seen over the treetops from Interstate 40, a couple of miles away. I still had to go to the Oklahoma Halfway House for sixty more days, so I would have a couple of months of free, but structured, living left. I guess this was supposed to ease my transition from prison life back into society before I was actually discharged formally.

Regardless, this day was the day I counted as being released, especially since my whole sentence this round, was either spent behind walls or double fences. I thought, today would be a new beginning, the first day of the rest of my life; a successful, drug, crime, and prison-free life.

My second wife Jenna, the woman I married not long after I divorced Maryjo, was to pick me up and drive me to the halfway house. Jenna had just moved from Guymon to Oklahoma City, so she would be close to me and have a place for us to live in when I got out.

I had spent my last few years at El Reno preparing for this day. I took all the Vocational Technology training available and any other class I could, eventually working half-days at the B.O.P. (Bureau of Prisons) regional dental lab; a vo-tech program I'd graduated from. I welded, on the second shift the rest of the day, in the prison steel factory; honing my job skills and making myself as employable as possible for when I was released. I was ready.

There aren't many sensations that can compare to the elation of getting out of prison. The longer you've been in, the more intense are the unexpected feelings of trepidation and fear that run right along beside your excitement and joy. Yes, I said fear; fear something will happen at any moment and wake us from our dreams-come-true, among other worries, like will my peppy still work after all these years when faced with a real, naked woman and not just a photocopied picture of one? Of course, there are a lot of serious life concerns for many long-timers getting out, but, for the most part, we are all very… happy.

I'd been sweating the remaining days. The nights leading up to my release were sleepless, haunted by turbulent dreams that something would go wrong again. I laid down on that last evening, trying to will myself to sleep so I would wake up and it would be time to go. Finally, there it was: daybreak.

"Maxwell, bunk and junk," the guard said when he came by. Four words of freedom.

I took a moment to see all my friends and Brothers one last time, then I was off to the laundry. My closest Brothers helped me haul my B.O.P.-issued bedding, clothing and personal property up the hill. There, the laundry officer checked off my belongings from when I had first arrived and signed me out. We then walked to the administration building, where I said my goodbyes to the Bros who were left on the yard after the last incident. I had some good Brothers and some good friends there, so a bit of my soul would remain and I would carry with me a little of theirs. After a few final hugs and a wave, I turned and went through the Admin doors on my last round to the business office to get my check. I had accrued a total of two hundred and thirty-two dollars and eighty-five cents to begin my future with. From there, I went to the warden's secretary for my release papers and, finally, the last stop: Property. That's where they have you change out of your prison khakis into street clothes, which your friends or family should have provided. That, or some Salvation Army crap the prison kept on hand. Every step I took my pulse quickened. I worried that an officer would holler, *Maxwell, there has been a mistake. Your release has been cancelled!* Each breath I took, I silently prayed not to hear those words, mad at myself for even thinking them.

My apprehension was some what justified. In the six months leading up to my scheduled release, every member of my little band of Brothers and I went to lock-up for stomping all the Oklahoma Skinheads off the yard. There are differences between the Aryan Brotherhood. Almost every State has its own branch and its own leadership: Skinheads, K.K.K., Dirty White Boys and groups like the Aryan Circle. Each are independent of the rest, but bound to hold to the code of ethics that governs the overall white brother-hooded community, with severe consequences when they don't. In this case, the Skinheads had an unholy arrangement going on with the prison's Captain of Security. Apparently, one of them had a, give and take, 'information' relationship with the Captain. When the Captain asked that skinhead's Brothers to cover for him, they agreed. They sold out for promises of favor, breaking the cardinal convict prescript, and in doing so ensured their own destruction. My impending discharge almost derailed when several of them ended up in the hospital. We lost Ricky to the surveillance camera tapes. Thank God they were too grainy to identify anyone else.

Not long after that, around thirty pounds of tobacco were found behind the toilet paper roll holder in the bathroom wall of the dental lab where I worked. Ever since they made all Federal and most State prison yards tobacco-free environments, a single small cigarette goes for five or six dollars and a one-ounce pouch can bring one hundred and fifty dollars. Tobacco in that quantity equals a significant amount of money, twenty to thirty thousand. An officer obviously brought it in, which makes it, in the minds of security and the administration a big deal.

They rounded up all of the dental lab workers, about fifteen, including myself and put us in the Secure Housing Unit, (S.H.U.). What we just call "the shoe". We spent a couple of weeks in the hole, until someone broke and told them what they wanted to know. The rat turned out to be the only one they kept locked up and let the rest of us out. The officer got scared and wouldn't return to work, so the police got a warrant and went to his house, catching him with more tobacco, weed and heroin packaged to be brought into the yard.

As a consequence, they fired us all and shut down the dental lab program.

Jimmy Maxwell

CHAPTER FOUR
FIGHT FOR WHAT'S RIGHT

A few weeks later, about a month before I was due to be released to ninety days in the halfway house, that I had then. Darold (D.K.) Ellsworth – a good friend who I'd celled with three of the four years I'd been there – approached me during a chow call.

"I don't know if you've already heard this, or if it's even true, but I figure if it is, you'll want to know about it…" He hesitated, rubbing his stubby fingers back over his bald dome, as if he was about to tell me something he'd rather not.

D.K. made the decisions for his particular group of A.B.T.s, the Aryan Brotherhood of Texas; I called everything for Oklahoma. We trusted and had backed the other more than once.

I took in the demeanor of the short, stocky con, I could see something was bothering him. "I'm listening," I replied.

D.K. said he'd heard that some Oklahoma independent whiteboys had sold a little, white Okie kid to a black Puerto Rican on A-unit.

'*Independent*', in these circumstances, refers to people who have no gang or family affiliations. However, they are still beholden to adhere to the same ethical standard as the rest of us, with similar consequences when failing to do so. This is regardless of whether they are a patch-holder or not, and bartering off some young white boy to be a sex slave, especially to another race, was definitely a violation of that standard.

"That can't be true!" I said, shooting him a sideways glance from my narrowed eyes. "But you can bet I'll look into it, to be sure."

I was more or less just assuming it was some bullshit story. I had people up in 'A' building who were supposed to ensure things like that didn't happen. Not to mention, on this yard, the U.A.B. strictly enforced racial respect and racial boundaries. Separatism reigns in prison. Every race governs their own people and, if something happens between different skin tones, it is discussed by those calling the shots and the outcome is handled. White, Black, Mexican or Indian, we all tried to keep the operation of the prison running smooth because we were all involved in different – some quite lucrative – money making hustles, that directly depended upon it.

Hell, when new people arrived on a unit they would be met by a committee of representatives from their own race to check their paperwork; namely their court documents to show they were not government collaborators, their gang affiliations, and help them find a cell with their own people, as well as give them a care package if need be. Or, if there's a problem, i.e.: their paperwork doesn't check out, or they are from a rival gang, send them out on a stretcher.

Occasionally, prison administrators send new people in when there were no cells of their race available. The "committee" will then tell the new guy, if he's not smart enough to figure it out for himself, that he must refuse housing and sit in lock-up until things get shifted around for them.

I marked D.K.'s account as something that needed to be clarified one way or the other.

When our unit was finally called, D.K. and I walked to chow together. We discussed the recent tornados and my wife's fearful trip down from Guymon through the thunderstorms with her cat, Cricket, and her little Pomeranian, Ruby.

After reaching the mess hall and getting our trays we went our separate ways – D.K. to go sit at one of the A.B.T. tables and me to sit at one of the U.A.B. tables. It was just a sign of respect that the rest of the population would leave our dining areas and those of a couple of other family's, such as the Aryan Circle and the D.W.B.s, empty for us. There were a couple of U-abs seated at two of our tables; men from different units who had already eaten.

I noticed Drew sitting by himself. Drew is a six foot five inch, bald-headed, thirty year-old with a pile of time. He had the job of watching over his Brothers, our business ventures and whatever else needed to be dealt with on A-unit. He looked up when I sat down.

"Hey, Brother, how's your wife doing? Did she make it alright through that tornado?" he asked. I told him she had, even though she and her freaked-out animals had to take cover under an overpass at one point. "Man, you got a good woman," Drew finished, making a face at the greens on his plate.

"She should be up to visit tomorrow," I said. Then I told him what I'd heard, even though I couldn't imagine it to be true.

"Well, if it did happen, it would be Shannon Fry and his bunch." Drew went on to tell me they had some slow-witted youngster down on Shannon's end of the building that they tormented on a regular basis.

I scooted up in my seat. "You mean to tell me that this could be true?" I felt my blood turn to molten lava as anger came surging up through my throat into my head. "How could you not know if something like this happened or not?" I asked, my voice grinding hard as a rock-slide.

"Look, Brother, I don't mess around with those people down there," he said. "But, we can go find out." We got up and threw our uneaten trays in the slop window and headed toward A-unit, a red wave of rage threatening to overwhelm me as we stormed up the sidewalk.

Suddenly, Drew pointed, "Shit, bro, there's that kid right there." I looked and saw a skinny, pimple faced youngster, walking up the sidewalk. He had dishwater colored hair that sat on his head like seaweed, and it was clear that he wasn't well-hinged by the slack look on his mug.

"Hey!" I yelled at him. He froze in the middle of the walk looking like a cornered rabbit. "Is it true someone sold you to a Puerto Rican?!"

"Y-y-yes," he timidly replied, trapped in the intensity of my growing anger.

"Who the hell did that to you?" I gritted. I felt my face flush, as my heart began to pound in my chest like an Apache battle drum.

The kid was trembling, afraid to tell me and afraid not to. "I'd rather not say," he said, pleading with his eyes.

"You don't have to," I exploded. "I already know!!"

I did know. Drew had said it would be Shannon Fry, if it were true. Shannon was a big ol' corn-fed peckerwood from McAlester, Oklahoma. He was strong as a draft horse, with a head on him like a gator-mouth pit, and was someone I already didn't like.

He and his brother had written to us from jail the year before and told us they were Okies who wanted to stay in Oklahoma, close to their families. However, the guy who testified on them was on the El Reno yard. They asked if we would help them out because the B.O.P. would not send them to a yard that housed someone with an obvious separatee against them. A *'separatee'* being paperwork an official files to make sure that two people who cannot exist peacefully, for one reason or another, on the same prison yard, do not end up on the same yard.

We discussed it as a group since this involved putting our people out on a limb for non-patch holders. It was my opinion that I would rather have solid people on the yard than a known snitch who could become a potential problem for us in the future. Besides, we had a couple of prospects who needed to put some work in anyway. In this case, *"putting in work"* is an act - violent or otherwise - that a member, or a prospective member, of a brotherhood performs strictly for that faction.

As a matter of fact, one of the prospects knew the Frys and spoke up for them, along with volunteering for the job. The vote was unanimous in favor of the Frys, so we sent our volunteer and another prospect to handle it... It was handled. The little Brother, Ace, wore a mask and got away with it while Cole, our volunteer, ran right out in front of the surveillance camera and went to lock-up.

The rat was gone and one of the Fry brothers, Shannon, made it to El Reno. Considering the next closest Federal prison they could have went to was out of Leavenworth, Kansas, or Beaumont, Texas., it was a pretty good favor.

Cole was still in jail for the assault when Shannon showed up. The Fry brother was grateful and thanked us for helping him, looking out for Cole until he got out of lock-up. They stuck together like wet toilet paper until Cole discharged, finally getting his patch right before he left.

No sooner than Cole was gone, it reached me that Shannon was up on A-block running him down, about something supposedly out of their past. I took Shannon out on the ball-field and asked him what kind of guy waits until their friends are gone to talk about them behind their back? He denied the accusation and tried to explain it away as a misunderstanding. I told him I would stand in the gap for any of my Brothers in their absence and, even though he was a big ol' boy, if anything else came up, we were going to go down through there; which meant we were going to fight.

So my taste for him was already sour when this latest insult to the dignity of the people of our State came up; the audacity and shame was more than I could stand. I had spent all this time looking out for my

Oklahomans to have one do this to another weaker, mentally challenged one at that, caused me to nearly lose my mind.

A crimson mist enveloped me and I made a bee-line straight for Shannon's building. By the time I got to the doors of his unit I wasn't concerned about losing my halfway house date.

Drew was working to keep up behind me, stress etched in his face. He tried to remind me that my wife expected me to come home to her and telling me he and the others would handle it. I was just too enraged to hear any of it. Somewhere in the back of my mind was a vision of Jenna in tears, but I couldn't stop.

I stormed into A-unit and saw Shannon leaning against a pillar outside of his room. He was listening to his Walkman and took the headphones off his closely cropped blond head when he saw me coming.

"Hit the cell," I snarled. This was it. I was tired of messing with the man. I told my other Brothers who were gathering to stay out of it and he and I rolled up into his concrete cage for war.

Shannon is about six foot three and a good two hundred and sixty pounds, but I am not a little man myself. I'm real close to six-two and weigh in around two-forty, so it was a heavyweight battle. That big catfish head of his could take a punch and I'm fairly infamous for how hard I hit. I never did drop him, but by the time the look-out reported that the unit cops were headed to our side of the building, his head was twice its normal size.

When I got back to my cell, I found out that I had a few contusions myself. However, nothing noticeable that would catch the attention of the staff. Somehow I had made it through my momentary loss of control without tricking everything off.

As my adrenalin subsided and with my anger and indignation expended on Shannon's head, my thoughts turned to Jenna and what a close call I'd just had. She'd be upset if I had gotten caught and lost my halfway house and good time. I forgot all that as soon as one of my bros and D.K. came through my door, telling me Shannon's head was all swollen up and he wanted a re-match before he went to jail. I told them to tell him to bring his ass down on my unit this time. We would clear out the TV room and box till one of us couldn't walk out, but Shannon was afraid there were too many of us down on my unit and wanted a more neutral spot, like the ball-field. *Is he shitting me?* I thought. I probably should have just stood my ground and sent word to either come to me or suck it up, but I was still mad, and to have that piece of crap call me out made me madder still.

D.K. and Mize, another of my brothers, were standing there with me.

"The cock-sucker is just trying to save some face and make sure I'm going to lock-up with him," I said. "If I wasn't going home in a month, I'd stab him full of holes for this."

"Yeah, this is chicken shit, but you are going home, so don't even think about it," they told me.

However, whether it stopped me from going home or not, I wasn't going to hesitate to at least rip into him again, so I headed out to the rec-yard. It was a nice spring day, *a good a day as any to fuck-off everything I'd worked so long for,* I thought. He finally showed up, wary of the possibility I had brought a shank.

To minimize the risk of getting caught, I told my guys to keep everyone away from the ball-field. After all, everyone is drawn to a fight, like bees to honey and we didn't want to draw a crowd. I'd wait for Shannon, by myself, out in the field where, hopefully, the police would really have to be looking to see a couple of dudes banging it out.

It wasn't a bad plan, except for the gawker factor. Everybody on the weight pile, hand ball, tennis and basketball courts were locked on target, even though they could not come out and gather around to watch the fight. Bereft of a front-row seat, they all did the next worst thing: they stopped what they were doing, stood and gawked from wherever they were.

When the guard finally glanced out the window, he saw everyone staring up the hill. He looked to see what the attraction was and there we were, two big bulls in a field duking it out like something out of a John Wayne movie. It didn't take long for the rec officer to call in the cavalry to break it up and take us into custody.

Shannon fared a little better this time and I had picked up a new shiner, but by now his head was looking like Slaw from the movie 'The Goonies', so they took him to medical first. I was sitting outside, waiting my turn, just seething at the fact that I was now going to lock-up. Everything that my wife and I had worked and planned for so long was going to be blown away like smoke in a breeze. I was so angry at Shannon, but also at myself for allowing him to do this to me and my wife. This second go-round was so plainly designed to ensure that I went to lock-up with him. I almost wished

I had taken a knife out there and punched a bunch of holes in him for the anguish it was going to cause her when she found out.

While I was sitting there cuffed, thinking about this, the officers escorting me first to see the Doc, then to jail, were asking me why we were fighting. I gave no reply. All I could do was sit there and growl in frustration and anger at the whole situation.

Though I may have had a good, even justifiable reason for taking Shannon on, as far as I was concerned, *'the man'* would never know the whys of this. Prison Law: no matter what, you never talk. I could not tell staff what Shannon had done to drive me to the point of taking this self-sacrificing action against him, no matter the cost to myself. That's just the price of the path I've chosen, but I would be lying if I said that it was not a bitter one to pay sometimes.

Anyway, after the medical process of being looked over and cleared of any internal injuries etc. the officers took Shannon off to one wing of the S.H.U. and me to another. They threw me into a cell by myself, which made contemplating my misfortune all the more miserable. I finally fell asleep with the thoughts of my impending visit with my wife the next day, our first visit since she'd moved, on my mind. I knew this would crush her.

I woke up the next morning with the Captain and Lieutenant at my cell door yelling at me. Apparently, there were a couple of hundred white boys piled up on the yard. They were all the members of one family or another from the other States backing my brothers, as they braced all the independent woods from every State. The Captain and the prison staff didn't know what was going on and I certainly didn't. I couldn't even see out of the window, because of the metal shutters that were bolted to the outside wall in order to keep inmates in the S.H.U. as clueless as possible. Nevertheless, it didn't stop them from demanding that I stop whatever was going on.

"We've gone to lock down. I need this yard moving. We have a steel factory to run here, damn it!" the Captain griped at me. I replied that I didn't know anything. I was obviously unaware of what was going on, and had no way of stopping it if I did. "I don't care! I know this shit is stemming from you and Fry's fight yesterday," he finished.

"Look, Cap, I'm not going to tell you what we were fighting about," I said. "But maybe… you should just open the yard back up and let the *rest* of the trash be taken out." They walked off muttering to themselves about them taking the trash out and me not liking the trash that they collected. I went and sat down praying this wouldn't affect my visit, but also dreading the betrayed look I would see on my wife's face when she saw I was in lock-up.

Right on time, 9 a.m. they came to get me for the visit. My heart beat pushing the blood through my veins with increasing urgency as it always did in anticipation of seeing Jenna. But my feet were trying to hold me back, like I was walking through concrete, trying to keep me from the impending scene that I was fixing to endure.

I stepped through the door of the visiting room and looked over to the normal seats Jenna usually chose to sit us at. As I walked in, I watched the bright, excited smile fall from her face in shocked despair at seeing me led through the doors in handcuffs, wearing an orange detention jump suit.

"What did you do?" she yelled at me, before erupting into tears. She knew what this meant. It wasn't the first time. However, after having her move away from everything she knew, with just her animals, to be with me when I got out, the betrayal she felt was evident. Jenna was bawling by the time she got moved from her normal spot to where the officer had me sit, which was right out in front of the desk where all S.H.U. visits had to take place. She was hitting me even before the guard made it around into his cubical.

At five feet three inches tall and one hundred and twenty pounds; with long, brown hair that hangs all the way down past her thin waist to her shapely ass, my wife can be the prettiest thing in the world. Along with the store bought big C-cup boobs I'd bought her when I was in the State Penitentiary at McAlester, she could make my heart skip a beat with just a smile. However, it tortured my soul when she was sad or staring at me with hurt in her eyes. Now she wouldn't even look at me.

I tried to get through her wall of tears, asking her to hear me out, that I had no choice, what had happened had caused me to momentarily lose my mind. I held her hands in mine, partly so she wouldn't hit me anymore and quietly relayed the story to her, as she sobbed. I told her how they had been mistreating this kid, eventually selling him to the Puerto Ricans and my uncontrollable reaction to it. The whole time she never acknowledged hearing anything I said.

I finished with my voice full of anguish and my cheeks wet with my own tears. That's when I was reminded of the reason I married this girl in the first place. Still not looking at me, Jenna pulled one of her hands from mine, sniffling she wiped the tears from her eyes. After brushing the hair back out of her face, she looked up at me with more love and admiration than I'll ever deserve. "I am so proud of you for being the man you are," she said. She also told me that I had done the right thing and we would deal with it whatever the cost.

She understood, too, that this was just something we would have to eat, because the powers that be may never know the righteousness of my actions, nor care if they did. I told her about the stuff going on in the yard that morning and that the Major, Captain, etc. seemed to be mad at me, so we could probably expect the worst. As close as I could figure, it would mean about another year. That girl just looked at me and told me that she would have been disappointed in me if I had done anything less. However, she did say, "If anything happens again, promise to send someone else!" I told her I would. Believe me, she let my Brothers know about it when we were all down visiting together a couple of weeks later. They replied that they had tried, but I couldn't be controlled, to which she just beamed with pride and said: "That's my man."

CHAPTER FIVE
HERO FOR A DAY

Anyway they took me back to my cell after my visit. My heart was heavy, but still swelled with pride at Jenna's courage. I was sitting on my bunk sorting through it all when I heard the sirens going off out on the yard, which meant for everyone to get on the ground wherever they were. Apparently, the yard had been reopened.

There were a couple of people up and down the run who had a damaged slot or two in their window where they could get very small glimpses of activity out on the compound. It was confusing. At first I heard someone saying it was a white boy thing. They thought that they saw two men in cuffs and one on a stretcher. Then it was a Mexican thing. Next, someone said they saw a black guy go by on the electric ambulance cart they have there. I gave up trying to figure out what was going on. I had a pretty good idea, but none of what I was hearing made much sense, filtered through the minds and the mouths of the prison grapevine. What I did know was that the yard was locked down again and that I was now probably in more trouble.

An hour or so later, I heard the gate at the end of the hall open. Apparently, the fallout of whatever went down on the yard was making its way back to the hole.

There is more than one level of S.H.U. units, with several halls of cells, and they pretty-much scatter all combatants as far apart as possible. So, the chances were pretty good to get at least one of them on the run to tell the story of what is happening on the outside. However, the only prisoner they brought by my cell was that kid I saw the day before.

I went back and sat on my bunk contemplating what that meant. Then, I heard someone tap a jail key on my cell door and say: "Maxwell!"

When I looked up, I saw Lieutenant Turnbull in my window. He was a burly, flat-top wearing, hardnosed gang task force investigator that I'd had on my case for the last several years. Before I could move from where I was, the lieutenant pointed at me with his key to emphasize his words. "I'm speaking up for you!" Then he nodded at me with an odd look of respect on his face and vanished. Huh? What? I jumped up and ran to the door to ask him what he meant, but he was gone.

Over the course of the next few days, I found out what had been happening on the yard and what brought on the Lieutenant's comment. Apparently, the confrontation between the white *'families'* and the *'independent peckerwoods'* was simply that every patch-holder, related to me or not, was mad because I was in jail for this garbage; because most of the "independent" people knew what was going on. They were afraid, or didn't want to deal with it themselves and left it to me, even though I was closer to going home than any of them. The end result of that summit was what I'd been hearing from inside of the S.H.U..

The other two cohorts of Shannon's who were involved in the whole systematic abuse and sale of the mental kid were smashed out. The Puerto Rican got stabbed and the youngster sent packing off to protective custody. He had to go, because there were people who believed all this could have been avoided had he spoken up sooner.

They were trying to sort out all of the commotion when the boy told the police that he could not live in General Population any longer, so they then took him to the Captain's Office. I was told when they asked him if he knew anything about what was going on, he spilled, filling in all the gaps that they hadn't already plugged by interviewing other people on the yard. He also told them about me and my asking him whether the abuse I'd heard about was true, along with my explosive reaction and the subsequent fight with Shannon. He also mentioned a whole lot of stuff that we didn't even know about.

They took him straight to medical and discovered that he had been tortured continuously over the previous couple of months. He'd been burned repeatedly all over his body with tweezers and different metal objects that could be heated over an open flame. He even had burn marks on his penis. His tormentors had made him stick it through one of the holes of the metal pan beds we sleep on, which are just a little bit bigger than a quarter. Then they slapped his penis around until it swelled so much that he couldn't pull it out from the hole, whereupon they burned it with the hot metal.

Serious whacko shit... and that, was where Lieutenant Turnbull's comment at my window had come from.

As the days went on the Warden, case managers and counselors made a point to come by my cell and thank me. Deputy Warden Whirlinger and my unit manager, who had always made it clearly known that he had no love nor tolerance for A.B. types, told me: "Thank God there was someone on this yard who was willing to stop something like this, however they could, even with the potential price of their freedom hanging in the balance." They also told me that they would not let it cost me a day, even if they had to defend me all the way to the Regional Office.

I was given two weeks in the hole and credited for time served. The rest of my sanctions were suspended and I was informed that my halfway house date should stay the same.

When I was let out of the S.H.U. it was by one of the officers who had taken the kid to medical when he'd came in. After he opened the door releasing me back on to the yard, he followed me out. He spoke with me and described the burn marks on the youngster and told me I deserved a fucking medal... not to be locked up.

Wow! Let me tell you, sometimes life's just crazy. My head was still spinning from the turn of events when I was met on the sidewalk by almost all of my bros and several of my friends, wanting to help me carry my property back down the hill. It seemed they were enjoying the benefits of being on the side of right for a change as well. I looked up at the sky, savoring the feel of the sun on my face, and listened to my friends fill me in on what had been happening while I'd been gone.

Anyway, nothing ever goes all the way, how you would like it to go. In the end, I did lose a month of my halfway house. Apparently, justifiable or not, I was still considered a violent man. Regional Classification pointed out that I'd had a few other violent episodes accredited to me in my time at El Reno already, so I just walked away feeling lucky I had any halfway house or good time credits left at all. My wife was feeling the same as well.

CHAPTER SIX
RACE RIOT

The day of my original release date came and went, with me holding my breath that nothing else would come up that might threaten my new date. I stepped down from being the C.E.O. of my small, twenty-five strong, band of Brothers and handed the reins over to Travis Withers. Travis was a big, bald-headed Brother with twenty-something inch arms, a normally even demeanor and a mind that had never been influenced by drugs. He was a good man with strong family values. I felt pretty confident sitting back relaxing, now working full-time out at the steel factory, just passing the days away, but, of course, the realities of the sudden, unexpected volatility of prison life still hung in the air.

One evening, about a week and a half past the day I should have originally went home, D.K. and I were standing up on the top run shooting the breeze. He nodded his chin for me to look down to the bottom run where I saw Travis and Owen, a big ol' crazy wood from Houston who had horns tattooed on his head, come storming heatedly through the yard doors with agitation written all over their faces.

They were followed by several others of our overall unit crew; all of whom were on the 'Wood Pile' soccer team. One of them broke away when he saw us on the top tier and, running up to us, he blurted out: "There was just a big fight on the yard. A couple of Mexicans jumped a white guy on the soccer field."

No sooner had he gotten those words out of his mouth, the Mexicans who had caused the problem came through the doors. Before D.K, or I had the time to get to our people to find out what had taken place, the guys who had told us about the fight noticed the Mexicans and charged. This, in turn, started an avalanche of white boys falling upon the opposition. I was told later by one of the counselors that the security camera tape was like nothing they had ever seen before, and he described our assault as a *'white wave'*, whilst adding that the security footage was going to be used in the future as a training tape.

Our units are long buildings that resemble the inside of a shopping mall. They are split in half by a couple of sets of double glass doors on both levels with an officer's cubicle located on one side of the doors or the other. Each side housed around two hundred people on its two tiers.

Under normal circumstances, I would describe the atmosphere between races as respectful, come and go, live and let live. Our Hispanic friends usually worked well with us to handle most issues of life. They even taught us how to play soccer, whereupon I became a goalie. However, not many yards have the unity of the white community El Reno has and that solidarity had only been strengthened by the recent Shannon Fry ordeal.

The U.A.B. had a surprisingly large treasury, considering it came from nothing more than monthly dues, stores, - a *'store'* being the business of loaning out commissary for a fifty percent mark-up, gambling rackets and tobacco percentages. We stayed away from the more lucrative drug scene. I wanted to try and keep our guys as close to home as long as possible.

My philosophy was that something unavoidable might come up, such as this, but if we could avoid heat then we should avoid it; because every family I saw *'moving'* in the drug trade whether they were black, white or Mexican eventually got swooped up and scattered to the four corners of the United States. This was something that might not matter much to the people from other parts of the country, but for those of us who were from, or had family in, Oklahoma, it would impact upon our lives greatly.

Anyway, we would often sponsor *'block parties'*, as in *'cell block'*, out of our treasury. On someone's birthday, holiday or for whatever reason, we would pull some money out to pay the resident pizza maker to cook up fifteen or twenty pizzas. We would ice down forty or fifty sodas and tear open a bunch of bags of chips, whereupon thirty or forty of the white residents would circle around in their chairs down on our end of the building and we'd feast, not causing trouble, or trying to lord it over the other folks. They had their own events like that. It was just a way of sharing and a way of bringing our community, as we saw it, together. We did a lot of things together as a community like play softball, football and soccer.

You can see why, when there was an issue, the response was always a total turn out. Usually, though, there was some point where the mobs on both sides held back long enough to let the heads of their families work their way to the front so they could meet and determine if the issue could be resolved without all-out war, or, more importantly, if it couldn't.

It's a guarantee, given the chance, that those guys in charge of the Mexican outfit where the two or three Hispanic offenders came from, would hold them accountable for their violation of race relations and have them smashed off of the yard. They had done it before, for a number of reasons. But sometimes tempers are just too hot and a small spark can start an inferno. With Travis right at the head of the pack, the whole place rolled out with everyone assuming that whatever had happened called for this action, D.K. and I included. Once they collided the time for diplomacy was past. It was war plain and simple. Someone said they saw a shank and it was an all-out attack.

My friend D.K. and I ran along the top tier as the mob on the ground floor flooded towards the other end. Another half-dozen whites or so came from their cells and were running along the other side of the tier; all trying to get to the Mexicans. D.K. and I raced through the dividing doors and down the stairs into the middle of the onslaught, caught up in the moment like everyone else. However, when we got there, there was no one to fight. There were three or four guys on every one of the Mexicans; hitting, kicking and stomping. Knives were really useless on either side. Even without them blood was everywhere. To be honest, the thing that saved me was that there was literally nowhere for us to immediately fit in; thus giving our brains a chance to catch up with our bodies. D.K. was the first to realize that we weren't needed. I felt him pulling me back telling me, "Brother, get back up here. You're going home, they've got this." He reminded me, if I didn't keep my hands and feet to myself, I would once again lose my quickly-approaching release date. Dammit! He was right and I'm glad he was there. Darold and I backed up onto the stairs where we could watch over everybody. It wasn't long before the alarm was sounded and the response team came. They came from everywhere, yelling for everyone to, "Lock down!" The battle was over, if you could call it a battle, so we made our way back to our cells.

The medical staff descended on the unit and attended to the injured. After they had cleared them off, security took over and rounded up four or five of the combatants who had taken too long to pull back and as a consequence had been caught red-handed, quite literally, by the officers.

Things settled down for the rest of the night, but the next day the C.E.R.T team, which stands for Correctional Emergency Response Team, and the unit staff came back with a list of people they could initially identify from a cursory viewing of the video surveillance. As they were taking one of my Brothers by my cell he hollered at me and asked me to call his wife and let her know he was going to be in lock-up. The guard escorting him was one who knew me. He said: "Hell, Maxwell, I think you're on the list also."

I told him if they were using the surveillance tape to lock up all the guys they were getting then they could use the tape to clear me as well… that I only had a couple of weeks left. He allowed they were reviewing the tape and, if that was true, he would try and keep me out of the S.H.U.. They locked up about fifteen off of my unit and I was waiting for my cell door to open every time we saw the security team come back down the hill.

Finally, my case manager and that same officer came to my cell. "Well, Maxwell, I'll be damned, we thought we were going to have to come lock you up for sure. You were right, the tape showed how close you came to diving in, but it also clearly shows you didn't. Your wife should be happy with you this time," my case manager said.

He told me that Jenna had called up there. Somehow, she had already got word through the convict's wives' and girlfriends' grapevine, which is more efficient than you would sometimes like, that something had gone down and she wanted to find out if I was injured or in trouble. He said he told her I was alright, but she would have to call back, because they were still reviewing things. He said he'd informed her I was not in the clear yet, but, at that time, I hadn't been locked up either. I sighed with relief and relaxed.

The fight had spread throughout the prison, so we were on total lockdown. Over the course of the next few days we saw the guards escorting one, two, three and four people at a time off to the S.H.U., both White and Mexican. By the time it was all over, we had lost over thirty people and the Mexicans most of theirs.

We were down for over a week when the Gang Enforcement officers came and got Darold and me. When we got outside, we saw other officers were bringing a couple guys from C-unit and one, or two, out of A and B blocks also. Drew, coming out of 'A' building, broke out in a big smile, relieved to see I was still there.

All of us were either lead speakers or seconds for our different families and groups. We were told we weren't going to jail... yet, but, that the Captain and Major wanted to see us. Still, we were a little apprehensive when we were taken into the Admin building, which was connected by a hallway to the S.H.U., especially when we were led into a room that held two large holding cells. In one, were five or six of our guys while seven or eight Mexicans were caged in the other. They had been pulled from lock up. I also noticed that with them were a couple of their shot callers, who had been brought in off the yard... just like us.

We were let into the side that held our guys; hugs and handshakes all around. Then the Captain and Major got our attention. They informed us that they had brought all the heads of every family involved together in the two cells, they were going to leave and give us a chance to get our differences worked out. If we could not come to a satisfactory conclusion, the next option was backing up the busses and scattering us all to the furthest reaches of the B.O.P..

As they left, I had Travis and Owen bring us up to speed regarding what actually happened, while our '*Esè* counterparts did the same in the other tank. We found out a fight had started over one of our players kicking the shin bone of one of their players during the soccer match, at which point a couple of the Spanish team players of the same clique had jumped in; kicking and hitting our player. This immediately incited the white players and observers to start fighting with the rest of their team. In no time, unbeknown to us in the block, the horn was blown, the fight was stopped and everyone sent back to the units. It was then that D.K. and I had seen Travis and Owen coming in.

The guy who'd got jumped on the soccer field was there. He told us the kick was unintentional, but admitted when the other player got mad and cussed him out that he took the fight to him, at which point the dude's homeboys jumped in. Travis told me that they had actually stopped fighting out on the rec-yard before they were all herded into the units.

With what information I now had, I, D.K. and a couple of the other family representatives pulled the head honchos of the Mexican group to the end of the tank and began discussing the whole thing. Their issues were with being mauled the way they were on C and D units without having had a chance to handle the problem themselves, especially considering the fighting had already come to a stop on the yard. Our issues were simply that we weren't going to tolerate being jumped by another race without an all-out response any more than they would have.

In the end we came to the agreement, with a couple of dissenters on either side, that tempers were high and had got away from *'everyone'*. The Mexicans acknowledged that the violation had started with them and we agreed that there was at least one point where the situation may have been handled in a more diplomatic fashion.

I semi-privately chastised Travis. I didn't get onto him for handling up, but for not taking the time to bring the issues to a cooler head, namely mine, to decide which way to go with it when he had the chance. Instead, Travis made the decision on pure, hot emotion. Not to say I wouldn't have done the same thing, but that was the more responsible way to run an outfit when so many people's futures are reliant on the decisions we make. Like a little kid, he said playfully: "Owen hit the guy first!" We laughed, but then he got serious and said he understood.

Publicly, I told the Mexicans they poured the gas on the firewood and the heat of the moment was just too hot to keep it from igniting. Especially when someone saw one of their guys reaching for a knife. The guy was present and claimed the fight had already started before he did.

The result was that they would smash out the Esès who had jumped our soccer player and not let them back on the yard. Almost every one already in the hole got shipped off to one end of the country or the other anyway. We, in turn, would work on our diplomacy. All agreed things had gotten out of hand too fast and that we normally got along to work things out. A few of our joint business ventures were also mentioned. After shaking hands, we called the Captain to send for the Security Major.

We told him what we needed to do. The guards took us out and the others back to jail. Then the Major sent some officers to take us cell to cell, to tell our people we had worked out an agreement with each other and, when we were finally let out, everyone was to stand down. The Mexicans were taken around to their people as well. I sent Drew and one of D.K.'s people to handle A-Block, some independents to B-unit and a couple of Dirty White Boys to C-unit. D.K. and I were then taken to D-unit where we went door to door; with him taking one side and me the other.

CHAPTER SEVEN
THE LAST GATE

We were slowly let up and eventually life got back to normal, right before my release date got there. As I said... *finally*.

I was dressed out in clothes Jenna had sent to the prison for me; a black pull over T-shirt and a pair of Levis. Excitement was vibrating through my veins. It was really happening after sixteen years... *God... it's really going to happen!*

My wife would already be outside waiting, because she had stayed the night at a motel in Yukon. El Reno is only ten or fifteen miles from O.K.C., where the halfway house was located, and Yukon is probably right in the middle. Even though, my wife now lived in Oklahoma City, we wanted a place to stop at before getting to the halfway house. Jenna and I didn't want to get behind and overshoot the time limit I was given of an hour to get me there on my *'first day'*. However, we hadn't been together since we got married at McAlester. We *needed* a little one-on-one and, regardless of the risk, we were gonna get it.

There was another inmate, a big, dark-haired Indian kid named Josh, getting out and going to the halfway house also. They had brought him in from the work camp outside the fences to go through the release process and get his paperwork. His wife was picking him up too. We talked and struck up a friendship, easy to do in our overjoyed states of minds. He was a good youngster anyway. Josh was mad at himself, because he hadn't thought of the motel idea. He said that he and his wife were destined to try and find a place to pull off on the side of a road somewhere. I told him Jenna and I'd just had a lot more time to think about how we were going to manage our first time than they had.

Lieutenant Turnbull and a C.O. I didn't know came back to the little holding pens they were keeping us in while we waited for that final key to turn. The Lieutenant said we would be let out the side gate and that both of our wives were outside. He told Josh and I that they were not allowed to come all the way down to pick us up, so they were parked waiting for us in front of the gun tower. Then the Lieutenant looked at me. "Maxwell, this has been a long time coming for you. Good luck," he said as he stuck his hand out.

I took it, shook it: "Thanks, L.T.."

With that, he turned and opened the door to the sidewalk that led to the final two gates, then we all stepped into the morning air. Damn, it smelled good, felt and tasted good! I figured when I got on the other side of these last gates the smell, feel and taste would be even better. I was trying to look down through the fences and concertina wire for a glimpse of my wife. I knew she was almost as excited as I was. I could see the cars and the women once we were through the first gate. I was right... the air was already tasting better.

Last gate! *It's really happening!*

The Lieutenant opened it. I looked at him and he nodded back confirming it was alright to continue onwards. I think that was the only time I'd ever seen that man smile. Josh and I went through the gate and turned to see both of our wives standing beside their cars. They were parked on the other side of some line they'd been told not to cross. Neither of us said anything. I was far too caught up in the moment. My whole world was standing, or I should say bouncing, from one foot to the other in excitement down at the end of this parking lot. She was wearing a knee-length flowery sundress that I knew would have no panties underneath. She was looking like a ray of sunshine to me.

We were walking towards them, with every step I took getting faster. As the distance closed, I could see the love and joy on my wife's face. Finally, she could be contained no more. Gun line *'be damned'*, she took off running. She ran to me and jumped into my waiting arms. I swooped her up, kissing her and hugging her tightly. Wow! I finally let her go and we headed for the car laughing and smiling while we loaded up.

As we pulled out of the parking lot I reached over and pulled her skirt up. Sure enough – no panties!

CHAPTER EIGHT

FREEDOM

I had Jenna's skirt pulled up and my hand between her legs before we even got out of the parking lot. It was already too late when I realized I needed to restrain myself and wait until we got to the motel to molest my wife, because at that moment she drove us right into the bar ditch. She was as worked up as I was. Eight years is a long time to lust for one another, so I reigned myself in. We laughed and I kissed her as I forced myself to pull her dress back down. Damn! But... life was getting better.

Jenna got us back up on the road. I sat back for a second and breathed in... *freedom*. It's hard to describe the emotions I felt! As close as I can come to a description is exhilarating, exuberant joy. The hairs on my arms were even standing up and dancing. I don't know how to express it as well as I would like, but Jenna and I were happy, that's for sure.

There is just something about being free that makes everything you see, hear, smell and taste more vivid; all the way down to the way the sun feels on your skin. I was thinking about this as we drove down the highway watching the trees and fields go by.

All of a sudden, I realized that there was something missing... that for the first time in a long time I didn't have a blanket of dread draped around my shoulders. For the last year or so I'd been living with the ever-present fear that something would happen and the powers that were in control of my life would change their minds about letting me out. I had made it – I was out and getting me back in wouldn't be easy.

Jenna and I were riding in silence for a few minutes, both of us anticipating our quickly approaching motel stop, when I noticed a phone laying in the console. I snatched it up. "Is this your cellphone?"

"Yeah," she answered.

"Wow! It's so small! I'm going to call Joe and tell him I'm out." Opening it up, I could see the dial pad, which was easy enough. However, after I had pushed the numbers in, I sat there staring at the phone in my hand.

Jenna noticed, "What's wrong?"

"How do you make it work? I put the numbers in, but what do I do now? How do I make it dial?" I asked with a lost look on my face.

Jenna was looking at me in total amazement. "You're kidding, right? Oh, honey, you're not kidding!," she said, when she saw me turn red in embarrassment. "I'm sorry," she went on. "You push the *'Send'* button."

"The what?"

"The green button. Damn, baby, didn't they have cellphones when you were out before?"

"They had them, but they were as big as breadboxes and very few people owned one. Pagers were what everybody had back then," I told her as I pushed the green button.

"I didn't realize how much catching up you were going to have to do," she said, with a little sadness in her voice. I noticed how smoothly that she merged in and out of traffic and thought of how fast everything out there was moving.

"Me either," I admitted with a touch of nervousness apparent in my tone as I watched the fancy little insignia flashing on the phone's screen to indicate that it was ringing.

Joe answered on the fifth ring. Joe Sanders has been one of my closest Brothers and friends for over twenty years. We had done time together in several prisons and he had just got out of El Reno fourteen or fifteen months earlier himself.

"Yeah?" he said.

"What's up... asshole?" I taunted him anonymously.

"Asshole? Who is this?" he demanded.

"This is your prison daddy. Who do you think it is?" I went on, teasing him. I looked over at Jenna who was smiling at me and shaking her head, she knew Joe from the visiting room. I'd been keeping tabs on him since his discharge; he was struggling, but adjusting.

By now, he recognized my voice, not to mention the fact that there were only a handful of people in the world who would talk shit to him like that, with me right at the top of the list. "Why hell, brother, what are you doing? When did you get out?" he asked excitedly.

"Just now! Jenna and I are headed to the halfway house. I wanted to call and tell you I was out. I've got a couple of other calls to make – I can't believe this little, tiny phone…" I trailed off.

"Yeah, I know… right? You probably didn't even know how to dial it as long as you have been in. Take care, bro. Call me when you get settled," Joe concluded.

"You're right about that. Looks like I have a lot to learn…"

I got a couple of other quick phone calls in, one to my mom and another to my friend, Tony Mac. Then, Jenna announced the turn off for Yukon and the La Quinta Inn was coming up; the motel where she had stayed the night before, so we'd still have the room when we passed by.

At that point, she got my undivided attention. I loved my wife and had been waiting a long time to be truly intimate with her; hell, we both had. I was excited, even a little nervous. I reached over and slid my hand up the inside of her thigh. When I got to the top where her legs met, I could tell by her wetness and the shudder that ran through her she was as anxious as I was.

"Honey, let me get to the motel first. We don't want to wreck and get killed before we even get there," she cooed huskily, with a slightly glazed look in her eyes.

I laughed and squeezed the inside of her thigh. "We sure don't, babe."

By the time we pulled in to the parking space of the motel we were both vibrating with anticipation. Jenna and I were kissing and climbing all over each other. When we fell through the room's door, I literally had her sundress pulled off over her head before the door slammed shut behind us.

I'm not going to lie… I had concerns prior to getting to this point, concerns I'd never admitted to anyone, even to myself and certainly dared not let show to Jenna. They ranged from worries of premature ejaculation to whether "it" would even work right there at the last minute. That might be hard to understand for most people and, overall, I kept those thoughts stuffed off in a dark corner of my mind, afraid that if I let them manifest into full-blown 'worries' that I might actually create a self-fulfilling prophesy. I had heard of this happening before and I knew it was mostly a psychological phenomenon. Unable to be completely rid of any fears of that nature, I just refused to think about them.

All that to find out love and lust conquers all. I had no time for worries nor doubts when that door shut. In that moment, there was only Jenna… we came together and the rest was a blur. The next thing I knew, it was time to break away from one another and get back on the road to the halfway house. We had allotted ourselves forty minutes and we did not waste any of it. All too soon it was over. Forty minutes was not even close to enough time to relieve the sexual tension that had been building between us since we had been together. It took some effort, but we pulled ourselves apart, with the fear of not being able to make it to the center in time hanging in the air.

As it was, we were still ten minutes late.

CHAPTER NINE

HALFWAY HOUSE

We pulled into the parking lot of the Oklahoma Halfway House, called O.H.H. for short, with a dozen lame-sounding excuses explaining why we were late upon our lips; ready to spiel them out to the execution squad who, we were sure, would be waiting to terminate my few months of early release for our brazen negligence right on the spot.

When we got there, we found it as active as a beehive. I actually had to fight our way to the front of the line of halfway house residents who were signing in and out, going from one place to another. When I finally did get up to the desk, I was told to sit and wait until they had time to process me in; hardly giving me a second glance.

Humph! I thought, *you mean to tell me I rushed through Jenna and my first intimate encounter, cutting it short, then driving in a panic that intensified every minute we went over our supposed maximum allowable arrival time, to find out they weren't even paying attention!*

Gone were the worries of a guillotine cutting off my halfway house time at the neck. Now I was just plain ticked off. Especially, when about twenty minutes later I saw Josh and his wife straggle in, make their way to the check in desk and get same brush off that we had.

Josh and his wife made it over to where we were and after sitting down told us the people behind the desk said… they'd be with us in a little bit. Josh told me he'd tried to give the desk clerk the flat tire story he and his girl had come up with, but before he even got it out the guy told him… *as long as we were there and checked in by count time*, which was still an hour away.

"No, once you are here you cannot leave again." Josh said was the response when he'd asked. Now, I was really pissed off!

Okay... I guess, to be honest, even though it was irritating, I was just glad not to be starting out my new life with a bruise already on my record. I was relieved for Josh and his wife Trish as well. Back when we were in the holding tank waiting to be released from El Reno I'd been talking to him, although briefly, about making this my last trip to prison and what I thought it would take to stay out. He allowed that he too wanted to remain free and do right by his kids. I encouraged him to stay away from the drugs scene, get a job and follow the rules. After sixteen years you develop a serious respect for freedom. Like I said, he was a good kid. I was glad he hadn't already got in trouble for being late either.

"Damn, stud, you were pushing the roadside stop to its limits weren't you?" I commented.

With a crestfallen look he replied: "Hell, we barely even got started when we got into an argument about things she'd been doing. We've been fighting the whole time!"

I took a better look at his skinny, blonde-haired wife. I could see the tell-tale signs of a meth user written in the lines of her face. My young friend would be fighting an uphill battle; the odds of him making it were slim, walking back into a situation like that. But, they had three kids... so what are you going to do? I looked over at Jenna and counted my lucky stars that she wasn't an addict and was a stable down-to-earth girl.

Well that's what I believed, anyway. As I thought about it, I was reminded that Jenna was far from perfect herself. We had our own turbulent crossroads years before, not long after Jenna and I tied the knot in 2001, halfway into my sentence. I was incarcerated at O.S.P. where, as I mentioned earlier, I'd bought her the beautiful boobs that proudly protruded from her once A-cup frame. A stupid thing for me to do and I strongly recommend against such generosity now, considering it was probably the catalyst to her meeting and having an affair with my baby brother, who had just gotten out of prison himself.

Don't ask me how we got through that; I couldn't accurately tell you and, in the end, I don't think I ever really did. However, I tried and believed, or convinced myself, after a lot of tears and promises from Jenna, that she tried also. At least she was scared enough of losing me that she stopped and moved to Guymon to comply with the terms I'd put on our continued relationship. Over the years, with her living a supposedly open book life, only two blocks from my mother in a small town where nothing much goes unnoticed, I had slowly rebuilt trust in her. Looking at Josh's wife and seeing how fooled he was, the pride I was just feeling about my wife was suddenly overshadowed by the awareness that there might be more than I knew with Jenna as well.

With some effort, I pushed that thought away. I didn't want to tarnish our start… everybody is human and it was a long time ago. I was out now and, even though it destroyed any relationship between Jenna and my father's side of the family, or any relationship to this day between myself and my youngest brother, she had stuck by me and, to my knowledge, faithfully. Sounds stupid now, I guess, but I figured that counted for something. She had regained my confidence and I loved her still, so I was feeling fairly secure sitting there analyzing Josh and Trish's future chances. He only had thirty days to do, before he would be home, I silently wished him the best.

Eventually, the desk Sergeant got all the residents signed in and out. Then he called Josh and I up to get us squared away. After we were officially checked in, we had to send our wives home so we could be given a quick overview of the grounds, boundaries and the routine for moving around them. Then we got settled into our rooms.

Back then, the Oklahoma Halfway House was the only halfway house in the State that housed Federal inmates as well as being the only facility in Oklahoma that was still co-ed. This was something that Jenna wasn't very happy about, but, honestly, other women were not my concern at the time.

This little reintegration weigh-station was not restricted to just Federal prisoners; it housed State inmates as well. Although, under different rules and guidelines. They were fairly equal, with the few advantages that there were leaning toward the Federal residents.

It had been converted from an old clinic into what it is now, with a front check-in counter at the entry where a couple of staff offices were also located. It was constructed from three single-story buildings, whose only security was unlocked, but alarmed, emergency doors and windows with screwed down, heavy-duty mesh screens on them.

The buildings and their attending, awning-covered sidewalks were placed in the shape of a 'U', creating a courtyard at their centre, while there was a wooden stockade fence that ran along the opposing side closing it off from the alley. This courtyard was a small grassy oasis right in the heart of downtown Oklahoma City that smelled of freshly cut lawns and pollen rather than the stench of dirty prisoners and sweat that I was used to. It contained two or three trees, a half dozen flower beds and several picnic tables and grills for the inmates and their families to cook and eat on during visiting hours; which was basically all day long on the weekends.

Your family could come and dine with you for every meal as well if they wanted to, because we took our grub around the corner at the Greek restaurant that had contracted for the privilege... and the paycheck, for the skimpy meals that they provided. However, it was nice to have the option to eat with your family and eat what you wanted, if you were willing to spend your own money on it, and of course it was also pleasantly ironic that we could chow down on kleftiko minus the original meaning of the word. The recreation and smoking area was right across the street from the center at Dewey Park. It was a little city acre the halfway house had commandeered for the purpose of its inmates. It had an eight-lane elevated commuter highway that ran almost directly over it. Out here it was graffiti-covered concrete and crabgrass, it even seemed louder and smelled of oil and hot rubber, nothing like the secluded visiting yard only fifty yards away. The park and the restaurant were also the main reasons for all the congestion Jenna and I had ran into upon our arrival at O.H.H.. Because, to go to the diner to eat, or to the park for recreation, you had to first pull your file with a paper itinerary in it and have the desk Sergeant sign you in or out.

As with anywhere I go, in Oklahoma, anyway, there are always a few Brothers on the ground, I immediately ran into Earl and Buddy. Earl looked like a taller version of Kidd Rock and fancied himself a hustler. Buddy was a stocky, bald, albino, he was pretty handy to have as a right hand man; but wanted to have his fingers in everything. They both took orders well, and to my knowledge were clean. I informed them that my main goal in life was to stay drug-free and out of prison, that I was determined to make a life for my wife and I. But, out of loyalty to the Brotherhood that I had helped to structure, and to a commitment I had made years before, I intended to pull the street thugs together, organize them and put a end to the Bros on the outside doing scandalous shit to one another and other good people. It was also my intent to keep drugs out of the upper echelons. I informed them that, when I fulfilled my obligation and had things going on the right path, I would be calling for an election to pass the torch to someone else. Even with a few bad habits and personality quirks they assured me that they would, and could, comply. I made Earl and Buddy intermediaries between myself and all the rest of the Brothers, so I would only have to deal with a handful of them. Eventually, I put four others in similar positions. I did not like the circumstances, but I had made a promise; it was what it was.

My status preceded me. Everyone on the street, including the staff at the halfway house, knew I was a U.A.B. ramrod coming right out of the Federal system. I was unaware that, at the time, the F.B.I. had even assigned a couple of agents to monitor my movements. A 'person of interest' was the term used when I found out two years later.

It seems as if I was doomed from the start...

Anyway, as biased as it was to begin that way, I suppose it had its perks. The staff at the center left me alone and didn't go out of their way to engage me. Omar, the cool, black night-time guard who usually took twenty dollars to let people slip out at night while he padded his count sheet, told me that he and all of the staff had been informed of who I was and that if I wanted to go spend the night with my wife it was on the house – free of charge. As tempting as this was, I had to decline; the road to get where I was had been too long and too hard to put my fate in the hands of others. Even though Omar was probably trustworthy, to a self-serving point, all it would take would be for one A.W.O.L. resident to get caught up by the city police for something and as soon as they found out where he belonged it would cause a lock-down head count at the center that would be completely out of Omar's control. Tempting or not, I had a lot more invested in my being there than most.

Besides, I just really wanted to make it and do the right things. I didn't want to start living outside the lines again. That had been my problem all my life. For some reason, I never thought the rules everyone else lived by applied to me. I was done... I just wanted to live the rest of my life inside the boundaries of society and outside fences topped with razor wire. Even with the Brotherhood: it needed a boost of honor and integrity on the streets and I felt that it was my duty to at least try. However, I told my guys I never intended to commit another crime, unless it was assault and battery... on those who couldn't get their heads out of their asses and wanted to be a plague on our people.

The next few days after my arrival at O.H.H. were the toughest. I had a lot to do and didn't know squat. I could also tell that I didn't feel like the other people. I was stiff and out of place. Nevertheless, I didn't intend to waste any time getting bogged down by fears of inadequacy. The very first day, I got on the desk phone and called every dental prosthetic lab in the O.K.C. area, big and small. I was a little disappointed when my best response was… *although they weren't hiring at the time, they would take my name…* I wasn't going to let that slow me down! My next move was to go out and look for a job. To do that I needed an I.D, so I filled out an itinerary to the Department of Motor Vehicles, which was across town off Martin Luther King Boulevard. At the time, my wife worked the morning shift as a waitress and couldn't come and take me, leaving it up to me to figure out the bus schedule.

After having done all I could to prepare for my first big solo trip out into the world, completely unsupervised, I went to bed nervous, which is something that I have previously never admitted to anyone. Not even to Jenna when she asked the night before whether I was going to be alright on my own. She must have somehow picked up on the apprehension I was trying so hard to hide. I just stuck my chest out and said into the phone: "I'll be damned if I'm going to be nervous about being free!" Actually, I wasn't trying to be cocky about it for Jenna's benefit, but for my own sake. I was feeling weird about my freedom and it made me angry; I did not want to be afraid to be free! I didn't want to find out, after all it took to be free physically, that I was still incarcerated mentally.

Bright and early the next morning, I shelved any trepidation that I was feeling. I knew this was a step that had to be taken and I was going to take it. Without any one knowing about the fear I felt inside, I pulled my day's itinerary out of the filing cabinet, had it signed at the desk and walked out of the door. As easy as that, I was on my own, headed down town to the city bus depot.

It was an amazing morning! This was early summer, the air was still, and cool. The smells, were of concrete and automobiles, but oddly enough it still smelled fresh and free to me. I could even hear the sound of nature, through the morning rush; birds calling, bugs squeaking - the angel singing… *Are you kidding me?* I thought! *This is great!* But… I still felt like a kid that was stealing from a candy store. I was looking about nervously; with each step that I took feeling like I was violating some cosmic law. My heart was pounding and my breathing became rapid. I wasn't supposed to be here; no fences, no walls, no cops to tell me I had to walk on a certain side of the sidewalk. I was overwhelmed for a moment. *Dammit… why do I feel this way?* I wondered as I forced myself to relax and stilled my trembling hands. *Was I always going to feel like this?* These emotions only got more profound after crossing my third crosswalk. I realized that people were hustling and bustling by me, on their hurried way, seemingly without a care in the world, whilst I stood in their path stoically; waiting for the crosswalk sign to tell me that it was okay to cross. It dawned on me that there was a difference between myself and the rest of the people on the street. I silently envied them their freedom and sense of belonging that made them comfortable enough to jaywalk, completely ignoring the crosswalk signs. However, I still could not seem to restrain myself from automatically stopping and pushing the button. Something was wrong with me, I realized sadly.

I made it to the bus station, found the right bus, made the right changes and arrived at the D.M.V. without any problems. When I got there, I went in and got my State I.D., making it the whole way there and back to the depot without a foul or suspicious look directed my way. It may sound funny, but I was proud of myself. It's strange how, when we are out in the world for awhile we take so much for granted; things you would never even notice unless they were taken away.

Walking back to the halfway house, I was experiencing the same social phenomenon I had on my way to the down town bus depot. At least my mouth wasn't so dry and my palms weren't sweating as much. I hated feeling… intimidated? I wanted to belong, to fit in, to overcome this confined mentality that seemed to be laying on me like a sodden blanket.

At my second stop light, standing there with my finger poised to push the crosswalk button, I watched a man in a suit and a couple of nicely-dressed women cut catty-corner through the street. Skipping across to get to a cafe, they were obviously taking a break from the office grind to relax and dine in. My envy for their level of carefree comfort in this fast-paced, bustling world, won out. I dropped my hand back to my side, squared my shoulders and, after looking both directions to make sure the way was clear, I took off across the street in direct violation of the flashing "Do Not Walk" sign on the opposite light post. Every step I took further into the street loosened the yoke of restraint that years of prison life had put around my neck and shoulders and, by the time the instep of my foot hit the opposing curb I was free! The yoke had completely disintegrated and fallen away. It felt great and, within three blocks, I was brazenly cutting across the roads like everyone else.

I got back to the center feeling like a new man. I thought I had discovered the key to mental freedom. I even encouraged the other long timers who were suffering the same afflictions to try that method. I wonder how many of them would agree with me now, or how many would point out the folly of my assertion, because if I could go back in time I would push that damned crosswalk button... because I, wasn't, like everyone else.

CHAPTER TEN
DRIVER'S EDUCATION

Anyway, with me now feeling like Superman, Jenna and I took advantage of everything that gave us an opportunity to spend time together. We found that one of the perks of being Federal over State was that our loved ones could come and check us out twice a week and take us to the church of our choice, as opposed to the State offenders having to go to predetermined, pre-approved places of worship only. All we had to do was get our itinerary signed and we were good.

Jenna had an apartment for us over on the Northside, not far from Victory Christian Center. She had been going there every so often and liked it pretty well. Although I wasn't much of a Christian at the time, I had promised to take her to church when I got out. However, while I was still in the halfway house we were not necessarily looking to get our worship on. We just wanted a church close to our apartment that was large enough so that we would not stand out. That way, I could check-in with the center from its gift shop's phone when I got there, head out and get home without wasting too much time. It was the same process after the service; call the center from the church and let them know you were on your way in. Victory church was perfect, being only two blocks away. We would always pick the longest service and, afterward, would often come back in time to hear some of the message. We became comfortable enough to make Victory 'our church' once I was formally out.

The first time we did it, though, I thought surely they'd have somebody watching us for something like that? Besides, whether I was a practicing Christian or not, I still believed in 'Big G' and I was sure that the eye in the sky probably wouldn't be too pleased with my using His chapel passes to go tear the bottom out of my o'lady's wishing well... I never said I was a choir boy and, really, after being locked up as long as I had, I wasn't going to miss out on any opportunities to be with my girl. After all, at least I wasn't sneaking out at night. Anyway, it wasn't only about having sex, it was about spending time at home with my wife, too.

Home was a little cookie-cutter apartment right off of 42nd and Ann Arbor. Although the complex it was in was fairly large, covering about a quarter square mile with single-story apartments, the units were crowded together and small.

The drive to our place wound around one end of the complex to the other, through several sets of parking lots that serviced separate buildings. However, although there were many parking lots, there was not enough spaces; which became a great point of contention to me later. It came to the point of me pulling people out of their apartments and announcing to the whole end of my complex which spots were mine and were, therefore, not to be parked in by someone else. My wife told me there was something wrong with my view of the world when she found me standing, looking out our front window with a ball bat in my hand... just daring someone to pull into one of the spaces I had declared were for my use only. In retrospect, maybe she was right.

Our apartment was the second unit from the end in a row of ten, laid out in the British style called terraced housing; which can best be described as looking like single story monopoly houses slid together side by side. Another building just like ours ran parallel behind us. There was a fifteen foot grassy gap separating the two blocks that all of the residents' backdoors opened out to, where people would sit small grills and lawn furniture. The place itself was small, square, efficient and all we needed at the time.

Jenna hadn't been there for more than a couple of weeks when I was able to first see it. It was still pretty bare; all she had for furniture was a couple of plastic chairs in the living room and a double mattress thrown in the corner of the bedroom to sleep on, which we beat into the floor every chance we had.

It wasn't long after that, due to my being able to spend more time with Jenna, that I realized that she had a problem with alcohol. I noticed Jenna always had beer or a bottle of wine at the apartment and she would often get drunk on our excursions. I would watch her, only taking a few sips off a Budweiser myself, fearing I could be breathalyzed when I got back to the center.

However, the magnitude of the problem wasn't driven home to me until Jenna picked me up from a job interview one morning on her day off. I had walked to the place and had an hour to kill. She must have downed a bottle right before I got in the car, because I didn't even see it coming. A few minutes later, we were in line at a bank's drive-thru trying to cash my Federal discharge check, when it seemed to hit her all at once... Suddenly, she was shit faced drunk! I was totally caught off guard.

I didn't have anything against a little drinking or partying now and then, but this was out of line! I was on a strict itinerary courtesy of the restriction put upon me by the halfway house; an itinerary that I was way off of just by being in the car. Not to mention, that I was a long way from where I was supposed to be. I was pissed off, which led to the two of us having a full-blown shout-fest right there; two car-lengths from the bank's teller. I glanced out of my passenger window. It seemed quiet and peaceful on the other side of the glass. It was around eleven and people were casually taking the opportunity to do their banking before breaking for lunch. There were three full lines of customers, who were all staring at us. I didn't even understand what I was dealing with, or where it was coming from, but I was mad. Finally, I just made her pull out of line, out of the parking lot and down a side street before someone called the police. It had came on fast and had only got worse; she almost side swiped a parked car and damn near ran into the back of another before I could get her to stop.

"Stop this fucking car right now! You can't even drive!" I yelled at Jenna. Then, looking at my watch I went on: "I have to be back at the center in forty-five minutes. How could you pull this shit?" I clenched my jaw and fumed as I yanked the keys from the ignition. Squeezing my eyes together in disgust, I sat calculating my whereabouts in a town I didn't know wondering whether I could walk back to the halfway house in time.

"Grive meee the frugging eeess. I caaan drive... you assehole," Jenna slurred at me.

"Are you freaking kidding me?" I yelled as I slammed my fist into the dashboard of her little, gold 2004 Toyota Camry. "Are... you... freaking... kidding... me?" I pounded out each word. "You can't even drive down the street and I have to be back.. and... I couldn't leave you like this, even if I knew... exactly, where I was at."

"I can… rive. Fuuucckkker! I was doing jussss fine," she screamed at me, drawing the word *'fucker'* out into its own rattling shout.

I sat there looking at her – stunned. I'd never seen this side of her. In the eight years we were married, she had never shown so much irresponsibility. Well, that wasn't entirely true as I said before, but since then we had never had words like this between us, not to this degree anyway. My freedom was on the line now. "What have I got myself into?" I asked myself, while my mind frantically searched for a solution. I didn't have a license… but, to hell with it, I decided. "Get out of the car. I'm driving," I said.

"Noooo," Jenna answered.

"I said get out, or… I will drag you out," I ordered. I was acutely aware that my time to get Jenna squared away and myself back was quickly ticking away.

I guess the tone of finality in my voice got through to her, because she just harrumphed and got out. Mumbling to herself, she came around and got into the passenger seat while I climbed into the driver's and put the keys in the ignition. At least now I had a plan. "Which way do we go?" I asked.

"I don' know. Rou tell me," Jenna countered with a snotty smirk.

"Bitch… you're going to make me kill you," I said and tried to start the car… but it didn't even make a sound.

"Ha, ha, ha!" Jenna blurted out.

"What's wrong? Why won't the car start?" I demanded.

"It's been so long since you dove a car you don't even know you ave to push the bake in before it will start. Ha, you dumb frugger."

I hadn't even thought of the fact that I hadn't driven a car in sixteen years until she pointed it out. It still didn't really sink in until I jerked the gearshift into drive and pulled around the parked truck Jenna had almost ran us into. As soon as I got moving down the road the realization I hadn't been behind the wheel of a car in so long jolted me like my piss hitting an electric fence.

The world outside of the car was… moving, so were other cars and people who were traveling in one direction or another. My body tensed as I scooted up in the driver's seat with both of my hands gripping the steering wheel. I imagine that I looked like one of those little old ladies you see out on the road every now and then who drive ten miles an hour, clogging up traffic.

66

Jenna laughed again, but not as spitefully. I even let out a nervous chuckle at my reaction to this unexpected circumstance and the enormity of what it appeared I was accomplishing, in the face of it.

My relief at thinking we might be alright was short-lived. I came to the end of the side street we were on and drove right into a traffic circle. *'Oh, shit...'* I thought. Everything was now moving towards me and me towards it. My mind scrambled through my memory for every rule of the road or scrap of information that could help me through this. I kept telling myself I knew how to drive... but I wasn't prepared to have to remember so suddenly, especially while so charged up emotionally. I really am pretty good under pressure and what I am describing is what was going on inside of me, not what was going on the outside. I held the car steady as all the other cars and myself came together at the non-stop, four-way crossing. I remained stoic and in control even as we merged with the lights and sounds like a kaleidoscope. My mind shifted into top gear to put all the motion into perspective with my hands and feet. Within thirty seconds I had passed through it and I let the breath out that I hadn't known I'd been holding in.

Damn it... that could have been a mess and I would have been right back on my way to prison. Even if no one was hurt, if I would have caused just a fender-bender there would have been no *'ifs'*, *'ands'* nor *'buts'* about it, I would have woken up the next morning back in El Reno. I was mad... but Jenna... she still didn't get it.

I saw an entrance to a clinic parking lot and turned into it. I pulled around to the back, as far out of sight as possible, and parked. I sat there, head down. I couldn't believe it; I had forgotten how to drive. *How does someone forget how to drive?* I was too crestfallen and unsure what to do next to even be mad at Jenna any longer. I couldn't leave her alone and I couldn't drive.

I must have been mumbling to myself, because all of a sudden Jenna said: "It's alright, honey. You'll get it back. It's juss been a long time. You didn't do too bad, really. I couldn't help but laugh. You looked soo scared sitting there with your nose hanging over the steering wheel... so intense."

I looked at her... she hadn't hardly slurred her speech at all when she said that. She even sounded a little bit like the woman I knew. Hope surged in my chest. The longer we sat there, the clearer she became until she asked: "How much time do I have to get you back to the center?"

Glancing at my watch, I said: "Seven minutes. Can you drive? If you can't, I'm not going to let you leave when you get there."

"Just move over, you big dummy. I've driven in worse shape," she said with a slight slur still in her voice.

"Please God let her be alright," I silently asked Him as she and I switched places. She regained my confidence by finding our way out of a completely unfamiliar area to get us back to the center just in time, dropping me off a block away so I could run up to it on foot the way my itinerary called for. *One thing is for sure,* I thought, as I was having the desk sergeant sign me in. *I am definitely going to have to relearn how to drive A.S.A.P..* I couldn't help but think... if Jenna would jeopardize me and my situation this badly so early in the game... what else was I in store for?

On the bright side of all that, I got the job I'd interviewed for. I would be welding for a place called West End Roasters. They made high-end coffee bean roasters for coffee companies. The foreman, however, told me I wouldn't be able to start for a week or two when the man I would be replacing was leaving.

It would be a good job, but welding was really my second choice. I had put a lot of work and training into learning how to make dental prosthetics while I was at El Reno. I was good at it and I could do it from A to Z, especially the metal work, which was a little more technical. My main plan was to try and get work at a dental lab long enough to get an understanding of how the business worked on the streets. Later I would try to start my own in Guymon, which didn't have any.

I found out the lab, who had taken my name when I'd called that first day – and had given me a glimmer of hope by telling me I would be placed on some list of future prospective employees, was in walking distance. Since I had a week or so to kill before I could start work for the roaster company anyway, I put in an itinerary for the McConeghie Dental Lab down on 15th and Western Avenue. I just wanted to go down and pitch myself in person, so they might put me a little higher on the list when and if they needed someone.

I walked in there, explaining that I had another job already and knew they were not hiring, but since I was really wanting to work for them at some point and I had some free time – thought I would come in and show them my qualifications. They turned out to be a group of the nicest people I've ever known and McConeghie was one the highest esteemed dental labs in O.K.C.. It was not the biggest, but it was the best. Before I walked out they had changed their minds about hiring and hired me right out from under the welding job. That was on a Friday and I started work on Monday, hardly more than a week after I'd gotten to the halfway house, so I'd actually landed two jobs in my first week and a half out. My wife worked and I was feeling pretty confident about our success.

The only thing over-shadowing our life was Jenna's drinking. It wasn't like she was a fun-loving drunk either. She could be... but she was an unpredictable drinker; one minute she was happy and laughing, most often too loud, then, like flipping a switch, she was yelling and screaming; making me want to choke her. On one of those church trips we made, Jenna got so obnoxious that I left her at the house and drove myself to the chapel, since driving was something I was now practicing every chance I had. The skill was coming back quickly. I was fully intent on driving myself back to the center as well, because I was afraid that I would hurt Jenna if I stuck around. On my way back to the apartment, I called and told my wife I had already checked-in with the center from the church and I would park her car in one of the secured parking lots downtown and walk my last two blocks back to the halfway house.

"Who's going to sign you in, dumb ass?" she yelled into the phone.

Grrrr... I ground my teeth together so hard I thought they would shatter. She was right. I wheeled the car back around knowing I was trapped. I pulled up in front of the apartment and waited for her to stumble out.

"Ha, ha, ha! Stupid mother frucker," Jenna spat at me when she pulled the Toyota's door open. I don't really believe in hitting women, but I was angry and very confounded by her. I threatened to slap the taste out of her mouth if she didn't get into the car and shut up, which only started her off on another tirade. So, at the end of my rope, frustrated to the edge of madness, I sat her back in her seat with an open-hand to the side of her face... and she stopped.

"God damn it, Jenna... I can't do this. I would never leave you for anything, but I won't be with a woman I have to slap around to get her attention. You need to get your shit together! I've got fifteen minutes to get back to the center and you need to be able to go in and check me in, then drive yourself back home safely. If they realize that you are drunk, they are never going to let you check me out again!"

"I'm sorry, Jimmy. I don't know what's wrong with me. I've just been alone so long and alcohol has been my only crutch," Jenna sputtered, then she started weeping.

Now feeling sorry for her, I stroked her hair and, hugging her, I told her it would be alright; hoping and praying in my mind that it would, then I drove us back to O.H.H.. She did pull it together and we made it through the desk clerk whereupon Jenna made it safely home.

There was a crowd of us guys and girls who kind-of hung out together at a gazebo in the smoking park. They had gotten in the habit of drinking on the weekends; I guess doing drugs too, but my negativity towards meth kept it out of my face. Up to that point I had declined drinking as well, but that day I walked over and grabbed Joey's cup. Joey was in his mid-twenties, medium-built with red hair and freckles to match. He had lost a couple of fingers in an industrial accident while at the halfway house and didn't do much but sit around and drink, waiting for his settlement check to come in. Joey only had a couple of swallows left in his cup of Mtn Dew and Everclear, but I drained it. That was not near enough, so I took Lisa's mug out of her hand and killed that also. Lisa was a pretty, blue-eyed, blond, rich girl who had somehow fallen into the hands of the Feds. She was ornery as hell and probably the black sheep of her family like the rest of us... she was cool though. Her and Joey had a thing going on.

Anyway, when I brought her cup down, which had been full, everybody just looked at me. "Don't ask," I said with a frown. Lisa gave me a knowing little hug and I walked off back to my room. From then on I drank, not enough to get into trouble, but enough.

CHAPTER ELEVEN
REALITY CHECK

Things were going good with my job and I started adapting to life. Driving came back quickly. I was able to get a bank account and a debit card. Jenna and I started buying furniture here and there for the house; enough to get by until I was completely released. Then I would go get her stuff out of storage in Guymon.

Earl and Buddy got out and started getting in contact with Brothers on the streets, laying down the groundwork and preparing them to start attending organized events and meetings.

Some days felt like things were going to be alright despite a couple of incidents involving Jenna's drinking. I started really questioning who she was when she used money my mom gave her to help her payoff an overdrawn checking account for beer and cigarettes. I couldn't figure out how she could have hid all her character defects from me all these years, but, as stressed out and angry as Jenna made me, she had waited for me and I was going to give it my best shot. However, the hopes and dreams that had sustained me for so long seemed to be crumbling before my eyes.

The circumstance that really broke something between Jenna and I was when she found out she was pregnant. We had not planned on that at all; as a matter of fact, Jenna had used the *'Morning After'* pill after our first encounter at the motel. In my case, it wasn't that I didn't want a child, I just thought it would be irresponsible to not have our lives on stable ground, and I figured that by the time we were stable enough we would probably be too old. We had talked about it long before I got out, but, Jenna, with her new body, didn't want to stretch it out of shape.

We had become friends with one of the waitresses from the Greek restaurant and were over at her house visiting when Jenna took the test and discovered she was, in fact, pregnant. She approached me as if scared I would be mad, but I only smiled and hugged her. She appeared relieved at first, then, over the next few days, she broached the subject of aborting it, which I flatly refused.

"I just wanted to make sure you really wanted me to have it. I wasn't really going to do it. Do you promise you will still find me attractive when I'm fat?" Jenna asked, lighting one of her cigarettes.

"Of course I will... you'll be more beautiful than ever. Don't worry, this might not have been something we planned for, but nonetheless, it's our responsibility now... and I promise you I'm really excited about it," I reassured her. "But, your going to need to give up smoking until after," I indicated the Marlboro she had between her fingers.

"I know," she said looking down at her hands which were pressed against her knees, the smoke, dangling from two of her slender knuckles. She seemed pleased, but I could still tell that something was wrong. I thought she was just unsure of how genuine my enthusiasm was, but I was completely on-board from the moment she told me... *what was that distant look on her face though?*

A few days later, the fragile fragments of my life that I had worked so hard to piece together were smashed asunder when Jenna came up to see me, sat down and told me matter-of-factly that she had lost the baby. If she'd had any doubts about whether I was truly wanting to have this child with her or not, they were washed away with the tears that I shed.

"How can you be so calm about this, Jenna?" I asked her through my sorrow.

"Miscarriages happen all the time, Jimmy," she answered in a hollow voice.

I looked at her... something about the way she said that... "You didn't do this, did you?" I frowned.

"No, Jimmy. I wanted to have our baby more than anything, but I didn't really want to get stretched out of shape, so maybe it's for the best," she said. She was squirming around, trying to light a cigarette. Looking everywhere... but at me.

"You did do something! What did you do, Jenna?" I asked her, my sorrow slowly turning into anger.

"Nothing... besides you said a long time ago we couldn't afford a child," she whined.

I snatched the smoke out of her mouth and crushed it, throwing it to the ground. "That's not a decision you make alone, which would be tantamount to killing my kid. Get away from me, Jenna!"

"I didn't do it! I swear," Jenna pleaded.

"For some reason I don't believe you. Leave!" I shouted with more tears welling up in my eyes... but now they were tears of anger – maybe even hate.

A girl and two guys from the center were walking by where we were sitting in the visiting area, they looked at us and hesitated. I glared at them whilst gritting my teeth – they moved on.

"I didn't do it, Jimmy," Jenna said again, trying to get though the wall in my heart that I was constructing as we sat there. "Just because I didn't want it doesn't mean I did anything."

"I really need to believe that. But at the moment... I don't," I said, then I got up and walked off.

She hollered at me before I got around the corner, finally bursting into tears herself: "I didn't know how much you really wanted it 'til now!"

I went to my room thinking: *How could she have done that? Did she do it? Could she really?* She hadn't even been upset until I was leaving. There was no doubt that I didn't know what she was capable of after some of the things she pulled while I'd been at the center. I wanted to believe her, but, out of all the things I had faced and put up with from her since I'd gotten out of El Reno, this one... this one could be a deal-breaker. *Shouldn't I be consoling her? Yeah... if she even acted like she'd needed it... How could she?* I was thinking too much... my head hurt.

Finally, I got up and went outside. The crew were out there as always since it was the weekend. It was just mid-afternoon on a Saturday and they were already well on their way to getting drunk. Thank God. I took a straight pull off of the one hundred and ninety proof whiskey bottle they were spiking their cups with... Wheeew... Wheee! If you have ever taken a straight shot of Everclear, then you know exactly what I mean.

Well, that started the ball rolling... and following my lead, we all got very drunk. I must have told Lisa what was going on, because she stayed pretty close to me. I didn't mess around on my wife, but I was needing some sympathy. I passed out on the picnic table. It was dusk when I woke up... to discover Lisa was hoovering my rooster right there in the open. I looked down at her and she looked up at me. "Where's Joey?" I asked.

Delaney, one of our drinking crew, was sitting at the end of the picnic table staring out the other direction, "He came and saw what Lisa was doing. You growled at him and he turned around and walked off," he said.

Damn it! What a asshole I was. "Lisa, stop." I said, pushing her hair out of her face. I knew she liked Joey and I knew that she would regret this later. I already did. Joey wasn't a friend, I didn't even know him, but I never feel good about hurting someone who has never caused me any harm, not to mention my wife. "Stop it," I said to Lisa, "I mean it," and I sat up, pulling away from her. I liked her, but this wasn't cool. I brushed her hair back out of her face again and told her to go find Joey. Then I got up and walked inside to my room and passed out on my bed. It was about 7:00 p.m..

About 1:00 a.m. I was woken up with the staff rolling the whole place out under the pretense of a fire drill. They were herding us all across the street to the park. I stumbled out feeling more hung-over than drunk. When I got outside, I found out that some guys in the East Building had been caught with a bunch of booze in their rooms; drunk and raising hell, so the staff was breathalyzing everyone.

They separated us by gender and started having people step up. It was a two-stage process and you had to fail twice in order to receive a misconduct report. If found guilty of any one of the various rules at O.H.H., the malefactor could have his or her time extended by losing previously earned good time credits.

As each offender stepped up to the front gates of the park, staff members had them blow into a little tube. If they got any reading at all you were put on the list to be retested after they were done with the rest of the residents.

I was quickly calculating the last time I'd had a drink. It had probably been 5:30 or 6:00 that evening. I really wasn't sure how long I'd been passed out before I woke up to Lisa devouring me, but it couldn't have been long, no more than thirty minutes. The sun went down at seven, so I could safely say it had been seven or eight hours, but I could still feel that one-ninety proof deep down inside of me. I stepped to the back of the line, wanting as much time as I could get before I had to blow in that tube.

I silently cursed myself for what a fool I was. I was scheduled to get out the following Friday. I still didn't know what to think about Jenna, but tricking off my discharge from the halfway house was not going to make anything better. I cursed myself again.

It was a nice night at least, warm with just enough of a cool breeze to make it pleasant. While I stood there waiting for my turn I noticed Joey was staying clear of me, so I walked over to him and told him I was sorry.

"It's Okay. She really wasn't my girlfriend, anyway," he said. He was fidgeting looking at the ground. I could tell he was hurt and just trying to save face.

"I don't know what happened here, but I wouldn't do you wrong on purpose, little brother. I've got nothing against you. I know that Lisa likes you... I think she was just trying to make me feel better about some stuff that was going on between me and my wife. It's messed up all the way around. Everclear is some wicked shit," I told him.

"Yeah," he agreed. "Do you think Lisa still likes me?"

"Yeah, she does. She is probably mad at herself right now," I said and patted him on the back. When he walked away, I looked up and saw Lisa watching me from the women's group. She was moving as far back as she could in her line as well. She threw a question up to me with her eyes. I just shrugged and nodded like I thought it would be alright between her and Joey. She nodded back and turned away.

There were about fifteen of us who blew hot the first time. Most of our drinking crew passed out early enough to slip through; Lisa and I did not. The center housed about one hundred or so inmates and the rest of the violators were from different parts of the facility. Lisa and I tried to hang out in the back of that line as well. Eventually, though, it got too short and Lisa stepped up at about 2:30 a.m.. It had been over eight hours, to the best of my calculations, since she had drunk anything. The first time she blew in the tube the results were inconclusive. The second time... she was clear. I saw her breathe a sigh of relief, flash a hidden smile at me, then take off back to the women's wing.

There were a couple more guys ahead of me, but my turn finally came up. After watching Lisa and a few of the other drinkers slide through I was a little more hopeful that I might make it. I'd been drinking a lot though, so I wasn't feeling real confident about it as I stepped up to the desk.

"Well, Maxwell, are you going to blow numbers, bud?" a stocky red-headed cop asked, holding the little white tube up for me to blow in.

"I hope not. I get out next Friday," I said.

I blew a .04... He let me try again and I blew a little bit less, but the thing about blowing numbers while you're incarcerated is that there is no cut off. Any is too many, because we're not supposed to be drinking at all.

"It's too bad we had to drag you out of bed to give you a write-up," the officer said a little sympathetically. He knew that the misconduct report would undoubtedly change my discharge date.

"Who exactly was it got all this started?" I asked the guard as innocently as I could.

"Maxwell, you need to let that go. You don't need any more problems than what you've already got," the night officer said.

I shrugged and went back to my room.

The guys who'd caused all the problems got beat up the next day, but it still didn't make me feel any better... or change anything.

Jenna and I went to church the next morning and I mean we really went to church. She was upset about my pending misconduct and blamed herself. She swore to me that she did not abort our baby. I wanted to believe her. I had no proof otherwise and now, on top of it, I had shame and guilt for what I'd let happen myself the day before. I marked it up as something I would never know one hundred percent for sure and chose to give her the benefit of the doubt. She had stuck by me, I told myself, but, though I loved her, I was starting to not like her very much.

As I was signing out to work on Monday morning, I saw a note in my file to see my case manager that evening. When I got in from work, I found there were enough people having to sign their misconduct reports for failing the breathalyzer that I was able to dodge the process that night. Tuesday evening I finally got corralled into signing my write-up too, which is just acknowledging that I'd received it, then I was told to look in my itinerary folder for the hearing date and time. I found the notification on Wednesday, telling me to stay in from work for my hearing on the following day, where I would be found guilty and sanctioned to lose 'good time'; thereby pushing my release date back further. Knowing my discharge date was on Friday, I wadded it up and threw it in the trash.

I crossed my fingers the next morning. I hoped, since I left for work while the night shift was still there, that I could make it out the door without someone realizing I wasn't supposed to be leaving. I figured they would know where I was, and, if they really wanted me, they could still come and get me... but that is what they would have to do.

When my time was up, my time would be up. I knew it should take at least twenty-four hours to process and stop my discharge. I was hoping I could make it until morning without the O.H.H. staff being able to send in a conviction and have the sanctions approved by the Regional Office in Dallas, Texas. All I could do was just make the process as difficult as possible... and hope... I could squeeze out the door.

All day long I sat at my work station, looking up at the phone every time it rang to see if whoever answered it glanced back in my direction. I was relieved when the day was over and still no men in black suits had come to take me away. I thought for sure the moment of truth would be when I took my itinerary up to the desk sergeant to sign-in from work, but he never even glanced up at me when he saw my name slid under his nose.

I wasn't absolutely positive, but I thought, *I've made it, they don't have time to stop me now.* Of course, I wouldn't be sure until I walked out the door the next morning with my discharge papers in hand.

I still didn't sleep easy that night.

The next morning, Jenna was up to the center early. This was the big day! We were excited, but nervous. The administrator of the halfway house was in the office with my case manager. I naturally assumed that they were talking over a strategy to try and keep me in custody. It seemed like they were in conference for a good hour, with Jenna and I looking over at every unfamiliar male who walked through the front door, wondering if it could be a U.S. Marshal or not. They are usually quite easy to spot, since they have a certain way of dressing and walking, like they are untouchable or something. We saw several who made us tense up, but, one after another, something they did or said exposed them as something other than an officer there to pick me up.

Finally, I was called into the office. The halfway house administrator, Ms. Chandler, was an older woman, her greying, red hair was pulled back in a tight bun giving her face a severe, sharp-nosed look. She had a hateful attitude to match. My case manager, Mr. Jones, was a slightly-balding, medium-size, middle-aged black man. Jones was a decent guy who did his job, preferring to see people succeed rather than fail. He had actually been pretty helpful to my wife and me while I was there. They were both looking at me as I walked into Mr. Jones' office.

"Mr. Maxwell, you didn't come to your misconduct hearing yesterday. Did you not get a paper in your file telling you to lay in from work?" Ms. Chandler asked, barely containing a sneer.

"No, I didn't see anything," I lied. "Just my regular job itinerary."

Ms. Chandler was looking at Mr. Jones with an accusatory glare. Mr. Jones asked me hurriedly: "Are you sure, Mr. Maxwell? Because I put one in there myself." The way he cut his eyes at the administrator, who was still looking at him with some weird, predatory look of triumph on her face, made me realize that it wasn't really me who was under the gun here. She was trying to blame him for not processing me in time. I knew he had previously been accused of being too easy on the inmates. This was the powers that be trying to shift the blame and use Mr. Jones as a scapegoat.

There are not enough good people working in the system as it is, so looking directly at him, I said: "Oooh... that piece of paper... the one that told me not to go to work, because I had a misconduct hearing at 11:00 am? Yeah, I saw it and I threw it in the trash. There is no way you can stop me now, Mr. Jones. You've been after me since I got here and if you thought I would make it easy for you to shaft me then you were wrong." Mr. Jones knew I recognized what was going on and he gave me a slight nod; his appreciation showing in his eyes.

"You're right, Mr. Maxwell. You're lucky Ms. Chandler there didn't want to upset any of the prospective employers around here by sending someone to get you. By the time you got back from work, it was too late."

I looked at the Administrator. "Why, thank you, Ms. Chandler," I said in my most sincere voice. "I guess... you would really be the one responsible for helping me. Thank you again. That was really nice of you. I promise I won't let you down. I'd even hug you if I could," I finished, taking a step toward her.

I thought she was going to turn purple. She made some kind of gurgling sound in her throat as she took a step back. "In all my years here I have never seen someone just not show up for their hearing! Your papers are signed," she spat. Then, tossing her head, she snorted and stormed out.

I turned to Mr. Jones, who was smiling openly now. "She's right. Your papers are signed. There's nothing she could really have done. You ensured that when you skipped by, signing your write-up on Tuesday instead of Monday," he said.

"I guess someone could have came and found me if they knew that," I replied, looking at him under my eyebrows.

"I had a lot of misconducts to sign that night and I was already working overtime as it was," he complained casually. "I was right about you, too. Thanks for what you just did." He grinned again and stuck out his right hand, sliding my signed discharge papers across the desk with his left. "I don't think I have ever seen her so flustered, ha ha. Good luck, Maxwell. Your P.O.'s name and number is on the front page. You need to call him when you leave here."

"Thanks, Mr. Jones," I said, shaking his hand and taking the papers. "Good luck to you, too. They need more people like you around places like this."

When I stepped out of his office door, Jenna was standing there with a leaden fear tormenting her face that only lifted when I held up the papers and said: "I'm free, baby!" Then she screamed in delight and jumped into my arms.

Maybe... things would be all right. I hugged her back and we headed out to the car.

Chapter Twelve

Rise & Fall

When we left the halfway house that day, I can't even begin to describe the feeling of freedom I felt. As Jenna was driving us home, I finally relaxed from the tension of the last week... well, really... of the last few years – I was really out. I sat in the passenger seat straight and alert; a sense of hopefulness permeated my mind. I lifted my chin, looking at the sky, letting the sun warm my face through the windshield's glass. Internally, I felt knots loosen that had been tied tight for longer than I cared to think about. With a slight smile, I turned and looked at Jenna. "We made it. Seems like just yesterday we were in the visiting room at McAlester talking about this day," I said.

She smiled back.

My sense of complete freedom didn't last long. When I checked in with my Federal parole officer, Steve Stone, I quickly found out that I still had to jump through hoops and dance to their fiddle. Once you get caught up in the justice system it seems like it never lets you go. On top of that, Steve informed me I needed to chase down someone in the State Department to dig up my State parole as well. It didn't really matter to me, I wasn't doing anything wrong. I complied. Now I had two parole officers... *'Freedom'*, what's that?

When I went in and met Mr. Stone for the first time, I must say I was fairly impressed. He was a tall man a couple of years younger than me, but old enough for his dark hair to begin greying around the temples. Steve was very clean-cut and well-dressed like all Feds are. I could see right away he was a very 'by the book' type. However, as he read me the rules and terms of my supervised release, I got the feeling that he wanted to see me be successful.

I told him about my dental laboratory job, that I was clean and intended to stay that way. I even told him some of my hopes and dreams for the future. As I expressed my sincere desire to make it, he warmed up to me and seemed fairly impressed in return.

Mr. Stone set me up on the *'Color Line'* for my urinalysis testing, which I assured him I would never fail. The Color Line is a system developed to manage all the Federal and State's drug testing. An offender is assigned a color, such as fuchsia and, yeah, I did say fuchsia; which just so happens to be the first color that I was given. They had hundreds of colors and every day except Sunday the worker bees at the piss collection place, who I'm not going to glorify with some highfalutin job title, since it is what it is, would put out a list of colors on its answering machine. Its clients, people like me, could call in and check it as early as seven a.m.. If your color was mentioned, you had to report to the piss place to give a sample sometime between the hours of eight a.m. to eight p.m. weekdays or nine to one in the afternoon on Saturdays.

It was a pretty convenient little system, especially since I worked only two miles down the same road from where it was located. It also helped that I had no worries in that department. I had quit doing drugs years before, while I was still in prison. I hated them and what they did to people's lives – mine and my kids... particularly. After decades of observing the devastation to individuals and their families, not to mention countless trips to prison myself, their negative effects were obvious and undeniable to me. Not only that, I knew if I didn't stay clean I would be doomed to fail again and I was determined to make it this time.

I was very meticulous about trying to set things up right. Jenna and I got a computer that I hooked up our banking through. Thanks to a couple of computer classes I'd taken in prison, I created an Excel sheet with all of our monthly bills in it, putting little equations in the cells to add them all together for our yearly total, etc. - pay days highlighted in green. The system was good and it gave me a sense of organization and control of my financial fate. I spent every morning tracking bills and keeping our money straight. Electronic money was new to me and I just knew, if I blinked, it would all be screwed up or stolen. Overall, though, it was not bad for a guy that couldn't even dial a cellphone that first day out.

Disciplined from prison and getting more sure of myself on the streets after the breakthrough I had at the halfway house, I was up every morning at four a.m.; jogging the half-mile to the gym down the street... workout... jog back... shower... breakfast... off to work.

We painted the apartment – naked – and turned our little plain-Jane shoebox rental into a cozy place to hang out; laughing and enjoying finally being free. The neighbor couple a few doors down even got a kick out of my freedom, after seeing me creep out onto the back porch bare-assed to put my paint supplies up. I was completely unaware of their presence until I saw the cherry glow from their cigarettes, whereupon I promptly assumed a similar color.

My dad had a '98 Buick Regal that he let me work payments out for. I studied for my driver's test and within a few days of my release I had a ride, insurance and a driver's license. All legal and legit. Not long after that, I was able to pick up a sweet little Harley Road-King pretty cheap.

I still had a few adjustment problems, but overall I was loving life. My future was looking hopeful and promising. My U.A.s were coming back clean. My parole officer was happy. I was happy. The only rule or law I was breaking was the one that says I could not be in the company of other felons. That one I broke into a million pieces.

I really threw that little restriction to the wind when my birthday came around. Although Jenna wasn't a big fan of the Brotherhood, she nevertheless organized, via the council, a party for me that included all my friends, bros and their families. On October the 17th, my apartment, its parking lot and the alley behind my unit were full of street-side A.B. members... old and new; all there to party and show their respect for what I stood for in prison and for what they hoped I would stand for now that I was finally back out on the streets.

A couple of Brothers went to the apartments in the building that backed up to our alley to 'ask' if we could use the grills they had by their back doors. I wouldn't let them just take them over without them at least trying to get the owner's permission. Either way, we ended up with five grills all fired up and spitting out wonderful-tasting hot dogs, hamburgers and B.B.Q. chicken. We stretched a big tent from rooftop to rooftop, sat the stereo outside and had a great time.

I'm not going to lie; it felt good to see so many people, Brothers and their families enjoying my birthday. For a moment, I even thought Jenna was getting into it, but she was becoming very suspicious and jealous of everything, even though she set it up. My little brother, Rusty, and his wife showed up. I heard him telling people: "No, I'm his real brother," which only drew him several blank stares back, until I explained he was my biological brother… Then it was all hugs and handshakes.

We were having a good time. I'm not so sure about the rest of the complexes' tenants; the boys had pretty much overran my end of the property, taking up every available grill and open parking space, which was something that particularly peeved me when other people did it. We weren't trying to be obnoxious and I made sure they stayed friendly. There were a couple of cool neighbors who came out their back doors to see what was going on. We offered them hotdogs and hamburgers too. The couple I had ran into a few nights before with nothing on, but a splash of green paint on my willy, took us up on it and enjoyed our hospitality. The rest of the residents, however, just peeked out through their curtains, or hurried into their cars. This wasn't really the impression that I wanted to make on my new neighbors, but what's a birthday boy gonna do?

Before the party wore out and people started to leave, I had the Brothers gently push the women, kids and all non-patchholding persons into the front of the house and out of the alley. Then we had a quick meeting and discussed the future of the U.A.B. on the streets and my vision for it.

I explained how we could start a newsletter to link the Brothers on the streets together with those who were in the State and Federal prisons. This would allow us to circulate to the Brothers as a whole what was considered acceptable behavior and what was not. Besides keeping the Hood connected and informed, I saw us promoting the good side of what we do, something the general public doesn't have any idea about and probably never will. Although we are often perceived, sometimes justifiably, as bad-to-the-bone, hate-fueled tyrants, that was not our intention from the offset and it's certainly not our raison d'être. There have been many unsung heroic deeds by people in prisons everywhere, where prisoners put themselves in the line of fire for what's right even when they know that their actions will mostly be ignored or misconceived.

My desire was to change what we do into something that helped our people instead of plagued them. I had read all the R.I.C.O. laws. If we stayed away from the drugs and ran it right we could achieve great things and avoid prosecution at the same time. We might even swing the public's opinion towards our concept of what *'white pride'* means to us, which boils down to *'caring for our people'*, rather than the overly simplistic stereotypical notion that we wish to raise ourselves by the expense and hatred of others.

I had a lot of support from most of the guys, but it didn't matter if I did or not, since the council was behind me and we were going to do it my way. I had Earl, Buddy and a couple of others organize and set up our monthly meetings. We placed Joe Sanders, as our new treasurer. He was still clowning me about not knowing how to use a cellphone when I got out; we laughed, then I punched him and gave him a big hug. The meeting broke and we went on with the party.

Over the course of the next few months our meetings grew larger, to the point that the only place that we could hide them was in plain sight; disguised amidst the B.B.Q.s we'd throw with our families.

The meetings didn't always go off without a hitch, but overall we were coming together.

CHAPTER THIRTEEN

KARYN

As the aftermath of my first birthday as a free man in sixteen years passed, I was steadily rolling towards a few more firsts out in society, such as Halloween, Thanksgiving and Christmas. My social skills were quickly becoming more sophisticated, but the coming events nevertheless left me with an anxiety I couldn't explain to myself, let-alone anyone else. The birthday party wasn't so bad, however. I was in my own element. The coming holidays involved my stepping away from that comfort zone into the world of *'normal'*, free-world citizens, which was something I needed very badly and secretly longed for. I was aware that feelings of comfort with my own kind, ex-convicts, was a symptom of a self-destructive mental shadow that hung over me and had been ingrained into the core of my mind since the first time I got released from a boys' home when I was eighteen years old.

I recognized it after so many wasted years in prison and so many failed attempts to break the cycle of recidivism in my life. If I wanted to make it, I had to free myself from those chains and become comfortable in the company of the average, everyday, law-abiding citizen. It may sound easy, but it's not. Ask any veteran who's returned from war. You always feel like you know something about the world, and by that I mean the 'dark' side of the world, that the average person is lucky enough to be oblivious to. Whether the feeling is founded or not, it still separates you from them and, in a convict's case, it limits his vision and his ability to thread into the weave that the fabric of society is woven from.

That's why I accepted when Rusty, my younger brother, invited me to a Halloween party with him and his friends. They were people he'd been stationed with when he was in the Air Force at one time or another and none of them had ever been to prison. Even though it brought back some painful memories and involved my dressing up in a costume, I felt it was necessary for my evolving into a truly free man.

As I've said, it had been a long time since I had been to a Halloween party and that's if you could even consider my last time *'going to the party'*. Really, I was just working the door of a nightclub that was having a Halloween theme.

Thinking back to that night brought back a deep sadness I thought I had long gotten over. It was almost painful enough to change my mind about going to Rusty's festive gathering. I felt ashamed as I looked at my current wife, Jenna, while memories of the love I'd found, and lost, at the last costume ball I'd attended so many years before took me on an unexpected and unwanted journey into my past.

Karyn Wagoner... I had pushed her memory from my mind years before I'd even met Jenna, because I couldn't bear the pain. The void created by not having Karyn in my life had been patched over whilst I was trapped in prison for all that time. As I contemplated my first October 31st on the streets in a decade and a half, I was almost overwhelmed with memories and emotions that I thought I had long since put to rest. It was a crazy, short love-affair, but it had nonetheless left me feeling – no... it was more like knowing – that Karyn was The One; that once in a lifetime One, when you know your soul has touched something special... something that was meant to be.

...It was 1993 and I had just turned thirty. The mother of my children and now ex-wife, Maryjo, and I had broken up. One time out of several, before I finally divorced her in 2000. She was living in Tulsa, while I lived in Oklahoma City. I was the maintenance supervisor over my apartment complex, which granted me a pretty nice little poolside place rent-free. The H.V.A.C. license I had earned during my previous trip to prison was coming in good for something.

I was also clean and sober – A.A. sober, although I moonlighted as a doorman/bouncer at a couple of nightclubs and more than one strip club a few nights a week. It just so happened I was working a nightclub on Halloween night, one of the *'beer only'* joints that allows eighteen and ups to go out, drink and party in a club environment. It had a live band and a big dance floor.

I went dressed as a bouncer and the only concession I made towards holiday attire was an pretend eye patch that made me look like Captain Morgan in a leather jacket.

I saw the two girls come in. They were both around twenty years old and both beautiful. One was blonde with curls and was dressed as Shirley Temple, while the other had come as Little Red Ridinghood complete with jet black wig, red shawl and a basket of apples.

I probably wouldn't have taken notice of them, because there were a lot of girls coming and going in all kinds of outfits at this club, but when little miss Red Ridinghood passed me she looked up into the one care-worn, brown eye that wasn't hidden behind my eye-patch as I looked down into her sparkling, blue-grey ones. It was for only a brief moment, a flicker in time, but it seemed like we'd both fallen victim to one of Cupid's drive-bys as something familiar passed between us. As she was led away by her friends into the noise and flashing lights of the club, I knew that she had felt the same reaction as I did. I had seen the surprised, blinking 'tell' on her face as she glanced back over her shoulder at me before she was swallowed by the partying throng.

The girls had arrived with two men who were dressed as the Lone Ranger and Tonto. They were both cheap, cheesy costumes and I could tell by their body language that they thought they were a couple of players on the prowl; whilst I also felt the notion that the Lone Ranger was hiding more than his face behind his mask. Whether he was or not, the girls didn't really fit with these two. But, I'd seen a lot stranger things working these night club doors. I knew I was giving them the once over because of my brief encounter with Little Red's eyes and I was aware that I was probably just projecting evil thoughts onto the guys she was with because I liked her, but I decided to keep an eye on them nonetheless. It was my job anyway.

The nightclub moved into high gear and I didn't have much time to think about them for awhile. The next time I saw them, no more than an hour and a half after they had came in, the girl in the dark wig was helping her friend Shirley Temple to the bathroom. Shirley could barely walk and Little Red Ridinghood, although far from in the shape her friend was in, was struggling to keep herself steady enough to help her. I couldn't imagine them getting that drunk on beer so quickly, but people bring drugs into the club all the time. However, for some reason, I didn't see these two as the type. As a matter of fact, the look in little Red Ridinghood's eyes was clean, clear and piercing. She might be a partier, but not a lush by a long shot.

As they disappeared into the bathroom, I looked over through the crowded, costume-filled bar at the table their party had sat at. The club was a pretty nice place and the night was going smoothly. Even in such a festive mood, people were just dancing and having a good time to the live band. There usually weren't to many problems at this club; I worked it with just one other guy who helped the bartender behind the bar most of the time. But I knew *'trouble'* and when I spotted Tonto and the Lone Ranger, I could sense right away that what was going on around them was the least of their concerns. They had their heads together like they were conspiring to pull a bank job or something, easily recognizable with my past prison experience. I wasn't sure what was up, but I didn't like it. As I watched, the waitress took over another bucket full of long neck Budweisers to their table. I noticed the two men didn't really look all that messed up.

"Sandra." I caught the curvaceous waitress as she was passing by.

"Yeah, Jimmy, what's up?" she asked. She swished her hips, knocking the patrons who were crowding her aisle out of her path, balancing a tray of empties in one hand the way only a seasoned club waitress can. I grinned at her *'I Dream of Genie'* outfit.

"Nice costume," I said when she stepped in front of me. She smiled and I went on: "You know that table you just took the last bucket to? Have they been drinking a lot over there?"

She glanced back. "You mean the Lone Ranger table? Not really. That was only their second bucket. The girls seem to be getting a lot more wasted than the guys, but I'd bet I haven't picked up more than two or three empties from either of them."

I nodded my thanks to her and Sandra swayed on through the crowd to the bar.

I was distracted and the next thing I knew I heard a commotion. Well, it was really just a little wave of tension that floats through a bar like dominoes falling back from something unusual happening, like someone hitting someone, or, in this case, Shirley Temple falling out of her chair.

The Lone Ranger was picking her up and trying to get the girl's jacket off the fallen chair while Tonto had grabbed Red Ridinghood's knitted shawl from the back of hers. Tonto and Red were arguing and she was trying to pull the wrap from his hands.

I watched as the Lone Ranger bundled Shirley Temple up and half-carried and half-walked her towards the door. They were ahead of Tonto and Red by several feet. Miss Grey Eyes, although pretty messed up, was clearly torn between not letting the masked man get too far from her with her friend and trying to shake off Tonto's hand from her arm.

As the Lone Ranger and Shirley Temple arrived at the door where I was standing, I stepped in front of them and asked if everything was alright; which gave Red a chance to catch up to her friend as well. Shirley Temple was almost out on her feet and the Long Ranger was trying to explain to me that she had just had too much to drink and he was taking her home. I had no reason to stop him at that point and he knew it.

I looked at the other two. Tonto had a hold of Red Ridinghood's elbow trying to guide her by me. The clear look in her eyes was gone, but the deep, piercing intelligence was still there; trying to look at me through a fog. "Are you alright?" I asked her directly.

Tonto jumped in, agitated, before Red could answer. "Why the hell wouldn't she be?"

I raised my eye patch and looked at him menacingly. "I was talking to *her*," I said.

"Well, it's none of your business. It's not your job to harass people who are out just trying to have a good time," he argued.

That was true and I didn't stop him, but I did move with them as they entered the parking lot. I knew something wasn't right, so before I let Red get by me, I asked: "How well do you know these guys?"

That question seemed to really irritate the pair of men. I ignored them while Red Ridinghood told me that they had just met them at another friend's party. She said they were from California, staying with relatives and weren't even from Oklahoma.

At that, Tonto pulled on Ridinghood's arm and she jerked it away. Looking at me she said: "I don't feel right. I didn't drink that much and neither did Stacy," referring to her friend. The look on the fake-painted Indian's face said it all. There was no doubt in my mind that they had been spiking these girls' drinks. Luckily, this girl had enough sense about the company she was in to drink slowly and sparingly.

I turned and took six or seven steps to the car that the Lone Ranger was trying to stuff a lethargic and barely conscious Stacy into. I grabbed his arm. "I don't think I'm going to let you drive off with these girls," I said. This guy must have anticipated my eventual involvement and turned with a knife already in his hand. I was a pretty good size guy at thirty and had seen my share of prison yard and barroom brawls. I was no stranger to a knife fight, so I kicked his feet out from under him and slammed his head into the bottom of the door frame, stomping his fingers as he tried to break his fall and knocking the knife from his hand. I finished him with a left that followed him all the way to the floorboards.

When I stood back up something struck my head. A bright, white light Hiroshimad across my vision, followed closely by a red haze that seemed to wash the white light away. I felt myself sink to my knees and I fought to keep consciousness, knowing from years of rubbing elbows with the most ruthless killers in society it could mean the difference between life and death. With those thoughts motivating me, I forced the red fog from my sight just in time to see Tonto getting ready to bring the steel pipe down on my head again. I had enough awareness to know that this time would finish me and there was nothing I could do to stop it. *All I'd been through*, I thought, *to be snuffed out in a parking lot by a punk dressed up as Tonto...*

All of a sudden, though, Tonto was screaming and spinning around – his steel pipe clattering to the ground. He was now trying to shake free the crazy girl who had jumped onto his back and was attempting to peel his skin away from his face with her nails. He reached back, trying to jerk Red Ridinghood from his back by tugging at her hair. He got his hand wrapped in it, but only succeeded in tearing off the black wig that she was wearing; revealing her straight, shoulder-length blonde hair from beneath. She was fighting to stay on him, digging trenches in his cheeks with her nails, but the match was uneven and he was just shaking her free when I got my feet back under me. I was mad now and all I wanted to do was protect this girl who had probably, literally, just saved my life.

I reached them about the time he had ran the girl into a parked car and had gotten a hand-hold in her real hair. I hit him square in the chin as he was rearing back to punch her in the face. The haze came over me again, but this time it was from anger and rage. He released her when he rolled over the hood of the car that they were fighting on. I lost sight of her as I followed him over the other side of the vehicle; pounding him down into the wheel well of a four by four truck that stood next to it. I beat him until I felt a hand on my shoulder and a calming voice in my ear telling me to stop.

When I came back to my senses and was able to pull myself away from a now-unconscious, beat up and bloody potential rapist, I looked back to see the blonde haired Little Red Ridinghood leaning against the car beside us; holding her friend with the curls wrapped in her red shawl. About that time, the car the guys had been driving peeled out of the parking lot. "There went our ride," my new friend said with a rebellious toss of her head. Then, looking at me with tenderness in her eyes, she went on: "You know you are hurt, don't you?" I realized I had blood running down my shoulder and back. I reached up and felt the gash in my head. Damn!

About that time Bill, the other bouncer, showed up. Looking over the situation he said: "Jimmy, you need to get out of here." Nodding his head at the gathering crowd, he continued: "With all this commotion and your past they'll take you to jail just because its you until they figure it out."

"You're right, Bill. Have you got this?"

"Yeah, man. Go, I'll take care of this guy," he said, pointing at the prostrate lump of evilness still spread-eagled in front of the four by four.

"You're not going anywhere without us... Jimmy, is it?" my newly-discovered blonde friend stated. "You helped us. Now I'm going to help you. Besides, in the shape you're in, you'd probably wreck before you even got out of the parking lot."

I looked at her. The adrenaline and the physical exertion had worn off whatever those boys had tried to slip them. She had that clean, clear look in her beautiful eyes again. "Well, I'm not going to let anyone drive my car without knowing their name first," I said.

"Karyn. My name is Karyn Wagoner. Now give me your keys."

"Nice to meet you, Karyn Wagoner My name is Jimmy Maxwell. By the way, how are you with super glue?"

"What?" she asked.

"I can't go to the hospital, either. If you're going to help me, I need to pull this cut back together..." I let my words trail off as I handed her the keys to my car. Then I helped her put her friend Stacy into the back seat.

Driving off, she said: "You're kidding about the superglue, aren't you?"

I looked at her closely... she was pretty, about five foot seven, slim, but very well-built; especially in the push-up bra she was wearing to enhance her costume. The most alluring thing about her, though, was the way that she looked directly at me when she spoke. I could tell she was honest. The way she stuck by her friend, not to mention me, told me that she was loyal; and the way she jumped in to help me, not knowing at the time if I was even in shape to come to her rescue, told me that she was courageous. I would have to be careful... she was dangerous. I could fall in love with her too easily, not to mention that it felt like I knew her already. "You don't owe me anything," I said. "I can take care of this. You may have already saved my life."

"And what do you think you did for us, Jimmy Maxwell?" Karyn said.

"I can't say I don't appreciate your help, but won't your people be wondering where you're at?" I asked.

"I think you've proven you're trustworthy, Jimmy... and there is no way we can show up with Stacy at her aunt's house in the shape she's in."

"Okay, then," I said. "Make a left at the light."

Once back at my apartment, I carried a now completely unconscious Stacy to my bed. I left Karyn to attend her friend and tuck her in, while I washed the blood from my hair and cleaned the gash in my head. My pupils were a little oddly dilated; a sign of concussion, but, other than the bitchin' headache I had, I didn't think Tonto had managed to crack my skull. Sometimes having a hard head has its benefits.

Anyway, Karyn came into the bathroom when she was sure that Stacy was alright and sleeping well. Seeing me with the super glue in my hand she said: "You really weren't kidding about gluing your cut shut? Sit down before you fall down and let me help you." I did and Karyn gently washed it again and cleaned it with peroxide before gluing the sides of my cut back together. I could hear her telling me, under her breath while she worked, how much I needed her. She was saying I had done a terrible job of cleaning my wound and, had she not been there, I would have surely got an infection and probably died. The whole time I could feel her fingers touching me and her nearness fogged my already cloudy mind.

Karyn did a good job and afterwards we sat there and talked on the couch for hours. I even forgot about my headache. She was not only cute and funny, but smart with an integrity in her I could see immediately. I felt something move inside of me... my spirit was reaching out to hers and hers towards mine, as if they recognized one another. It was a little disorienting.

Maybe it was the concussion... but, regardless, I was intoxicated with her from the word go.

We talked about everything... from where I learned about super glue, which led me to explain about boxing in a boy's home for an old coach who never failed to fix us up when we got hurt. I told her of my previous legal troubles and subsequent trips to prison. She told me about her folks and friends back in California and about how her and her friend, Stacy, were here hoping to get in on the ground floor of a new software company that was starting up in Oklahoma City.

As we went back and forth telling each other our life stories we got closer and closer until Karyn was leaning her head on my shoulder. I stroked her hair now and then as we talked and we eventually fell asleep on the couch with my arm around her; the side of her pretty face pressed right into my chest.

When we woke up... I was in love. What sealed it was when I gently brushed a strand of hair out of her face and she snuggled into me sleepily. Then, opening her beautiful eyes she smiled and said: "I think I belong with you." That is when I kissed her for the first time. I remember thinking that nothing else in the world mattered at that moment. Although it started out a sweet little kiss, it quickly turned into a passion-filled, fiery furnace of urgent desire. Soon we were rolling around in each other's arms as we kissed, touched and explored one another. Pieces of our clothing were being shed with every movement until our bodies were completely nude; all except for one sock that I couldn't kick loose in our heated, emotional, sexual frenzy. Ultimately deciding I didn't have time to waste on it, I left it hanging half-off and flopping around. I took to her like a man who's been lost in a desert takes to a cool, mountain stream. I dove in and immersed myself in her. Waves of passion, were splashing off of her too as she released the same lusty, emotion-filled intensity that I did.

We rolled around the couch, the floor and even broke the coffee table as we found and shared each other. No sooner than we would stop to catch our breath and talk some more than one thing would lead to another and we were back at it again, completely forgetting about my head injury. We were young and she brought out the best in me. A couple of hours later we seemed to finally expend ourselves. We lay exhausted. Karyn was wrapped tightly in my arms as we talked and laughed quietly together; finding ourselves totally into one another within just twelve hours.

That's how Karyn's friend, Stacy, found us when she came out of the bedroom. Karyn had managed to wake her up a few hours earlier and explain what had happened and where they were, so she wasn't overly alarmed when she came stumbling out of my room. She looked at us laying, as far as she could tell, naked under a blanket on the couch together... and said: "Oh my God, Karyn... you are such a hooch!" Karyn must have told her friend that she liked me and that there was something special building between us, because Stacy said it with an approving smile on her face and laughter in her voice.

Karyn threw a pillow at her while trying to stay covered up. "You can go fuck yourself, Stace," she said. Then she went on: "Stacy, this is Jimmy, the guy who saved you... us, from... who knows what last night."

"Yeah, you sure did. Thank you, Jimmy. They definitely spiked my beer. I only had a couple of beers earlier at another party and by the time I finished my first one at the club things were already getting blurry... and I've got the worst headache ever."

"Me... too," I said. They both smiled at my little joke and Karyn gave me a soft kiss.

Then she and I got our clothes on and we all talked while the girls went into the kitchen and made breakfast. My head hurt if I thought about it at all. When I went to the bathroom the world tilted sideways on me and I stumbled. Karyn told me there was no way she was going to leave me like that, but they would need to go back to Stacy's aunt's and explain why they hadn't come home all night. However, Karyn said she was coming back to stay with me, at least until I could walk without getting dizzy.

I had to sleep the rest of the concussion off, so I threw Karyn my car and apartment keys and told her to do whatever she needed to do. She kissed me deeply and passionately before she and Stacy walked out of the door. As I fell asleep on the couch, listening to Bob Seger quietly moan out *'Night Moves'* over my stereo speakers, it occurred to me, that I'd never given my car keys to anyone before. *Huh, maybe Tonto did crack my skull,* or... maybe, I was in love.

I woke up and Karyn was already back. She was leaning over me, gently pushing my hair apart to inspect my wound. "I can't believe your glue thing worked like that," she said. "How are you feeling?" My answer was to reach up, pull her face to mine and kiss her as meaningfully as I could.

Karyn and me spent the next ten days closer than two spoons in a drawer. We talked, we loved, we saw movies and went out to eat. It was a warm week for early November, so I rode Karyn around on my Harley. There was just enough crispness to the air that made her hold herself as close to me as possible. I would pack my saddlebags with a picnic and a blanket and we would hunt out the most remote roads. We'd follow each smaller one until we were just completely secluded out in the middle of the country somewhere. With no sounds of the world around us except the buzzing of insects and maybe an old pump Jack squeakily drawing oil out of the ground, Karyn and I would spread our blanket, eat and make love. Afterwards, we laid naked in the sun, my arm under Karyn's head looking at the blue sky, talking about what we could see in the clouds. Pretty soon, we were seeing our future in them. She and I discussed her moving in with me and… who knows where else we would go from there. We both knew we belonged together and that there really wasn't anything to think about, except… what to do about it. It was an amazing feeling.

But our happiness was not to last. The dark forces in this universe never want what God has planned for you to work out and, after we had only spent a mere week and a half together, struck with calm surety. Karyn's grandfather had a stroke and she had to go back to L.A.. We talked on the phone every day, but those days were before cellphones and the calls mounted up, so we wrote letters as well. She was going to return to be with me, but the doctors weren't sure when, or if, Karyn's granddad would get his motor skills back and be able to take care of himself. I talked to my parole officer about transferring my paper time to California; it wouldn't be easy, but he said it could be done.

Sad and lonely, I fell off of the wagon somewhere along the way. I started doing and dealing drugs again. The last phone call I had with Karyn I told her I almost had the money I needed together and I'd be flying out there to her in a few weeks. Drugs are bad, though, and the more I got caught up in them again the more I got caught up in them again; to the point where Maryjo had to drive to O.K.C. and kidnap me while I was passed out. She took me to Tulsa to dry out and save me from the self-destructive path I seemed determined to follow. Little did she know of the turmoil that my heart was in.

I did dry out… but the damage was already done. An undercover informant had already made a *'controlled buy'* from me, so within days I found myself sniffing the oatmeal of County jail.

I tried desperately to call Karyn, but I never seemed to get past the switchboard and I couldn't remember her parents' address. It felt as if I would never be complete again; as though one of the crazy sons of bitches that they cage up in the psycho ward had snuck free in the night and somehow carved out my heart.

It was five years before I finally gave up hope that she would be able to find me. There really wasn't much chance of it in the first place… I didn't have any family in the city back then and I had kept her away from the people that I knew. The time we were together we spent alone and immersed in each other. I knew Karyn was trying to find me, but I also knew she'd be thinking I had abandoned her. She would have no idea why I wouldn't call. Once she had checked with all the hospitals and discovered I was not laid up from an accident or something, eventually she would assume I was just another asshole who talked a good game and never meant a word of what I'd said. I don't know what she did or what she thought. I'm sure it was horrible for her… I know it was for me.

Anyway, that was long ago, but it was my last Halloween on the streets for a long time and, the thing is, no matter how many years pass while you're in prison, your memories seem to stop and start when you walk in and out of those cold, steel gates. So, for me, that distant Halloween was also my most recent, and all those thoughts and feelings that had lain buried for so long rose up to bite me like a zombie in pigtails the next time that the night of all hallows came around.

Jenna and I walked into Rusty's costume party dressed in black and white striped outfits to resemble a pair of escaping prisoners, only to find a girl dressed in the exact same Red Ridinghood outfit that Karyn had been wearing so many years before; all the way down to the push-up bra and basket of apples. She wasn't as pretty and didn't have the same look in her eyes, but it was enough of a punch in the face from yesteryear that I almost stumbled from the barrage of memories blasting back into me.

The rest of the night I proceeded to get drunk, avoiding the costumed female fraud as much as possible. Occasionally, I would catch myself staring across the room at her, but that box where I kept Karyn's memories locked up tight would start jumping around every time I did, so I drank myself into oblivion…

The remainder of my first Halloween party in over a decade and a half ended up being just a blackout night, with no memory at all from that point on.

Jenna was mad the next day. Apparently, even though I may have avoided the Ridinghood knock off, I still must have said more than I should have on the subject while I was in a drunken stupor. I suppose my social skills were also probably not-so-polished that night either, because I wasn't asked to attend any more of my brother's friends' get-togethers.

CHAPTER FOURTEEN
TONY

Over the course of the next month I had other Brothers and friends show up at my door. Tony McMullen, known to all and sundry as Tony Mac, made a point to come by and check on me. He was my best friend; the best friend I've probably ever had, or ever will have, and he was not even a 'Brother'. We had walked through the early years of prison together, long before there was a Brotherhood in Oklahoma... back to back, climbing the food chain on pure courage and grit. My destiny was to eventually go on to lead the Brotherhood and his, after getting saved down on H-Block, Oklahoma's very-own subterranean Supermax, to becoming a well-known traveling evangelist.

But, that's not who we always were. Tony and I had been on the streets together before, back in the late Eighties and early Nineties. In our 'gangster' years, when drug dealing and drug house robberies where as commonplace in our lives as going to the grocery store. We stuck to robbing the dealers who were known for fucking people over and working with the cops, in a warped parody of Robin Hood virtue, which hadn't quite gotten around to passing on the spoils to the peasantry.

However, we did graduate into robbery-for-hire, which puts you right on the edge of the fence of right and wrong; our version of it at least. The thing I appreciated about Tony was that he had the same moral compass I had. We always researched the hit beforehand and always turned down the jobs if we found out there would be women and children there, or, if there was reason to believe the marks were 'good people'. We were pretty ruthless on the job. We had to be. We tried to look over the situation carefully ahead of time to avoid any accidents that either of us would find hard to live with. Being an outlaw with a conscience really leaves you walking a tightrope; it also means that sometimes you have to pass up a few things when your belly is hungry.

But… shit happens. You go through a door and find yourself in a circumstance that you may not like necessarily. Someone is there who shouldn't have been, or you're robbing someone and you realize in the middle of it that maybe the mark you're hitting is better people than you were told. Either way, once the ball starts rolling down hill there is no stopping it until it reaches the bottom, regardless of what it may hit on the way down. In those cases, all you can do is manage it as best you can.

Tony and I didn't find ourselves in that spot often, but it happened on occasion. Like the time we hit a gun collector; although at the time we didn't know we were hitting a gun collector. We thought we were taking down some low-life who was always ripping people off and trying to take advantage of drug-addicted women. That's what Tony's younger half-brother, Kenny Ray, told us anyway.

When you rob for a living, especially if you're bound by certain ethics, some days you're swimming in money and drugs. Other times, you might go all month wondering where the rent money is going to come from and how you're going to keep the lights on for your family. This was one of those times.

Tony, Maryjo, who I'd just married then, and I were sitting around my kitchen table. Unbeknown to us at the time, Maryjo was already pregnant with our first daughter, Echo. We were listening to Kenny Ray describe to us how *'this guy'*, who was *'no good'*, always had a lot of money and was looking to buy a couple of ounces of meth. This was back in the days of P2P, the good stuff, and, unless you were buying it in bulk or right from the cook, would cost an average of one thousand two-hundred dollars an ounce. Not a big lick, but enough to get us by.

Kenny told us the guy was as skittish as a new colt and would never let Tony nor I near him if he saw us coming. Tony was six foot five and three hundred pounds with a head on him the size of a five-gallon bucket. I wasn't near as big, or ugly, at two and a quarter, but I was muscled and mean-looking before I even started frowning.

Kenny, on the other hand, was a typical skinny, wire-haired junkie. He had a sunk-in, acne pockmarked face and looked a little more treacherous than Maryjo did; although those appearances were a little deceiving. Even with that, the guy would not trust Kenny too far, either, which left us trying to figure out how to lure the mark to us. Maryjo, Tony and Kenny talked me into letting Maryjo participate in baiting the mark, citing the fact that he would feel less threatened and more likely to think he would be able to take advantage if he thought he would be dealing with her primarily. Not to mention, she was extremely alluring and hard to resist with her svelte shape, Asian eyes and long jet black hair. Anyway, all were true and rational reasons and made too much sense to refute, so accepting their logic, I put together a plan.

"Okay, Kenny," I said. "You tell this guy you know a girl who is trying to get rid of a couple of ounces of uncut crank. Say her old man's a dealer and went to jail. She wants to get off of them cheap and get his ass out of County. Maryjo you go along, tell the guy you don't know much about the business; say I've always handled it. You just know you need sixteen hundred for them both to make my bail... Play the naive, innocent wife. He should jump on that with both feet. Kenny just be damn sure you take care of her and make certain he brings the money back here to get the dope."

All in all, not a bad plan. I would have liked it better if my wife wasn't in it, but Kenny would be with her until they got back to the house where Tony and I would take it from there. Besides, Maryjo might look like a harmless, little half Asian girl who couldn't or wouldn't hurt a fly, but she had been through a lot and had the street savvy and underlying toughness that made her a lot more than meets the eye. Of course, if I had known she was pregnant already, I would have nixed the whole deal.

Anyway, I told Kenny to go make the call. When he got off the phone he said: "Okay, Jimmy, the guy jumped on it. He wants me to bring Maryjo to the McDonalds on Admiral." He was looking at his older brother and me expectantly. I could tell he was excited by the way he was bouncing from foot to foot, but I saw an underlying fear there, too, in the ashen pallor of his skin. "You'd better be right there with her every step of the way until you get back here, Kenny," I warned him.

"Don't worry, Jimmy. He will," Tony assured me, looking at his brother with a meaningful glare.

Maryjo jumped in as well. "Honey, you know I can handle myself. Besides, this is easy peasy... bat my eyelashes... *'I don't know what I'm doing... You'll have to come over and weigh it.. blah... blah'...* I'll do it just like you said. It's a good plan."

I didn't answer her. I just looked at Kenny. "You heard what I said," I told him in a quiet, even tone that assured him he would not survive if he let anything happen to her, Tony's brother or not.

They headed out the door and took off in Tony's four-door Plymouth to meet the mark, while Tony Mac and I checked our guns. I had guns... I love guns. I usually armed us - and the rest of the crew, when we had something bigger. I had a 16-gauge Ithaca, a 12-gauge sawed-off pump shotgun, a Llama .45 automatic, a .38 Smith & Wesson, a Charter Arms .38, a Mac-ten with the trigger mechanism filed down that would spit out three or four rounds at a time when you stroked the trigger and a mini-fourteen banana clip and all. I kept the little arsenal tucked away in my closet ready for World War Three, except for my .45, or .38, which never left my immediate reach.

Anyway, this wasn't anything perilous, so I tossed Tony a .38 and leaned my sawed-off pump against the bedroom door. That's where we were waiting when the car pulled up. We heard Kenny walking them up to the porch and then make up some excuse to turn around and get back in the car, saying he'd be right back. He wanted to go pilfer the dude's car since it was still sitting at the McDonalds. Kenny was a small-minded thief, at least when he was strung out... like he was now.

My house was just a small, rectangular, two-bedroom affair. It had a wooden front porch and a three-foot tall chain-link fence around the yard. There weren't any worries of the mark seeing us in the bedroom, even though the windows faced the porch on the east side of the house, because like most tweekers I know, we had tin foil and blankets covering the entire windows, except for that little tiny hole in each one so we could see out when we felt the need to.

My step-daughter's room was right on the other side of the bathroom, but Stephanie was at school at the time. The west side of the house was made up of the living room, which was only a sheetrock wall away from where Tony and I were standing. There was a small kitchen behind that, which led out to the back patio.

We could hear Maryjo and the guy come in the front door. She was telling him: "You'll have to weigh it yourself. I'll just go get the dope and the... I think my old man calls them *'triple beams',*" referring to the scales.

"He is the one who messes with all of that. I don't even know how they work," Maryjo was saying as they entered.

I could hear the excitement in the guy's voice. "Be sure and bring a spoon and some water, so I can try it out, too," he was saying to her, planning on shooting-up right there in front of my pregnant wife, but Maryjo had left him in the living room and was turning the corner of the short entryway to the bedroom by the time he finished his statement.

She nodded and quietly mouthed: "He's got the money," as she passed us running into the bedroom.

Tony and I took the three steps down the entry hall into the living room... Two more steps and I was on the mark... "Get down on the fucking ground!" I yelled as I hit him with the buttstock of my sawed-off shotgun, knocking him off his feet. Tony was right behind me covering the guy with his gun, as well. He stepped on the side of his head, holding him down, while I frisked the man.

"Whaaaat-t-t's going on," the guy stammered in total shock.

"Just shut up! Where's the money?" I demanded, while I was feeling his pockets with my spare hand.

The guy said it was in his sock, so I reached down and ran my hand over the man's legs. I found the money stuck in a pouch strapped to one of the guy's calves. I also found a small .380 semi-automatic in a little ankle holster strapped to the other one. "What did you plan on doing with this, you piece of shit?"

"N-n-n-othing... It's only to protect myself," the man countered. He was having a hard time enunciating with Tony's size fourteen boot on his face and neck, holding him pinned to the floor.

I shook the guy down and removed his wallet and a few other items from his pockets. Then, I had Tony step off of his head where we could sit him up and look him over. He was as tall as me, maybe even a little taller. The man had a receding hairline and what he had left was buzzcut to the scalp. He was slim-built like most junkies and had an average face. I leaned down and handed him his glasses, which had slid across the floor during the fracas.

"What do you think, Bro? What do you suppose he was going to do with that gun?" I asked my partner, only taking my eyes off of the guy long enough to count the money... One thousand one hundred, huh?

Tony stayed quiet, keeping his attention on the job at hand.

"The mother fucker only has eleven hundred on him! He was going to bulldog his way through, maybe even rob Maryjo!," I muttered sourly; now glaring holes through the man.

"No… no… I would never do that. I just figured, if I couldn't negotiate a deal I would at least buy one of them. The gun is just for protection. I swear! Look, man, take the money… I've been robbed before. I've got references… I won't tell. You don't have to kill me." The guy was pleading, almost crying.

"Just shut up," I said, although how he was acting and sounding was precisely what I wanted to see and hear. I was reading him for weakness… to confirm that he was not a viable threat to me or my household later. I was looking through his wallet for his I.D., address and other basic info… *'leverage'*. After all, even though Maryjo and I were moving soon, I was still robbing this guy in my own home… and just because this guy was supposed to be your average shady dumbass, I still needed to be careful.

The guy must have realized his situation was pretty precarious, since every chance he had he looked at Tony or me and pled his case; repeating that he didn't know where he was at… and he would never tell, even if he did. Tony would periodically tell him to *"Shut up"*, while I was looking through the things I had taken off him, trying to discern for sure what kind of guy we were dealing with. He certainly acted like a harmless, cowardly junky. I was counting on it; neither Tony nor I had any intention of killing this guy. Not to say we wouldn't if our lives or our loved ones lives were at stake, but in anything we ever did, it was never the plan and was always the very last resort. Of course, I didn't normally rob people in my own home either.

As I was going through his wallet, I found several gun auctions and gun collector cards, identifying him as someone who had more than just a passing interest in owning a single gun. "What's the deal with these gun dealer business cards? How many more guns do you have?" I asked as I leveled my sawed-off at him to emphasize my need for him to be truthful.

He admitted he had several more at home. The seeds of worry for my household started to sprout. I continued to look through his wallet and between the cards I discovered a torn off matchbook cover with a phone number written on it. The number seemed familiar.

I told Tony I would be right back. Leaving him with the mark, I went back to the bedroom where Maryjo was waiting. "Jimmy, I feel bad… he trusted me..." she said when I walked in. She could hear his frantic pleas with us in the living room and it unnerved her a little bit.

"Maryjo, he had a fucking gun. He didn't even have all the money he needed to make the deal you offered him, the deal that he came here for. Don't sweat it... I don't know if he was going to try anything or not, but at the very least he was going to try and undercut you. There is no reason to feel sorry for him." Once I had consoled her, I went on: "But I found this phone number in his stuff. It looks very familiar. See if it matches any of our numbers." I gave her the matchbook cover and went back out into the living room.

I was making the guy tell me again why I should let him go... trying to read his threat level, when M.J. came out of the bedroom and showed me the matchbook cover. She held it by her thumb against the same number in my address book, where he couldn't see it.

Most of the contacts in my little book weren't all that important, but, there were a few I did business with who I considered good people, ones I wouldn't necessarily hurt unless they tried to hurt me. In this case, the number he had belonged to my best connection. They were the kind of people who didn't let their number float around with just anyone.

Dammit! I thought.

To Tony I said: "Bro, we might have a problem here. This freaking guy knows my people. As harmless as this dude acts, he might be more than he appears. I can't afford to let someone go who might come back and shoot up the house. I've got the kids to think about."

The guy couldn't hear all of what I was saying, but he got enough of it to know the stakes had changed and for some reason he might not make it out of there. "Oh my God, please, please I've got a family, I'm good people. I would never tell," he cried.

"I'm not worried about you telling. I'm thinking you might not be as harmless as you want us to believe and come back here and hurt one of my kids... and as much as I hate it... that's something I cannot let happen... no matter how I feel about what I might have to do to stop it."

"No... I am harmless, I swear," the mark said, throwing his hands up. "I have a daughter also, I know how you feel. I've been robbed before, I didn't do anything then, I promise."

"Brother, I'm sorry," I said to Tony. I knew Tony didn't ever want to kill anyone again. He was my best friend. I never meant to get him into something like this. For that matter, killing someone is the last thing I want to do as well… but, it's kind of like letting a zombie live because one of them is your brother and you haven't got the heart to chop his head off and, three days later, you come home to find he's eaten your wife and two children. Dammit… damn it!

Tony looked at me. He was down for whatever needed to be done, but I could see the stress and concern gathering in the corners of his eyes. "I understand, Jimmy. I even agree… but damn, this went from making a little money to serious shit real quick."

The mark's lips trembled… "I swear… I won't try anything, I'm just as harmless as you thought I was. I've got references… I've been robbed before," he repeated for the third or fourth time.

I squinted my eyes together and rubbed the back of my neck in frustration. A bad call here could be bad all the way around. None of us intended for this to ever be a debate. My morals were struggling with my intellect. I knew I didn't have the right to put everyone else into something this deep. Kenny Ray was back by then also, so it involved Tony, Maryjo and Kenny at this point, as well as, of course, the mark himself. Every sense in me told me I didn't really need to worry about him, but what if I was wrong?

I knew who our mark was now. At least I knew he was not the worthless, unconnected piece of crap Kenny Ray had convinced us he was; and this was something I was going to have to talk to Kenny about later. When I'd had the guy tell me about his guns, which he did openly and honestly, an AK-47 was on the list. I remembered seeing it over at my contact's house. This guy was standing in the garage with the assault rifle leaning against the workbench when I walked by. I mentioned the gun when I was inside and my friends told me that the guy, our victim, was a friend who supplied and worked on all their guns. He was some kind of whiz with firearms. That's about all I knew, but it was enough to make me have to think this through.

You would think that realizing he might be 'good people' would save him automatically, but the damage had already been done. I knew if it was me, I would be back to level the whole house. You can think what you want; it was not an easy decision. Like I said before, being a hard case with a conscience left you walking a fine line between right and wrong sometimes.

"I'm going to ask you this one more time," I said, looking at the mark. "How many guns do you have?" He told me again and it was the same as before… The AK, a .357 Magnum, a .44, two .38's, a 9mm and the .380 that I already had. I believed him… and in the end the softer side of me won out, but I needed leverage.

"Alright, brother," I told Tony. "I will let him go, but not with all that firepower in his hands." I looked at the guy, "You're going to take us to your house so I can get your guns and then I will cut you loose."

"But my wife and daughter are there," he cried.

"Well, I can take you out and bury you in the country somewhere, if you'd rather," I said. "Hear me… and hear me well. I'm not letting you go as long as you have those guns in your possession." I was looking him straight in the eyes, waiting on his answer.

He was sweating. I could see by his jerky, panicky movements that he was conflicted, but he nodded. I had already decided to risk letting him go, but the bottom line was I wanted to be away from Maryjo and Kenny no matter what happened from here on, just in case. I shifted my head towards Tony, who read my thoughts, we'd worked together like this so many times before. He herded the guy out to the car.

The weather was good, it had rained a shit storm the day before, but the sky's were clear now, it was late summer the sun was out and warm enough to have dried up most of the water.

Once there Tony asked: "What do you want to do?"

I was sitting behind the guy, pointing a pistol at his back through the passenger's seat. "I don't know, bro… The wife and the kid is a problem, but I have to have those guns."

Tony asked the guy how old his daughter was.

"Five," the guy replied.

This just keeps getting worse and worse, I thought to myself.

The man cared for his family sincerely. He told me where he lived, but cried and pleaded the whole time for us not to involve them. Neither Tony nor I had any intention of involving his family, especially since his daughter was only five, but we couldn't let him know that.

"Just drive around a little bit, brother, and let me figure this out," I told Tony. Tony made the guy take us to his car. Basically just to pass the time and look over the damage Kenny might have done to it. He had parked it at the McDonalds where he'd gotten in with Kenny and Maryjo.

When I saw the car it sparked an idea. "How many cars do you have?" I asked the guy.

"Two," he answered, "Mine and my wife's."

Once again, Tony knew what I was thinking. He looked at me through the rearview mirror, a slight smile on his face for the first time since this had begun. "That will work," he said, pulling back onto the road heading in the general direction that we knew this clown lived.

I looked at the man, "Okay, this is what we're going to do. You're going to take us to your house-"

The guy threw his hands back up in the air. "Nooo, my daughter is there," he started blubbering, cutting me off.

"Put your freakin' hands back down and smile, dumbass, before I shoot you for being stupid," I said. I respected this guy's concern for his wife and daughter, but he had me so irritated my teeth were grinding. "We're not going in your house with your kid there. Why do you think we've been driving around for thirty minutes trying to figure out how to do this? What we're going to do, asshole, is find a payphone where we can see them drive off and you're going to call your wife and tell her you broke down at McDonald's and she needs to come and get you. Your daughter is too young to leave alone, so she will have to take her with her, capice?"

"Oh, yeah, yeah, that'll work. Thank you," he said.

"Don't thank me, dickwad. That's just how we are, but don't think for one second just because I don't want to have to hurt anyone here that I won't blow your fucking brains out if you try anything when we get in there," I snapped.

"No... I promise I won't," he replied, the relief of knowing his family would be out of this was evident in his voice. I almost hated robbing this guy. I was going to kill Kenny when I got back. This guy was a knob, but he loved his family and, from what I could gather, probably never fucked anyone over in his life, but at this point there was nothing to do except finish it. Besides, we needed the extra money from the guns anyway.

We got lucky and found a payphone we could drive up to right on the other side of the entrance to the R.V. park he lived in, north of Admiral and Mingo. We could even see his trailer and extra car from where we parked.

I instructed him in what to say, stressing the importance of his need to convince his wife there was nothing wrong other than him needing her to come get him. With a gun pointed at his back, he made the call while we listened. He was motivated and he did a great job. It was only a few minutes before we saw his wife loading up their daughter in her car. Another moment and she was pulling out on Mingo right across the street from us on her way to the McDonald's to get her husband.

We all felt relieved as the car drove out of sight. Our mark sighed audibly, while me and Tony kept our relief to ourselves. I knew Tony well enough to see the tension loosen in him. I felt the weight lighten as well, but I still had a job to do and we didn't have time to waste. "Let's get moving," I said.

Tony drove us across Mingo Avenue and right up to the front of the guy's mobile home. He lived in a long Airstream that could be pulled behind a pickup truck. It was large as far as Airstreams went, but smaller than most of the other trailers in the park. I had lived in one of them when I was younger with my dad and step-mother, so I knew it was going to be tight once I was inside.

I told Tony to sit there while I took the guy in and got the guns. I reminded the mark that if he tried anything slick Tony knew where he lived now. Having prepped the man with as much threat logic as I felt was necessary, I ordered him out of the car. Playing the part of a casual visiting friend, I kept him covered with the snub nosed .38 I had stowed away in my jacket pocket as we ambled to the trailer.

Once through the door of their little home my senses jumped through the roof! The motorhome was stacked high with stuff on both sides of the isle. As we walked through the first room, I picked up two guns that were laying around haphazardly; one on a countertop and the other on a bookshelf. I backed him down the narrow pathway through the cluttered little hovel they called home, fully aware, as he opened each passageway door, that I was now completely in his environment. He knew where everything was at any given moment and I knew absolutely nothing. "If you breathe wrong, your wife and kid will come home to find your body on the floor. Do you understand? I want every gun you mentioned. Don't reach for them, just tell me where they are," I told him, the high stress of the moment giving my voice an even more menacing tone. As I backed him through the cluttered home, he would point at a spot and I would retrieve another gun. The hairs on my neck were standing straight up and the tension in my shoulders ran all the way down to my trigger finger. He knew how serious the situation was and moved slowly and deliberately through the trailer as I loaded the guns, one by one, into a gym bag that I had taken from below his kitchen table.

Finally, we reached the master bedroom, if you could call anything in this little trailer *'master'*. There I found the AK-47... it was in pieces. "What the fuck?" I said.

"I was cleaning it," he replied. He had it tore down all the way to the trigger mechanism. Every little piece was laid out on a section of unfolded newspaper.

I didn't have time to waste trying to figure it out here, so I rolled it all up in the newspaper and stuck it in the bag. "Is that all of it?" I asked.

"Yes... Yes," he said.

"Don't fucking lie to me. I'll come back if you are," I demanded in my most threatening tone. I was conscious of how ridiculous this whole thing was becoming, considering he and I both knew I wouldn't know the difference until I was long gone and I wouldn't be back.

"It's all there, I swear," he said.

With no choice but to accept what he told me, I retraced my steps down the aisle toward the only door that the place had, making him keep his hands in plain sight. Once we got there, I told him he was going back out to the car with me. I didn't want him to be able to grab a gun I may not know about and shoot at us from inside the home while we were leaving. Before we stepped out, I told him he'd better make our parting look good and friendly as well.

The sun seemed brighter when we came out, and the wind had picked up a nice breeze. I felt like a weight had been lifted off of me and I could see the relief on Tony's face too. The mark and I walked to the car like we'd been friends forever. When we got there, Tony told him: "You did good... now don't fuck it up by doing something stupid. Just keep up the show until we're long gone."

When I was settled in, I told Tony to roll, but before we split, I reiterated to the mark to mind what Tony had just said. I also reminded him that there was a whole crew of us, so even if we did get caught, there would be someone to settle the score. He nodded his understanding, waving to us as Tony and I pulled off. We could hear him saying: "Okay... glad you could stop by. Come back anytime..." before we drove out of earshot.

"Wheeew…" I said, blowing out a breath and a big knot of tension I'd been holding. "That was a trip!" I told Tony about the cluttered interior and the high-wire situation inside. He breathed a sigh of relief of his own. "What do you think, Jimmy? Do we need to worry about him?"

"I don't think so. We made a good call. He's got too much to worry about himself. Nevertheless, I'll be glad when M.J. and I get moved," I said.

We headed back to the house and I called my gun fence on the way. By nightfall, I had all the guns sold except for the AK-47 and I had it put together.

As I said, Tony and I had history. We had been through a lot and were as close as any two brothers could be. I watched him go from who he was then to who he is now. I saw him get saved in prison, then get out and go on to start a prison ministry; I saw him buried in Oklahoma's toughest maximum security pit only to rise from the depths to open the State's congressional sessions each year in prayer. Tony was my friend, a true friend. He had come a long way and wanted to see me succeed as well, so he visited and tried to counsel me now that I was out. Naturally, he was of a mind that I needed to let my responsibility to the A.B. go and talked to me tirelessly about what I could do with my past to help guide others to avoid the same pitfalls in their futures.

CHAPTER FIFTEEN

BRANDON

Tony had also been keeping tabs on my kids for me since he'd been out and told me my youngest son, Brandon, was getting into trouble and needed to be with me. I called Maryjo and found out that, in fact, my son was already in juvenile detention. His probation officer, who was at his wit's end with Brandon, was even threatening to put her in jail too, because she could not pass a U.A. herself. She begged me to do something.

It was really not the best time. My relationship with Jenna was often strained, not to mention we didn't really have much room in our one-bedroom apartment, but I had been an absentee parent long enough. Knowing it would have its rough spots, but accepting them, I called Brandon's probation officer, then gathered my forces, which included Tony Mac and my father, and we went to see the judge in Brandon's defense.

It's not very easy to get out of prison after sixteen years and have a judge award you custody of your teenage kid. Especially one that's already been having trouble with the law. But, as a testament to the stability I could already show in my life, and the support I had, we walked out of that courtroom with my son in tow.

Brandon had grown up never knowing me on the streets. I'd been sent downriver the last time when he was six months old. He had been coming to see me periodically in one visiting room or another, at one prison or another, his whole life, from Oklahoma's subterranean supermax, all the way to the Federal prison that I'd finally discharged from.

Although all of my kids, including Brandon, loved and respected me and never doubted my love for them, my youngest ones, Echo and Brandon, both held an underlying resentment towards me that stemmed from my absence in their lives. As much as my son wanted to be with me - at sixteen years old, he felt like he'd managed fine so far without me telling him what to do and resisted my authority now I was out. It didn't help that he had out-grown me by a half inch, which only added to his rebellious sense of bravado. Anyway, he seemed happy enough to be with me, at least happy he was out of juvey.

His attitude didn't really come into play until he found out I actually intended to be a parent, something neither his mother nor I had ever really been. Brand was torn between his love and desire to finally be with me, a thing he'd longed for all of his life, and the free and easy, unsupervised lifestyle he'd enjoyed with his mother, who had no control over him. Like all of us at sixteen, he thought that he was all grown up.

He did respect me, though shadowed with a healthy touch of fear. That and the fact I could send people after him to bring him home from wherever he was, gave me a measure of control over him he hadn't ever experienced before. Don't get me wrong; Brandon was a good kid with a kind heart. To my knowledge, he'd never hurt anyone. He was totally different than me, who was mean as a rattler at his age and was fighting full grown men out in the oilfield pits… and winning. Not Brand, he claimed he was a lover, not a fighter. He was lucky he didn't have to grow up with my father or stepfather, I decided. However, he didn't like being held down and our small apartment only got smaller when Brandon took over the living room as his bedroom.

For everyone's sake, we did the best we could and tried to have fun. I was clean and still working at the dental lab and Jenna was waitressing at night. Her drinking was still bad and it made the apartment that much more uncomfortable when we would have fights about it, but, in the beginning, we adjusted pretty good. I had a ex-con friend, Dwayne Mossenbacher, who had gotten out and put together a small but successful remodeling business. As a favor to me he put Brandon to work, teaching him the basics of construction. We seemed to find a balance with all of us working.

With my son and I home alone in the evenings, Jenna's alcoholism and paranoia got the best of her. Somehow, she got it in her head that while she was gone, Brandon and I were running around chasing skirts together. She quit her job… and… the apartment got even smaller. Subsequently, so did our income. Jenna hated working anyway – and had *jokingly'* told me many times while I was still in prison that she just wanted me to get out so she wouldn't have to work any more. I wouldn't have minded carrying the load, but the timing and the reasoning couldn't have been worse. I became resentful as I looked at the bills mounting up and my, now inadequate paycheck disappearing; so we fought more and she drank more and, consequently, I drank more as well.

It was pretty lame now that I think back on it. Anyway, we fought enough that it began to make life miserable for all of us. She would do things like grab the gear shift when we were going down the expressway at two in the morning and try to pull it in *'park'* with me on parole, which didn't end pretty. Another time Jenna, drunk and mad at something that her pickled mind would just seem to create out of thin air, leaned back and started kicking my windshield. When the glass started spider-webbing, I backhanded her and held her face in the seat by her hair until I could get pulled over. I was becoming someone that I didn't like.

My son was a serious point of contention between us; the apartment was just too small. I thought about selling my car or my Harley to fund a bigger place, which was saying a lot, because, at that time, getting my face in the wind on my bike was the only true joy I had.

Eventually, Jenna decided to go back to Guymon until I either got a bigger place or sent my son back to Tulsa. I understood Jenna's angst; she had waited a long time for me to come home and now she was having to share me and our home. I was torn... my son had waited a lifetime and needed me also. I knew Jenna was just wanting me to chase her, but I had my hands full with my job and the bills that all fell on me now.

As for my son, I was always having to have Tony or someone hunt him down in Tulsa. I would either let him go to visit or he'd get a ride up there and didn't want to come back. His girlfriend was there, his friends were there and his new-found love of Methamphetamine was there.

I spent hours talking to him. I understood better than he realized how he felt going all those years without me, because I missed him and his sister every day of their lives, as well.

I told him how I'd been involved in speak-out programs, because of the deep sorrow I felt for the mistakes I'd made. Mistakes that had pulled me out of their lives. How I had tried to prevent other families making the same mistakes I had. I tried to steer him away from the crowd he wanted to hang out with and told him how drugs only destroyed lives. I had countless stories and examples from my own life, as well as others. Like most kids, it went in one ear and out the other. "Yeah, dad, that's easy for you to say, You're in your forties and you've already lived and done everything you wanted to do. I'm just a kid who wants to have fun," he'd say.

I related a story to him I used in every speak-out I ever did, about a eighteen year-old kid I knew, named, Kyle Gryder. He'd been out stealing a motorcycle to go joyriding on when the police spotted and started chasing him. Kyle was a quarter of a mile ahead of the police when they ran a red light to keep up with him and got blindsided by another motorist. It killed the officer driving the cruiser. Kyle was apprehended and charged with murder, receiving an eighty-five year sentence at eighty-five percent required time in. Do the math. The kid never intended to take a life… but, as I told Brandon, it still happened. Anything can happen when you put yourself out there like that. Brandon just shook his head and told me that I was probably just making the story up.

We would make frequent trips to Tulsa to see my youngest daughter, Echo, and my new grandbaby, Haven Rain. I had got out just in time to be at the hospital as my beautiful daughter was delivering her into the world.

Overall, I tried very hard, not that there wasn't more I could have done. Had I been more proficient in the art of parenthood, or just been a little further along in the evolution of myself… who knows what could have been. I still don't have all the answers, I can tell you that, even though I fully intended to walk the line and do the best by my children and Jenna as possible, I still had areas of my life which were self-destructive, as sure as if I was caring a bomb around who's timer had already started it's countdown.

CHAPTER SIXTEEN

BROTHERHOOD

The *'Brotherhood,'* the very organization I was partly responsible for and was determined to lift up and structure into a honorable, functioning entity on the streets, turned out to be the chink in my armor. Well, I can't really blame my troubles on the Hood. The blame resides with me, in the mentality and psyche that goes with staying connected to prison and consorting with everyone that was still moving in and out of prison as a way of life. As much as I saw myself as a beacon of stability and hope for my brothers to find organized, understanding help on the streets, the fact was I was pulled into their world, crowds and scenes on an even larger scale than I had been warning my son against all along. It's hard to preach against something, when you're seen to be standing at the head of it.

By then, our Brotherhood "BBQ's" had grown in attendance. I tried to keep Brandon out of sight of what I was doing, not wanting to glamorize that outlaw, gangster lifestyle. It's difficult to be the right kind of example, when his whole life, he's been told stories about his dad doing exactly that. Anyway, with Jenna gone off to Guymon, I used Buddy's niece, Sheena, to organize the other brother's wives into cooking brigades and entertain the families while the men and I took care of business.

Sheena was a pretty, slender, blue-eyed blonde who loved the Brotherhood, motorcycles and the spotlight of 'head woman' that these events put her in; the place my wife would have normally been. With Jenna absent and Sheena working so close to me, we eventually started having an affair. Sheena was spontaneous and creative sexually; working hard at trying to win my heart in lieu of my wife's eventual return. She even gave me her little, brown-and-tan toy Chihuahua, Mr. Big. Not named for his diminutive size, but for his big heart. He became my little partner in crime and loved to ride with me stuck down in my leather coat. Right or wrong, it was what it was and Sheena was a good hostess when called on to be. She was not so much in love with me as drawn by the excitement and power that she perceived came with the rank.

As I said, the Hood was coming together. However, it wasn't all smooth sailing... there were times where I had to exert my authority at meetings in the only way the young hardheads these days understand.

I really didn't have a lot of tolerance for the Brothers that came into the hood five or six years before, while I had been out of State custody, hammering out a place for the Hood in the Feds. It seemed like a whole crop of people had came into the Brotherhood who didn't know where my authority came from in the first place. I didn't really want the responsibility I had so long ago taken on, knowing it could very well bring me down and pull me back into a life that I wanted to leave behind. I didn't have time for bullshit; the older members knew and were glad that I was out and planned to take things to a new level.

Things went well for the most part, although there were a few incidents. When our little get-togethers became too large we moved the meetings away from my place. We used the *'Midway'*, a strip club where I had been given permission by Rudy, the owner, to hold them in a sectioned-off part of his bar. Occasionally, we used a nearby lake, or Buddy's backyard. The bar was cool, because when we would have a closed session we could go unseen. The arrangement worked well for Rudy; he had been in prison for pandering and, while his sister ran his club, she had let the place pick up a black, gang-banger type of clientele. He thought our presence might swing it back around to a more middle-class, Caucasian customer base; or at least a less-rowdy one. This arrangement ended one night when we came rolling in fifteen-deep, freaking out the five or six gangbangers that were in there. Of course, it probably didn't help that the Brothers wouldn't let the white dancers strip for them. Once one of them was overheard trying to call in his homeboys – apparently trying to intimidate us – I gave the go ahead. My crew, already chomping at the bit to get at them, beat the posturing loud-mouths through the bar and out into the parking lot. My brothers and I barely got out of there before the cops showed up. We cured Rudy's problem, but, needless to say, we were asked not to come back.

We moved our gatherings out of the bars, public parks, lakes, *etc.* and just stuck with Buddy's for awhile. Buddy had a huge house with an extremely large backyard. It worked well for us, because, even though it was square in the middle of Oklahoma City, the back property was still fairly secluded. His driveway led under a long car port that was shared with the house next door, so, when we had his extended driveway packed with cars, trucks and motorcycles, the space between the two houses was almost completely blocked off from the view of the street. The rear fenceline and surrounding easements were dense with trees and bushes as well, effectively obscuring Buddy's yard from his neighbors' prying eyes.

At this point, with our attendance passing the thirties – forties, we started feeling the need to conceal our growth and rightly so. As I've said, but wasn't aware of at the time, the Feds were already watching us. Buddy even thought he saw someone across the street trying to take pictures of what was going on in the backyard. I didn't believe him, I thought it was just his drug-induced, albino imagination to be honest. It was a year later, when I got a visit from the F.B.I., that I found out he had not just been envisioning it. In my defense, I had a lot going on at that particular meeting. Not only was I having an issue with a couple of the street council members over their lack of respect for the 'no drug business at our open get togethers' rule, which also meant don't just drive around the corner to conduct it either. There was a very good reason for that rule; it was called R.I.C.O. (Racketeering Influenced Corrupt Organization Act), which especially included drug activity. The Brothers who have had to deal with the Federal government before always seem to have a deeper understanding and respect for the devastation that the Feds were capable of inflicting.

On top of that, the mandatory call for all the Brothers within a hundred miles to show up pulled in a few unfamiliar faces. Three of which were young Brothers in their late twenties and early thirties who came rolling in late after most of the business had already been discussed. With the relevant issues worked out, we were relaxing, enjoying the warm weather – eating the grilled ribs and the potato salad that the women had prepared and drinking a couple of beers. However, out of respect for the new arrivals, we ran the kids and the women back in the house to bring the three up to speed. 'Crazy Pete' was the leader of the little group. He had shoulder-length brown hair and narrow, ferret-like eyes. I could immediately sense the hostility emitting from his short, stocky frame. He was followed closely by a young and respectful blond-headed Brother, who is now passed, may he rest in peace, named Bobby Glass. They had another Bro in tow, whose name I can't recall.

From the start, Pete came into the meeting jealous and petty; expecting to be appointed a seat on the council. He'd been taking orders from an idiot ex-brother named Redwood who was not high enough in the structure of things to be clued in to the master plan that I and the others had devised years before. Redwood was sitting in a minimum-security prison somewhere, high on meth pretending to be a big ballin' shot-caller and convinced this guy – for his own self-serving reasons – that he should be the one running things on the streets.

I already had a low threshold for ignorance, so when Pete started telling me what Redwood told him to do... I just shut him down. "I don't care how he told you to do it," I said. "What I'm telling you is how *we're* doing it. Do you understand that?"

Pete was squirming around and wearing an obstinate look on his face, whilst the rest of the guys gradually surrounded us to see what was happening.

"You better listen to him," Brian Cyphers, one of my oldest and most trusted Bros, told him. "You came in while Jimmy was gone to the Feds. The people you are talking to in prison have far less authority than he does. Trust me on that; he's running this shit."

I stepped in. "I don't really have time to hold your hand," I said, irritated at the whole disruption. "You can't do what I can do... or you already would have-"

"Why can't I?" Pete jumped in, cutting me off.

Getting angry, I snarled: "Because I'm Jimmy fucking Maxwell and you're not! That's why," daring him with a glare to say anything else. He kept his mouth shut... but the insolent little punk couldn't restrain himself from rolling his eyes. He may not have intended for me to see it, but I did.

"Oh, hell no..." I said. I stepped over and gave him a straight left from my shoulder to his chin. "Come on, tough guy. Let's see what you got." He stumbled and tried to grab me. I steam-rolled over him, driving us both through the wooden railing of the porch stairs and then through a section of stockade fence, before I beat him to the ground. Some of the Brothers standing around were taken aback at the suddenness of my attack. Others were smiling a smug smile, as if they knew what was coming from the moment Crazy Pete and his posse came swaggering in with a chip on his shoulder.

"Listen," I said, to everyone there, but specifically to Pete. "I have personal plans I've put on hold in order to get this Hood up and running out here the way it could and should be. In a year we will have elections. The people who are eligible to be elected to the council seats, especially my seat, will have to be clean and sober, but, until then, this is how it is. If you don't like the way I'm doing things, then vote me out and put someone else in my spot and I will go on about the business of living my life."

Brian and the rest of them told me that they had my back and appreciated what I was doing. I looked at Pete. "What about you… do we understand each other now?" I asked, helping him up off the ground.

"Yeah, Brother, I got it," he replied, rubbing his jaw.

I looked at my watch. 1:20 p.m. Fuck! I forgot to call the color line and on Saturday they close at one! I silently cursed myself and crossed my fingers hoping my color wouldn't come up when I called. Sure enough… my color came up. That was the second time in two weeks that I had missed a U/A. No matter how sincere I was about being clean, my parole officer was getting suspicious and increased the frequency of my tests.

Three weeks later I got a call from the State Penitentiary at McAlester, telling me that Crazy Pete had ran off with a couple of Brothers' money there and they wanted a hit put out on him. I called a special closed meeting and excluded myself for reasons of bias and had the council make the call. I was getting discouraged, it seemed like it was one thing after another. Drugs were destroying us… and, as strong as I was, I was helpless to stop it. I could even feel myself getting pulled closer and closer towards its jaws.

CHAPTER SEVENTEEN
MAKING A STAND

Things started turning for the worse. My son went to stay with my brother, Scott, in El Paso, Texas, where he was supposed to learn a trade, but with his first paycheck he caught a bus and went back to Tulsa. I was tired of chasing him down.

Missing those U/A's had my parole officer on my case. Not to mention, I'd also been pulled over on my bike and blew enough numbers in the breathalyzer for a *'Driving While Impaired'* charge. It was just a misdemeanor, but enough for me to lose my allowable drinking privileges and give me my first taste of legal troubles since I'd been out.

The bills were streaming in. I broke my own rule; I picked the phone up… "I want in," I said, "I need the money." That's all it took for me to step back into the dope game… and it was not long before I was using again as well. When that happened I was full tilt in it: sex, drugs, motorcycles and rock 'n' roll.

Jenna came back from Guymon right in the middle of my fall. I came clean to her about my affair with Sheena, but we fought so much that I kept finding myself back in bed with the little blonde, which only made mine and Jenna's relationship harder. The pretty blue-eyed Hood rat had somehow gotten under my skin. It got to the point that I became blatant with my cheating; seemingly with very little control of myself in that area or concern for what my wife thought. Jenna claimed I was demon-possessed at the time. She allowed she could look in my eyes and see a hollow man not the noble, honest, loving man that she knew me to be.

As for myself, I didn't know what was wrong with me. I was honest. I told my wife everything. However, I was unwilling to stop the affair.

Regardless of Jenna's shortcomings I was still guilt ridden, my only firm stance was that I refused to leave her, no matter how hateful she was when she was drunk, or how much the other woman in my life wanted me too.

Jenna tried everything when she came back from Guymon – except not drinking. She yelled and screamed, she cried, she pled with me to stop seeing Sheena. When that didn't work, she tried to immerse herself in the life that I was living, doing drugs and having sex with me and the women that I was sleeping with… even her arch-nemesis, Sheena. Don't get me wrong, it weighed heavy on my heart that I was harming someone who I loved. I also became aware that I didn't want to actually lose my wife, even if I had a litany of grievances that I held against her. But, it was as if I was caught in a rip tide, I could see and feel it, but couldn't get out of it.

With drugs back in my life my extramarital affairs increased exponentially. As can be expected when stepping across the line, back into the shadowy world of drug use, and shady clandestine drug deals, so did my level of violence. Sleeping around and beating people up were becoming commonplace.

My friend Tina; a short, emerald-eyed, buxom brunette whom I had met in the process of one such drug deal or another became the woman I slept with when I wasn't sleeping with Sheena. Jenna liked her simply because she was Sheena's nemesis: the enemy of my enemy is my friend. Anyway, that worked for me.

Tina was not only good in bed, but she was a good connection. She would go out of her way to give me anything I needed. In turn, I looked out for her.

When she got ripped off I found two of the guys who'd robbed her. Then tricking them into a meeting, I let her watch as I beat them senseless with a pair of candlestick holders. She loved and was loyal to me from that day on. But, regardless, I could see the intimidation that I was causing, even in the people I cared for. I was getting out there. I was losing it! Every day that I stayed in it, I became more and more of the man I thought I'd left behind. In more ways than one.

How could I be caught back up in this shit!? I demanded from myself in one of my moments of clarity. I was fully aware of the whirlpool that I was being whipped around in… again. I was also fully aware that, no matter how strong a swimmer I was, if I stayed in its spiraling current I would eventually be sucked down the vortex and drowned in the dark life-destroying depths of the drug world once more, just like everyone else.

My P.O. was catching on and wanted to put me in rehab. He gave me every opportunity, but I kept talking my way out of it; not wanting to lose my job nor be confined any more. I can't tell you how many times I have wished since then that I'd taken that route, but honestly I thought I could make it on my own. I can be very determined and I knew the road I was on was not where I wanted to be.

One day I was riding my scooter; coming back from visiting a biker friend and his wife in Ada, Oklahoma. Mr. Big was tucked down my shirt. I had taken a different route, which took me down a small, two-lane blacktop. I realized that for some reason the winding, tree-lined road looked familiar. It wasn't long before I knew why. As I topped a hill, off in the distance over the horizon, I could see the familiar prison tower that belonged to the Lexington high-medium security correctional facility right outside of Purcell. My heart sank as it came into full view. It was a bad prison; complete with gun tower, two or three rows of sixteen-foot high chain-link fence, topped with strands and strands of concertina wire. It's a prison I've been in more than once during the twenty-five years of incarceration that I had chalked up by then. It was a prison's prison... not as ominous as the thirty-foot, whitewashed walls and towers of the Oklahoma State Penitentiary in McAlester, but a sobering omen nonetheless. As I was driving up to it I started thinking about how sure I had been when I got out of El Reno that I would never be doing drugs, cheating on my wife, or be going back to prison again. The thought then occurred to me that I could no longer be so certain of that.

I pulled over on the side of the road and sat and stared at the ugly, paint-chipped exterior of the suffocating concrete buildings. As I looked at the bar-covered, bulletproof windows, through all that chain-link and razor wire, I mentally reached inside one of those cells I had been housed in so many times before; purposely remembering the lost and hopeless, abandoned feelings which I and everyone else around me had felt. I forced myself to enter the mind of one of those inmates who, I was sure, at that very moment, was peering out of his window at me sitting on my bike looking at the concrete fortress he was in. I knew what he was thinking, smelling and feeling; I knew he envied me and wondered what I was doing, where I was going... how it felt to be free. I also knew from experience that it made the oppressive weight of incarceration that much heavier.

I looked down at Mr. Big, who was stretching his face up at me with a questioning look. "I know, little buddy," I said. "I'm screwing up. If I don't do something... something right now, I will end up back in there. This is a sign." Looking at my little friend, I went on: "What do you think? It's time to get a grip, isn't it?" Mr. Big's response was to give my nose an affirming lick.

I looked back at the prison... some poor bastard was sitting there thinking they would give anything to trade places with me, for just one more chance. I had sat in those same windows thinking the same things about people I'd seen going by before. How often I had wished for, just... one... more... chance... and... wasn't this it? I solidified my resolve... Yes! It was time to change the coarse of events in my life. No more dope, no more Sheena. I needed to pass on the responsibilities of the street Hood to someone else. Someone clean. Then follow through with my plans to move to Guymon and start a dental lab business. That is, if I wanted to have a life and remain free. Aware that, if I stayed, I was only going to organize it into something that would warrant a racketeering case, considering that a good many of my Brothers, now including myself, were hip deep in the dope game. Tucking Mr. Big tighter into my leather coat, I kicked the powerful Harley engine into gear. I roared off down the road, feeling truly confident in myself and my future for the first time since I fell off the wagon back in the halfway house.

I quit drugs that day and began making plans to pass the torch for direction of the Hood to someone else. I loved them, they are my family, but it was necessary... I'd paid enough. I also broke off my relationship with Sheena. With that, I finally started getting the upper hand on the battle I was fighting within myself and started making real strides towards getting my life back. I was determined to rebuild my sense of integrity and get back on the road to fulfilling my hopes for the easy, peaceful future I had dreamed about those last few years in prison.

~ ◻◻◻◻◻◻◻◻◻ ~

Brad stopped us again. "Tape, tape, tape..." he said, pulling back from his view-finder and waving his hands. "This is one of the best interviews we've had. Hold up. I don't want to miss getting anything on film!" With that he scrambled to reload his camera. The rest of the technicians busied themselves with their jobs.

I stretched the best I could in my chains, eliciting the attention of the guards who'd been leaning against the door. Then I looked around the white walls of the cinder-block room that we were in. There were some property bins stacked against one wall and a couple of grey metal filing cabinets against another; some kind of storage room, I gathered. There was nothing on the walls other than a red fire extinguisher and the ubiquitous, to any public building, emergency exit map that was encased in plastic and screwed to the wall by the big blue steel door.

"Brad's just saying that, isn't he? I mean you've had to have done hundreds of interviews?" I said to Sara, who was trying to get comfortable in her chair.

"We've done over a thousand actually," she said. "And, yes, you stand out as one of the top five ever. Our bosses will probably do this whole segment on you and Brandon."

They seemed sincere, but I couldn't help but wonder how many other people they'd told that line to, to get what they wanted. "I'm not that special; just a guy who has been fucking up his whole life."

"Yeah, but you seem to be acutely self-aware of it, understand and regret it more than your average inmate," Sara countered.

Tracy was back, checking and dabbing at any spots on my face that may show a glare. She was close enough for me to notice that she still smelt good, which made me all too conscious that I probably didn't. "Do you want another water?" she asked.

"No, or I'll end up having to stop to pee," I replied. Then, looking back at the pretty producer, I said, with the weight of my past mistakes heavy laden in my voice: "I've had to live with more regrets than most. My son being at the end of this hall is a good example."

"We will talk about that when I get you guys together, but at the moment I'm curious about something…" Sara glanced at Brad. "Are we ready yet?"

He had just slapped in a new cartridge and was leaning forwards to his camera. Sticking his thumb in the air he said: "Yep, let's do it."

Sam stepped forward to check my mic one last time then slapped his sound marker together.

"Rolling…" Brad said to Sara.

Fussing with her hair a moment, Sara looked at me. "You obviously were trying to stay out and have a life. Even when you got off of the path you realized you were screwing up, and it appears that you caught yourself on your way down. What happened?"

"Well it might take a minute to answer *that* question," I squirmed, not only because my ass was falling asleep, but because the ignorance of it all was almost unconscionable. "Y'all may as well get comfortable, because this one's a long story… and not a very easy one for me to tell."

PART II
CHAPTER EIGHTEEN
CHOICES

L ife is a tricky bitch. If you don't hold it close and treat it with respect it'll turn on you quicker than a rattlesnake with a tooth-ache.

The night that turned my life in the direction that it is now in began simply enough. A few weeks after I had broken it off with Sheena I told Jenna that we were going to get us something to drink, grill us some steaks, and spend a quiet evening at home together. I left the choice up to her whether we would go to the liquor store for a bottle of Sailor Jerry's rum or the convenience store for some Budweiser. She was trying to make up her mind as we were riding down the street; her butt perched on the back of my Harley.

As we passed the Victory Christian Center we could see it had an event going on by the cluster of cars that were in the parking lot. I remember saying over my shoulder: "That's where we really ought to be going." But we rode right on by the drive that led down to the church, right by the proverbial road to redemption and down that hard road upon which I always seem to find myself. Of course, I didn't notice the Devil laughing at me and I gave it no more than a passing thought as I lost sight of the parking lot's lights in my mirrors. Like most things in life, after calamity strikes, a person goes back over the course of events and tries to say: *"If I would have just done this one thing differently everything would have turned out alright."* Hindsight is twenty-twenty. However, its also irrevocable.

Regardless of whether Jenna heard me or not, she didn't say anything regarding my comment; only saying that she would prefer a bottle over beer.

We found ourselves back at our apartment, sitting on the rear porch under our big folding umbrella, which was stuck down the center of the wrought iron patio table. We relaxed in its matching chairs, sipping on mixed drinks of rum and coke, as the day melted into night. It smelled green back here in the alley. I glanced up, appreciating the way that the streaks of orange and black stretched across the sky as the last glimpses of the sun fled over the horizon.

We had the stereo on in the house and we were listening to Elton John singing *'Someone Saved My Life Tonight'* coming over the speakers. Jenna was clinking the ice-cubes around in her drink with her finger. She looked at me out of her big, brown eyes and smiled as she blew out a steady stream of cigarette smoke. "This is nice," she said.

"Yeah it is," I agreed, smiling back and taking a sip of my drink. I recall sitting there and thinking how good I felt about having made a firm decision to work on my marriage with my wife; determined to be a faithful husband. I was enjoying the feeling of my moral compass and character finding their way back towards pointing true north again.

That's when I looked down at my phone and saw a number in my missed calls that I didn't recognize. Curious, I pushed the call back button. Sean, Sheena's fourteen year-old son, answered on the second ring. When I asked him if he had tried to call, he told me that he had been trying to find his mom and thought that I might know where she was. Sean went on to say that, since he'd tried calling me, he had been able to get in touch with her and she was on her way to pick up him and his younger sister, Jessica.

While I was on the phone with Sean I could hear his father, Stan, Sheena's ex-husband, saying in the background: "What's that motherfucker doing calling *my* house?" amongst a few other things. The "motherfucker" Stan was referring to, presumably, being me. I felt my blood heat up. I didn't say anything to Sean about hearing him, I just hung up the phone.

Stan, in my opinion, was just a fat, jealous, drunken blowhard that had convinced himself and his kids that he was a tough guy. However, his little front yard victories in which he was able to beat up one, smaller, out of shape neighbor or another, didn't impress me.

I knew I should just sit and enjoy the evening with my wife. After all, I had a lot to make up for. Before I even said it, I also knew that it wasn't going to go over well when I announced to Jenna that I was leaving and would be back shortly.

"What do you mean, Jimmy? You said that we were going to have a nice quiet evening at *home!*" Jenna yelled back at me; clouds of hurt building in her face.

I'd been sitting there stewing about Stan running his head while I'd been talking to his son. I was trying to let it go, but... I couldn't. I knew Sean and Jessica would be gone and I thought that putting this guy to rights would give me some peace of mind as I closed out that chapter of my life... I almost listened to my wife, but instead I replied: "Don't worry. This has nothing to do with Sheena. Stan is the only one over there. I'll be back. It's just something I need to do."

"You promised!" she said with tears welling up in her eyes.

I kissed her on the forehead and wiped the moisture from her cheeks. I went on to tell her: "This won't take but just a minute and I *will* be back." Ignoring her sad, skeptical look I went out the door and threw my leg over my black and chrome 2001 Road King. I revved my engine as Jenna turned away from me; shutting our apartment door as she did so.

It was a warm June evening. Stan lived down off of N.W. 23rd and Portland; only four or five miles as the crow flew. I rode over to his house full of indignation and Sailor Jerry's rum, intent on bouncing his fat ass around his front yard and secretly relishing the idea. At the same time, I was slightly concerned about how Sheena's kids were going to feel when they found out that I had kicked the snot out of their dad.

When I pulled up in his driveway I could see right away that Sheena had already been by and picked up Sean and Jess. The house was quiet and dark except for one dim light that showed through the kitchen window. Confident that Stan's children were gone, I sauntered up the steps to his porch and banged on the front door. A minute later he answered. When Stan opened the door and saw me he looked around quickly to see if I was alone... "Jimmy! W-what are you doing here?" he asked. By the look on his face it was evident that he was very surprised to see me, which goes to show how little he knew me.

Stan was in his mid to late thirties, bald-headed and weighed in around two hundred and sixty pounds. He was a fairly large man, but his size was mostly running to fat despite his age.

"I heard you running your mouth while I was on the phone with Sean earlier," I snarled. "I'm here to find out if you got something to say to my face."

"Oh, man, I didn't know that was you. I didn't mean nothing about you..." he stammered. "Hell, come on in and have a drink with me," he went on quickly, trying to change the mood and ease my tension. I could smell the whiskey on his breath before he'd even mentioned having a snort.

Although I had gone there to fight, my main purpose was to put him in his place and check his loud mouth; meaning to make him either live up to his words or swallow them. Whether I could whip him or not didn't matter to me. By the lump in Stan's throat, he and I both knew which way that had gone. I'd already accomplished my goal without having to beat his face in. Something that would have undoubtedly caused a never-ending enmity towards me from Sheena's kids. Feeling like Stan now understood I wasn't to be taken lightly and that he needed to walk softer around me, I accepted his offer.

I'm not sure why. I've scratched my head a thousand times since then, wondering. To be honest, I guess, I felt a little sorry for the guy. He was so obnoxious and mouthy when he was drinking that no one, not even his kids, could stand to be around him. Even though he worked at Budweiser, provided a good home and was relatively stable, his drinking made him a fairly lonely man. Not to mention – I was already full of rum myself.

Whatever my motivation was, I strolled up in his house and we sat down at his round, wooden kitchen table. He had a comfortable home, glancing around his kitchen I could appreciate the wood work that went into his matching stained cabinets. Sitting there I helped him polish off the rest of a bottle of Whiskey, while we talked about my recent split with his ex-wife and my determination to straighten up.

At one point, I realized how drunk I was getting and asked myself what I was doing still there. A small voice told me that I needed to leave and get back to Jenna while I could still ride. But, I was already too drunk to listen and with one more drink I was completely obliterated.

The conversation turned towards his estranged girlfriend, Jolene, and how she had taken up and ran off with some other guy, which got us both grumbling.

"Couldn't I pad a few of your guys pockets to have this guy Joe, I think his name is, put in the hospital?" Stan finally got around to asking me. He was leaning his elbows heavily on the table and looking forlornly at the bottom of his empty glass. We had already established that there wasn't a single drop left in the bottle when we prepared the last drinks. Joe was the new boyfriend. When I asked him why he wouldn't just do that himself he explained that he didn't want to look like the bad guy.

"Hell with that!" I shot back. I stood up, having to catch myself from a sudden case of vertigo. Then I grabbed Stan by the shoulder. "You need to go over there and D.D.T. that dude; throw Jolene in your truck and bring her ass back home, your damn self. Come on… I'll go with you," I drunkenly volunteered. That small, sensible whisper that had echoed around inside my head earlier had been drowned in the last quarter bottle of Jack Daniels.

The next thing we knew, we were pulling up in front of the trailer-house Jolene and her daughter, Sabrina, were living in with this new guy. When I saw the tall, skinny, brown-headed *pretty boy'* on the porch, I bailed out of the truck. Stan was already yelling at him. When Joe started cussing and yelling back, I whipped out my lock-blade and headed up the steps after him. Jolene and Sabrina had come out onto the porch and Joe shot between them and ran into the house with me only three steps behind him. Jolene, a short blonde with as average a face as I've ever seen, tried to step in my way and block me from entering the trailer, but I brushed right by her and Sabrina going in after him; only to find that he had ran out of the back door.

About that time Stan caught up with me. "Come on, you crazy motherfucker! Jolene has already called the cops!" he warned. He pulled and pushed me towards the door, telling me to take his pick-up and get the hell out of Dodge. Why he wasn't coming with me I didn't know, but I climbed into Stan's brand new big, white, king-cab truck that he was so proud of and took off. Barely able to drive and feeling like I had left a man behind, I drove to the closest place I could for assistance… Sheena's house.

CHAPTER NINETEEN
SNAKE EYES

Sheena and her kids came running out when I swerved into the driveway, folding up the passenger side mirror on one of her carport columns. "Oh my God, what has Jimmy done to dad!?" I could hear Jessica scream. She was obviously panicked and fearful that I'd done something to her father to be out driving his truck, alone.

Sheena came out to the truck. "What's happened?" she asked, tension straining her voice. She turned and yelled at her kids to go back into the house. With a worried look torturing her ocean-blue eyes, she went on: "What are you doing in Stan's truck?"

"Come on," I said. "We've got to go back and get him. He's still there…" and I went on to blurt out the story as coherently as I could. I slid over so that she could drive. Still confused at how Stan and I could be together and none too happy about it, she drove us back down I-40 towards the trailer court where I'd left him.

Sheena called her sister-in-law, Lauren, to discuss the absurdity of it all. They finally gave up trying to figure it out and just laughed at the odd things people do when they're drunk off their asses. Shaking her head, still in disbelief, she switched lanes and took the Rockwell exit.

Halfway through the loop she suddenly quit laughing and handed the phone to me. We could see the red and blue flashers of the police cars out in front of Jolene's trailer. "Oh shit! Stay down…" Sheena gasped. I was so intoxicated that I just started whispering to Lauren on the phone, as if the cops somehow wouldn't be able to see nor hear me. I was *'stupid'* drunk and thinking that the whole thing was just a big joke! I got the seriousness of the situation real quick, however, when we were spotlighted by one of the police cruisers and another one whipped out of Jolene's yard to pursue us.

Sheena, close to panic, drove past the turn-in where the police cars were now coming from and tried to dodge down the next trailer court avenue. The cop jumped right in behind us; running Sheena and the truck up onto a yellow guardrail. The police threw down on us. Sheena, confused and upset, exited the truck without any resistance.

"Passenger, come out with your hands up!" the officers yelled at me.

The rest pretty much passed in a blur, with me slowly registering through my inebriated haze that I was going to jail. While I was sitting handcuffed in the back seat of the cop car, the officers paraded Joe, Jolene, and Sabrina by, so that they could identify me through the window; with each one nodding and saying variants of: "Yes, officer, that was him." I barely remember going through the booking process after that.

When I woke up I found myself in a plastic boat, which is a canoe-shaped portable bunk that jails and shelters keep on hand when they are over-crowded. I was in a cell in the Oklahoma County Jail.

Scratching my head, I slowly recalled what I could of the prior night's events. What I had done and with whom rose foggily to the surface of my mind like the Ghost of Christmas Past. I remember looking into the mirror and asking myself: *W.T.F.?* What was wrong with me? I didn't even like Stan. Why was I out running around with him, let alone getting myself jugged over him? Sure, a night in County might have been worth it for cracking his head, but for helping him? I was astounded... and disgusted, as the magnitude of what I was probably facing sunk in. I remembered the officers taking two matching switchblades off of me and my heart grew very heavy. I sat on the edge of the commode with my arms resting on my knees. I stared at my hands wondering who they belonged too, feeling like the person they were attached to could not possibly be me.

I was aware that I really hadn't done anything and I also knew, or rather hoped I knew, that I had never intended too. But when I called my wife she told me Sheena had found out I was being charged with 1st degree burglary and the prosecutor was pushing for a home invasion charge. *Holy Crap!* I thought. I'd only been out for a little over a year! With this there was little doubt that I would be going back to jail and, if *'the powers that be'* had their way, for a very long time.

Later that day we found out that my bond was set at twenty thousand dollars. My wife and Sheena, though despising one another, pooled their resources. In other words, my wife allowed Sheena to post my bond, they both signed for me and within a couple of days were able to make my bail. I was released at two in the morning. The sleepy, bald-headed, night-duty officer told me in a tired grumble that there was a note requiring them to inform the Feds if I were going to be released. He'd got no answer when he tried the number attached. As he unlocked the outside door, he suggested that I get a hold of the parole office the next day and let them know.

Since Sheena had put up the money and supplied the bondsman she was naturally the one who came and picked me up. I knew this was the beginning of an already old problem when she pulled up in her sugar daddy's stretched-out Lincoln Continental and smiled at me. It wasn't a regular smile: it was the smile of a mouse that had just sprung its trap on the cat. But I was grateful to be out of jail, so I didn't complain as I climbed into the car's red, plush interior.

"Take me to Stan's. I want my bike," I said. When we got there, my Harley wasn't sitting in the driveway where I had left it. After not getting any answer at Stan's front door, I walked around the side of his house to find my ride locked behind a gate in his backyard. Mad because my bike had been moved in the first place, I began looking in the trunk of the Lincoln for a piece of chain or rope that I could use to pull Stan's fence down. He finally came out on his porch. "What's my bike doing in your backyard?" I growled.

He had his pick-up pulled up across the front of his house. "Look at my truck!," he said. He was pointing at the big dent right behind the driver's door where it met the frame. It was down low where the cops had run Sheena up onto the guardrail. "Who is going to pay for my truck?" He was wearing a pair of pants with no shirt on; his fat gut hanging over his belt, jiggling around grotesquely as he paced back and forth nervously along his railed porch.

"What the fuck does that have to do with you having my scooter in your backyard?" I scowled.

"Well, someone has got to pay for this dent," he replied, still pointing at the damaged truck, but staying up on his stoop close to his front door.

As hard as it was for me to believe, I realized that this piece of shit, who was almost as responsible for me going to jail as I was, had been intent on holding my Harley hostage had I not gotten out. "I *know* you're not thinking of trying to hold my bike! I will tear your whole fucking house down and leave your fat ass buried in the rubble," I snarled, heading for him.

Sheena grabbed my arm. "No, Jimmy, you'll go back to jail and we'll never get you out this time. Or your bike back. Hell there's a cop car coming down the street right now!" I glanced down the lane and saw not just one, but two, squad cars slowly cruising the neighborhood.

"I'll give you your motorcycle, Jimmy, but this is messed up... Look at my truck," Stan whined.

"I know you're going to give me my motorcycle, Stan," I said. "Of that there is no doubt." I was still amazed at the depths of this guy's stupidity and I was getting madder thinking about what would have happened had I not been there. "As a matter of fact, I've had it with you..." I told him as he was heading around the side of his house to open the gate for me.

That's when Sheena jumped in front of me. "Let it go..." she said, staring hard at me and nodding for me to look back over my shoulder, where the police cars were just pulling up to the front curb.

The police officers, one short and stocky and the other tall and lean, both sporting the traditional flat-top haircut, came walking up the driveway wanting to know what was going on. Stan and I denied any problems and Sheena jumped in trying to smooth things over as well. I told them I was over there to pick up my motorcycle, which my friend was watching for me whilst I'd been in jail. Stan had already unlocked the gate for me to roll it out. While Stan and I were out of earshot, I assured him, through clenched teeth, that I would deal with him later. I pushed my bike back up to the front of the house, still thinking about how much trouble Jenna would have had with this clown, trying to get my bike back, if I hadn't been able to get out of jail. *He's lucky he didn't know me in the old days,* I thought to myself. The cops, seeing that we weren't fighting, listened to Sheena explain away whatever they *'thought'* they'd seen whilst driving by.

When they saw my bike the tall cop said: "Oh... I see what the tension is all about now. That isn't just a motorcycle, it's a Harley!" Apparently, he was a fan. He looked at me and asked if they were going to have any problems out of me later.

I was still bristling, not wanting it to show. I didn't even look at him. "No... can I go?"

"Sure," the one in charge said. "But, we'll be around, so go home if you don't want to end up back in jail."

I nodded then hit my electric starter and roared my bike to life. Stiff and staring straight ahead, I told Sheena that I was going home and would see her the next day. She stuck out her bottom lip and said that she loved me and would call me later.

I was not only pissed off at Stan, but I was pretty disgusted with myself too for more than one reason. The least of which was getting thrown in jail behind that piece of crap... but even more, for my thinking of being with Stan in the first place. I had vowed off of hard liquor because I'd been known to turn into a real idiot when whiskey drunk, so in the end, the responsibility for this was all mine. Not to mention, I was now fully aware that the door I had worked so hard to close on Sheena's and my adulterous affair was now thrown wide open. I drove home back to Jenna.

When I pulled up to the apartment I could see Mr. Big's pointed ears and little brown and black face through the living room window. He was hopping around on the back of the chair that sat against the glass. He knew the sound of my Harley. Jenna always knew when it entered the complex, because Mr. Big would start dancing his little 'my daddy's home' dance.

The next day, I called and apologized to Sabrina and her mother Jolene. With special emphasis on Sabrina, to assure her that I never meant to scare her. She laughed saying: "Oh its alright, Jimmy. I knew you were after Joe. He's an asshole, anyway."

Jolene wasn't quite as cheery about me running up in her house with an open bladed knife in my hand. But, she accepted my apology and told me that she was sorry for getting the cops involved.

She said that the detectives who called her to the station had told her that they knew me and were bragging about how they could put me away for seventy or eighty years this time. Upset, she told me this was way out of hand and she didn't want that, especially since she knew it had been all Stan's doing anyway. Jolene told me that she would not go to court against me if she had any choice. However, she also admitted that when it came to going to jail, she was a real chicken-shit and were it to became a choice between testifying or being held in contempt, that she *would* testify. I told her that I appreciated her honesty and, after apologizing again, hung up.

Thinking about the description Sabrina and Jolene gave me, of how crazy I looked, standing in the middle of their living room, snarling and going after Joe with that knife in my hand, I wondered what a jury would think about all that coming from a fourteen year-old girl; even if she told the jury that she *knew* I wouldn't have hurt her, or her mom. I mean... I absolutely *knew* I wouldn't have, and I still felt like an asshole. What would people who didn't even know me think? I reflected back to the forty-five-year sentence that I'd gotten the last time for a *miniscule* amount of meth... and I began to worry.

Next I called the color line to check and see if I was supposed to go in and get U/A'd that day... Sure enough, my color was on the list, so I went down to the place that took our samples. When I got there, I discovered that the Federal probation office had called and cancelled my contract with them. I called my parole officer, Steve Stone, and was referred to his supervisor, who told me that Steve was out of town. After I told him that my color had come up and the U/A place wouldn't let me piss for them he told me that it was just standard procedure. Then he went on to tell me that I should come in and they would take a sample from me in the office.

That sounded like a trap to me... and having just made a twenty thousand dollar bond I really didn't want to go back to jail just yet. Plus, what the detectives told Jolene had me more than a little concerned. Forsaking my job at the dental lab, Jenna and I decided to go to Tulsa for a few days until I could determine the seriousness of the situation. Maryjo, my oldest daughter Stephanie and youngest son Brandon had a fairly anonymous place up there. At least the lease and utilities weren't in any of their names. I knew that with a little detective work its whereabouts could be ciphered out, but it would take a little time and, after all, I hadn't really decided to make an all-out run for it yet. I just didn't want to be picked up by the Feds before my court date and lose that option before I made a decision. That's if they were even after me.

Sheena started flipping out. She was mad because I was out and spending all my time with my wife. When she laid it on me that if I did not come stay with her she would have my bond revoked, I got mad. Sheena later told me that she wouldn't have really done it, but that was enough for me. I felt honor-bound after that to shuck those chains. At that time, I still had full intentions of showing up for court. Even though the Feds would be waiting to take me into custody when I did. Of course, that was contingent upon having some reasonable belief that I wasn't going to be completely hung out to dry over it. But, for all intents and purposes, I would be on the run until I decided what to do.

To confirm my fugitive status, not two days later, Sheena called to let me know by voicemail that a Federal Task Force had raided mine, hers and Stan's house all on the same day, back in O.K.C..

The chase had just became official....

CHAPTER TWENTY
DRUG HOUSE

I didn't want to step back into the drug world, but I needed money while I was laying low, so I started running drugs between the city and Tulsa. I had a little network of friends and Brothers who were loyal to me. Some were dealers and some were sellers already; making it an easy niche to fit into. However, as the marshals turned the heat up, I realized things weren't moving near fast enough. I needed traveling money and I needed a gun. So, I decided to rob a heroin supply house that Maryjo had put me on.

Maryjo was a *'functioning'* heroin addict and she knew several dealers. Her having been my partner in crime back in the old days, when I robbed just to feed and clothe our family, made her well-aware of what I needed and was capable of doing to get on my feet. Not to mention, the particular drug dealer she thought I should hit was one I'd had words with a few months earlier.

...Long before I was on the run, Maryjo asked Jenna and ne if we would help her beat her heroin addiction. We agreed and had her come to O.K.C.. Once she was with us we got her on the waiting list to get into the Referral Center. The Referral Center was a pretty successful jumping off point for drug addicts that were serious about quitting. It got them dried out, assessed their needs and referred them on to the next full facility treatment center that best suited their goals. But... there was a waiting list.

For two weeks my wife and I put up with Maryjo trying to *'kick'* heroin. I had to use every favor and connection I knew, which weren't very many in the opiate world. But... I knew enough to keep her in *'Lortabs'*, *'Roxys'* and whatever else she needed to get her through the roughest parts. She was getting to be a real pain in the ass by the time a bed became available at the center. She'd even started to squirm around with the idea of not going in at all.

"The hell you say!" I exploded the first time that Maryjo mentioned '*...maybe needing to do the treatment center thing at another time*'. Teddy, her current husband, was whining about her coming back to Tulsa. He would tell her that her dogs needed her – that the house was falling apart – that she wasn't going to make it anyway... *etc.*, *etc.*. He was a loser with a capital 'L'.

"After all the shit I've put up with; running all over town to keep you '*well*' until you got a bed – you're going?" I demanded in frustrated aggravation. "And if Teddy, or anyone else, comes down here to get you I'll beat their head in and toss them in the dumpster out back." I pulled my ball bat out from behind the front door and leant it against the wall to emphasize my level of commitment. She slumped back on the couch. She knew me well enough to know I meant what I said.

The day Maryjo was to check in finally came. We were in a clinical intake room with fake plants, generic paintings and all, waiting for the plump, dark haired receptionist to get done processing a sullen, Gothic-looking young lady who was obviously only there at her mother's behest; since she was the one doing all the talking. Maryjo was sitting next to me fidgeting nervously when someone called her phone. I could tell by snatches of the conversation that it was her heroin connection in Tulsa. I told her to put the phone up, but she argued that it "...was just a friend." The next thing I heard was: "Oh... Ummm... really, Mark... yeah I'll be there." Then she jumped up with the phone still in her hand and said: "Come on, Jimmy, this is going to have to wait. I need to go back to Tulsa."

At that point I blew one! Completely oblivious to the other three people in the room's gasps and stares, I snatched the phone out of Maryjo's hand and shoved her back in her seat. I cursed the people on the other end of the line. I told them we were sitting in the waiting room of a treatment center at that very moment, which I damn near had to carry Maryjo into. In my most menacing tone, I promised them if they ever called her again I would come to Tulsa, kick in their door and take everything that they had. Then I smashed the phone right there in the floor.

Maryjo was used to my explosive temper and occasional, overwhelming outbursts. She just sat up straight crossing her legs. Never even glancing in my direction, she straightened her long dress and said with her most dignified pout: "Well... you didn't have to break my phone. I knew you weren't going to let me go, anyway."

I looked up and saw the receptionist watching me. She had her fingers poised over the buttons on the phone in front of her... ready to call 911, security or whatever else depending on my next move. The mother just watched me with a firm, almost understanding, look on her face; even giving me a slight nod of approval, whilst her daughter just looked hopeless and frightened; apparently now abandoning her own thoughts of escape. Aware of them for the first time since the phone call, I mumbled with embarrassment: "I'm sorry. I didn't mean to frighten anyone. You don't know what it took to get her here."

The receptionist nodded and removed her hand from the phone. "No problem. I completely understand."

Maryjo lasted about a week before I got a call to come pick her up. She had been kicked out for smoking in the bathroom! Somehow, she'd just let them catch her...

At any rate, the heroin connection I'd made that heated and frustrated threat to was the one and the same that Maryjo thought I should rob. Mainly because they were who she knew the most about. She was able to tell me when the three people that normally worked it would have the most cash together for their recoup. Supposedly, upwards of ten grand and a couple of guns. A nice little fugitive fund 'if' everything was everything. Taking them down worked nicely for me, since in the end they had played a significant role in derailing my ex-wife's recovery, and I generally like to do what I say I'm going to do.

Maryjo gave me the whole layout; how many people were usually there, when they had the least amount of traffic, as well as where the safe and guns were kept. She told me how Mark, or Sharon, who was a tough ol' bulldyke, walked around with rolls of cash and a pill bottle full of balloons of heroin in their pockets.

She also told me that they would never open the door for me. When a man came to the door, the male occupants of the apartment would let someone they knew in, but would never unlock the door if they didn't know them, especially if they looked like me. However, if they saw a girl through the peephole they would let them in without hardly a second thought. Then lock the door back and walk away, apparently, not perceiving a female as a threat. Maryjo indicated that so many women came over there that they would do the same thing even if the person answering the door didn't know them, just assuming someone else did.

Jenna and I talked over the idea of using her as my decoy girl, but she had been there once with Maryjo. It would be a toss up whether they would remember her or who she had come with, or not. But with Sharon being a dyke and especially the guys they weren't likely to have forgotten that hot little hourglass shape of my wife, even if her pretty brown eyes and waist-length dark hair escaped their memory. Besides, I was very protective of Jenna and tended to keep her at a distance from my activities. Using Maryjo was out of the question, for obvious reasons. So, I pulled up a tough, little, dark-haired hooker friend of mine named Heather who lived in the city to help with the job.

Heather was pure prostitute from her four inch stiletto heels up to her push-up bra. She would have been gorgeous had it not been for a couple of scars on her face that she'd acquired from the tough street life she'd led. She was still very pretty and down as they come, and jumped on the opportunity to make some money.

After a huge argument with Jenna about *'why'* she couldn't go with me, I left her at a friend's house and went and picked up Heather. We talked the plan over while we drove the ninety miles from O.K.C. to Tulsa.

In Tulsa we met up with Maryjo. She was riding with Phillip, an old ex-con friend of mine, and his wife Della. I had come up with an old, nickel plated, single action .38 that looked like it might fall apart in my hand just holding it, let-alone shooting it. But, even as raggedy as it was, I still wanted bullets. Della was the only non-felon in the bunch and she carried herself like your everyday law-abiding citizen. She had green eyes and well-groomed, shoulder-length, dishwater-blonde hair, and wore a pressed, baby-blue pant suit that would have been appropriate for any office job. She was the obvious choice to send into Walmart to get me some ammo. Naturally, sending the only *'non-felon'* female with us, alone, to get a certain type of ammunition – she came back with the wrong kind.

Maryjo was freaking out trying to tell me that the dope house would be filling up with people. "There is no telling who will be coming and going if you don't get over there," she complained.

So, after altering the plan a little and adding Phillip into the mix, I decided to take the house anyway. Robbing an armed dope house with an empty gun is not a very smart thing to do, in my humble opinion, but desperate times call for desperate measures. I had not come all the way from Oklahoma City to end it as a dry run.

Phillip knew Sharon, Mark and a couple of the Mexicans that periodically lived in the dope house. Phil had a pretty decent little heroin habit himself and had frequented their drug repository almost as much as Maryjo had. He allowed that even though he was a tall, lean, bald-headed, tatted-up ex-con, he wouldn't have any problems getting in. However, he didn't really want to expose his complicity in the robbery if it wasn't necessary. Phillip and I went all the way back to the boys' home and he'd had my back many times before, so I knew I could count on him in a pinch.

My plan only involved him as a lookout and recon. Since he knew them, he could go in as a customer. If there were too many people already there for me and Heather to handle, he could call me off by sending me a blank text. Or, if someone noticed that there wasn't any bullets in the gun and tried to make a move on me, he could step on up to cover my back. Short of that, there really wasn't any reason to make our connection known. If it went the way it should, Phillip would also be in the aftermath as just another one of the victims; able to report back to me if the police were called or if someone had recognized me.

Considering it was later in the morning than we'd planned and people would be showing up randomly, along with the lack of bullets, the convenience of his relationship with the pushers made it worth a few balloons of heroin from the take for the added insurance. I told Phillip I'd give him thirty minutes to re-con the situation before I showed up, then I pulled around to the back of the apartment complex and let him out.

The connection lived at 122nd and Garnett Street in a fairly large, mid to high-end three-story apartment complex. The rectangular buildings were long and tall with entryways staggered down both of its main sides. The grounds were covered in manicured trees and bushes. Its roads wound themselves through and in-between the buildings, so a person loitering around would not necessarily stand out as long as he wasn't looking too shifty.

I backed my Regal into a parking space right around the corner from the mark's apartment, so it would be close. Then I went back around to sit in Phillip's and Della's blacked-out, King Cab F-150 with Della, Maryjo and Heather where we waited.

"Are you all good with this?" I asked Heather when I climbed in.

"Yeah, but what if they stay between me and the door and don't let me unlock it?" she replied, looking nervous for the first time.

"They're not going to do that," Maryjo jumped in. "They probably won't even notice that no-one knows you for a few minutes. But, if you don't hurry there's going to be a whole lot more people in there to deal with!" For some reason Maryjo had been snapping at Heather all morning as well as giving me a steady stream of advice and details that I did not need.

"Maryjo," I grated, "I know what the fuck I'm doing. You've told me everything I need to know. Now sit back and hush. You'll get a fix when this is over." Then looking at Heather, I continued: "When Maryjo and I were married I used to do this on a weekly, sometimes daily, basis, just to put food on the table and diapers on the kids. Don't worry. I will not leave you hanging. I'll be coming through that door if I have to knock it off its hinges, but a quiet entry and a quiet exit is what we are aiming for... Okay?" I looked at my phone and seeing there wasn't any blank texts from Phillip said: "Now, are you ready?"

"Lets do this," Heather said, sticking her chin out and showing that determined toughness that I chose her for in the first place.

We walked around the side of the building and I pointed out the Buick as we passed by it on our way to the front. The apartment that we were looking for was a couple of doors down. The entry was perfect for a dope house. There was a ten-foot tall bush placed in a way that, once a customer walked up to the door, they were out of the view of the casual passerby, whilst at the same time being observable to the occupants of the place through a peep-hole in the door. However, it also made it more convenient to rob.

When we got to the apartment, Heather went to the door and I stepped around the corner out of sight. I could feel my pulse quicken as the adrenaline started to surge through my body. I even had a little bead of sweat run down the nape of my neck. Back in the day, this would have been as easy as breathing, but I hadn't undertaken a robbery in a long time. Before that thought could take hold I heard Heather knocking and someone letting her in...

Not taking any chances, I came around the bush and hit the door before it could be closed all the way. Pushing my way in, I slammed it behind me and yelled: "Everybody on the ground!" I brandished the gun with extra emphasis at the four guys, who were sitting at the kitchen table chopping up dope, with Phillip sitting amongst them trying his best to win an Oscar for best supporting actor.

Sharon, who had let Heather in, was the head honcho of this outfit. She was a medium built, blonde-haired woman in her early forties, who had a permanent scowl etched in her face from years of dealing with junkies, day in and day out. When I entered, she was still standing by the door. Joni, Sharon's girlfriend; a plump, soft blonde, was laying under a blanket on the living room floor watching T.V.. Heather pulled out a knife. I told her to empty out the plastic trash can on the floor and watch Joni.

Meanwhile, I dragged Sharon into the kitchen by the neck with one hand and pointed the gun at the men with the other; repeating my order for them to hit the floor. As I pointed the revolver at them menacingly, I moved it from one to the other quickly, so that they couldn't see the cylinders clearly and discover that they were empty. I thrust them all down to the floor and frisked them quickly. With my most vicious snarl I stuck the gun in Phillip's face and asked him if he felt like being a hero. He allowed… that he did not. The rest complied pretty quickly.

I searched Sharon and threw the money and pill bottle that was in her pocket into the trash can, along with her and Joni's cellphones. Heather collected wallets and cellphones from Mark, Phillip and the other two that were on the floor beside them.

"Where is the safe?" I demanded, glaring at Sharon.

"There is no safe," Sharon replied, licking her lips nervously and glancing hopelessly at the front door. I realized that she was probably expecting more people to show up at any time.

Leaving the gun with Heather, I grabbed Joni by the hair and started dragging her back to the bedroom where the safe was supposed to be. "Well, maybe your girlfriend will be able to show me then!" I leered at Sharon, while Joni struggled and pleaded. "Its not me doing this to you, sweetheart," I directed to Joni. "Your girlfriend there obviously cares more about her money and drugs then she does about you."

"Nooo!" she cried as I tugged her down the hallway.

At that point Sharon jumped up. "Alright – alright, I'll show you. Just leave her alone!"

Keeping a hand locked in Joni's hair, I followed Sharon into the bedroom, secretly thankful that Sharon had broken so quickly. Since I don't know what I would have done with Joni past trying to scare them into compliance, anyway.

I left Heather *and Phillip* to watch the kitchen as I retrieved the small safe that was hidden in the closet. After that I herded the two women back out to the living room and had Heather tape everyone's hands and feet.

Leaving them secured face down on the floor, we left carrying the safe and the trash can of phones and wallets with us. It was still quiet and peaceful outside. There was no sign that anyone had raised an alarm. Relieved, I hit the remote button; popping the trunk as we were rounding the corner on the way to the car. We tossed everything in the boot before we climbed in and pulled out casually. I exhaled for what seemed like the first time since going through the door. Heather was excited from the intensity of what we'd just done, but as soon as the adrenalin wore off she collapsed and was asleep within two miles of the job. I looked over at her sleeping and smiled. She was still holding her closed, lock-blade knife tight in her fist while the rest of her jiggled gently with the motion of the car. She had done well.

I drove across town and got a room at the Ramada Inn. Then I let Maryjo know where we were, so when Phillip could manage to extract himself without raising suspicions, they'd know where to find us.

Once they were there, I divided up most of the balloons of heroin between Maryjo, Della and Phillip. There was only three a piece for them and two each for Heather and me. We'd timed the heist to catch them right before they re-upped.

Phillip told me that he didn't stay long, but he'd been there to hear Sharon and Mark discussing their suspicions of Maryjo's hand in the robbery. My name wasn't mentioned specifically. However, someone pointed out that Maryjo's ex, who just happened to be me, used to rob the more unsavory drug dealers around town before going to prison the last time.

Phillip reported that the two extra men who had been there, and were only victims by happenstance, had spouted off about what they would do to us if they ever figured out who we were. Pretty big talk from guys who didn't even move a muscle while I was in the other room looking for the safe. Having, to their knowledge, only Heather to guard all four of them.

A few days later I heard that Mark and Sharon had hired someone to try and track the assailants down. The bounty hunter collected all the phone numbers of the cellphones we'd taken and was calling them in the hope of someone answering. Never fearing retribution in the first place, I took it in stride as part of the game. I was confident that the bounty hunter *really* didn't want to find me anyway, and just as I suspected, the more suspicions pointed towards me, the less interest the bounty hunter had in confirming them. Around that time the message was sent *to me* that the police were never called and never would be.

At any rate, I waited until I'd gotten rid of everyone before cracking the safe. Only to find, less than two grand, one 9mm automatic and a few Phentenal patches inside of it. Not the ten thousand and one time score to hold me over *'quietly'* that it was supposed to be.

So... it was back to square one – running *'ice', a* form of grown methamphetamine from Oklahoma City, where it was plentiful, to Tulsa, where it was not.

Robbing people wasn't something I wanted to get back into, anyway. I'm a man who can make myself do what needs to be done when it needs to be done. But, as I have gotten older, my sense of what's right and wrong has evolved.

I even felt a little pang of guilt for knocking over Mark and Sharon's place. I didn't know them, but I hadn't heard anything particularly bad about them either; other than the argument that we'd had whilst I was trying to check Maryjo into treatment... I really had no justification for mistreating them. Finding out that they weren't involving the police only confirmed that they weren't all bad. I never had feelings like that back in the old days. I guessed that I was just losing my edge, and that's a sure sign it's time to stay away from the heavier shit.

CHAPTER TWENTY-ONE
NO TURNING BACK

Well, at least I had a little recoup money to work with. As I bounced back and forth between cities, Jenna and I stayed with whoever we were dealing drugs to at the time. However, as the manhunt for me intensified, the Federal Marshalls somehow started showing up at houses I'd been holding up at, particularly in the city. I began sticking closer and closer to Tulsa and only venturing into O.K.C. for the pick-up.

As my court hearing for the *'Burglary One'* eventually approached, I was still on the fence about whether to come in or not. The rumors, which turned out weren't true, but appeared to be at the time, pointed towards Sheena as the source of the information that led the marshals to most of my safe houses in the Oklahoma City area. That, and the threat she'd made about pulling my bond if I didn't forsake my wife for her, was enough to no longer feel beholden to live up to the bond she had made for me. Still, I was not sure that I wanted to be on the run for the rest of my life.

My world was already getting smaller and some of my friends were catching unnecessary heat due to my fugitive status. They would just tell me not to worry about them and do what I had to do, and so on. They all knew how long a sentence the no-justice system had given me the last time, over what people don't even go to prison for anymore. Me and my friends were all very aware of the devastation the Oklahoma court system could reap on certain individual's lives. As well as, that I was one of those individuals that, for whatever reason, could expect the worst.

In hindsight, I wish that I could go back and face my problems head on and take my chances. But, I was getting strung out on the drugs I was transporting – logic and reasoning were not my strongest suit during that time. Sometimes the harder you fight against the noose, the tighter it gets.

When my court hearing was a week away I made one last run to Tina's to pick up some dope. She looked at me with her soft, green eyes and told me that she would help me pay my attorney if I showed up for court. I still intended on it, even though the bondsman told me that the Feds had a plan for catching me there, if I did. I told her I'd most likely be there, but in case I didn't, she needed to keep her house clean and pull the pictures of me that she had got from my place off of her walls. I told her if the cops discerned how close we were, they would never leave her alone. She said that she didn't think that they would come there. I implored her not to count on it and to be ready. Honestly, as I headed back to Tulsa, I still didn't know what I was going to do.

Back in Tulsa I went about collecting money that was owed to me. Jenna and I were living exclusively out of motels by then. Mr. Big, my little guard dog, rode along with us, watching my back.

The last night before court we were hiding out at a Motel 6 on the east side of Tulsa. Counting up our assets, we had less than a thousand dollars, close to two ounces of ice, a fully loaded 9mm, my bike and the Buick Regal. We had long since run out our credit and debit cards. We had to abandon Jenna's Toyota, because I had caved in the windshield to stop Jenna and Maryjo from driving off with my money after M.J. had got kicked out of the referral center. We'd even lost everything we had at our apartment, except one pick-up load that Tina was able to slip in and get for us. Our lives were a total bust already.

Laying up together in that motel room the night before my arraignment on the 'Burglary' charge. Jenna and I talked about what we were going to do that next day. Deep down I knew I should head back to Oklahoma City. I knew it. But, Jenna had waited for me to get out for so long and even though she really wasn't what she pretended to be while I was in, I nevertheless hadn't really done right by her while I was out either. She laid in my arms, crying, not wanting me to go.

Jenna had now also developed a drug habit. Even worse, as much as she denied it, she was not equipped with the right moxie and street savvy to navigate in the world that I had exposed her too. She would be eaten alive if I was not there. Along with the weight of that fact was the ton of guilt I had over the way I'd handled things when I got out. The thing is, regardless of what blame I could lay on her for my actions, when push came to shove, I was responsible for the wrongs that I had committed and the pain that I had caused her. The guilt that I carried crushed my common sense.

I didn't want to go back to prison forever. I knew that my only chance, although at the time I believed it to be only a slim one, was to face my legal issues head on. I was aware that if I didn't, it would be like throwing gasoline on the fire that my fugitive status had already ignited. Without a doubt it would burn out of my control.

"Jenna, I should go in." I said it softly as I held her in my arms. My chest wet with her tears.

"No... I don't want you to." She cried and squeezed me even tighter with her arms.

"You know, honey, this... this is the point of no return. If we don't go back to O.K.C. tonight the ante goes up on me. I'm not going to spend the rest of my life in prison. I'm so tired of that life, I'd rather be dead," I told her.

"Well if you die, I die. I'd rather be dead than without you again." She snuggled up closer, putting her face right under my chin, as she talked quietly. I could smell the sent of the shampoo she'd used in her hair.

"I'm serious, Jenna. There are only two ways this could end – me in prison forever, or dead. I'm not suicidal, but honey I'm not going down easy and I don't want to get you into something like that," I whispered. Then I kissed the top of her head and stroked her hair.

"We could keep those Phentenal patches and if we get into a shootout we could put enough on to O.D.. That way, if something happened, we would die together," Jenna cooed. Then she smiled as she wiped the tears from her eyes. "It would be romantic and a perfect ending to our story. I don't want you to leave me alone again... *ever!*"

I looked at her and brushed a long brown strand of hair out of her face. My heart warmed seeing her smile for the first time in days. "Yeah, but the problem is..." I whispered softly, "this is not a story and shit seldom ends the way that you would want it to in real life."

She just snuggled closer. "Romeo and Juliet," she mumbled in a sleepy voice before she drifted off.

When I woke up it was mid-morning and too late to change my mind. I still considered calling my bondsman and asking him if he could get me another day to get there, but what was done was done; there really wasn't any second guessing at this point. Besides, I had already been on the run for months, as it was.

By the time we left the motel it was well after checkout time. We rolled our little caravan, me on my bike and Jenna following in the Regal with all of our stuff, over to the house of a big slug named Fat Randy.

As Randy's name indicates, he was fat. He was also quite worthless, although back in the day he had made a name as a fairly renowned pool player. Anyway, he was just fat and sweaty now. The kind of guy who had a house and a little dope sack, so he had *'friends'* and a couple of little whores hanging around now and then. He was scared to death of me; he called it respect... whatever, I've been around long enough to know the difference. As I said, he had a house, one that wasn't on the list of possible places to look for me and he wouldn't – couldn't - tell me 'no'. So, we went and hung out at his place until I figured out what our next move was going to be.

I really didn't have a plan. Jenna suggested that we just pack up the bike and ride to the Grand Canyon just to be free and see what we could see. Mr. Big was down for the idea. It wasn't a bad thought, really, but it was already September and even though it was still fairly nice weather to ride in, it wouldn't last. Besides motorcycles, especially Harleys, draw cops in like flies to a horse's behind. We would eventually be pulled over just so the cops could have a look at us. Something that we couldn't afford. Most importantly, though, was with Jenna and Mr. Big on board I wouldn't be able to run if the Law got behind me. I would never endanger them like that. Jenna might not have taken what I'd told her the night before seriously, but I knew the reality of our situation and I didn't want her that close to me when the end came.

Mr. Big, Jenna and I laid up in Fat Randy's living room, napping on the couch and selling a little dope to the people that would occasionally stop by while Randy stayed crashed out in his bedroom.

About mid-afternoon, Randy's home phone rang. I let it ring on through to the answering machine only to hear Maryjo's frantic voice yelling for someone to '...*pick up the damned phone!*' When no one did, it immediately started ringing again.

Snatching it up, I said in my best 'anybody but Jimmy Maxwell' voice: "Hello?"

On the verge of hysteria, Maryjo blurted out: "Is Jimmy Maxwell there? I need to talk to him right now!"

"Well, I don't think he's here right now. Can I take a message for him for if he comes by?" I'd reverted back to my own voice, expecting my ex-wife of fifteen years to recognize it without having to openly acknowledge that it was, in fact, me on the line.

"Who is this? I don't have time for games!" she screamed into the phone.

"Just tell me what is wrong and I will make sure that he gets the message," I reiterated, trying one more time to get through to her.

Maryjo was just too over-excited about whatever was going on to comprehend, so she continued in an exasperated voice: "I Need to talk to Jimmy Mother Fucking Maxwell right Now! This is an emergency!"

I gave up. Aggravated, I finally grumbled: "Yeah, what the hell is so important that you have to call on a landline and make me confess it's me... giving up my location, if by some chance, the phone at Dale's place is tapped?!"

"Jimmy? Jimmy is that you?" Maryjo went on, as if she hadn't even heard me.

"*Yes*! What the fuck is wrong with you?" I shouted.

"Oh I'm glad I got you. A State and Federal Task Force just kicked in the door at my old house. They also crashed Pete's house looking for you! So don't come over here to Dale's, we're getting ready; expecting them to show up any time." She had just moved in over there and it was a likely place for the police to look for me.

"You couldn't find a cellphone to call me from?" I asked.

"No. Hell, if you're over at Fat Randy's you should just stay there. That should be a safe place," my ex-wife went on.

"Well it fucking was until you picked up your landline and called this landline and made me get on this god forsaken phone, confirming my presence at this flippin' address! I mean, Maryjo, if you think they are on their way over there – even if they are not listening right now, they can see on your phone the first place that you called after they stormed those other houses. That's how detectives do things," I told her. "So now I have to leave here and I really don't have any place lined up to go to yet."

"Well, I'm sorry. I was just trying to let you know what was going on. It's just like when we were married, I still can't do anything right!" she bitched.

"That's right. It's the reason we still aren't married," I teased.

"Fuck you, Jimmy Maxwell! I'm just worried for you. I love you. Let me know where you end up," Maryjo said, laughing as she hung up.

I love and trust Maryjo. She is the mother of my children, street wise and down as they come. We had been through a lot together, but when she gets excited her mouth runs ten steps ahead of her brains sometimes. So, I hung up thinking to myself: *'Not on your life, honey. Not on your life.'*

Although that wasn't a thought specifically for her, as far as I was concerned, the only way I was going to feel comfortable was if *no-one* knew where I was. Because one leak leads to another until you're not just up to your neck in hot water – you're caught up in a raging flash flood.

"What have I gotten myself into?" I scolded myself silently.

CHAPTER TWENTY-TWO
GETTING OUT OF TOWN

I turned towards Jenna. "Grab Mr. Big, We've got to get out of here. Now!" I growled; already starting to feel the added pressure from my decision the night before.

Jenna had caught my side of the conversation. "What happened... what did M.J. say?"

I told her what Maryjo had said. I also told her that it was unlikely anyone was listening to Dale's phone yet, or that the cops would even pull his phone records. However, it was still a link to our location if some industrious flatfoot was smart enough to think of it. Sure as hell, if I decided they weren't that smart, that is what would turn out to be what bit us in the ass.

Jenna started gathering the few items we'd brought into Randy's throughout the day. I went out to the car and re-organized what was left of our lives in the trunk and backseat of our Buick; packing my bike's saddle bags as economically as possible.

I still didn't have a clue as to where we should go. Only knowing that we needed to steer clear of anywhere that the cops could associate with us in some way. Hell, motels aren't even safe; not in T-town, not if you are using your own I.D., which at the time was the only one that I had. In their boredom the police working the graveyard shift sometimes ran warrant checks on the registers of the lower rent motels. Even having someone else rent the room for you left you open to trusting that person, more or less, as they hold the straight razor over your exposed jugular vein. Not a good idea anywhere... but, especially not in Tulsa, the capital of *'shake and bake'* methamphetamine; which makes it a breeding-ground for cutthroats and

snakes who would sell their own mothers for another box of ephedrine pills
or a *'get out of jail free'* card.

Not to say there aren't good people mixed in there too. I have known
many. But, who's got the time, or can afford to take a chance to figure out
who is whom when your freedom, or maybe even your life is on the line.
It's better to just not trust anyone, unless you already know you can. Even
then, you'd better cover your ass to the best of your ability. Me, being me, I
had everyone acting like they were my best friend and wanting to help, even
if they really didn't. I forgot how lonely it was to be on the run. Of course,
we were now getting high a couple of times a day, which wasn't helping my
trust issues, nor my cognitive reasoning skills, at all.

I'm not going to lie… the way Maryjo sounded on the phone had me a
little panicky; as if there was a whole militia out to find me and might show
up anywhere that there a was a small tie to me… at any time. Even driving
was risky, since the car and the motorcycle I was using were registered to
me and were included in the police B.O.L.O.. It didn't take a genius to
figure out that what we needed to do was get out of town. But, trying to
leave right then, when the task force was out in full force and could get
lucky and spot us, wasn't a good idea either. We needed a place to go to
quick.

My son, Brandon, had given me a number to a friend of his named
Calvin. I gave Calvin a call looking for a fresh place to lay low. There, I
could sell some of the speed I had and Jenna and I could decide where to
go next. Calvin answered on the third ring. I told him the situation. "I
need a place to park these vehicles and get out of sight for a day or so until
it's safe to leave town."

"They ain't chasing you right *now* is they?" Calvin asked. Then he
murmured: "Ummm… yeah, yeah, sure, man, come on over."

Taking the backstreets, I followed the instructions he gave me to his
house off of 21st and Sheridan.

From the outside it didn't look bad. It was a modest tan and brown,
square, single-story house with a couple of steps leading up to the front
door. There was a short, fairly well built, tow-headed, twenty-five year-old
standing out front waiting for us when we got there. I could tell he was a
'wannabe' gangbanger by his sideways ball cap and ridiculously oversized
shorts. "Calvin, I presume?" He nodded and I asked him where I could put
my bike that would get it out of sight. He led me around to the back. He

didn't have a fence, but the backyard had a row of trees and bushes that blocked off his property from the street. Calvin showed me a small break in the hedge and I rode my heavy motorcycle through it into the yard and pulled my bike up behind his house.

The car wasn't as conspicuous, but I still had Jenna back it up the driveway, bringing the rear bumper up against his already chipped siding, so no-one could see the license plate. With the vehicles stowed away and our ties broken from all known associates, I was feeling secure for the first time since Maryjo had called. More like the first time all week.

We followed Calvin into his house. Crossing the threshold of his two bedroom crib was where normal, clean and conservative ended. The living room was crammed full of shit. There was a raggedy couch and cushion chair somewhere in there. However, you couldn't sit on them, because he had crap piled everywhere. The junk littering the living room consisted of a folded up bed frame, a dresser or two, baskets of parts, tools and who knows what else. Calvin was a thief, so along with his personal clutter was other people's things that he'd never found a buyer or a use for. It looked like a hoarder's house with just an aisle to walk through.

Once past that, on our way back to my son's friend's bedroom, which was the only place in his house to sit down, I glanced into the kitchen. Naturally, every dish was piled in the sink and along the counter with food still caked on them. The cockroaches stopped their house party and stared at us with their antennae as we walked by. We stepped over the garbage that was over-flowing from the trash can right inside the kitchen entrance.

Calvin led us down the hall past a closed door on the left. He said it was another bedroom, but that it was a total wreck and had more stuff in it than the living room did... I could only imagine.

The bathroom was on the right. Calvin's bedroom and base of operations was a little further down. It was cluttered as well, but it was at least livable - a little oasis, in a desert of broken glass, sharp metal spikes and prehistoric cockroaches. There were dirty, bent spoons for fixing dope and other drug paraphernalia laying around on every table or dresser top. There were spots on the floor where different things had been spilled. When Calvin leaned over and picked a pill up off of the floor that he admitted that he'd dropped 'days ago' I told Jenna to keep Mr. Big on the bed. I didn't want him to lick or stumble onto something that might hurt him.

Mr. Big did not like Calvin from the word go. It took me a little longer to come to the same conclusion. When your dog doesn't like someone that quickly you should probably listen.

I gave Calvin some speed to get high on for helping us out and he went to jabber jawing, bragging and trying to impress me and Jenna with his 'I'm a down hustler' mumbo jumbo. We were grateful that we had a place to hold up, so I just let him blather on and even gave him a deal on a gram or two. But the more he talked, the more he slipped up and said things that made me suspicious of him... and, the more Mr. Big snarled whenever he came near.

Once while he was running off at the mouth with one of his stories, which I was paying very little attention too, I caught the end of what he was saying. "...and I tells them police I didn't care what they had on me I wasn't goin to work fo'em anymo." He hurried into another story, but I heard what I had heard – I thought...

I looked at Jenna and asked her if I'd heard him right. She nodded. "I *think* so."

Mr. Big already knew... If we didn't hear Calvin admit to being a rat, Mr. Big damn sure did and was letting me know about it. He snapped and growled every time Calvin tried to approach the bed – *his* bed.

Loosening my 9mm, which was in the makeup bag Jenna had sat on the floor by my feet; that not only held my pistol, but my scales, baggies and other drug-dealing paraphernalia, I said: "Dude, I have never seen my little man there act like this towards anybody before? What is wrong with you?"

"Yo wha – what you mean 'G'?" Calvin stuttered.

"I mean Mr. Big doesn't like you and I'm trying to figure out *why?*" I said, staring intently at him. My hand tensed when he shot a spiteful glare at my little guard dog, who once again snapped at him for getting too close to the bed. Seeing the flames in my eyes, Calvin quickly dropped the hateful look that he'd directed towards my tiny, two-pound partner.

Jenna grabbed Mr. Big up protectively at the anger that had flashed across Calvin's face. "Yeah, he never acts like this, even when he doesn't like someone... he's never like this," she said, looking meaningfully at me.

"Well, bro, it's not like I'm some piece of shit or something and that's why." He dropped his fake urban accent and pled his case defensively.

My eyes squinted and my thumb drew back the hammer of my already chambered automatic. "Maybe, maybe not. You have a lot of spills and miscellaneous shit laying around. I've been trying to keep an eye on him, but he may have licked up some meth oil or something. He could be just high and paranoid and you've been moving and talking way too fast. But if you ever, even think about hurting my dog… it'll be the last thought you'll ever have," I promised him.

In his frustration and tension, he decided that he had a few things that he needed to do. Leaving Jenna and me at his house, he left to go make a couple of deals and sell what he'd bought from me. He babbled off a half a dozen other things that he was going to attend to as well, which I didn't even listen to either.

Once he was gone, Mr. Big was visibly less tense. I'd really hoped what I'd said about him licking meth residue off of something wasn't what was going on with him. I loved him way too much to want to risk his little mind and heart, but if it hadn't been that, then it meant we had other problems.

"So… what the fuck was that he said about… not telling the cops anything… *anymore?*" I asked Jenna.

"Honey, it sounded like it to me, but I didn't catch all of it and can't remember exactly what I did hear," Jenna admitted. "But Mr. Big won't even let him come near us. Something's wrong. And if it was because he'd got into something he wouldn't be so calm now," she said, pointing at him. He was casually walking around sniffing Calvin's blanket; undoubtedly looking for a suitable place to hike his leg. Had he done so, I doubt that the smell could have beaten the aromas that already choked the atmosphere.

"What do you think, little buddy?" I questioned Mr. Big. "Do you think this guy's likely to trade us in to get out of that case he was talking about catching last month?"

Hearing me talking to him he came over, ducked his head and rolled over on his back so I could scratch his belly. "Yeah, we'd better go ahead and get out of here. I just don't trust this guy and if he could get us busted he'd have access to the car and my bike, he could be talking to the police now for all we know." Mr. Big licked my pant leg like; *'Yeah, what do you think I been trying to tell you? Let's go, Dad'.*

"You're right," Jenna said, lighting a cigarette and blowing a nervous stream of smoke out from between her lips. "But it's after midnight. Where are we gonna go? It's not safe to drive around this late."

165

"Where we should have went in the first place. To a motel. Out of town," I said, pulling my pistol from her cosmetic bag and sticking it in the waist band of my pants. I threw my black leather jacket back on and, picking up Mr. Big, added: "Let's roll."

Jenna didn't waste any time gathering up the few little things we'd brought in with us. We were headed for the door when Calvin showed back up.

"Where are you guys going?" Calvin asked anxiously – too anxiously in my opinion. It didn't help the way his eyes darted around while he puffed like a junkie needing a fix on his smoke.

"We're leaving, going back to the City, we should have never stopped here in the first place," I lied. Not willing to give him any more information.

"Oh, man, y'all can wait 'til morning, can't you? I know your dog has got you tripping on me, but really, you're safe here, at least 'til morning," Calvin said, trying to convince me. He continued: "But even if you do, you should leave one of your vehicles, so you're not riding double hot."

"We're out of here and that's the end of it," I stated flatly. The more he tried to persuade me, the more certain I was that he was up to some shady shit and the madder I was getting.

Seeing my agitation level rising, he relented. Some of his arguments were even fairly sound, but my suspicion of him had already reached the point of no return. Now, the more he said, the more I was sure he was one of those bottom feeders who would sell their own sister if it profited them in some way. The only thing that saved him was that I knew I was high and had been so for days. He was lucky I was self-aware enough to know that my dope-fired brain may have been a factor in my *'feelings'* about him at the time. However, that shit only goes so far and he was right on the edge of me not giving a crap whether his strangeness was my own imagination or not.

Before I let Jenna pull out of the driveway, I pulled my bike into the street and made a trip around the block to check things out and see if he'd already brought the heat down on us. With it looking clear, I stopped in front of the driveway and motioned Jenna to follow me.

We headed north, the opposite direction I'd told Calvin. I was shooting for Skiatook via the back roads. It wasn't far, but far enough from the hustle and bustle of city life that, hopefully, the cops there didn't go around checking the motel registers for warrants.

Somehow, on the dark back roads, we missed Skiatook altogether. The hour was getting later and I knew we needed to be off the road. I was not sure whether I was right or wrong about Calvin. I am convinced that leaving his house was a good call, even today. However, driving around back country roads in the middle of the night on a Harley Davidson is like a matador waving a red flag at a bull to any night-shift cop who we might run across. We needed a town, a motel, any motel, not to mention gas. Jenna waved me over and showed me that she was down to less than an eighth of a tank. I told her we should just pull off onto a deserted dirt road and sleep until morning. We were obviously off course and I was feeling antsy about pushing the odds of us being on the road so long, so late.

She didn't want to hear it. "I don't want to spend the night in this car again. I just want to find a motel and be able to relax in a clean bed!" she bitched through the car window.

"Whatever. If some cop tries to pull us over, you'll be wishing we had," I countered. However, I didn't insist on it. I wanted a bed too. Besides, sitting on some dark side-road with your lights and engine off has its own set of risks. Honestly, though, I wanted to make Jenna happy also. She'd already had enough hardships to deal with as it was.

CHAPTER TWENTY-THREE

BARNSDALL

I pulled back onto the two-lane black top, quickly bringing the big Harley engine up to speed. Jenna followed in the Buick close behind. It was a pretty nice night out for mid-September; cool enough to keep the bugs down, but warm enough to not feel the chill in my leather coat, goggles, and riding gloves. I was cruising about seventy, thinking about how much I loved riding and how free I felt, as we came up on the town of Barnsdall. It was so small and quiet that I didn't even see the dim lights of the little hamlet until I was almost in it.

My first feeling was of relief. *Alright motel and gas*, but as we wound our way into town and the highway turned into Main Street, it was obvious that the little community closed up shop when the sun went down. I didn't see a soul, or any lights on, other than a few glowing street lamps most of the way through town. We had passed a couple of service stations, but they were as dark as the rest of the businesses and I didn't see any signs of a motel anywhere.

The main street ended in a 'T'. To my surprise, across the road on a fairly well-lit, derelict parking lot was twelve or thirteen high-school-age kids. They were just hanging out, partying, sitting on the parked cars and folded-down tailgates of their pick-up trucks. The complete contrast to the rest of the town caught me a little off guard. When I turned the corner, I steered over to the parking lot to ask directions from one of the youngsters. I got all the way around the curve and was pulling over when I spotted the brown and white County sheriff's car sitting in the shadows across the street. He was, apparently, keeping an eye on the youthful get-together. I tried to ignore it and act as though I had no concerns whether there was a cop watching or not. When I stopped to ask one of the teens if there was a motel or open gas station in town, Jenna pulled the car up beside me.

The youngster indicated that there wasn't anything available at that time of night. He pulled his John Deere hat off and ran his fingers back through his blond hair while he was thinking. "There might be an open motel in Pawhuska, ten miles on down the road," he said. Then, spitting a brown stream of tobacco juice on the curb, the kid went on to tell me that would be the closest gas station, as well.

Thanking him, I asked Jenna what her gas gauge read. Worry drew her brows together and she replied that the needle was now hitting the little post that held it. "We'll make it," I assured her. Without looking over at the cop, I warned: "Drive very carefully." Then I pulled back out into the road.

Honestly, I wasn't that nervous. I'm a good rider and the way we stopped and asked directions should have just made us look like late night travelers. Besides, after riding so far with the cool breeze in my face, I was as clear headed as I could be under the circumstances. However, I stayed extra alert and was careful as I rode to the stop sign at the next inter-section. Under the red octagon was also a road sign pointing motorists towards Pawhuska. I stopped, hit my blinkers and pulled out smoothly heading down the highway with the borough ending as abruptly as it began.

I cranked my bike up to the highway's speed limit, quickly putting some space between myself and the County cruiser back in that parking lot. I checked my mirror to see that Jenna wasn't having any problems either. She was a hundred yards behind and I watched her pick up speed leaving the town. All of a sudden, the sheriff's car appeared behind her and hit his red and blue lights. My heart took a jolt. I can't describe the feelings that those damned lights send through a person, especially if you are bound for jail.

Thinking that they were pulling her over and knowing that she was riding dirty, I cranked my throttle all the way back and shot off like a rocket, trying to draw the cop's attention. He immediately abandoned Jenna and came after me. Most Harley's aren't really built for speed. The low gear ratio did allow me to accelerate from sixty to a hundred miles per hour almost instantly. However, only having five gears impeded any hopes for speed over one-twenty or so, in spite of the 1450 c.c.m. engine. It wasn't long and the County car was right behind me, even coming up beside me now and then.

I pulled the gun from my waist band and was considering shooting one of the tires of the cruiser when I saw a frightened female face staring out at me from the passenger window. A male cop was clearly in the driver's seat, but the female passenger was dressed as a civilian. *Where did she come from!?* I realized at the speeds we were going, a tire blowing out could be fatal to the occupants of the car. Determined not to be taken, but unsure of what to do, I stuck the pistol under my leg and focused on losing the officer on the winding and hilly two-lane, rural highway.

A hundred and twenty miles an hour, in the dark, takes up most, if not all, of your attention. My heart was racing just as fast as the pistons in the v-twin. The black ribbon of road was rolling up under me so fast that the yellow dashed lines appeared solid, while the air I was blasting through stretched the skin of my face into a mask of pure concentration and threatened to blow me off the back of my bike. My universe was cut down to the flashing lights in my rear-view mirrors and only reached ahead of me as far as the arch of my headlight beam. I was vaguely aware of the dark, blurry shapes of trees, fences and the occasional turn off that led into the sable velvet of the night. The world flashed by like a fast-moving, video-race game after you've hit the nitrous button. The moon was out, but just enough to give off a soft glow that added to the affect.

I had gained a little ground on the cop behind me, but I knew, unless I did something drastic, that I would not be able to outpace him enough to lose him. My mind was desperately grasping for ideas. I crested a hill and *'in the blink of an eye'*, I spotted at the bottom a dirt road that led off to the north. I jammed my right foot down on my rear brake and squeezed my front hand brake with all of my grip; effectively locking up the wheels of the big bike.

My reasoning for wanting to take to a dirt road was born out of sheer desperation. It occurred to me that even though I would have to slow down myself, I may be able to kick up enough dirt and dust that my pursuer's vision would be impaired to the point where he would have to slow down even more than me. Not to mention, if it didn't end well for me, I would be off of the main road and away from where Jenna would have to witness it.

All that streaked across my mind, and my decision was made. My body reacted within a millisecond of my glimpsing the turn-off. My wheels locked up. I slid a good forty or fifty feet down the hill, trying to decelerate enough to make the turn. It was very close, but I was just going too fast as I topped the hill. I skidded right on past the mouth of the dirt artery and into the dew-covered grass of a bar ditch.

I could hear the cop slamming on his brakes behind me, trying to slow down too. Now in the ditch, I abandoned braking and tried to throttle my way back up onto the highway; fishtailing back and forth in the muddy grass. When I'd almost reached the shoulder of the road again, I hit a soft patch of soil and my front wheel went out from under me. I'm not sure how fast I was going at that point, but it propelled me over the handlebars and onto the grassy shoulder of the highway. I rolled a couple of times and landed on a knee. There was no time to wonder if I was hurt or not. My mind was focused on the screeching of the officer's tires as he was sliding to a stop behind my wrecked motorcycle...

Where the fuck was my gun?

I assumed it had come with me as I arched through the air. Not wanting to leave it behind, I frantically drug my hands through the grass trying to locate it; giving the deputy time to exit the cruiser and throw down on me with his sidearm.

"Stop! Put your hands in the air!" he yelled. The stocky, dark-headed officer was aiming his pistol at me in a two-fisted stance from behind the protection of his open squad car door.

Realizing that the search for my firearm was futile, I finally acknowledged the frightened sheriff, who was continually and alternately ordering me to: "Freeze!", "Stop!" or "Get on the ground!" He claimed later that I reached into my leather coat like I was reaching for a gun. I don't remember all that. What I do remember was thinking about what I had told Jenna just the night before. Standing there facing that scared, shaking, officer; the type most likely to kill you, in my opinion – and his gun, I realized how much I'd meant what I had said to her. This officer probably was going to shoot me, but that was the only way he was going to stop me. I braced myself for it. I've said before, I turn a little kamikaze when my back is up against the wall and God has watched out for me more times than I can count.

I raised my hands, but kept moving across the road to the south. Frustrated, the mounty continued yelling orders at me; informing me of his intent to fire if I didn't comply. I grimaced as I ignored them and kept moving, daring him to pull the trigger, expecting the impact of his bullets at any moment. When they didn't come, I turned and ran through the other bar ditch I'd been approaching. As I dived over the barbed wire fence, I tucked and rolled back to my feet and within three steps I was enveloped by the welcoming blanket of the night.

Three more steps - and the earth disappeared from underneath me... The ground had a crack in it like something left behind after an earthquake. However, in Oklahoma, it was much more likely to have been created by some strange form of erosion. Luckily, it was only four feet deep, but the unexpectedness of it caused me to land flat on my back in about five inches of muddy run-off water. Splash! "Oomph," I groaned. My mind quickly scrambled to register what had happened and reorganize the strange tilt of the earth's axis and lack of gravity. After the brightness from the cop's spotlight, I could barely see the edge of the pit, but my eyes adjusted quickly as I climbed back up onto the grassy field and ran into the pasture.

My leather jacket was thick and heavy when it was dry, but now wet, it was like wearing a sandbag. I shucked it and kept moving. The field I was in appeared to be one smooth, low-rolling hill after another and for the most part was clear of trees and other foliage that could aid in concealing me. However, the grass was tall in spots and the ground seemed broken in places. I lost the lights of the highway scene when my flight took me down into a low hollow that stretched a hundred yards across and a couple of hundred from end to end.

Off to the right, I barely caught the shine of moonlight reflecting on dark water. I stopped running and listened for any sounds of pursuit. Not hearing any, I quietly moved towards the shimmering light wanting to get a better look at the little body of water I'd almost ran by. I knew I should be putting distance between myself and the road while I had the chance. However, I was on foot and the posse, which would be showing up at any moment, would not be. The ones who were, would probably have dogs and, even though the field was a rolling hill here, I may get over the next rise and find it be nothing but flat grasslands for miles. Aware of this, I couldn't afford to pass by a potential hiding spot without first evaluating it.

I squatted, with my heart beating a samba, desperately willing myself to calm down and think things through. I was looking out across what turned out to be a fairly large cattle pond. The dark and murky water was at least fifty paces across and another seventy-five or eighty long. It sat in a wash with its far ridge climbing up sharply out of the water for six or seven feet only to roll off down another hill. It was scarcely visible with the shadows from the encompassing embankment and a few wispy clouds, defusing the already dim moonlight.

CHAPTER TWENTY-FOUR
THE CATTLE POND

I was already chilled from my first contact with the water back in the hole, but it wasn't anything more than an inconvenience. I didn't think this pond's temperature would be any colder. Making my decision within seconds of stopping, I moved around where I could crawl into the watering hole right off the grassy edge. I needed to get in it without leaving behind any visible signs of my entrance. I was careful to ease into the wet murk as smooth and silently as possible. Sound will carry in the cool night air and would be a certain auditory giveaway of my present location.

At first it was only eight to ten inches deep. I slid on my stomach through clay that had been pounded to the consistency of soft mud by hundreds of cattle who had waded in the shallows up to their fetlocks to get a drink from this prairie oasis. It made it very smooth and quiet as I used my hands to pull myself out into gradually deepening water. When it became deep enough that I would have to tread water, I pulled my shoes off, so I wouldn't have to struggle to keep my nose above the surface. I headed straight through the middle, trying to reach the far bank where it was deeper in shadow. It wasn't long before I felt the bed of the watery basin rising back up; forcing me to crouch lower and lower, so that only my head remained exposed.

Once across the small lake and nearing the other shore, I could make out a little more of the landscape. There was a slice in the south bank where a creek had washed it out when the rains caused the pond to overflow. It made for a winding trench in the otherwise smooth, rolling topography. I could see it only held a trickle of water now and a lot of mud, which would make it easy to track me were I to take that route. I noted it, but continued past it. I was going to have to chance going to ground right under their noses. I didn't really like pushing the odds that way, but I had already decided this was probably my best option before I slid into the water.

As I finally reached the shadowed cove, I could see quite a few big rocks sticking up out from the surface. My guess was they'd been piled on this end as protection against erosion. I could feel a few more large rocks on the bottom of the pond. I was moving with my body floating out behind me just pulling myself along by grabbing one under water hand hold after another. When I got as far from the other side as possible, where I knew the police were all going to start showing up at any moment, I found a shallow spot between submerged rocks and dug out a trench in the muddy bottom. Laying on my back, I stuck my shoes under me, then worked a couple of large, flat rocks from the lake bed and placed them on my stomach and upper legs; effectively holding my body down.

Seeing the glow of floodlights from the arriving search party coming over the top of the hill, I smeared mud on my face. Then I gathered some moss and a few strands of reed from between a couple of standing rocks and smeared them on my hair and forehead. Somehow, the police had gotten their cruisers onto the rancher's land and within minutes the other side of the wash was lit up with their red and blue flashers and bright search lights. I knew that the hunters could not see me without direct light, so I watched and listened until I saw the probing beams of a spotlight swinging across the top of the water towards me. Then I lay my head back, with only my nose sticking above the surface; hidden beneath the vegetation that I'd lain on my face. I watched with pond-bleary eyes as the glare of the light swept over where I was laying just inches below the water.

As I'd feared, when they discovered who I was the man hunt intensified. There was a helicopter or low flying plane throwing light down on the pasture further south. There were also K9 officers and their dogs searching down the creek bed that I'd seen when I was swimming across the pond. Luckily for me, once they had cleared the lake by scouring the surface with their floodlights, other than the occasional back tracing sweep, the search for me seemed to concentrate in the direction I'd originally been running before I'd spotted this watering hole.

Every now and then, water made it up my nose and down the back of my throat; making me want to burst up and out of the quiet, calm, pond in a coughing fit. You would be surprised at what you can control when your life and freedom is at stake, so I clenched down tight every muscle in my body; swallowing and enduring the moisture that trickled down into my lungs.

A couple of times, thankfully when the roaming search beams were pointing in another direction, one of my rubber-soled shoes would slide out from under me and pop up to the surface with a quiet '*baloomp*'. I would frantically reach out and snare it from under the surface, like a shark on a midnight swimmer, and return it to its place underneath me.

Whilst allowing time for the search to move on, I laid there thinking about Jenna. I knew that she didn't have much gas and I wondered if she had turned around and headed back for Tulsa, or if she'd continued on. Chancing the gauntlet that she'd have to drive through would be dangerous, but knowing her she'd probably try it out of fear for me. Unfortunately, I thought that she was very likely to end up in jail herself, considering the officer probably saw her pull up and talk to me back in Barnsdall along with her being the initial focus of the attempted traffic stop. I hoped, whatever she chose to do, she and Mr. Big would make it. I contemplated what I would do if she was arrested... where they would take her and Mr. Big... and if I would be able to break them out or not. Of course, I realized that before I could do anything for them, I needed to get out of this pond and back to civilization.

As one set of searchers' lights winked out of my immediate area after another I evaluated my circumstances. The stakes would be even higher now. I had to assume they had found my gun, that they knew who I was, and that the Feds were aware of my approximate location. I was safe for the moment, however cold and wet. The nearest town was miles away and was not an option, since Barnsdall would be a buzz with gossip about the harrowing chase of a desperate fugitive that had started right outside of their community. That left me effectively stuck out in the middle of nowhere.

Jenna and I had discussed what to do if we were ever separated. If it was possible, we were to try and meet back up at the last place that we'd seen each other, twelve hours after whatever had caused us to run in different directions. Then again, twelve hours after that, if one of us didn't show. I lay there wondering if she was in jail and if she would have the resources to get all the way back out there to look for me the next day if she wasn't. I had all the money in my pocket, so even if she didn't go to jail she may be stranded on the side of the road somewhere herself.

I lay there, momentarily taken over by a fit of shivering that I couldn't control. I watched the water's surface above me vibrate as I tried to gain control of my muscles. After the fit had passed, I looked around to make sure that the turbulence on the water's smooth, glass-like surface had gone unnoticed. From my vantage point, I could no longer see any lights, cars, officers nor hear anything in the air. I estimated that it was around 4:30 a.m. Not knowing where the searchers were, or when they might be back, I took the opportunity to make my underwater hiding place a little more secure and comfortable. I needed to get my head out of the water, so I could hear someone approaching up any of the hills. My biggest concern was that I could be spotted in the rapidly approaching dawn by amy person who may walk up and look down on the water from the embankment behind me, with me being none the wiser. It wasn't practical, or possible, for me to lay there for hours with my whole face submerged. The pre-dawn had already made it easier for me to see what was around me, so I needed to hurry, before it got full light.

As I'd said, there were jagged rocks piled along this bank, with several of them breaking the surface. Finding a large flat rock that was a good two feet across and just as long, I dislodged it from the muck and sat its edge on another submerged rock that was at the head of my little shallow, body-shaped trough. I then raised the front of it out of the water seven or eight inches and slid two large, square stones I'd dug up as well under either side; making a little cave with enough room for my head to fit in and remain above the water-line. It was propped up out of the water in a haphazard manner so, once I laid back in the trench and pulled the rocks back on top of me, I was able to put my head inside and under the rock made lean-to. By hanging more moss off the front of the small cavern I found myself fairly comfortable, able to hear, as well as see what was immediately in front of me through the hanging grass. I relaxed with the reasonable assurance that anyone looking down from the hill behind me would only see a cluster of moss-covered rocks sticking out of the water.

I then took inventory of what I had in my pockets: a wad of money that the water couldn't hurt. A camouflaged coin bag that held all my dope, which despite the fact that a lot of it was sealed up in zip-lock baggies, was sure to be ruined after being submerged for so long. And lastly, an AT&T track phone, which I knew was no more than a useless piece of plastic at this point. I frowned as I watched the murky water pouring out of its little holes when I held it up in the dim light. Nothing that would help me out of my situation. I didn't even have my watch. I'd lost it in the wreck.

There was no reason to move from where I was until the search was completely over. I didn't want to be spotted and lose the small advantage I'd gained. Of course, I knew if I didn't move out before daybreak, I would be stuck where I was until sundown again, because once the Feds knew I'd been flushed out and had run to ground out here, they wouldn't miss the opportunity to at least stake out the area to see if I might pop back up. As the sun was coming up over the horizon, I consigned myself to the fact that the safest thing to do would be to wait them out. I laid back and thought of what a fucked-up mess I'd made of my life.

Dammit, I thought, wasn't it just a year and a half ago that I'd gotten out with so much determination to live right, stay away from drugs and never have to spend another day in prison again? I tried to remember what exactly had gotten me here. My motorcycle wrecked, two ounces of ruined dope in my pocket; a wanted man, being hunted like an animal and facing another couple of decades in prison!

If I was to be honest, I could probably lay most of the blame at the feet of my infidelity. A noble man cannot lie and cheat on his wife and still maintain the integrity that the foundation, his strength for everything else he is, has been built on. No matter how much he might justify it. To be incorruptible, you have to be uncorrupt. Like the Bible says, a little leaven leavens the whole loaf. Who knows?

I didn't want to think about that; I'd spent so long trying to convince myself that what I was doing was acceptable since Jenna had cheated on me while I was in, and she was a raging, unpredictable alcoholic once I'd got out. None of which, I realized while laying submerged in that pond assessing my life, excused my actions, or changed where it had brought me. I knew that when I stopped and looked hard enough at it, the extra women in my life were what had led to my downfall. That and the Hood. Underworld organizations are always going to be solidly entrenched in the drug world and, eventually, it was money and business that finally cracked my resolve to stay out of the mix. Looking back, I remember clearly seeing my world start to spin, picking up speed as it spun, throwing my life out of control.

Well, I told myself it is what it is, at this point pushing self-pity out of my head. I can't change anything in the past; all I can do is deal with the here and now and I resolved to do what I needed to do, to get through my immediate problems. I needed to figure out how I was going to get out of the middle of nowhere with no freaking vehicle without being spotted. I could beat myself up about what a fuck-up I was later.

As the morning wore on, no-one popped up over the rise and I didn't hear anyone trampling through the grassy fields. I decided to get out of the water and crawl up to the top of the hill, so I could see the road and be close enough to get help if I saw it heading down the highway. Just maybe, Jenna had made it and would be out there somewhere on that road looking for me – my only hope of not having to hike my way out of there.

I didn't even know the term water-logged could apply to a human until I crawled up out of that pond and onto the bank. I felt like an over-bloated sea sponge. I literally sloshed and was so heavy I could barely move. My wet Levis, shirt and shoes just added to the effect, as did my white, wrinkled, fish-belly looking skin.

The sun was well up by the time I'd come out of the water. I flipped over on my back, looking up at the blue sky, soaking in its warmth. As I lay there, I realized how thirsty I was. Drinking out of that stagnant, parasitic cattle-pond was not a temptation I would give into unless my life, literally, depended on it. I didn't know how long it would take me to get out of these back hills and the last thing I would need was a case of diarrhea to go along with the already formidable obstacles that I had to overcome.

Laying there on the bank, I could hear the highway over the next rise. It seemed like I could pick up the sounds of quite a few Harleys traveling up and down that road. There was a motorcycle rally going on the other side of Pawhuska. I wondered if Jenna had called my friend Mike Gardner, who was the big wig prez of our home grown bike club: 'The Rogues', and if he might've had some of his Brothers out making a few trips up and down this stretch of highway to help me. Even if that wasn't the case, maybe a passing rider would aid a fallen biker. Surely they had heard there had been a chase out here and that the rider was still at large? The only problem is that, these days, I'm just as likely to wave down an off-duty biker cop as a down-for-the-cause one percent-er; willing to put himself out there to help me.

Regardless, I needed to get up to the top of the knoll and get a look at what I could see. Flipping back over, I jumped up in a squatting position and looked around to make sure that I was still covered by the low-lying hill, then crouching, I moved up the slope. Thirty yards from the top I had to drop back down and belly-crawl through the grass, because the dips and breaks in the surrounding hills were leaving me exposed to the road in places.

Before I even got to the top where I could see the highway closest to me, one of those dips in the landscape let me glimpse a section of the blacktop a half mile or so further down the road. There I could see a white Crown Vic sitting pulled off on the shoulder facing the direction of the highway that I had fled from the night before. It wasn't marked, but it was obvious that it was some form of law enforcement; probably one of the Federal fugitive team who'd been dogging my trail for months already. It was just what I'd feared. I abandoned my quest for the top of the hill and headed back down the slope.

Back by the edge of the watering hole, I lay there listening to the sounds of the highway just a hundred yards away. I could hear cars, trucks and more motorcycles; mostly Harleys, motoring by. Occasionally, a vehicle would drive very slowly along that stretch of asphalt. I could tell it was someone looking for something, but could only assume it was the car I'd seen. Jenna would have hollered or got out, wouldn't she?

If she came, would she see the government car staked out down the road and read it for what it was?

Hours later, I did hear what I knew in my gut was Jenna cruising by. It was a diesel half ton, not my Buick, but the music was blaring and the sound told me that the truck was moving slowly down the road. I couldn't be sure, I just *'felt'* it, so I jumped up trying to run in a low crouch back up the hill to reach the crest in time to flag her down if it was. As soon as I neared the spot where I had seen the Crown Vic earlier, I slowed and cautiously peered through the break in the rolling mounds and, sure enough, it was still sitting there. I dropped to the ground trying to crawl the rest of the way up the grassy slope. I wanted to at least see if it was Jenna, although I was aware that I could not expose myself to the watching car even if it were.

It was still another ten yards to the crest of the hill when I heard the truck rolling on down the two-lane blacktop and my heart sank. I knew that I'd already exposed myself to the white car if he'd been looking in the right place at the right time, so I could only hope that my luck was better than his. At that moment, I was shielded by the tall grass, so I lay there looking at the sky. I waited, hoping to hear the sound of that truck coming back by and praying the stalking observer's patience would run out and he would roll off before it did.

I realized how lucky I was that the season had not turned cold yet. Here in Oklahoma, the weather can change as often in a day as a woman changes her mind. Other than that one cold spell, which had brought on the fit of shivers in the pond, I was doing pretty good. Laying there in the tall grass with the warm sun shining down and a cool autumn breeze blowing across me, it was almost serene. I looked up at the clouds, seeing different pictures and shapes in them, amazed at how flat the bottom of them were, as if they were all just sitting on a giant invisible pane of glass. Not for the first time, I thought about what an artist God was, if he was real.

What-the-hell... is... that?, I almost said aloud as I squinted up into the sky. It wasn't a helicopter, but it was moving slow. I soon realized it was a small plane. The way it was climbing and circling was what made it look even slower than it was. When it got over me it dipped down like it was trying to get a better look. I frantically pulled grass on top of me, trying to cover myself as much as I could, but still feeling naked to the eyes in the sky. *What the fuck! Why are they looking for me so hard?* I thought. They'd obviously found the gun and they may even know where and how I got it. I was used to being treated differently because of my past and my high standing with my *'affiliates'*, but damn, you'd think I was leaving a string of dead bodies behind me. The Feds must be pissed... and, maybe, there was more being laid at my feet than I knew. It was obvious that they were wanting to get me off of the street and I could expect no mercy from the court if they got me alive.

Not knowing what that plane saw or what was coming next, I abandoned the idea of catching a break and somehow spotting Jenna out trying to help me. For all I knew, she may be in jail and I was probably risking myself out in the open on wishful thinking. It was only a few hours before sunset, so I crawled back down the decline, knowing if I'd been spotted, the safest place for me was back in the water. Reluctantly, I gave up the warmth of the sun and the relative dryness of my mud-caked and stiff clothes and waded back out to my watery sanctuary, resigning myself to be safe rather than sorry. Besides, I couldn't move from the gully until nightfall anyway.

CHAPTER TWENTY-FIVE
HUNTERS' HEAVEN

A couple of hours later, as dusk was once again throwing shadows over the pond's surface, I emerged from the putrescent water and clambered ashore. What a mess this was! Once again I was completely water-logged, not that I'd actually ever got over the sensation in the first place. I dug in the grass and retrieved my little bag of useless, or at the very least, contaminated dope. I hadn't had time to examine it, but on the off chance it wasn't as bad as I feared, couldn't bring myself to discard. My cellphone I'd hidden too, hoping in some optimistic part of my mind to dry out. I stood up to my full height for the first time in eighteen hours.

I'd torn holes in the knees of my jeans in the spill I'd taken from my bike and they had only ripped further in my flight from the scene and subsequent submersion in the water. The lower legs of my pants now hung uncomfortably below my knees. I tied the loose threads to keep from stepping on the bottoms and making them worse; unwilling to abandon the protection that the legs of my Levis would afford me walking through high, bug-infested grass, thickets and brambles. I was well-aware I looked like a mess and that anyone who saw me would automatically be suspicious, whether they knew anything about the quiet, ongoing manhunt or not.

I let the sun settle all the way below the horizon while I made my preparations to move out of my hidden little cove. As ready as I could be, I headed off north, back towards the highway I'd came from. At the summit of the rise I could see that, as long as I timed it between traveling vehicles, I would be able to cross the road safely without being observed. Then I could ascend into the wooded hills I'd noticed earlier, moving in the opposite direction I had last been reported traveling.

I didn't realize what an exhausting toll laying submerged under water like that, for so long, would take on a body until I went back over that barbed wire fence and sprinted for the other one across the road. I could already feel the debility of my body by the time I was crossing the other barbed barrier, and by the time I was twenty yards further into the field I could feel my lungs and muscles fighting me. The thirst that I'd been ignoring all day came hammering home as I doggedly made myself run the remaining eighty yards across the open land to the tree-line.

Once there and safe from exposure to any motorist that might just pop up over the rise, I bent over with my hands on my knees trying to catch my breath, surprised by my fatigued state. From the security of the first dark stand of trees I entered, I looked back up and down the highway as far as my vision could extend, to see if my open flight had flushed out any persistent, unseen observers. Seeing no-one, I felt for the first time like I'd beat them, the cops, the Feds, everyone looking for me. Even though I still had a long way to go before I made it back to civilization and, even though I would still have to avoid detection the whole way, I'd shaken my pursuers. I was free and not a soul had any idea where I could be right then.

There were a few more little patches of open ground that I had to traverse before reaching the safety of the densely-forested hills, which stretched on for miles. Getting there unseen was no problem; the sun was now completely down, with the moon not much brighter than the night before.

When I entered the forest, which I later discovered followed a rocky ravine clear up into Kansas, I found that the moonlight was blocked by the dense canopy above and it was pitch dark below it. *Wow*, I thought, *this is a trip*! I was having to just trust my sense of direction as I felt my way from tree to tree through completely dark sections of forest. Every now and then a dim moonbeam would lance to the ground where breaks in the leaves and branches overhead allowed; giving my mind a brief respite from the overwhelming feeling of being lost in utter blackness. As I fumbled from one consuming shadow to another, I moved cautiously in the inky maze, trying not to break a leg or poke an eye out on a low-hanging twig or branch. The terrain was full of gullies and ravines and would have been fairly formidable in the daylight, but in the dark it was treacherous.

When I stumbled into a barbed wire fence that was strung from north to south I knew, for all my scrabbling around, that I was heading in the right direction. Pawhuska would be to the northwest. Although it was ten miles away, It was the next nearest town where I might be able to call in some help, or steal a vehicle to get back to Tulsa. Crossing the fence and ripping my crusty pants even further, I continued my trek confident in my instincts.

Traveling up and down the sharp hills in the dark was tough mentally as well as physically. Thirsty and hungry, I was already tired after only a couple of hours. I found myself climbing down into a deep cut in the land, sliding over huge flat rocks and having to hold onto one small tree trunk or another to keep from falling down the slope. Once at the bottom, it flattened out a little and the dense forest was split by a small creek. There was open space directly above it in places and with nothing to block the glow of the moon I was able to see partially. I could make out the sparkling water and hear the quiet gurgling of the small stream as it trickled around rocks and over small dams of fallen leaves and twigs.

Water! Glorious running water!

I wouldn't go as far as to say that just because it was moving it was completely safe from certain intestinal complications, but it was what Indians and settlers survived on for hundreds of years so that was good enough for me. I found a place where the water ran over a fallen log and let it run into my cupped hands. It may sound funny to be so damn happy over finding this rocky, leaf-choked creek, but I was parched by then, which I knew was playing a huge part in my unnatural exhaustion. I drank greedily from the run off for ten minutes before gingerly stepping over to the other side, trying not to slip and fall on the squelching, grasping bank.

After two muddy steps utter darkness blanketed me once again and the bank appeared to turn vertical. That was not actually the case, but I had to hunt, mostly by feel, for a break in the rocks and find trees growing in the slanting slope to pull myself up. This side of the deep ravine was formed in terraces. I'd climb up ten or twenty feet to find a small, overgrown, rocky, leafy ledge then have to search out another spot to climb up to the next one. I was tired and ready to rest, but I wanted to get to the crown of this little mountain first. However, on the third fairly flat patch of ground I found, I crawled up onto it and just laid there.

Looking up through the tops of the trees, the onyx night sky almost seemed bright compared to the complete sightlessness down below amidst the thick foliage. I could hear bugs chirping and smell the musky leaf-covered soil. My mind was shutting down. I'd drank so much that I was now sated, but I was physically exhausted and mentally drained. I felt myself drifting off... My last thought before I slept was of my sticking my dope sack under some leaves, so if God forbid, I was to be awakened surrounded by gun barrels aimed at my face, I wouldn't have that sack of useless meth in my pocket.

I crashed hard, but woke up within a few hours. The night was still pitch, but the temperature had dropped. Only slightly refreshed, I sorted out my thoughts. Remembering my earlier determination to reach the summit of this sheer, rocky slope, I rose and set off. Having no idea how far it was from the top, I climbed another twenty feet... to find myself there.

As I crested the ridge, the ground leveled off and I found myself looking through the trees at a clearing. Visible by the moonlight was a sheet-metal cabin sitting not thirty yards away. At first I was a little apprehensive; not wanting to run into any of the rural residents this close to the highway scene from the night before, but the windows were dark. As I circled around, wary of dogs who might give my stealthy reconnaissance from the tree-line away, I realized that there were no roads nor even ruts that led up to this place. Could I be that lucky? Could it be empty? I stepped out into the open and walked over to the structure. Standing on the side of the building, I banged the flat of my hand on its tin wall and listened from under a window. Nothing – not a squeak.

Confident that the place was abandoned, I went around to the front door and turned the knob to find that it was unlocked. I opened the door to get a better look, but couldn't see much by the meager moon rays that came through its three windows. What I could see was mostly clutter. I let my eyes adjust as much as they were going to and spotted a small steel-spring cot with a torn and raggedy mattress lain on it. Throwing caution to the wind, I walked in shutting the door behind me and immediately stumbled over a pile of unidentifiable refuse on the floor. Recovering my wits, I trod gingerly through the ramshackle room to the bed. Too exhausted to care about anything, I crawled onto it, still in my cold, damp, muddy clothes. Seeing – actually feeling - my way, I found some kind of blanket that had been thrown on the floor at the end of the cot. I pulled it up over me, dislodging a family of mice and who knows what else that were making their home in its long-abandoned folds.

I vaguely remembered that I'd forgotten to retrieve my little camo bag when I'd woken up on that ledge and climbed up here. I passed out again thinking that I was going to have to go back down and get it before moving on. This time, I didn't wake up until the sun was beaming through the windows and morning was well on.

When I did, I lay there for a couple of minutes letting my thoughts catch up with me. I realized I'd left myself completely vulnerable to discovery by sleeping so soundly so close to where the search for me had been focused. Holding my breath, I concentrated on the very air... listening for any sound that would seem out of place. All I heard were the normal country morning noises; birds mostly, chattering at each other as they swooped around trying to catch bugs to take back to their nests. Far off I could hear the faint sounds of a big-rig rolling down the highway. The road must have curved a little to the northwest also, which would make sense since it was headed for Pawhuska too.

Having decided I was alone, I swung my legs down and sat up. A couple of mice scurried out from under the bed. I smiled, watching one of the panicked little critters trying to run so fast on the hard linoleum floor that he wasn't even moving. He looked like a cartoon character. All he needed was a little puff of smoke behind him when his frantically churning legs finally gained traction and he darted around the corner of an old newspaper-filled milk crate to join his little partner. "Don't be afraid, little fella. This is your house. I'm just passing through," I told him.

I sat there looking around this little haven of hunters' heaven and took in what I couldn't see the night before. It was a twenty-foot square, wood framed, tin-sided shack with a gabled, corrugated sheet-metal roof. The floor was wood, although covered in linoleum where it wasn't torn up. The two by six trusses in the ceiling of the cabin were left exposed, but the walls had been sheathed in light paneling. However, the shelves and a countertop had been built into the underlying studs. There were a few faded and dusty framed pictures that appeared to span three or four generations sitting on the shelves and an old calendar hanging from a nail on the wall from 2003; seven years out of date. A good sign, I thought to myself. On the south wall I saw a gun rack, although there wasn't any firearms hanging in it, it did hold a big wooden bow. Thinking that might come in handy, I went over to take a closer look. The bow was intact, but it was un-strung and I could not find the bowstring stashed in any of the gun cabinet compartments. My search only turned up a few rounds of .22 and 30/30 caliber ammo.

The bow and bullets made me wonder what else may have been left here that was still good. I saw empty cans and other miscellaneous left over crap on the counter next to the door, but nothing immediately jumped out at me that would aid me in my journey. There were several bags of what appeared to be trash piled together in the middle of the floor and a couple of stacks of old milk crates loaded with different things in them. I found one that had some fishing gear, but most of the stuff in the plastic boxes was junk. It was dusty and dirty, but overall, in its day, I could tell this place had probably been a great getaway for some grandfather, son and grandson passing on the family hunting and camping traditions.

I kicked the bags on the floor around looking for a container to carry water in, when I ran upon a sealed jar of black olives. *"Oh man,"* my stomach exclaimed with joy. I immediately opened them, drank the juice and popped several in my mouth. Realizing that there may be a treasure trove of things cached in here if I looked hard enough, I dug through all the bags, shelves and cupboards. In the end I came up with a couple of cans of hominy, one can of glorious pork and beans, and a tin of Vienna sausages, which disappeared into my mouth before I even stopped my search.

I piled all the useful items that I'd found in the middle of the floor; the food of course, fishing line, lures and a few hooks, some cord, the blanket, and a dry T-shirt that appeared clean, but smelled of the musty old cabin. Keeping an eye out for anything to make a small backpack out of, I came across a square piece of tarp. Piling everything in the tarp, I carried it outside and set it on the wooden picnic table that sat out front under a tree.

This little place was sitting on the peak of probably the highest of the surrounding hills. I could feel a light, cool breeze blowing across the clearing in front of the house. The sun was up high enough to give some warmth to the day. I estimated that it was probably 9:30 or 10. It was nice up here, I thought, and it was only going to get nicer. I stood there a moment and let the sun shine down on my face soaking in – *freedom*!

Scouting around, I discovered the cabin truly was inaccessible for a full-sized vehicle due to the density of the surrounding vegetation. I didn't see any obvious footpaths leading in and even though I could hear the highway, it had to be at least a couple of miles away from this remote little paradise.

Taking off my shirt, I hung it over a limb just to be free from it for a little while and feel the sun. Then, I pulled out my cellphone to give it a closer inspection. Although there was no water that came out of it this time, it still felt like a useless chunk of plastic in my hand. However, I laid it on the table in the open sunlight, hoping it would possibly dry enough to work.

Taking my newly empty olive jar and another small plastic coke bottle, I went back into the trees. After finding the general spot where I'd climbed up the hill the night before, I descended to the small, babbling stream. Everything looked so much different now that I could see things clearly. The steep hillside was still choking with fallen branches and leaves on its rock-covered terraces, but without the eerie, foreboding blackness of the night, it now just seemed like a casual climb through the woods. There was even a place down by the creek that I'd been wary of in the dark because it looked like it might've been a cave, which in this part of Oklahoma could be the lair of a bear, boar, or mountain lion. Even *that* possibility couldn't detour my trek in the dog-tired state I was in the night before, but it turned out to be nothing more than some bushes that formed an arch at the top, where one slope met the other and had grown across the bottom of the gully. It even took quite a stretch of the imagination to reconstruct the shadowed image that I imagined in the dark.

Once I'd gotten my fill of water, I topped off the containers that I'd brought with me. Standing there at the bottom of the slope, I looked up at it trying to judge where I'd passed out and hid my dope sack the night before. First, second, or third tier, I couldn't remember for sure right then, so I climbed up and searched them all. Forty-five minutes into it, still not finding my little camo bag, I gave up my quest. I had other things to worry about besides a bag of water-logged dope. I figured the drugs were still there in the baggies even if they did get wet, and may still be potent when dried out. However, I doubted it would be *'saleable'*. *Whatever*, I thought. *If I really need to, I can come back and go over this hill more thoroughly some other time.* Right then, I needed to concentrate on getting back to town to find out what happened to Mr. Big and Jenna. Thinking about the cabin, the woods and the stream, I mused that I wouldn't mind staying here for a few days if they had been with me, but they weren't and I needed to find out if they were alright. Abandoning the search, I hiked back up to the top of this low-lying mini-mountain and back out into the warmth of the sunlit clearing.

Going through the supplies I'd scrounged up from the cabin, I discarded what was not absolutely necessary to keep it light as possible. I made a rough knapsack out of the tarp and packed what was left inside it. I gave the clearing and cabin one last look, again thinking it would be a safe place to hold up for a couple days if it wasn't for the worries over my little tribe. Grabbing my shirt off of the limb, I threw the knapsack over my shoulder and headed off through the trees, in what I assumed was the direction of Pawhuska.

CHAPTER TWENTY-SIX
NOT OUT OF THE WOODS YET

I hiked across the crown of the small mountain. The going was much easier; it was relatively flat and the trees weren't as dense. I came across a gravel service road just two hundred and fifty yards from the little lodge. Following it to its crest, I looked down from the road's elevated vantage point and checked my bearings.

The gravel lane I was standing on wound down to the bottom of my mountain and out across grassy, sectioned-off farmland. Sure enough, there was the highway a mile and a half away meandering towards the general direction that I needed to go as well. I reasoned that I couldn't miss my mark if I kept that two lane black top a couple of miles off my left shoulder.

There was a farmhouse sitting on my side of the highway that the service road I was on went by on its way to Highway 11, which meant I was on that homeowner's land. Having seen all I could see from my slightly exposed perch, I turned and headed down the other side. I strolled along in the middle of the gravel path, enjoying the casual, unobstructed walking while it lasted; confident that I was its sole traveler and was hidden by hills and trees all around.

It went on for a mile or more, then ended at an active well-head; its pump-jack moving up and down squeakily in a synchronized, never-ending rhythm. The drilling road had taken too much of a northerly direction for my purposes anyway. I had only stayed on it because of my reluctance to give up the easy going, so I took to the woods again traveling west with the intention of keeping the highway to town within reach.

It wasn't long and I had to cross over another barbed-wire fence, informing me that I was leaving one tract of land and entering another.

Here the forest was dense enough that the rancher had no need of metal fence posts and had just strung his wire strands from tree-to-tree. I love the country, particularly the woods; the smell, the sounds and the feel in the air as you move under the forest's cool, leafy canopy; especially through rolling mountain ranges. They're like a natural obstacle course down steep, leaf-littered hills, over moss-covered boulders and at the bottom of almost every ravine is a deep-cut creek with washed-out dirt cliffs that have grass and trees hanging precariously out over the water.

This was just like that, bringing back nostalgic memories of hiking through the woods when I was a kid and lived, for short periods, up in Wabash, Indiana, and Marysville, Ohio. It was beautiful and definitely made for pleasant traveling. If it hadn't been for my underlying sense of urgency to get out of there, I could have lingered in some of those spots for hours. As it was, I kept moving; only stopping long enough to drink water and scarf down my can of pork and beans.

I came to a break in the woods where I was going to have to cross an exposed, flat half-mile stretch through waist-high grass and brambles before I could reach the next protective tree-line, which climbed up the far ridge. There was no way to tell how visible I would be once out in the open. I could hear the highway faintly again. Whether I would be in sight of it or not I couldn't tell yet. I was also concerned that a landowner checking his cattle and fences might spot me. There's no reasonable reason for hiking across the middle of nowhere, unless you were in trouble of some sort, or had an orange vest on and a shotgun over your shoulder. *But, looking like I looked?* Either way, he would probably report it and I'd be back to square one.

It still had to be done, so hesitating only briefly, I headed out into the field. After taking just five steps into the grass and bramble-covered pasture, I could already tell this was going to be much harder on me than the physical exertion and slow going of climbing through the woods. The thorn bushes were thick and interwoven into the sea of tall grass; the snagging thistles grabbed at my pant legs pulling them and ripping them further with almost every step. The mid-afternoon sun was beaming down, adding sticky sweat to my aggravation. Bugs were brushing off of the blades of grass and flesh-tearing twigs and were burrowing into my sweaty skin. I knew if I wasn't already eaten up with ticks and chiggers from crawling through the grass on the hill by the pond, that I would be infested with them by the time I got across this. I resigned myself to it and pushed on, stopping occasionally to look and listen. Dreading the thought that if someone in a truck or jeep popped up I was going to have to drop down and belly crawl through the rest.

Finally, the thorn-choked grass gave way to smooth, rocky, moss-covered ground right before I reached the wood-line. What a relief! When I had first seen that stretch of field I had assumed it was going to be a refreshing respite from the hilly woods. Maybe I wasn't the country boy I thought, because I didn't see that torturous gauntlet coming at all.

Back in the midst of the cool trees, I trudged another couple of miles in the general direction of Pawhuska. I came upon a dirt road that led through a patch of land that was only sparsely covered with bushes and trees. The double-rutted, dirt road forked with one branch going south and the other continuing west up to a cattle guard, before ending at a two-lane highway that ran north and south. *What the hell!? This didn't have the feel of Highway 11.* If it was the same road it must have curved around sharply for me to be running straight into it. My sense of direction couldn't be that far off... I hoped.

Before I broke cover I got off of the dirt road and ducked back into the woods. Then I moved in to get a better look without being exposed to any passing motorists. When I got closer I was able to see that there was a small, ranch-style house sitting seventy-five yards off behind a wrought-iron gate on the other side of the mystery asphalt lane. I could see the carport had a work truck and another, newer pickup parked in it. From where I was, I couldn't tell if anyone was home or not. However, I could see three or four dogs running around the yard.

This was the first sign I'd seen of a habitation that may be of some use to me since I'd been out here. I couldn't pass by without trying to exploit the resources that could be gained from it. The work truck was pulled off to the side and appeared to be an extra utility vehicle. However, it seemed likely that somebody was home with the other pickup there. When I'd gained a better angle, I could also see why the highway had a different *'feel'* to it. A mile or so down a rolling hill, the tarmac ran into the original road, so this was just a branched off thoroughfare.

I looked southeast across the relatively bare piece of land, scouring the nearest tree-line for a potential campsite. Unwilling to put an innocent farmer or his family in harms way, I needed someplace to hold up and wait for an opportunity to approach the ranch house when no one was there. The potential of gaining clothes, food, a phone and possibly a vehicle was worth waiting out at least a night. Besides, I was going to have to pull up somewhere in a few hours anyway.

At the bottom of the southerly fork of the dirt path I spotted diamonds of sunlight reflecting off of some white, tin paneling. Thinking it might be some type of shelter, I moved toward it. When I got near enough, I saw it was an abandoned and tireless travel-trailer. It had been pulled out here and set back in the trees, tucked into a lazy curve of a creek, which made a deep, but dirty, little watering hole. There was also a nice fire-pit out in front of it. The several paths around the place, and the way the grass had grown up around the blocks the trailer was sitting on, told me that the campsite had seen a few seasons. Inside the camper I found a couple of sleeping bags, a hunting knife and a few other survival tools.

Resigned to stay there until morning, I went outside, stripped down to the buff and bathed in the creek. I also scrubbed out my crusty clothes the best I could without soap. Feeling good and somewhat refreshed, I wrung my clothes out and hung them over a branch to dry. I sat naked out on a log and ate a can of hominy that I'd opened with my new knife and drank my remaining clean water.

Reeling off a couple of strands of fishing line and setting the hooks, baited with beetles, I left them floating out in a deep part of the creek from the bobbers I'd found in the trailer; not really expecting anything to bite, but unable to resist the opportunity to fish whilst I had the chance.

Once the lines were set, I got the sleeping bag and laid it out on the bank at the edge of the camp. Then I stretched out to let my skin soak up the last, warm rays of the setting sun and breathed in the welcoming scent of the pasture. I was worried about Jenna and knew I had to get out of these woods soon, but I was actually enjoying the relaxed atmosphere. I didn't relish getting back to the rat-race and police chase, which was just waiting to pick up where it left off when I got back.

I had no bites by the time the sun went down and as it dropped below the horizon so did the temperature. The only clothing that had dried was my boxers, so I retrieved them from where they were hanging, then I toted the sleeping bag back into the trailer and laid down for the night. The Coleman lamp I'd found had no fuel, so I lay in the deepening darkness, listening to the country sounds as they carried through the cool night air. I could hear a cacophony of cicadas, crickets and other bugs calling to each other out in the trees; a dog barking somewhere and the Jake-brake of a semi far off on the distant highway. It seemed like hours before I fell asleep. However, when I did. I slept soundly rolled up in the warm sleeping bag.

When I woke up the sun had just crested the treetops and, with me wrapped in the insulated material, was already making the trailer uncomfortably warm. I got up and went outside to check my clothes and the fishing lines. The clothes were dry, but there was nothing on the hooks. I hadn't held out much hope to catch anything in that muddy creek anyway. Nevertheless, it was fun to try and it would have made a great story when I got back if I had landed the big one.

It was cooler outside with the morning breeze and I piddled around the camp eating my last can of hominy and whiling away most of the morning. Pretending, for the moment, that I was just out camping instead of at large in these woods as stranded fugitive on the run.

At one point, I walked up the dirt road far enough to see across the rural highway to the country home I was staking out; relieved to see that there was only the work truck that sat in the same place it had been the day before.

Determined to get myself to Tulsa that day using the phone or truck from the house, I went back to camp and put everything back the way it had been. The only thing I took was the knife. I even left the fishing supplies I'd brought from the mountain cabin, not wanting to disappoint the hunters or their kids when they came out the next time.

Setting out toward the ranch house, I ran from one sparse tree or set of scraggly bushes, which were scattered across that open stretch of land, to another – ducking down to hide whenever a motorist drove past. As I was closing in on the road just adjacent of the country house, a combine tractor came rolling by. His high vantage point caused me to hug the ground behind a puny two and a half foot tall mesquite bush. As soon as he and his tractor were out of sight I decided not to waste any more time, or take any more chances, by skulking around out here acting suspicious.

Standing up, I crossed the remaining twenty yards to the gravel drive. Three or four dogs took notice of me and came running out to investigate as I climbed the iron gate. It's been my experience that if you act scared of a dog they'll sense it and intuitively feel that you must be up to no good, bringing out their protective and aggressive instincts. However, if you take on the roll of alpha dog, ignore the lesser hounds and act like you are in charge, they tend to give way with no more than curious acceptance.

Deciding as I was coming down on the other side of the fence to face the oncoming dogs with as little concern or wasted time and attention as possible, I turned and strolled toward the house. The biggest dog, who looked like a Heeler-Chow mix, circled around eyeing me warily, his two cohorts flanking him with no more than a couple of quizzical yaps. I glanced in their direction and turned towards them as if they caused me no apprehension at all, which in my state of mind, really weren't my biggest concern. I walked right up the porch to the door.

Knocking, just to be sure, I hesitated for a few seconds and then tried the knob. The door was locked and looked pretty solid. I needed to use the phone that was in here and maybe, if I was lucky, the keys to that truck would even be hanging on a peg inside. Not to mention, I was thirsty and hungry as hell. To avoid breaking through the door in sight of the road, I'd need to go around to the back.

I came off the porch, scattering the pack of dogs that had crept up to sniff hesitantly at the ballsy intruder. With confident, purposeful strides I headed through the carport on my way to the back door.

Looking at the work truck and hoping its keys were in the house, it occurred to me that behind this locked fence it may just have the keys hanging in the ignition or tucked above the visor. By veering my course I was at the Chevy within ten steps. I could see through the window the door wasn't locked. Opening the door, I climbed in to the driver's seat and, sure enough, right there inserted in the ignition were the truck keys!

It's about time fortune smiled down on me for a change. *"But could it really be this easy?"* said the little voice from the negative side of my brain. Ignoring the voice, but still feeling my hope sink, I pushed in the brake and turned the key – my fingers crossed in some part of my imagination. Nothing… not a sound. *"I told you it was too easy to be true,"* said the voice again. Pushing that pessimistic thought to the side, I looked at the gauge and saw it had a full tank *Why would you have a truck with so much fuel in it out here if it didn't work? Oh hell-* I never finished the thought. This was a freaking five–speed stick-shift! My heart surged back up with optimism as I was pushing my left foot down on the clutch and reaching for the keys again… B-r-r-ramm, Brrramm…clack-clack-clack. The diesel engine roared to life! When it settled back down to its rattling idle, I put it in gear and powered around and down the driveway.

With the dogs finally deciding I was up to no good, they started barking and charging at the truck as I spun gravel under the tires headed for the gate. At the last minute, thinking about the damage I might cause the truck, as well as the gate, which would be much harder to repair than the barbed wire fence, I turned and cut down the yard and barreled right through the four strands of twisted wire, down through the shallow bar-ditch and came screeching out onto the road. My heart surged! I was almost home free... if my luck held.

I went about thirty yards south down the highway. Then, looking in my mirror to see if any cars were within sight of my fence-destroying escape from the yard, I saw the black skid-marks where I'd sped out burning rubber onto the road. They were pointing out the direction I was heading as sure as a street sign. Grabbing control of my urgency for flight, I stopped and casually turned my vehicle around. Once my front bumper pointed north, the opposite way of the tire tracks, I drove back by the house I'd just stolen the truck from. The dogs were loitering around the damaged fence and they looked up as I drove past baring expressions ranging from bemusement to contempt.

Surveying the interior, I saw a John Deere cap laying on the metal clipboard in the center of its single bench seat and put it on my head. I pulled it down low, trying to disguise myself to look as much like the actual owner of this truck as I could. The interior of the truck was just as utilitarian as the rest of the vehicle. Other than the clipboard and hat, there were only a few receipts scattered on the dirty dashboard. Laying in the passenger seat was a grey work shirt with the name tag 'Bob' stitched over the left breast pocket. 'Bob' was apparently a small man, because the shirt didn't fit. The back of the truck had toolboxes lining its sides and was equipped with an extra fuel tank that had a hand pump sticking out of it.

I drove six or seven miles on that road, finding that it curved back around and came into Pawhuska on the east side of town. Hoping the whole way I didn't drive past 'Bob,' considering that whoever he was, was either in Barnsdall or Pawhuska at the moment, I breathed easier when I got through town and was able to take the turn off onto the northeast-bound highway toward Bartlesville.

Once I was clear of Pawhuska and going a completely unexpected direction, I clicked the AM-FM radio on and listened to old rock and roll. I sang along, tapping the steering wheel to the beat of Eric Clapton's version of *'I Shot The Sheriff,'* and Janis Joplin singing about *'Me and Bobby McGee,'* while I drove the twenty miles to the next town, feeling more confident of successfully getting back to T-town with every mile. I realized then that I was a little surprised I was going to make it, considering that it was three nights before that a cop had me standing at gun point in the middle of the highway, in the middle of the night, in the middle of nowhere.

In Bartlesville, I had to go through town to find Highway 75-South to get back to Tulsa. I drove very carefully, never forgetting for a moment that any unwanted attention could end in another hot pursuit. However, I almost wrecked trying to take an exit when in my search for the highway I spotted a Taco Bell! I hadn't realized how hungry, or thirsty, I was until I saw that sign. Making it there unscathed, I detoured around to the Taco Bell speaker and ordered twenty tacos and the biggest coke they had.

Pulling up to the window, I was self-consciously aware of how I looked as I dug damp and moldy money from my pocket. "I'm sorry it's wet, I've been cleaning cattle ponds all morning," I said to the cute brunette who was handing me my bag and reaching for the nasty bill in my hand. She smiled, but wrinkled her nose as she gingerly took the twenty.

"That's quite alright. Have a wonderful day," she chirped, pinching the banknote between her thumb and forefinger.

Choking around a big slurp of Coke as I was getting my change, I replied: "I will! Thank you – you, as well." Driving off, I remember thinking that a Coke never tasted so good!

From there I jumped onto the big six-lane turnpike, just fifty miles due north of Tulsa. I drove no more than two or three miles over the speed limit as I shoved taco after taco into my mouth.

CHAPTER TWENTY-SEVEN

TULSA

I made it back to Tulsa without incident. Coming in from the north end of town, I took the Pine Street exit, which was only a couple of miles from Stephanie's house. I knew it was dangerous to go there. The Marshalls had stormed her place a couple of times already looking for me. There was no doubt it was under constant surveillance of some kind, but there was a back way in and I needed some information.

Stephanie's home was tucked in next to a large field a block off Utica, where Laramie Place and Wheeling Avenue come together. There was a thick, thirty-yard wide tract of trees behind my daughter's house that ran from the east end of the field, west, all the way to Utica. On the other side of the tree-line was a six-foot tall chain-link fence that cordoned off an old, abandoned industrial park the next block over. The grass and weeds over there had been left to grow chest high along its border; leaving the area between a little strip of urban jungle.

Parking my stolen truck in a secluded spot on the other side of the industrial park, I cut through the back. There wasn't any vehicular access to Steph's place without going all the way around to Utica. However, on foot, you could squeeze past the rusty gate and cut through the grounds of the huge, dilapidated, corrugated steel warehouse. There was a path through the tall, weedy grass to a hole in the border fence. It led all the way through the strip of forest to Stephanie's back fence.

Once I got there, I scoped out the area leading up to my step-daughter's place, looking for any signs of someone paying too much attention to her house. There was a car I didn't recognize in the driveway. However, it didn't have a law enforcement's look or feel to it.

Not wanting to waste any more time finding out what had become of Jenna and Mr. Big, I hopped over the three and a half foot tall chain-link and hurried across Stephanie's yard to her door. I opened it quietly, not knowing who the car might belong to. Cracking the door, I could see across the living room and into the dining room. Stephanie was sitting at the table facing me, talking to a guy that, from behind, didn't appear to be a cop, but nevertheless, someone I didn't know.

My thirty-five year old step-daughter, Stephanie, is only five feet four inches tall and weighs one hundred and fifteen pounds. But, she's a blue eyed, brown-headed, little pistol-packing hellion who hates the cops! However, she is very loving and loyal to me. The fact is, our whole family which includes my ex and all my kids, biological or not, remain fiercely loyal to one another, to me especially, with Stephanie probably my most adamant defender of all.

Nevertheless, Stephanie and her brother, Eric, my step-son, grew up in the 'Gangster Years'. Whether I raised them right or wrong, they are what they are and what they are is 'Down'. All of my kids are. I knew I could trust her to be able to see me at the back door and not give me up to the person facing her if he was someone to worry about. I pushed the door open far enough that she could see my face.

Apparently, there was no need to worry about her visitor. When she saw me her face lit up and tears of relief and happiness sprang to her eyes. She jumped out of her chair. "Oh my God, you made it! We were so worried," she exclaimed, running over to hug me.

I glanced at the medium-built, blond guy while she was squeezing me. "Who's that?" I asked suspiciously.

Now that he had turned around, I could see that he didn't have that official stick up the butt look that most police officers have. "Oh, he's just a friend. He's cool," she told me, then turning to him she said: "Hey, Bill. Maybe you'd better take off and I'll call you later."

"Alright," he agreed. He grabbed his coat and on his way toward the door he nodded to me. "It was nice to meet you, sir."

I nodded back as he headed out to his car.

Stephanie looked at me with a beaming smile on her face. "Don't worry about him. That's Ashley's brother... thinks he's a player... over here trying to get him some," she laughed. "Where the hell have you been? Jenna told me what happened."

"So she's not in jail?" I questioned with relief. "Where is she at?"

"She's at Dale's. I'll call her in a minute. Tell me what you've been doing the last three days... We've all been worried sick!" She talked as she padded from window to window closing curtains and blinds.

I related my harrowing tale to her, while she hunted up a pair of jeans and a shirt that would fit me before I took a shower.

"That's fucking crazy. Are you trying to make them kill you? They want to, they told me so. Don't give them the excuse they need, Jimmy." She looked up at me with moisture in her eyes. "'Cos you know I'd go completely postal crazy on their asses and kill 'em all!"

I laughed and kissed her on her forehead; not saying anything about where my state of mind was on that subject, just telling her I loved her as I turned away heading for the shower. Over my shoulder, I said: "Call Jenna and have her meet me at spot three."

Spot three was the McDonald's on Admiral and Memorial on the east side of town. Spot two was the little Muslim convenience store just a few blocks from Stephanie's – too close. I had another meeting spot out on the west side as well. They originated when I was running drugs from O.K.C. to Tulsa and had people scattered around selling for me. That operation was now ended, with my dope somewhere back on that leaf-covered hill in a water-logged camouflage bag. Still, Jenna knew where all the spots were and I could count on her to meet me there.

Steve, my step-daughter's real father, was in the kitchen when I got out of the shower. Steve was good people and, being half Comanche and half Cherokee, pretty down and crazy himself. Over the years, we had developed a mutual respect for one another. He appreciated my fierce loving, protective streak for Eric and Steph. "Jimmy, there are police all over out there," he told me through a cloud of cigarette smoke and nodding his dark head toward the curtains.

Drying my hair with a towel, I peered out of the window. I didn't see any, but Stephanie went out the front door to take a look. I left off drying my hair and sat down to put my shoes on. I noticed for the first time that I now smelled of soap rather than pondweed and dirt. "Have I got a story to tell you," I told Steve. "I've been in the woods for three days!"

"I figured you were still stuck out there when we hadn't heard anything," he said. "I told Stephanie not to worry and that if anyone could make it, you could."

"Thanks, brother…" I was saying, when Stephanie came running into the house.

"They're coming, Jimmy! One up each street!" she yelled.

Steve was looking out of the window now. "There's a couple black and whites—" he was confirming, but before he could finish, I was already out of the back door.

Over the months I'd already been running and dodging the Feds, I'd put a lot of thought into the layout of that house in relation to escaping undetected from it. I was confident when I hurdled that back fence and disappeared into the wooded stretch that, unless they had really studied it, or had a helo in the air, they wouldn't even think to stake out what was two streets over. I was gone in a flash, on my way back to the farm truck.

While I had been in the shower Stephanie had got a hold of Jenna and told me she was on her way to the spot, so I headed straight there. When I arrived, it was already late afternoon. *Where did the damn day go?* I thought.

I circled through the McDonald's parking lot, looking it over, then parked on the back side where I could see all the entrances either directly or through the glass windows. I spotted Jenna inside looking for me. I smiled when I saw her hopping from foot to foot excitedly the way she does when she's torn between anticipation and impatience.

Taking in the parking lot and the rest of the customers; not seeing anything suspicious, I decided she hadn't been followed and stepped out of the truck. Standing there beside it, I waited for Jenna's continuous, sweeping glance to come back to me. When she saw me, the light and beaming glow that lit up her face reminded me of when I had walked out of El Reno to her less than eighteen months earlier. *God how did I allow us to fall so far?*

I reminded myself that self-recrimination was not a luxury I could afford at that point and pushed all thoughts of it out of my head. Jenna ran jumping into my arms, hugging and squeezing me through her tears. "I've been so worried! I saw your bike wrecked and all the cops with their guns out. No-one's heard from you and I thought you may be hurt or dead! I've had people driving me up and down the highway looking for you for two days!" She blurted all that out so fast that her words were running over one another, only broken by the sobs of joy that she was fighting back.

"I'm fine. I'm fine. Everything is alright now," I told her as I held her and brushed the tears off of her cheek with my fingers. I asked where the car was, because I still hadn't seen it. She told me that she had made a deal with M.J. and Teddy to give them my Buick if they would go and get her car and fix its busted windshield. "You what?" I almost shouted. "That deal is off!" *They must really think they are slick,* I thought, while shaking my head at Jenna.

Jungle, an acquaintance of ours, came walking up rubbing his hand nervously over his bald head. He was a tall, lanky, middle-aged part-time junkie; meaning he would get his shit together for a few months and disappear out of the dope world. Then he'd fall off again and pick up right where he left off as if he'd never been gone. He wasn't a hardcore bad-guy.

Jungle and I already had an understanding; a couple weeks earlier he'd gotten some stuff from someone that was selling for me and hadn't paid, so I hunted him down and with a gun pressed against the back of his head retrieved what belonged to me. There were no hard feelings by either of us. It was just business. In that world you have to set your standards, because dope-fiends will push what they can get away with to its limits. However, when he walked up, he did so warily, then stood a good ten or fifteen feet behind Jenna, giving us our privacy.

When I noticed him, Jenna told me that Maryjo had sent him to drive her, because she didn't have a car any more.

"Give me your phone," I said. When she handed it over to me I called Maryjo, who answered on the second ring, "You and that bitch-ass ol' man of yours need to get my mother freaking car back to me – *NOW!* What the fuck are you all thinking leaving Jenna without a vehicle?"

"She's the one who made the deal…" Maryjo whined defensively. "We are supposed to go get your other car for her tonight."

I stepped back pulling Jenna with me as some idiot in a red pick-up sped by almost hitting us. Aggravated, I flipped the fat, bald-headed driver off then snarled into the phone, while I watched the guy shoot around the corner. "You can't drive that Toyota through the toll-gate without a windshield. If you don't know that, Teddy damn sure does. Now where are you? I want my car."

"Well hell, Jimmy, we were just trying to help. We figured that you wouldn't mind helping the mother of your kids," she countered with her usual passive-aggressive guilt trip.

I silently hoped 'Hot Rod' in the red truck, would whip back in so I could let off some of my growing frustration. "Maryjo, that line don't work on me any more and you know it. You and that piece of shit you're married to, get my car over to spot one. I'll be there in thirty minutes."

"You're a fucking asshole, Jimmy." Then, lowering her voice, so Teddy couldn't hear her: "But I love you. We'll be there. We really weren't trying to take advantage of Jenna. We will still try to get your other car up here and maybe you could loan this one to us for a while. It would at least throw the hounds off a little bit."

"I'll think about it," I huffed. "Just get over there. I lost all my dope and my gun. All I have is what I have in my pocket and a few more hundred that people owe me around here. I need all the assets I have right now."

Hanging up, I looked up at Jungle and asked him what he was driving. Like my acknowledging him dropped an invisible barrier, he stepped up and said excitedly: "Damn, brother, it's good to see you made it! I drove your ol' lady out to Pawhuska looking for you."

Seeing my slightly jealous and suspicious look, Jenna jumped in and said quickly: "Honey, I didn't know if you were hurt or not. Della drove me twice in her truck and Jungle took me yesterday. Billy was supposed to take me out there again today, but we didn't have the gas money."

"Yeah, Jimmy. Jenna was scared to death that you were laying out there hurt. Man, you know I just wanted to help you, brother," Jungle explained. He picked up the suspicious friction in the air that always starts cracking like static electricity when someone you don't know very well goes out of his way to help your ol' lady. Whether in the guise of helping *you* or not. A guise is often exactly what it is.

Anyway, Jungle looked genuinely abashed at my skepticism, because since the gun to the head incident, he had sort of became one of my biggest fans. Sometimes it just works that way and other times it's just an act, but the man really lacked the maliciousness of the latter... and with the hurt look on his face, I decided he was at least somewhat sincere to see me alive, well, and still free. "Right on, brother. Thanks for looking out and helping as much as you could," I said, slapping him on the shoulder with a grin, which made him instantly beam with a wide smile himself.

"Where is Mr. Big?" I asked Jenna.

"He's in the truck, and he has been missing his daddy, bad," she replied.

I looked at Jungle. He pointed out his truck, which was parked only a few spots down from my stolen one. I wiped mine down quickly and locked it, keeping the keys with me. I knew I probably wasn't done with it yet, but didn't want to drive around in a stolen vehicle any more than I had to.

Before I even got to the white, Ford 150 he'd pointed out, I could see a little brown head in the passenger window. Mr. Big was standing on the seat with his front paws on the arm rest, looking out at me as if he was afraid to hope it was really me. He saw me look at him and smile and his little ears quivered with excitement. "There's my boy," I beamed. He almost did a back flip in pure joy. I can't even tell you how much I loved that little guy. We loaded up with Mr. Big jumping up in my lap trying to lick my face to let me know how much he had missed me.

I settled down in the passenger seat and Jungle drove us the twenty miles across town to meet up with my ex and retrieve our transportation. On the way, Jenna caught me up on what had been going on with her while I was gone. She had, apparently, collected and used up several hundred dollars funding gas and rides out to look for me, as well as motels and drugs for herself. *Selling drugs, then turning around and buying them back at a higher price is about as smart as giving up our car, then having to pay someone to take you out to look for me*, I thought. Sometimes Jenna could be quite the snake in the grass herself. However, she wasn't made for the *'...smile to your face, then cut your throat...'* world that lays right under the *'injectable-drug line'*. What I mean by the injectable-drug line, is where recreational drug use ends and hardcore intravenous drug use begins. Anyway, I mentally started a list of people I might have to take the time to deal with on my way out of town, or before I got caught, or killed.

Jenna also told me I couldn't count on Tina, because the Feds had tracked my movements to her place via the snitch hotline back in Oklahoma City, and with all the pics of me she had up on her wall, they had roughed her up and were now watching her house.

Mr. Big licked my hand, while I watched the populated, wooded hills of Sand Springs flash by. I was thinking about my close call and wondering how Jenna and Mr. Big were going to fare when I was gone. Which, if I didn't do something soon and get out of town, and the State, probably wasn't too far off in my future.

CHAPTER TWENTY-EIGHT
JUNGLE

Hearing me list off our losses over the last few days and counting up our dwindling remaining assets, Jungle broke into my thoughts. "Listen, you don't have to get a motel. My sister and I inherited a house. She can't know, because she's a real bitch and would probably call the cops if she found out, but... she won't be over there until tomorrow afternoon," he said as he switched lanes getting ready for the up coming exit. "The electricity is on, you all could get a little food and a few blankets and crash until M.J. and Teddy drive your other car back from O.K.C. in the morning."

"I'd like to save the fifty dollars a room would cost me, but I don't know about being somewhere that someone might call the Law on me. I need to rest a couple days, not have to take off running again," I told him, scratching Mr. Big behind the ear.

Jungle leant forward so that he could look at me across Jenna sitting between us. "No, bro, if she did somehow slip up on you before I got back over there in the morning or M.J. shows with your car, all you'd have to say is that John – that's my real name, let you stay there overnight. She would be mad at me, 'cos we've been fixing the house up to sell, but *it's my house too*." He emphasized the last words to assure me that he had the right to allow whoever he wanted to stay there.

Still not real comfortable with the idea, but feeling that wad of money in my pocket, which seemed a lot smaller since I'd just counted up the things that I no longer had to rely on, I nodded. "Yeah, man, I guess it'll be alright, but don't leave me hanging there."

"No, I wouldn't do that. I don't want to have to argue with that bitch any more than I have to. It'll be fine," he assured me as he was pulling into the Phillips 66 station's parking lot.

I could see Maryjo and Teddy pulled off to the side with the hood of my Regal up. I told Jungle to pull around in front like we were giving them a jump; standard procedures for a meet.

Teddy was a short, bald-headed snake in the grass that seemed to have everyone, except me, snowed into believing that he was a good guy. He was only still a Brother then, because I didn't know then what I know now and I didn't believe in ex-communicating a brother on *'personal dislike'* alone. Teddy looked the part, at least to the weak and gullible. He was stocky built and had tattoos all up his neck, whilst his arms were sleeved out.

When we pulled up, I took in the scent of the exposed engine as Teddy went about hooking up the jumper cables like a good boy. He knew better than to speak to me. My dislike for him was common knowledge and he was fully aware that the grace I afforded him on account of Maryjo and the kids was as tenuous as a hair-triggered landmine. Whilst he busied himself by play-acting our subterfuge, I took my ex-wife off to the side and told her the plan, which, of course, she liked; since it involved me loaning her my car. "Really... I shouldn't," I grumbled, taking a drink of the Pepsi I'd commandeered from Jenna. "You guys weren't driving up and down that road out there trying to help find me."

"Jimmy, you know we would have, but none of us have a valid license and the car had been seen out there already," she countered. The warm September breeze blew a strand of her jet black hair into her face. As she moved it out of her eyes, she looked at me, hoping I believed that was the reason why they weren't out there helping Jenna, and not because they knew I would squash their deal to get my car. "You know that I love you and would do anything for you."

"Yeah, I know your motives were genuine," I admitted after chugging once again on my Pepsi. "That's the only reason I'm doing this. Jenna and I already discussed why she wasn't using our car to look for me. To be honest, it's a good thing it wasn't out there. The road was staked out the whole first day. I couldn't have moved if I saw it. But I know Teddy's motives were not based on the same logic as yours and someday I'm going to take his punk-ass out." Glancing over at him, I caught him looking away from us quickly. I guess something under the hood needed his urgent attention. "Remember," I finished. "All this depends on you two retrieving my other car." Turning my eyes back to my ex, I wondered – not for the first time – what the hell she saw in Ted. She had to know there was something not right with him.

I looked off down the grassy hill. "It sure is a nice day," I mused aloud. Jenna was letting Mr. Big sniff around to find a place to mark his territory, to let any wolves in the neighborhood know that '*Mr. Big*' was here. Smiling, I studied the woods. This far west, they were dense and stretched far and wide. I felt secure, knowing that most police couldn't hope to catch me if I could make it into one, such as the woods that lay all through the Shell Creek hills.

"Anyway," I said, breaking away from my thoughts. "Load up and follow us. We're stopping at the grocery store and then Jungle's going to let me into his house. When you get back from the City, I want you to take the Camry to the windshield place on Admiral, then come pick us up from there. I'm still not sure how Teddy figures to drive through the toll-gates with it the way it is, but I need it if you can get it. At least you'll be driving the Regal back and won't be in harms way."

On my way back to get in the truck I stopped and told Teddy to wrap it up. I couldn't help but add, with a knowing, hard look, that even if I had gone to jail, I would have never let him have my car, no matter what Jenna might have agreed to. Aware that he was just a hair's breath from destruction, he just nodded and ducked his head; busying himself with winding-up the cables. He shut the hood as I waited for Jenna to climb back in the middle of Jungle's truck, with Mr. Big in her arms.

We drove across town stopping only at a Homeland grocery store to pick up some food and beer. I was still starving. Those tacos I'd devoured earlier had barely put a dent in my hunger. Then we traveled the last few blocks to Jungle's mom's place. She had died and left her house to Jungle and his sister. It was tucked away in a nice little neighborhood off of 41st and Memorial.

When we pulled up, the first thing I took in was the lay of the land. It was a flat, suburban neighborhood; its streets lined with rectangular homes. No clutter – not many trees nor bushes and very few fences from what I could see; leaving a person's field of vision clear and penetrating in places through to the next block over. If I got hemmed up here it would be hard to get away on foot.

The house itself was a conservative, but nice, well-made brick home. Once inside, I could see that it had obviously just been remodeled. The carpets had been cleaned, maybe even replaced, the walls were freshly painted and there were new appliances in the kitchen. I could smell air freshener and furniture polish. They were ready to start showing the house to potential buyers.

Jungle was right the electricity was still on. So as Jenna and Maryjo loaded the refrigerator up I walked through the house looking it over with an appreciative eye. I used to be a maintenance supervisor over an apartment complex back in another life, so I noticed the little things like fresh caulking around the fixtures and new grout between the shower tiles. This was a three-bedroom house and it took a lot of work to get it into this shape. "Nice job," I complemented.

"It's taken three months to get this place looking like this." Jungle stood up a little straighter in subconscious acknowledgement of my approval.

"I can see why your sister might go postal if she caught us in here. We'll just stay in this back bedroom and keep out of the bathroom and kitchen as much as we can until you come and get us in the morning," I volunteered, whilst at the same time surveying how hard the windows would be to get out of in case of the necessity.

"I appreciate that, Jimmy. My sister really did put a lot of time and money into this place to get it ready and she's supposed to show it for the first time tomorrow afternoon."

Jenna came in with an arm-load of blankets with her purse perched on top. Mr. Big followed close behind, since she still smelled like food from putting our supplies in the kitchen.

"When is the last time Mr. Big ate—" I was saying, when Maryjo came bursting in.

"There is someone pulling up in the driveway!" she hissed at Jungle.

"Oh fuck! My sister must have told some of the neighbors to call if they saw anyone over here!" He made a pained face, before he sprinted down the hallway.

"Damn it," I groaned, pissed off that this clown had misled me into believing that he had some control of this house and his sister; which was obviously not the case by the frightened look and body language that he telegraphed at the news.

"You stay here with Mr. Big, Jimmy," Jenna directed me. "We'll act like we are the only ones here." Jenna and Maryjo then hustled down the hall to go join the commotion that I could already hear between Jungle and his sister.

"That guy is pissing me off," I told Mr. Big. He looked at me with his little bow-legged stance and gave me a look that told me not to worry, because he would protect me. I smiled as I bent down and picked him up. "My little man, we'd better just be quiet and hope that she goes away." He tried to lick at my face to acknowledge that he understood. "Don't do that, son. I don't know where that tongue has been," I whispered to him, holding him right up on my shoulder. He just looked at me and licked me again. "Aaah, ya little shit," I added, whereupon he just smiled at me.

We listened real close to what was going on in the living room. I could hear Jungle and his sister arguing; picking up that his sister was by far the dominant one of his family, probably by default, being the only really responsible one left of it.

However, dominant or not, Jungle seemed to convince the woman that he was just letting the girls stay the night and that he and Teddy were planning on leaving anyway. She wasn't hearing any of it and only seemed satisfied when Jungle and the two girls agreed to leave. She followed closely while she herded them out to the cars. I came up the hallway and watched through a crack in the blinds as all three vehicles drove off in the same direction.

Breathing a sigh of relief, I put Mr. Big down and we walked back up the hallway to the last bedroom. Exhausted, I shucked my britches and shirt and laid down on the blanket Jenna had made into a pallet. No sooner had Mr. Big settled down beside me, he jumped back up. His ears were twitching as he stared at the door. He was growling real quietly to let me know he was hearing something potentially dangerous to us and for me to not make any noise until he figured it out.

That's when I heard the front door open. I brushed my hand down Mr. Big's back and smoothed down his hackles. "It's probably just your mommy, son." He gave me an 'I'm not so sure about that' look as he stamped his little feet, but he quit growling. Soon we both knew it wasn't Jenna by the noises coming from the front part of the house. There were doors opening and closing, the sounds of light switches flipping on and off. The house was being searched. I had no way of knowing by whom, but it didn't have the sound of the police, so my assumption was that Jungle's sister had returned.

Me and Mr. Big were in the last room at the end of the hall, which the intruder was working their way down from door-to-door. Whoever it was would be on me soon, so I jumped up to pull my jeans on. My little buddy positioned himself between me and the door. His hackles bristled up around his shoulders again, but sensing the need, he kept quiet.

A fairly large, blonde woman – Jungle's sister I presumed, showed up in the door before I could get both of my shoes on. Seeing me standing there shirtless with one shoe in my hand, she bellowed: "I knew it! I should call the Law on you. This is my house!"

I jumped in before she could finish. "Hold on, Jungle... John, your brother, said that this was *'his'* house and gave me permission to be here."

"I don't care! I'm calling the Police – *and,* you have a dog in here!" She spat her words out, looking down at my little guard dog, who was now jumping and snapping at her in defense of his master.

"You don't want to do that," I was saying, while cramming my other foot into my shoe. She turned and took off down the hallway, pulling out her cellphone as she went.

I heard more noises coming from the front of the house. "Jimmy, are you alright?" Jenna yelled. I could hear the commotion as Jungle's sister encountered my two ex-wives coming through the kitchen. I gathered Mr. Big and our stuff and headed down the hallway too.

There is no mistaking a girl fight when you hear it. They are very vocal and fight with their words as much as their fists, claws, and teeth. "Fuck you, bitch! You ain't calling nobody!" I heard Jenna declare. The words *"bitch", "whore",* and *"skank"* echoed up the hallway from them both, blended together into a caterwauling cacophony of sound. At the same time, accompanied with the clatter of them both crashing into things in the kitchen and dining area as they fought.

I rounded the corner about the time Jenna scratched the woman across the face with the car keys in her hand. I yelled at them to stop. The girl didn't really want any more anyway and Maryjo was stepping up behind Jenna making it clear that she was on the verge of jumping in to finish her off if she didn't comply. Jenna, breathing heavily and with a fierce look on her face, was saying: "I knew this bitch was coming back as soon as she turned off behind us. She was calling the Police when I jumped on her..."

I could see the broken cellphone laying in the corner of the floor. Then Jenna spat at the other girl. "Bitch, your brother said we could stay here tonight."

By now, Maryjo, ever the mediator, was in Jungle's sister's face trying to explain that we had no reason to believe her brother didn't have the right to allow us to stay, considering he had keys to the house himself. *Where was Jungle, anyway? Apparently, he didn't see the need to turn his truck around when he saw the other two vehicles come back.* I'd have to discuss that with him later...

I handed Jenna Mr. Big. "You done good, honey," I said as I smoothed down her hair. Turning to the woman she'd been fighting with I continued: "Look we don't want any trouble. We thought it was alright to be here. Just calm down and we will leave." Whether the woman called the Law or not, I don't know. We just grabbed a few items from the refrigerator that we'd just put in there and hustled out the door, leaving Jungle's flustered sister standing in the dining room bearing the expression of a sulking child.

I had Maryjo and Teddy drive us back to the McDonald's where my stolen truck was and told them to follow me over to the *'Gateway Motel'* on Tulsa's west side. It sat right off the turnpike leading to the City, so they could come right back by there with my other car.

The Gateway was just a little, seedy thirty-five dollar a night motel, which advertised in flashing neon: *'WE HAVE PORN'*, right under their *'vacancy'* sign. I was tired and thinking I should have done this in the first place as we pulled into the parking lot.

M.J. went to rent us a room, so that my name wouldn't be on the register. The Gateway was a notorious crankster hangout and definitely on the list of places that night shift, city and County cops checked out.

When she came out, Maryjo pulled me to the side. "Jimmy, don't get mad, but Teddy and I were talking and we think you're right. It probably isn't safe to drive your Toyota back at night like this with a broken windshield. Maybe we can figure something else out," she said.

"Ha!" I laughed, almost snorting my contempt. "That piece of shit ol' man of yours knew that from the start. It was all game to get Jenna to agree to give you the Regal. I was wondering how far he'd play that out now he knows I'm back."

She looked at me. "Please don't do anything, Jimmy. You know the Arabs at this motel will call the Law on you quick."

Giving her the keys to the stolen truck, I looked over at Teddy: "Get the fuck out of my car. Get your shit and get the fuck on down the road. Now! Before I change my mind."

I stood there watching them moving their possessions from my car to the truck, whilst Jenna sneaked Mr. Big into the room, so that the weirdoes who ran this place wouldn't freak out if they saw we had a dog. As if it mattered, this hostel was already as ragged as it gets. It stank of guilt-ridden sweat and missed opportunities. Like some dog fur would matter…

Teddy said something to Maryjo and she complained to me that one of the headlights was busted out whilst adding: *'Was I going to send her off, in the dark, in a stolen truck with only one headlight?'*

"Yep, I sure am," I stated flatly. "Feel lucky that Teddy gets to leave on his feet at all."

She just flung back her long black hair with an irritated jerk in a perfect Cher imitation. "You're an asshole, Jimmy."

"Yeah? Really, not so much."

I raised my eyebrows, glancing at Teddy, to remind her of the words I'd just said. He was already behind the wheel of the truck – staring straight ahead like a first-time felon getting his mug-shot taken.

She got my meaning and climbed in beside him; shutting the door. Then she barked at Teddy: *"Go!"* and they drove off.

I stood there watching the truck speed away, shaking my head. *What was it she saw in him?* I asked myself once again. Oh well, it wasn't my concern any more and I walked on into the room to Jenna and Mr. Big. *God, what a dump,* I thought. *Oh well, at least there's porn!*

CHAPTER TWENTY-NINE
COOKING CLASS 101

Not wanting to give up our room any sooner than necessary, Jenna and I stretched the next morning out until checkout time. Jenna brought me up-to-date on what had been happening in my absence, whilst I thought about our next move. I wanted to know who'd tried to help her find me and who hadn't. One, she said, that offered assistance, was Billy Ray. I knew him, supposedly. At least, he'd claimed too know me and had told her, out of respect for me, of course: ...*and I'm the Pope of Rome...*, that if she needed anything, to get a hold of him. She went on to say Billy was a pretty good Methamphetamine cook. *'Cook'*, in this instance, referring to a back-alley chemist. With my stash lost and wet back in Osage County somewhere, I decided to take him up on his generous offer to her. Besides, I had come to the conclusion that I needed to learn how to make meth myself. It occurred to me how far I'd fallen from my firm policy against drugs. However, we needed money, and being on the run is not conducive to holding down at nine-to-five job. With that, Jenna and I set out across the river for Sand Springs to find Billy Ray and his o'lady, Pam's house.

Once over there, Jenna couldn't remember exactly where they lived. She said it had been late at night and the place was tucked way back off of the road behind another house. We spent an hour combing neighborhood after neighborhood. Eventually, she remembered enough to get us into the right area and all of a sudden she shouted: "It's right there, right there – stop!" I backed-up and pulled into the driveway she had pointed out.

No wonder it was hard to find. The driveway that led to it served a large, old colonial style home that faced the street. It also accessed Billy and Pam's above-garage apartment, which was tucked fifty yards behind it. Jenna was extremely pleased with herself ...and I was a tiny bit pleased with her, too. We weren't that bad off yet, but the way things were going, we needed a little luck.

Billy and Pam's place was just a square, little upper additional floor over the garage accessed by steep, wooden stairs that led up to a small, railed landing and their front door. The whole thing had been built on an incline that climbed to the alley, which cut down the center of the block.

Sand Springs is a beautiful outskirt city just west of Tulsa. It's built on the densely-wooded hills and valleys that are sandwiched between the Arkansas River and Shell Creek Dam. The whole community rolls up and down with the landscape.

When we pulled up, Billy stepped out of his front door onto the landing that sat at the top of the twenty-foot stairway. He looked around nervously from his high vantage point and quickly waived us up into the apartment. Once we were up the stairs and inside, Billy shut the door, turned around and hit me in the shoulder. "Damn, man, you made it. I told your o'lady that I thought you would. Do you remember me from Connors when I was doing time in eighty-seven?"

He did look familiar and I was sure that I had heard his name before, but whether it was on good terms or not I couldn't remember.

Billy was a skinny guy like most junkies – like I was becoming. He was fairly tall; just an inch or two shorter than me, with short, bushy hair, a seventies pornstar mustache and a pox-marked face. The way he looked didn't bother me. But, the way his eyes darted off whenever I looked too intensely at him made me a little uneasy. However, I almost expect some anxiousness out of people who have known me in my most violent days, so I didn't jump to any conclusions.

His next words reinforced that my assumption was, at least, part of it. "Man," his eyes got big. "I remember when you beat ol' Mountain Man down behind the gym." Then he looked at our wives and went into story mode: "This guy, David Little was his name, was a huge son of a bitch. When your old man here got done with him, in all of about thirty seconds, medics had to come get him on a stretcher. The cops locked the whole yard down. There was so much blood that they thought he'd been stabbed, until they wiped it off and found out he just got his big ass kicked! Over money wasn't it, Jimmy? Man, brother, I'm glad you made it... I already told Jenna anything you guys need... I was going to drive her out to Pawhuska to look for you. Did she tell you that?" He puffed nervously on his cigarette and blew a cloud of smoke in the air right before offering me the pack.

"Yeah, she told me." I waved the smoke out of my face and shook my head. "I don't smoke," I replied through squinted eyes. The smell of the tobacco got on my nerves.

Although I was leery of him, I thought maybe his shiftiness was just a product of being a junkie. Possibly mixed with him being a little intimidated by me. I wasn't sure yet. He was trying to make up for it with promises of aid, for which we'd come for in the first place, so I shelved my suspicions for the moment.

"This is Pam, my o'lady," Billy went on, introducing me to his girl. Pam was a large boned, well built, semi-pretty girl with brown hair, brown eyes and a deep tan from working her garden. "Her Sugar daddy pays the rent for us here. It's all good, brother. You can stay here as long as you need. I haven't got any dope right now, but we can make some tonight."

Pam, his wife or whatever she was, nodded her head anxiously.

Their apartment was compact. It had four rooms counting the bathroom. We entered the living-room that had a large bay window looking down on the driveway we'd just driven up. Through an archway on the right was the kitchen and a door to the alley. It wasn't as far to the ground back there due to the incline. To the left was the bath and their single bedroom. Overall, not a bad little place. The garage below was theirs as well.

The only problem I could see was that if somehow Johnny Law was able to sniff out my trail to this place I would be trapped. There was nowhere to go.

We spent the rest of the day gathering amphetamine pills and a few other supplies. That night, I got a crash course in cooking methamphetamine – 'shake and bake' style. I've been taught several ways to make speed. Put more accurately, there's been several people *try* to teach me. Most ways involve glassware; namely test tubes, beakers and so on, or making a pressurized tank to hold some farmer's stolen anhydrous. But 'Shake and Bake,' although not my favorite form of methamphetamine, was still pretty good when cooked right. The supplies were easy to get and it's extremely simple to manufacture. Exactly what I needed to keep us in untraceable cash, as well as supply our own increasing drug habit. It

217

wouldn't solve all our problems, but it would be a good asset in my fugitive's tool bag.

We sent the girls and Mr. Big off. Billy's o'lady didn't like the fumes and I was sure my little guy's lungs didn't need to be in contact with the toxic gases that would be the byproduct of the evening's events; especially since he already had a little case of asthma.

After they left, we got down to a cooking lesson: *'Methamphetamine 101… with Professor Billy at the helm'*. Billy really took to teaching; showing me what to do, how much of this and how much of that to use, and why. Why pressure is important in a chemical reaction and how it enhances the quality of the finished product. All the while, shaking the pressurized bomb he held in his hands. He taught me the signs that appear when the pressure is becoming too great for the plastic two-liter pop bottle that we were using; continually shaking it then passing it back and forth. Hence the name: *'shake and bake.'* He demonstrated when and how to bleed the pressure off, which was the source of the toxic and dangerous, not to mention distinctive-smelling, fumes I mentioned a moment ago. He showed me the whole process all the way to the finished product. He was a good, thorough teacher and I picked up the basics all in the first round, even though the fumes alone had us higher than the International Space Station.

When the girls got back, we got even higher still.

CHAPTER THIRTY

TRUDY

We stayed with Billy and Pam for a few days, sleeping downstairs in the garage. There was no room for a car, since one side was packed full of stuff; couches, bed frames, camping equipment, tools, boxes... you name it, although the air held on to the tang of gasoline beneath the aroma of musky furniture. The garage was stacked to the rafters except for a small area in the back, which had a spring cot and a dresser with a lamp on it that served as a makeshift bedroom. The other side of the garage had a little less debris. It contained the washer and dryer and therefore had piles of clothes stacked all around them. To put a car in there would have taken a couple of hours of work and it would probably be at the expense of the sleeping area. As it was, that little alcove with a bed in it was pretty cozy and it gave Jenna and I a measure of privacy. However, being right in the middle of Sand Springs, with its squared off blocks and grid-lain streets and alleys, it seemed to me like a trap that could snap shut at any moment.

After expressing my concerns to Billy, he told me about a woman he knew named Trudy, who lived in the hills on the other side of Shell Creek. He said she had a small cabin on the back part of her property that she'd probably rent us, especially now that I knew how to make speed. Billy allowed that she was sprung bad on dope. He said that in just a year she went from being a college professor, wife and mother of three, to a jobless junkie that just wanted to smoke meth and get freaked.

Billy was the kind of guy who got off on the power that having a dope sack gave him over other people. He thought a story like that was funny. I knew that there was something about him that I didn't like from the start. However, Jenna and I were getting desperate and we needed the help, so I shelved my distaste for using a woman's addiction against her and set my mind to do what I had to for Mr. Big, Jenna and myself to get by. But… I truly despise that drug and what it does to people's lives. So, although I told Billy we'd go talk to Trudy, I determined to try and not take any further advantage of her. It's funny, the people you feel the sorriest for are usually the ones that bite you the hardest and sometimes deserve every bad thing that happens to them.

Jenna and I drove Billy out to Trudy's, winding our way on a picturesque, rural, tree-lined road the other side of the dam. Eventually, we came to a nice, fairly new, red-brick home that was built at the foot of the nearby hills. You could see the roof of the house and the garage doors that the short driveway led down to, right off of the road. The rest of the house was obscured by trees. Billy wasn't lying she lived just far enough out in the sticks for her property to be butted up to open woodlands, the way I liked it.

When we arrived there was another couple already there. Billy recognized their Jeep and told us they were cool and, also, *in the game';* meaning they dealt in meth too. We didn't see the girl he *knew* would be with the guy, but the dude was in the driveway working on Trudy's truck. Billy went inside to tell the ex-professor about our interest in renting her cabin.

Walking over to the man after Billy went into the house, I introduced myself. "Hi my name is Dirk Zimmerman. What have you got going on there?" Indicating the question was directed at the open hood of the truck with a wave of my hand.

The guy wiped his hand on his pant leg before reaching out and offering it to me to shake. "My name is Chris and that's my o'lady, Sueanne," he replied, pointing toward the tall, good-looking brunette who was coming out of the door into the garage. "I'm trying to help Trudy get this truck running right. It runs fine for a few minutes then bogs down with no power at all," he explained, shutting the hood of the grey King Cab pickup.

"That's my wife over there. Everyone just calls her J-bug," I said, nodding toward Jenna.

Chris had a medium build and was bald headed. He was clean-cut except for the tattoos that were showing from underneath the cuffs of his sleeves. "Have you ever done any time?" I asked.

At that he took off telling me his life story. I noticed Jenna talking with Sueanne, also trying to get a bead on what we were dealing with. She already knew to go by J-bug or Julie Zimmerman if she was pressed. Chris told me that he had done a couple of short hauls in the Department of Corrections and named various prisons in Oklahoma that he had done time in. "What about you?" he asked, looking at *my* tattoos. I noticed a funny shine in his eye when I told him I'd been to prison, but not in Oklahoma.

He seemed satisfied and went on to tell me of his latest adventure. He was a meth cook as well and had been out in the woods gassing off his dope when Osage County cops, the same agency that had been after me, came up on him. He said that he had to take off and hide in the forest for a day and a half before he could get back to town. I sat listening to him in growing fascination, while he described the tale. He finished by telling me how badly he was eaten up with chigger bites and how many ticks he had to remove when he had finally gotten out of the woods.

"Where did this happen? When?" I asked.

Amazingly, he described the basic area and time frame that my ordeal had happened. I wondered if he was trying to pull my leg or something, but there was no way for him to know about me and my latest escapade. I sat there listening suspiciously, scratching at my own chigger bites, while he described how bad and extensive his own were.

It was very strange and it bothered me. I thought: *could it be, that while the cops were looking for me that they almost stumbled on this guy out in the same woods? And now... I have ran into this same guy several days later at this random location?* I don't like weird shit, and ninety-nine point nine percent of the time there is not anything that's unexplainable. It always means something. But, in this case, I really couldn't think of any way Chris's tale could be linked into my own, or any way he could possibly know about mine.

A couple of seconds later I almost changed my mind. Billy stuck his head out into the garage to wave us in and as we were walking toward the house Chris said to me: "I know who you really are."

That caught me by surprise and I had to keep a tight grip on myself not to show any reaction. Even if he did know me, which is not unusual in this part of the country, I'd already decided that his story had to be one of those rare, naught-point-one coincidences, but it was strange, nevertheless. I just gave him a fixed stare: "What do you mean? Who I really am?"

"I know you're Jimmy Maxwell. I saw you in O-four. Someone pointed you out during a transport. They were taking you to the prison in Lawton. You might know my dad, Gary Preston?" He went on to name a few others that he knew I would know; trying to appease my suspicious look by proving he was one of the fellas with the references that he was giving me. When he finished, it was obvious that he knew who I was. I also knew enough of the people he'd named, including his dad, to know he was probably at least semi-trustworthy. He ended his speech by telling me he wouldn't tell Trudy my real name.

Billy was waiting in the hallway. He said he'd told Trudy we were looking for a little place to rent out of the way somewhere and that he thought she might want to hire out her little cabin. He also said he'd told her my name was Dirk and I had some little petty thing I was on the dodge from the Law for. She'd indicated that would be alright because she needed the money and, if I could cook dope, that would be an added bonus.

When Jenna came in, we went on back to Trudy's room to meet her for ourselves. Trudy was a strange one to figure out right from the start. She was around forty-five, fairly pretty with brown hair, brown eyes and not shaped too badly for a woman who probably hadn't worked out a day in her life. Trudy was a cross between an academic flower child and hell-bent hard drug addict. She still had a way to go, but her life was one that was headed for total collapse. It was true, she had a nice home and a nice piece of land, but the payments were behind; she was struggling to keep her electric on and her truck was in disrepair. At first glance, I truly felt sorry for her.

We introduced ourselves as Dirk and Julie Zimmerman. I told Trudy that we called *'Julie'* J-bug for short, since that's what I called her most of the time, anyway. We talked to her for a while; with Trudy telling us her story, and us... basically making one up. After a while she gave us directions to get to the cabin, so we could see if it would serve our purposes before we went any further.

Jenna and I followed a stone-lined path fifty yards into the forest before emerging into a clearing. In the middle of it was a small, one room, elevated shack. The whole thing was no bigger than a motorhome and not much wider than one either. When we got closer to the little woodland shanty, we could see the place had seen better days.

The electric lines were down and the grass and weeds had grown up waist-high around it. We had to stomp our way to the small porch, where I used the key Trudy had given me to unlock the door. Trudy said she'd been using it as a storage unit, so the inside was almost as cluttered as Billy's garage. The smell of damp crept softly into my nostrils. To the right was the kitchen area, where a short countertop that jutted out of the wall separated it from the rest of the one room space. In the *'living-room'* the ceiling was raised up to its rafters, making it appear larger. The end over the kitchen was framed straight across, creating an open, sleeping loft with a short, built-in ladder to access it. Pretty cool, I mused, impressed with the nice way the builder economized space.

There was a sliding glass door on the other wall. It opened onto a small deck and looked out over a clearing that had a wooden picnic table next to a big Sycamore tree; a nostalgic tire swing hanging from one of its thick limbs. It was really quite beautiful. It would take a little work to get the place cleaned up and the electric back on, but I thought it would be fine for what we needed to weather the winter.

Jenna and I talked about it on our way back to the main house. We both liked Trudy and decided it wouldn't be right not to tell her what she was getting into. Someone else was bound to tell her who I was eventually, anyway. Plus, if she was cool, then she would be our first line of defense from anyone coming around inquiring about me. A nosy cop would have to start by talking to her and she could then warn us.

When Jenna and I got back up to the main house we had a talk with Trudy. I told her who I was, while of course down-playing the whole thing. She said everything was cool and that she would help us as much as possible. I went on to tell her about the downed power lines and she said we could run cables from her house to the cabin, straight through the woods, until I could restring the wiring on the poles. She even went on to invite us to stay in the main house until we could get it strung. She was acting almost *too* nice and helpful, but we marked it up to her being lonely, not to mention happy to have someone out there who could make meth. I imagine she thought that having a good-looking couple about who she could possibly freak with wouldn't hurt either. Something Jenna and I both picked up on. I hoped that, along with those reasons, there was a measure of just being good people in there as well.

We really didn't mind the *'freak'* part of her. However, right then I was not in the mood for it. Not with me covered in all those chigger bites. We decided that we'd show Trudy a good time when I healed up. You can read a woman, their moods and mindset a lot more clearly if you are sleeping with them. Now that Trudy knew who I was, it would be that much more important to know where Trudy's head was at during any given moment. Besides, Jenna occasionally liked pulling another woman into our bed; if she perceived the other woman posed no threat, that is.

We told Trudy about the police chase, my bike wreck and that I'd left two ounces of uncut *'ice'* hidden on the side of a hill out by Pawhuska. I asked Trudy to download a Google Earth application on her computer, so I could find a safe way in, via satellite, to retrieve my dope sack now that the heat was off. She did and, after studying the satellite imagery, I discovered the shiny corrugated rooftop of the hunter's cabin a mile and a half off the highway. It was perched right on top of a small mountain encircled by trees with no access road, just like I thought it would be. I was also able to map out a couple of back-ways into the area.

It wasn't long after telling her the Barnsdall story that she started asking disturbing questions, such as: "Do you think there is a reward on your heads? How bad are they wanting you?" Then Jenna found my real name and prison number written down on Trudy's computer desk... She cut her eyes down to it, so I would look. I felt the hairs on the back of my neck stand up and my internal alarm go off like a tornado siren. I asked Trudy what she was doing with it? The ex-educator said she was looking me up to see if there were any rewards or information about me posted online, *'so she could warn us if there were'.* It had been a mistake to tell her the truth. Jenna was even giving me the side eye as if to ask whether she should jump Trudy's ass or not.

"How the hell are you supposed to be able to deny knowing what my name is, if you have Google and Department of Corrections inmate searches for me engraved in your hard drive?" I asked Trudy. I looked her in the eyes, my suspicion apparent in my gaze. She shifted, taking a drink of her coke and looked away.

I had told her not to worry and that if the Law caught me there I'd go to my grave denying she knew who I really was. I promised to protect her, or anyone trying to help me, from legal repercussions for harboring me, regardless of the cost to myself. Including, if it were needed to keep them from prosecution, claiming that I'd kidnapped and forced them to aid me. But, they had to do their part by not leaving a contradictory evidence trail.

I told Jenna that she was going to have to change her plans. We wouldn't be spending the winter down in the cozy little cabin on the back of this chick's property. She agreed reluctantly, but asked if we could at least stay at Trudy's a few more days. Despite the warning signs, Jenna liked it there. We hadn't been stable in months; being constantly on the move, and this was the first time we'd really thought we might have a chance to hold up for a while. I felt bad for Jenna, and Mr. Big, who had taken over the duties of guard-dog at our comfortable, country hide-out. I told her we could, but I knew I was going to have to find something quick.

However, it was the very next day that I heard Jenna talking on the phone with, what sounded like, the Barnsdall Police Department. She was trying to find out about my Harley. We'd asked my bro, Joe, to go get my bike out of impound for me, so Jenna was trying to find out how much it was going to cost. I was all for getting my bike back, but I'd intended to call the impound yard for the information we'd need from somewhere in town the next time we were there.

I walked up and mouthed: "Who are you talking to?"

All of a sudden she got really agitated and had a worried look on her face. "I am his wife... but I don't know where Jimmy is. I just want to get the bike back, because it's part mine too. Yes, yes, of course I will contact you if he gets in touch with me. Thank you... I have to go..." she assured the person on the other end of the line and hung up. Then, turning to me, she said: "That was a Federal marshal I just talked too. The impound place told me that there was a Federal hold on the bike, so I called the Barnsdall Police Department and they transferred me somewhere else and I found myself talking to a Fed!"

"Why didn't you wait until we were in town to make that phone call?" I grumbled, slapping my hand down on the table.

Jenna jumped a little at the sharp noise. "I star sixty-seven'd the call. I'm not stupid!" Jenna proclaimed.

"I hate to tell you this, *honey*, but I doubt that star sixty-seven works when you're dealing with the police station," I said, rebutting her defense with exasperation thick in my voice. I turned to Trudy: "Does your cellphone have this address attached to it in *any* way?"

Trudy replied that it had a couple of other addresses attached to it as well. But, if they had the ability to get into the phone records, it would eventually lead out to her country home.

"Fuck! Jenna start putting our stuff back in the car."

"But... I star sixty-seven'd... I thought it would be alright. I don't wanna leave yet," Jenna complained.

I walked into the bedroom with her. "Maybe it did block the number, honey, but it's a chance we can't take. Besides, you said yourself that you don't trust Trudy anymore after the computer incident. Now pack up."

"You're right. I'm sorry... that was stupid of me to call the Police Department. I wasn't worried until I found myself talking to that marshal." I heard the sadness in her voice as she began gathering our things.

I found out later that Federal fugitive hunters showed up at Trudy's the following morning.

CHAPTER THIRTY-ONE

WALMART

When we got back to Sand Springs, Jenna and I held up at Billy and Pam's again; staying in the makeshift bedroom in the garage for a couple of days. While we were there, Jenna talked me into letting her go strip at one of the local strip clubs. I allowed it simply because our money was short by then.

There was no doubt that we needed to be getting out of Tulsa. However, once away from everything and everyone we knew; without any money nor a gun, it would just be a matter of time before I had to do something crazy and risky. We were basically stuck until we could put something together. I had to at least come up with a firearm, so I could take care of us in a pinch. Jenna stripped and I started putting together the ingredients I needed to make speed, along with trying to find someone to take me back out to Pawhuska to look for my dope. I didn't want to take my car; knowing its description may draw attention that I couldn't afford.

One night while Jenna was working at the 'Landing Strip', an upscale stripclub – as stripclubs go – on Tulsa's east side, Echo called and asked if I could take her to Walmart. Haven's first birthday was coming up and she needed to get a few things. I jumped at an opportunity to spend time with my daughter and grandbaby. I knew at any time I could split town, and/or the State, not to mention get caught or killed so, even though it was risky, I still got over to Echo's place on occasion to see them; enough that we had a little system worked out.

She lived in 'Sandy Park'; a rundown, section-eight apartment complex on the west side of the river: a place the police had staked out even when they weren't looking for me. The complex only had one road that circled around on itself accessing the different buildings. I would drive past Echo's turn-in and park a couple of parking lots away. Then, by cutting across a couple yards on foot, I could be at her front door fairly quick inconspicuously.

This day Echo knew I was coming and she and my son Brandon met me at the rendezvous spot. "Hey, dad, thanks for coming," she said, smiling when she saw me. I couldn't help but notice how much she looked like her mother when Maryjo was young, with her long, brown hair, brown eyes and smooth complexion. She was carrying Haven and all the traveling bags that go with an infant wherever they go.

"I want to go too, dad," Brandon announced as he strutted up beside his older sister.

That was fine with me. I hadn't been able to spend much time with him since I'd been on the run. It was then that Echo informed me that their mother wanted me to swing by and pick her up too, so she could get something for our grandchild's birthday as well.

Jesus Christ, I thought. I'm on the goddamned F.B.I.'s most wanted list and running around on a family outing as if half the State wasn't out looking for me!

However, I really couldn't begrudge Maryjo for wanting to go with us. The only time Echo could put up with her mom was when I was with them, so I made the trip out to Dale's, where M.J. was living full-time now, and picked her up.

When we arrived at the Mega Walmart in Sand Springs we all piled out and into the store. No sooner had we entered it, the girls headed off to the women's and makeup departments, leaving Brandon and me standing there looking at each other stupidly. Soon he took off on his own agenda as well.

Finding myself alone, I headed for the electronic section of the store; the same thing I always did when I went into a Walmart. I would eventually work my way around to the children's toy section to pick something up for Haven's birthday, but I'm a guy and the first thing guys go for in Walmart is either the automotive, electronics, or the sporting goods isles, regardless of what we actually go in there for in the first place.

I was perusing the new and cool electronic gadgetry when Shawn walked up. I ran into him every now and then over at my buddy Dale's, because he was dating Valerie, Dale's daughter. Shawn was a fairly normal looking kid in his early thirties, with short brown hair and a neatly trimmed goatee. However, he was squirrelly as hell. I didn't know him well, but we knew each other enough for him to know my situation. He was into fake I.D.s and identity theft. At one time I had even talked to him about making me a phony driver's license.

"Hey, Jimmy. What are you doing here? Was that Maryjo and Echo that I saw over in the women's department?" He was fidgeting nervously while he spoke – obviously high on speed.

"Yeah, that was them. We're here to get some things for Haven's birthday," I replied, absentmindedly picking up a radar detector that advertised: 'I'd 'Never get another ticket'. *I could use one of them*, I thought, before putting it back on the shelf.

"Oh, that's cool… I guess you heard about my break up with Valerie, didn't you?" He continued talking as we walked down a couple of isles together.

I hadn't; his relationship issues not being something that would have been mentioned to me. Even if it had, I wouldn't have heard it anyway.

"No," I said, "But I noticed that I hadn't seen you around there in a while." Shawn put another item onto the growing stack of stuff already in his basket. I wondered casually how he got the money to pay for his burgeoning basket of goodies. However, I really wasn't concerned with him enough to put much thought into what he was doing. I was just walking around talking to him as I boosted a twenty pack of lithium batteries, which is one of the main ingredients of street-manufactured methamphetamine. Soon enough, he went on his way and I meandered off on mine.

Eventually I made it over to the toy section and picked out a present for my granddaughter. Ready to leave, I started looking to round up my little clan. With the batteries on me I wanted to go out by the back register through the *'Home and Garden'* section, so I wandered back that way to look it over. When I got there, Shawn was checking out by the back register as well. He said he'd just seen Maryjo and Brandon headed out to the car. Hearing that, I stepped in line behind him at the register. I noticed he had quite a load in his basket by then.

As soon as I fell in next to him, he started carrying on a continuous conversation with me. All the while, handing one item after another over to the young clerk behind the cash register. Again, I wondered where this bottom feeder came up with the money to go on such a shopping spree. But, the sun shines on every dog's ass at one time or another, so I didn't pay it too much attention. It wasn't until I saw him writing a check and passing it over the counter, followed shortly by an I.D. that I could see right away wasn't his, that I realized what he was up too. He was working a scam and, by engaging me in such familiar conversation since I'd walked up, dragging my very *'wanted'* ass into it with him.   Extremely irritated, I walked off when the cashier started having trouble with Shawn's check and informed him that he was going to need to call in his supervisor. *What a dumb ass!* Shawn knew that I was already wanted by the Law. I was pissed that he had drawn me under a spotlight. To my relief, it didn't seem to be escalating into anything more serious as I left.

I made another round through the Walmart considering whether I should drop off the batteries I'd shoplifted or not... deciding I needed them. Everything seemed cool, so I weaved my way back through the store, approaching the same counter in the home and garden section that I'd been at before. There was no-one in line at the register and no signs of Shawn. When I walked up to pay for the birthday present that I had picked out for Haven I encountered the same young clerk: "Hey, you're back. Would you mind talking to my supervisor about that guy you were with earlier?" he asked, reaching for his long, flexible intercom mic to call him.

"What? I wasn't with that guy. I just run into him now and then. Why, what happened?" I asked.

"He was trying to pass a bad check and took off running. I'd appreciate it if you would talk to my supervisor."

"Not on your life, dude! I don't even know that guy and I'm not getting involved." I snarled a little bit to back the persistent clerk off, then turned and walked away.

From there I headed down the first isle I could where there was not any surveillance and unloaded the batteries behind a planter. Aggravated that I had people paying attention to me, but not overly concerned now that I was clean, I went wandering through the store again. I was planning to check out at another register when I ran into Echo pushing Haven in a cart. "Hey, Dad, have you seen mom or Brandon?"

I told her I hadn't, but I'd ran into Shawn and he'd told me they had already left the store. When I showed her what I had picked out for Haven, Echo informed me that my granddaughter already had the same toy at home. We walked back through the toy section of the store and spent twenty minutes, of good quality, family time together, laughing and joking with one another while I fawned over my beautiful granddaughter and picked out something else.

By the time we checked out, I had all-but forgotten Shawn and his lame-ass attempt to burn the store. Echo and I paid and left through one of the regular cashiers in the front. I was carrying Haven whilst Echo was pushing the shopping cart that contained the gift I'd purchased along with a few items that she had picked up herself.

Night had fallen while we had been inside.

As we exited the last set of sliding glass, automated doors we were suddenly approached by a couple of police officers. "Sir..." one of them said. "We would like to talk to you about the guy that you were with earlier in the store." I glanced around and saw three more officers scattered around, doing one thing or another. But, I could tell their attention was not far from me.

Standing there with my one year-old granddaughter in my arms, there was nothing I could do except stay quiet and still. I could not endanger Haven nor Echo by making any sudden moves. However, my heart was pumping out adrenaline at double-time, so that my mind was running on high octane; trying to put my current situation into perspective and assess any possible avenues of escape. With Haven in my arms, there was only one thing I *could* do, no matter the cost. That was to just stand there and say calmly: "What guy?"

At which point Echo jumped to my defense and announced that we were there as a family and that there was no one else with us.

The store manager, who had a snotty look on his face, strutted up and pointed over to a police car. "Well, that must be your wife in the back of that car then."

I looked over and saw Maryjo looking sadly at us from the back of a city cruiser. "She's not my wife," I replied, "just a girlfriend. I brought her and her kids out here for a family outing. What is she doing in their, anyway?"

The young, tall, dark-headed officer who had taken the lead on bracing me as I came through the doors stated that they had stopped her to talk about the same guy. The store's surveillance tape had revealed that we had all communicated with the man in question at one point or another. When they ran Maryjo's name through their system, they found that she had warrants. Then, while searching my ex before sticking her in the car, they discovered a few store items tucked away in her pants.

Standing there holding my panic in check by sheer grit, I thought: *are you freaking kidding me!* I told the officer, very aware that at any moment they were going to ask for my name and want to run my I.D. as well: "Look, I don't know that guy from Adam. He is just one of those people you seem to run into everywhere you go and eventually start having short conversations with. I couldn't even tell you his name. I can tell you that everything that we have on us we have a receipt for."

Echo was chiming in, in her agitated way, that we were just minding our own business. At that point I took the opportunity to hand Haven back to her and informed the officers that if that was all they needed, I would like to go to the bathroom. Naturally, they denied my request.

Free of holding my grandbaby in my arms, I checked my peripheral vision frantically for any avenue of escape; anything that I could reasonably believe would be successful. I'd already ascertained that I couldn't beat these officers in a foot race. Every one of these five officers, three white, one Hispanic and one black, were all in their mid twenties to early thirties and seemed pretty fit. Not that I wasn't, but there was a long way to go to clear the parking lot, or get around one of the corners of the building. We were standing right in the center of the huge storefront where the main doors are located. Holding onto every nerve I had, I clamped down on my flight drive and forced myself to face the scenario with the attitude and reserve that a truly innocent citizen caught in an unusual circumstance like this would. I decided that until a better opportunity presented itself, my best play was to continue to try to bluff my way through.

I was standing there in a white, wife-beater T-shirt and jeans. With all of my tattoos clearly visible. My only consolation was that I had my long, identifying hair tucked up under my ball cap. I was just lucky that the investigation was centered around finding the guy that fled and not me. For the moment, anyway.

It was about that time the officer dealing with me asked my name. I could overhear Echo talking with another officer telling him that her name was Echo Maxwell. Knowing they may ask one of them to verify my information, since I didn't have any other identification, I said loud enough for her to hear me and, hopefully, Maryjo also; sitting in the car that we were standing beside, that my name was "Jimmy Ballard." Jimmy Ballard was just one alias out of many that I had memorized, just in case of something like this. This one was actually Jenna's deceased brother's.

Just like I had figured, the officer's next request was to see my I.D.. He took it pretty casually when I replied that I didn't have one and asked for my date of birth. I popped off one, eighteen, sixty-one. *Awww Fuck...Dumb ass!*, the left side of my brain yelled at the right, immediately recognizing my mistake. One of the reasons I was using that alias was because, besides the fact that he was dead and he looked similar to me, his birthday was just a day after mine... in October. Although he was older than me, it should have made it easier to remember. However, I had memorized several names, dates of birth and social security numbers and mixed the months up before I could stop myself. *'Shit!'* I thought. I held myself back from making any panicked corrections and waited for him to call it in.

When I heard him say: "One, eighteen, sixty-one."

I jumped in and said: "Did I say one-eighteen? I meant to say ten-eighteen. You must have me nervous."

The officer just looked at me fleetingly then said into his mic: "Correction... ten, eighteen, sixty-one."

He then started asking me questions about *'the guy'* I'd been seen talking to in the store. At which point I stated, flatly, that although I'd seen him at several different stores and restaurants with my pseudo family. ...and yes... we had gotten to where we would say hello and sometimes even idly chat about nothing for a few minutes when we would run into one another, I nevertheless did not know his name. I told them that at one time I think he may had said it was Steve or something like that. But, honestly, I really never cared enough about him to remember it.

One of the officers that were standing around asked: "Are you sure... he's not hiding out in your car?"

At that point, I started to feign agitation to cover my raw nerves and subdued panic. "Hell, yeah, I'm sure he's not in my car! Matter of fact, let's just go have a look. I told you I don't know the dude, so why in the hell would he be in my car?" Echo was also spouting off similar indignant comments to their persistent accusations.

This was what the officers wanted, anyway, so the one in charge nodded: "Sure, show us."

Still desperately seeking to exploit any viable point of escape, I wanted to separate the officers and get as far away from the center of the store as possible.

When we approached my car, we found Brandon standing on the other side of the Buick. "What's up, dad? What's going on?" he asked.

The cops could see he didn't fit the description of who they were looking for, but, after taking his name, one of them called it in to check for warrants anyway. The other called in the tag number of my car.

I told Brandon it was nothing; that they were looking for some idiot we'd been seen talking to in the store. I opened the car door to show the officer behind me that there was no stowaway, hot-check-writer hidden in the back seat. Standing there with the driver's door open, the ignition key in my hand, I contemplated whether I should just jump in and try to drive off. I was now far enough from Echo and Haven to not cause them any harm. The officers, if they weren't able to stop me, would have to run all the way back to their car, or call to have one of the other officers jump into theirs. It was something that I definitely had to consider. As desperate as I was feeling, I knew that trying to bulldog my way into my car and out of there, although it was the best opportunity at running that I'd had so far, would still be a gamble with the odds stacked against me. However, things were going pretty good and riding out my bluff seemed to be my most likely chance at success. So, taking a tighter grip on my nerves, I threw the last remnants of will power I had against the door in my mind that I'd locked my panic behind when this first started. I sucked it up and decided to play it on out... and shut the car door.

One of the cops then told us, Brandon now included, to come back over to where the other officers were. As we were walking back to the front of the Walmart the other policeman asked me who the car was registered too.

I said plainly, so my son could hear and understand, not to call me 'Dad' again. "The car belongs to their real father, and he's going to kick my ass when he finds out about all of this."

The officer who'd told us to follow him back to where Echo and the other cops were waiting then inquired what the name of their real father would be?

"James... Maxwell," I replied. Not wanting to say the name *'Jimmy Maxwell,'* and set off any ringing bells.

The officer who had run the license plate was listening to the radio earpiece in his ear; the same one that they all had. "Our records show that the car doesn't belong to James Maxwell," he said.

Now I knew damned well that they did, because I was the one who registered my car at the tag office and put the tin plate on it. I obviously couldn't say that, so I just blustered out. "Hell, I don't know about all that. I just know that's what it says on the insurance verification that's in it."

The officer just shrugged and seemed to take my word for it. However, no sooner had he seemed satisfied, the cop who had originally taken my name and date of birth stepped in: "Are you sure that your birthday is on the eighteenth?"

Inside my head, I was shocked for a moment; panic threatening to overwhelm my will and push its way through that door, locked or not. The alias I was using, as I have said, belonged to my wife, at the time's, dead brother. She was the one who told me his date of birth and social security number. On the inside I was yelling: *could that girl have not known her own brother's birthdate? Or, is this cop just trying to test me for a reaction?* Not letting my thoughts show on my face, my mind calculated my response in milliseconds. Whether it was wrong or not, I couldn't act like I'd made another mistake. There might be typos all down the line, but a man knows his own birth date.

"Yeah, I'm sure," I said. I noticed a group of shoppers walking by looking at us like we might have something contagious. Glancing around at the cops, I knew how they felt.

The officer persisted: "Are you absolutely positive?" He said it with a slightly accusatory slant to his voice that I'm sure was taught to him at the police academy. In… *'How To Make Your Suspect Second Guess Himself - Class 101.'*

I answered him right back from a page out of the convict's *'School of Hard Knocks'* handbook. "I said I was sure, didn't I? I know when my freaking birthday is!" But, I was still wondering if Jenna could have given me the wrong date or not. However, I had to stand firm and just feign indignation at being questioned about it.

"Well, your State I.D. says the nineteenth, is why I asked," the officer went on.

I just shrugged, not needing to really say anything else, but thinking that I was going to choke Jenna if I made it through this. The officer shrugged also, then he and the rest of them seemed to relax. Collectively taking on a waiting, but defensive, stance.

Still looking for any opportunity to get away, I reminded them again that I needed to go to the bathroom. The lawman told me to wait. They were almost through with us, only having one identity left to clear. I settled back, crossing my fingers mentally. I was starting to feel the strain from holding my emotions in such tight constraint; to remain outwardly looking calm and impatient, but at ease, while on the inside my guts were writhing like a ball of snakes.

Then, suddenly, they all tensed at once; with a couple of them touching the little earbud receivers in their ears as the information on the last I.D. that they were waiting on came in.

"Alright, Mr. Maxwell. Turn around and put your hands behind your back," the dark-haired officer who'd been dealing mostly with me said. My heart hit the tarmac and I almost stood up before I remembered I hadn't given them that name. Then I noticed that they were all looking at Brandon instead of me.

"What the hell has he done? He's just a seventeen year old kid?" I interjected.

"Sorry, sir," the officer told me. "We have an outstanding warrant for his arrest."

They were making him empty out his pockets and asked whether I or Echo wanted to take his property with us; more or less directing the question at me, since Echo had the basket and the baby in her arms.

I stepped up right in front of Brandon to take his things. Now face to face with him and standing in the light, I was acutely aware that at any minute the police officer who stood right beside us would note the strong family resemblance.

To say that I was feeling a little impatient and in a hurry to end this little drama would have been an understatement. I stood there watching my son as he pulled out a huge bulging wallet. The officer took it from his hands to find it overflowing with I.D. cards and licenses with different faces and names on them. As the cop flipped through them quickly, I recognized that one of them belonged to Shawn. "Why have you got so many I.D.s on you, Mr. Maxwell?" the officer holding the wallet asked.

Brandon only shrugged.

I couldn't stand it any longer. "For Christ sake! I'm done!" I threw my hands up, acting like a father at his wits end with this son. More than *'acting'*, at that point, I really was pissed off. I now knew that the little chicken-shit Shawn had run by and dumped all his B.S. on my son before he scurried off into the dark like a cockroach. I turned and took Haven from Echo's arms, along with the bag she had in her hand. "Help your brother," I told her. "I can't believe this shit!" Then I stormed off towards the car; leaving her to get what property of Brandon's that she was allowed to take.

As soon as I was out of sight of the officers, I quickened my step to reach the car as promptly as I could. Then, holding Haven close to my chest, I climbed in, started the car and moved it about four parking spaces down; far-enough away that I would see the police coming if they'd had a change of heart, and close enough to rein Echo in when she came along. All of my calm reserve was threatening to shatter at any second due to the extreme tension that I'd held in check for over the thirty or forty minutes that this little drama had taken to play out. I was also aware that it was not over yet and would not be until Echo, Haven and me were well away from there.

About that time I saw Echo come out from between two cars. She was peering toward the spot our car had been in the last time she'd seen it. I was just further up the same row, so when I pulled out she saw me and hurried to get in. When she was seated, I handed Haven back to her. I realized that my reserves of calm were almost depleted, but we weren't out of the woods yet. Or, rather, the cop-filled parking lot. I once again suppressed my flight drive and slowly, but purposefully, drove to the nearest exit pointing us back towards Echo's apartment.

As I'd feared, it wasn't over yet. Just as I pulled up to the exit, one of the police cruisers fell in right behind me. My last nerve was strung tighter than a bow's string. Seeing that he didn't have his blinker on, I fought myself to keep from engaging mine. The address that my daughter had given them was straight ahead and I didn't want to appear as though I had anything to hide. However, I knew that at least one of the officers was aware I didn't have a license. I was having the desired result so far by playing my cards cool, so I took my hand off of my blinker and, when the traffic permitted, drove straight across the road and headed down Charles Page Avenue with the cruiser following closely behind. I saw the turnoff for Main Street, which I knew held the Sand Springs jail and police headquarters. I prayed silently that the officer behind me would take that turn as I drove right on by it.

I didn't realize that I was holding my breath until the cop-car's blinker started flashing and I let it all out. Echo and I watched as the car turned and disappeared from sight. I pressed the gas and hurried to the next left leading under the interstate and *away* from Echo's apartment. Knowing that my cover could be blown at any moment, I told Echo I would find her and Haven another ride home. The police now had her address and would be looking for me there as soon as they discovered I was not Jenna's deceased brother – Jimmy Ballard.

Chapter Thirty-Two

Cook Mountain

We headed back to Billy Ray's house as quickly as possible. I called a friend, Deena, on our way and asked her to meet us there. I wasn't going to hang Echo up with me any longer than necessary. She and Haven needed to be taken back home safely and I needed to get my car off the street at least. Besides... I had left Mr. Big with Billy and Pam whilst I'd gone on my ill-fated family outing.

After sending Echo and Haven home I talked to Billy about what my next move should be. The Feds would know I'd been spotted in Sand Springs and they would undoubtedly be centering their concentration for me on this part of the world now. While I waited for Deena to get back and take me to pick up Jenna from the *'Landing Strip'*, Billy came up with the idea that I could hide out at the cookers' cabin; a remote place in the woods where several meth cooks went to shake and bake their dope. It was in the forested hills on the other side of Shell Creek and was supposedly only accessible by a long, rutty dirt road that wound down the back side of one of the hills that they called a mountain.

The owner of the cabin and the land it was on was in jail and not expected back any time soon. The drawback, I was told, and the reason it hadn't been suggested before, was that different people would show up out there at different times to cook dope. Not to mention the power, water and gas were off, with winter fast approaching. However, being short of any other ideas, I agreed to check it out.

When we went and picked Jenna up I told her what had happened and what our new plan was. She was a little miffed that I had been out with my kids and ex-wife as a family, but mostly she was amazed that I had made it through the gauntlet once again.

"Jimmy, there is a reason that you're not getting caught," she speculated. "I don't know what it is, but there is a reason. A man doesn't just keep slipping through their fingers like that, without there being some purpose for it."

"Yeah, maybe," I replied, catching the scent of her hair as she tossed it over her shoulder. "I'm just glad I made it. But, if we don't get out of this part of the country, my luck will be sure to run out sooner or later."

The next day we all loaded up in Deena's black, Extended Cab Chevy and headed out to the country. From their descriptions, we needed to look over the cabin's hazardous, dirt access-road before we tried to drive my Buick out there. We drove west on Highway 64. About five miles out, we took the Phillips 66 exit – *'spot one'*, and drove down 177th. We wound our way in several more miles, behind Shell Creek Dam. By the time we'd gotten all the way out there we were seeing very few cars. The road was lined on both sides with thick trees and underbrush dense enough that we could barely see all the hills and creeks through the foliage.

At the top of the hill there was a dirt turn-off on the southern side of the road. It went over and through the bar ditch to a beat up, corrugated tin gate. It was half closed, sitting in the middle of the overgrown dirt road that led off into the trees. Billy got out and pushed it open so we could drive through. He then closed it behind us, running to jump in before we started down the thin, tire-worn trail.

In short stretches the road shaped up a little bit, but, for the most part, it was slow, careful going. The scenery was beautiful and the canopy of trees completely covered the road for most of the trip. In early October the leaves were still thick and green on the trees, though beginning to show hints of the coming autumn colors, so we weren't able to see any further than twenty yards into the wooded hills – sometimes no more than ten. *So far so good*, I thought, *just my kind of country*. Especially, when I was hiding from the Law!

The road was a winding, twisting, trek that rolled around the side of a little *'mountain'*. It climbed up and down a couple of deeply-rutted switchbacks and circled around an interesting rock formation or two. We drove for a mile and a half, then as we crept down one last eroded ravine, we came to our biggest hurdle yet: a washed-out culvert, near the bottom of the ridge. I tried to tell Deena, who was driving, to stay up high on the rocky berms that were left by the rain-runoff, passing over it with one set of tires on the exposed edge of the culvert, and the other set on the rocks. But, she allowed that she had been there before and bounced her way on through. This was why everyone thought it was inaccessible by cars, because her deep wheel-welled and tall truck barely made it.

Going at it like that, I could see why they'd told me that only people in trucks traveled out there. However, I thought I saw a way for the Buick if I was behind the wheel.

Taking notes as we went on down, I found that was our last obstacle before rounding a curve at the bottom of the rocky, tree-studded cliff. That was where we found a small clearing with a giant Cyprus tree right in the center of it. The tree probably reached as high as the top of the surrounding hills and right behind it was a little house, snuggled between the foot of the cliff and a deep ravine that ran through the thick forest along the west side.

From the way they had been talking, I'd gotten an image in my mind of a run-down, dirt-floored, ramshackle shack, but this was a fairly new construction. It was just a long, rectangular place. However, it was newly-sided and had nice, tight-fitting doors and windows. Sure, the power and water were off, and there was no gas out in the propane tank in the back, but, overall, not bad as far as hideouts go.

I could see the potential for a place to hold up for the winter and I knew that Mr. Big was going to like it out here too.

However, no sooner had I opened the door to let my little man out on to the ground, than Deena and Billy both stopped me. "Be careful, Jimmy. All the people that cook out here have just been throwing their excess chemical trash, used syringes and everything else out into the yard," Deena explained.

I snatched Mr. Big up off of the ground and handed him to Jenna. Then I wandered around the outside of the house with Billy, while Jenna and Deena went in to look at the inside. Sure enough, as we approached, between the big tree and the house, I spotted a pile of discarded meth trash along with an array of regular junk that had just been hurled out through the door. The trash-pile stretched all the way to the tree and halfway around the house to the wood-line.

We rounded the side of the house to look at the back door. It accessed what was meant to be a garage, but it had been converted into another room. *It's even worse around here,* I thought, kicking a used syringe out of my path. I spotted countless two-liter bottles, hoses, wads of tape, jars and empty chemical containers that had been used for meth manufacturing on our walk to the side door, whilst I could smell decaying trash scratching at the back of my throat, which around there even over powered the green renewing scent of the forest.

"I'm going to have to clean all that shit up before I can let Mr. Big out of the house," I told Billy, booting another syringe and an empty Coleman fuel can out off my way in disgust.

"Yeah, good luck… Like Deena said, they've been throwing this stuff out of here for a while now."

I could see by the embarrassed look on his face and the way he shuffled anxiously from foot to foot that 'he' was one of 'they'.

Now I'm not any choirboy and I can see the benefits of having a place like this to do my 'cooking'. By necessity, I was even planning on doing some myself. But, damn it, man, can't you dig a pit and throw all your shit in it? Out of respect for Mother Nature, if not for the people that own the place?

We stopped before we went in and I looked at the electrical setup. The meter was gone, but the electric tree on the side of the house was still intact, as were the lines running up from the house to the very tall pole that brought service in. I told Billy that I could jump the gap that the meter left with cables, but he ventured that they had already tried that. I studied the top of the electric pole and examined the wires coming in. I nodded. "The fuse is pulled up there. I guarantee that top line is hot. They probably pull the fuse from the transformer when there is no paid service out here. That way they don't have to fool with coming down that road any more than they have too."

Running my fingers back through my hair I said: "I bet I can get this on."

"Well that would make it livable and I have a big Coleman heater that you could bring out here to keep the chill off." Billy brushed a spider off of his arm, then pointed to the south where the power lines were coming in. "Look, bro, no-one else knows this, but if you follow those electric lines through the woods and climb down and back up the gorge over there, within five hundred yards, you'll run into a dead end road where you can park a car for a quick getaway."

I looked it over a moment before I grunted and followed him inside. We went in through the door to the converted garage. I could see that whoever had lived there before had tried to make this part into a den. They'd even put a pool table in it. But, somewhere along the way, it reverted to a store room for more junk. The pool table was now damaged and collecting dust, in those spots where there wasn't stuff piled on top of it. I could tell by what I'd seen so far that this used to be a pretty nice place and still had the potential to be so again. I was thinking that all I would need to do would be to clean the place up, get the power on and scare off the riff-raff.

Jenna came to the inner door from the kitchen, which was up a couple of steps. Mr. Big was prancing right beside her. "I love it, Jimmy. This is nice," she said, smiling and waving her hands in a way to indicate that she was including the whole layout. Mr. Big was wagging his tail and looking at me as though he agreed.

I stepped up into the kitchen and followed her through the house, swept up in her enthusiasm. Deena was trailing close behind. The living room had a big bay window facing south that I realized we would have to cover at night. It gave us a view of the big Cyprus tree and the only real access, which was from either the woods out front or the road coming in. It had hardwood floors. The only things in the room were a raggedy day bed that could also serve as a couch, a chair, coffee table and an end table with a lamp on it, which obviously didn't work. Everything in the house was dilapidated and beat-up from unconcerned abuse. The hardwood floors even had a few char marks where either a would-be chemist almost burned the place down, or someone made a campfire in the middle of the living room floor. My money was on the chemist, but I wouldn't have been shocked to find out that some idiot had thought a campfire on a hardwood floor was a good idea either.

We moved on to the bathroom, which was in good shape with the fixtures still looking new. Naturally, the toilet was a mess. I checked the water, but of course there was none. Further down the hall we found two bedrooms; empty and surprisingly clear of debris. The night time visitors probably didn't bother coming back this far into the house. It would be as black as a panda's tail out here after dark.

When Deena saw the extra bedroom she announced that she could stay out there with us. That way we would have an extra vehicle and another set of eyes. She had a point... and as I expressed to Jenna, the girl was one of the few people in the world that would know where we were, so it might be a good idea to keep her close.

Jenna said she wouldn't mind the company anyway, so we agreed.

Deena had a little friend named Aaron that tagged along just about everywhere she went. He was eighteen or nineteen, but appeared younger because he was shy and withdrawn, at least from what I could see. He wasn't a dumb or bad-looking kid, with his moon pie face and sandy, blond hair. He just didn't have anybody, or anywhere, to go and seemed lost. More often than not, he would just sit quietly in the corner somewhere until you had an errand for him to do, then he seemed pretty eager to please. Especially if Deena wanted him to do something. Anyway, he was helpful at times and he was another loose end, so he stayed too.

Deena was a pretty, dark haired, dark eyed, country girl. Her hair was cut in a bob making her look a little sassy. She came from the heart of Kansas and was down to earth. She carried herself as though she was trustworthy. However, in our world, you never know, so it was smarter to keep her and her little pet Aaron closer, where we could keep an eye on them.

Over the next few days we started moving supplies out to the remote cabin. Air mattresses, food, clothing, ice for the ice chest and the Colman kerosene heater that Billy had mentioned. I managed to get my Buick Regal down that dirt path, past the obstacles and tucked in behind the house out of sight. At that point we mainly started using the truck.

Next, I had to get the power on. We needed the refrigerator and lights. I also suspected that being this far out of town there would be a water well. Maybe with power, we would even have running water. It took a couple of days, but I finally located a twenty-foot ladder. It was still too short to reach the top of the huge telephone pole where the fuse was hanging out of its housing some three feet above the transformer.

Back in the late eighties, I was housed at a minimum security prison in Prague, Oklahoma. There they'd send us out on work crews to help the city workers of the surrounding towns. I worked for a city electrician. I learned quite a bit about how power came into a city and its distribution, as well as how to reset the fuses on a line when some poor squirrel or something had fried itself and blown the breaker.

Electricians have a long, extending pole with a hook at its end, designed to fit into the eye hole of the fuse bracket. With it you can lift fuses out and set them back in again, so they can be re-engaged. Knowing the basic idea, I knew that I could improvise. I found a long pole and climbed as high up the ladder as I could, then I hooked the eyehole and shoved the fuse back into place. There was no doubt whether there was power running through that top line or not, because sparks leapt and crackled from the initial contact and the smell of plasma wafted into my nostrils.

I climbed down and told Aaron to turn off all the breakers in the house. Then, after taking a pair of jumper cables from Deena's truck, I bridged the gap where the electric meter was supposed to be. Not knowing what the people who came before us may have done to the wiring of the place, we each took a different part of the house to monitor just to make sure that we didn't start a fire. Once we were in position I started flipping breakers. The lights came on, even the lamps that were plugged into the wall sockets.

All of a sudden Jenna yelled for us to turn them off! I could already hear the gushing water that was spewing somewhere in the house. Sure enough, we had a water well!

I turned them off then ran back to the utility closet that Jenna was pointing at. Someone had stolen the hot water tank! Water had just came spewing out of the open feed line, almost spraying her down! We laughed – we had water! Capping the line off was not a problem and the original tank would not have worked anyway, since it ran off of the propane line along with the floor furnace. I made a mental note that I needed to steal an electric one to replace it.

Shoot, with power and hot water we would be shitting in tall cotton!

After that Aaron and I, well mostly I, Aaron was turning out to be lazier than I first thought, started digging out a deep, five-by-five foot pit: a place to throw and burn all the garbage that was scattered around the house. Our little hideout was starting to shape up.

It occurred to me that I needed to get another gun when, while watching Mr Big happily chasing a grasshopper through the tall grass, I saw a good-sized mountain lion slinking into the ravine that bordered the southwest side of our cabin. There were a lot of wild animals out there. We'd seen deer and what appeared to be a small pack of wolves while we were exploring. Besides, I'd already ran off a couple of *would be* meth cooks who had wandered down the hill thinking that they had free reign like they'd had before. I let a few that I knew come cook down there. I was still taking lessons and took a little cut from what they made for letting them take care of their business, but that wasn't always without conflict either. As I said, I was no choirboy.

Anyway, it was time to pick up another firearm.

CHAPTER THIRTY-THREE

TRAP

Trudy had two or three guns out at her place. While we stayed there I would take them along with Jenna out on Trudy's land for target practice. I wanted Jenna to know how to defend herself in my eventual absence. Since we had some money and drugs in our pockets, we decided to pop in on Trudy and make her sell us one of her guns. I was about at the end of my rope with her, and the rest of the fake people I'd been having to deal with. They all had an angle or an agenda and, for the most part, were just pieces of shit. I was growing less concerned about their feelings by the day.

I unseated my Buick from the trees and bushes behind the cabin. Then Jenna, Mr. Big and I drove back up the mountain carefully and back out onto the blacktop. We caught Highway 97 and headed out to Trudy's place.

When we got there, I saw that the Jeep Cherokee that her sometimes boyfriend / trick drove was parked in her driveway. He also just happened to be an ex-cop. At the time I didn't have any reason to think, other than my wary, suspicious sixth sense, that Trudy was working with the police, nor that she had told this guy about me. He had been there before when I was around. But, as we entered this time, I immediately got a weird vibe and Mr. Ex-cop went white as a sheet and couldn't get out of there fast enough.

On top of that, Trudy told us that the day after Jenna's blunder of calling the impound yard the Feds had called her phone back.

My hackles rose instantly. "You talked to the Feds?"

Trudy went on to say that she'd told them that she thought we had left town. She was sitting there looking at me innocently and nibbling fervently on a bagel that she'd picked up from the bed stand. My eyes swept the room. The place was the same visually, but the atmosphere was palpably different. I could almost smell the tension mixed with the faint stench of… fear?

"Did they ever come out here and see you?"

"No. I just talked to them on the phone. They really want you, though. I've had people out here that were on the run from the Law before, but not anyone on your level."

I could see beads of sweat formulating on her forehead.

"It's hard for me to believe they would tell you all that and not come out here to see if I was here for themselves." Skepticism was thick in my voice. I studied her through squinted eyes… She was lying. *'Something'* was wrong. "We came out here, because we need one of your guns," I concluded.

"One is in the pawn shop. All I have out here is that rifle," she replied, pointing reluctantly toward the scoped .22 long rifle that was leaning in the corner.

"Well, that will have to do. We need it." I pulled a couple of twenty-five dollar bindles of dope out of my pocket and threw them on the dresser.

"But.. but, Jimmy, that one is not really mine," she complained sourly.

"So – give them the dope, but I'm taking it," I told her as I stepped over and picked it up.

"Where y'all staying? Can I meet you somewhere? What if I want to get in touch with you, or give you some money?" she asked. Finished with the distraction of the bagel, she was squirming nervously now.

"I'm getting out of the State. Nobody knows where we're at and I'm not telling anyone."

"But, Jimmy, doesn't anyone know? What about Billy? If the cops came messing with me, can I send a message through him that will get to you?" Trudy pushed.

"Yeah, whatever. Jenna, let's go… *Now!*" Every nerve in my body was firing off electrical impulses of warning. Something was wrong.

What I didn't know and didn't find out until later was that Federal Marshals had came out to Trudy's as opposed to calling her that next day. John from the main Federal Fugitive Task Force, out of Oklahoma City, had shown up on her doorstep. He had gained her complete cooperation by promises of rewards and so on. John had looked over her guns. He knew that I would want to replace the gun I'd lost in Pawhuska., so he hid the pistol that she *hadn't* pawned and left out the rifle, so I would have to take that instead. I now wonder, were I to have shot someone with that gun on my way out of there, if he would have lost his badge?

I also found out through the investigation that he had left his number with her and that when we'd arrived there she'd texted him and told him that we were there. John, apparently, had texted her back and told her to try and hold us up, or at least find out what she could. Then they started rolling immediately; trying to get their posse together and on the road, hoping to trap me. However, they knew that I was armed again, which meant they weren't going to approach me unless they were totally prepared.

Of course I didn't know any of this at the time, but my spider senses were on full alert for some reason. So, I just pushed by Trudy, who was stalling us by talking; wanting to hang out or go with us.

"Now - I said!" snapping at Jenna. "Get in the car. Something is up around here."

"What do you mean by that?" Trudy whined, whereupon I noticed crumbs of bagel still on her lips – accompanied by a slight tremble .

"You're right," Jenna agreed, jumping in the passenger seat. "I feel it too. Get out of here, Jimmy!"

"Trudy, you're lucky I don't have time to find out what's wrong here," I glowered at her. Something inside me was yelling for me too… just fucking *move!*

"Yeah… Jimmy. You're right. You probably should leave," Trudy conceded, looking to the ground shamefacedly.

I shot her a last glower of disgust before throwing the gun in the car and jumping in after it. We then peeled out of her driveway in a cloud of grit and dust.

Trudy lived about two and a half miles down Overlook Drive, which I knew from studying Google Earth maps was a dead end road. There was no way out using a vehicle if we took the other direction. Leaving me no choice, but to head right toward what I now felt in my gut was a fast approaching, rolling militia trying to head me off; either due to Trudy or her ex-cop boyfriend.

Making it down Overlook Drive without running into a blockade wasn't my only problem. Once I reached Highway 97 again, if I turned west, there would be six or seven more miles to go; heading straight back toward Sand Springs before there was even a turn-off. Shell Creek and its wooded hills paralleled the south side of the small two-lane highway with no access roads across it. I was going to run right into them if I went that way, which left turning east.

However, the situation wouldn't be much different. There wasn't any way to get off of that stretch of highway either. Not until I reached the end of it, where it tee'd off seven or eight miles from where I was. There, a right turn would take you back towards Tulsa and a left, well, I didn't know yet...

I knew that the task force would most likely be coming from Sand Springs. That was the quickest and easiest way out here. It was also where they had been concentrating their search for me since the Walmart escapade. With all this going through my mind, I sped as fast as I could toward the end of Overlook Drive. Jenna and I were both convinced that the police were so close that they could smell my aftershave. We had our fingers crossed and were saying silent prayers that we'd make it off of Overlook before we ran headlong into the police. When I got to 97, I hung a left and headed east; away from Sand Springs. From what we were told later, we must have just made it out of sight before the cavalry descended upon Trudy's house once again.

I wasn't taking any chances. I sweated being closed off at any moment; knowing that some of the police might be coming from the Tulsa direction. I didn't relax and, even then, not completely, until I'd reached the end of Highway 97 and took another left. I breathed a little easier when I was heading away from Shell Creek, Tulsa, as well as any approaching cavalcade of State or Federal law enforcement who may have been on their way to my last known whereabouts. Not for the first time, I wondered why they wanted me so bad.

Taking a left turn, I eventually found our way, after following several dirt-winding out of the way lanes, to Old Prue Highway. From there I was able to drive us in the back way to the now-familiar, double rutted access road and back down to the hideout.

CHAPTER THIRTY-FOUR
EYES IN THE WOODS

Safely in the woods once again, I tucked my car back in behind the cabin. I pulled it far enough into the trees that encroached up to the back side of the small house to completely hide the vehicle's presence from anyone approaching from the front.

Over the course of the next week, we cleaned up and secured the place. There was really only one direction that you could come in from. We ran electric wires out to a branch on the big tree and installed a spotlight that was equipped with a motion detector and pointed it up the drive and across the clearing.

I also ran across a battery-operated, motion-activated Halloween prop that looked like a skull, and it would blare out the theme song from 'Halloween' the movie whenever the eye-beam was broken. I hung it up on the barbed wire fence right around the bend in the road. That way, we would be warned of anyone creeping around up there as well.

After that, we just kinda settled in - hunting, exploring, target practicing. I spent a lot of time cleaning up the yard, burning the debris… and, occasionally, making a little Methamphetamine.

Maybe it was the meth… but I started getting a very uneasy feeling, like someone was watching me. I had already thinned the visitors who came out there down to a select few. It had gotten around to the general riff-raff that there was somebody staked out at the bottom of cook mountain who had a gun and didn't want company. But you never know… *Cops?*

I kept my rifle with me and when I got the vibe I would pick it up and look through the scope toward wherever the tension was coming from. Occasionally, I would unload the semi-automatic's clip into one of the targets I had sat up out in the woods; firing the rounds off in the general direction that I thought I was being watched from. Then I would give a verbal warning to anyone that might be out there. I really didn't want to shoot anybody, but I wanted whoever it might be to know that I was feeling high-strung and that if they surprised me, a shooting would very likely happen. I wanted people to be wary about coming around and it worked. I found out later that it almost got *me* shot more than once.

Like I said, I wasn't a choirboy and we were cooking Methamphetamine ourselves. I had culled through the cooks that I'd learned from and had them down to the best three; Rob, Billy and Rebecca, with Rebecca being hands-down the most fun to cook with, for obvious reasons. However, Rob or *'Uncle Cracker'*, to Jenna and I, was probably the best out of the three and it was him that was out there with me the most.

Rob was dark-headed and fairly healthy for a dope cook. Most who'd been at it as long as him generally reassembled the Crypt Keeper, or one of his kinfolk. He was pretty level-headed and didn't bug out when he was high, which I couldn't stand. Anyway, I liked him for the most part.

One night, we were shaking up a batch the way we usually did; throwing that pressurized chemical bomb back and forth between us, seeing who would break first and crack the seal to let off the pressure before it exploded. We would hold it around the door frame just in case it did; the whole time talking shit to each other about it getting scary. However, we believed that mixing the chemicals under pressure was one of the key ingredients to good dope, so we pushed the envelope and had a pretty good time doing it. The girls stayed in the other end of the house, telling us that we were completely crazy.

This night, we had just finished the hazardous part of the process and were pouring off the oil when Billy Ray called me from the top of a hill. He said that he and his buddy, someone I had only met in passing, but knew to be a meth cook too, needed some supplies in order to finish up their own little midnight cook. Billy asked if they could come down.

"Hell, no! You're not bringing anybody that I don't know down here. Besides, were busy!" I barked into the phone.

"Well, could you bring us what we need up here to the gate?" Billy whined.

"No! We don't have time," I scolded him.

I could hear the guy in the background saying, "Tell Jimmy that we will give him a cut off our shit if he'll help us."

"That fucking guy knows my *name?* What the hell is wrong with you, Billy? Bring your asses down here, then," I snapped.

I told Rob I was sorry, but I needed to look this guy over before I let him go on his way, not to mention the few choice words I needed to slip into the ear of Billy Ray.

They arrived as we were setting up to gas off our oil; the final step before *'drying'* to create powdered Methamphetamine. When they came through the door, I slapped Billy upside his head with one hand, while gripping my gun in the other. He cowered back while he gathered his wits from the open-handed slap I'd given him.

"What the fuck are you doing telling people my name and showing them where I'm at!" I snarled at him.

When my eyes turned to Tuck, the short, frizzy-haired guy who Billy had in tow, he jumped to Billy's defense. "Look, Jimmy, you can trust me. I'm cool, I knew who you were when we met before. I just didn't say anything, because you obviously didn't want to be known." He was standing there with his hands up, staring at the gun that my hand was white-knuckling through watery, pale blue-eyes. He continued: "Maybe he shouldn't have brought me out here. But, I'm a good cook. You've had some of my dope before. It was the blue stuff. And if you help us I'll throw a quarter of this batch back down the hill to you." The guy talked a good game and by now Billy was totally agreeing to kick some back to me as well, along with blubbering out a fake-ass apology.

From behind me, Rob said: "Hell, Jimmy, give them what they want and send them on their way. We have enough and I need your help, bro."

"I'll be after my shit in the morning," I grumbled before handing them a gallon jug of Muratic acid and some thin hose. Before Billy climbed back into his car, I warned him not to let anything like this happen again. I stood there feeling uneasy as I watched them leave.

Rob and I finished up the batch we'd been working on and I took my split. We then wound down for a couple more hours before I sent him on his way too. Something still wasn't right…

The next morning, which was really just the latest part of my night, I had Deena and Aaron go into town for some things from the store. I told Deena to go pick up my cut from Billy and Tuck while she was at it.

Jenna and I needed some *'alone time'*. Plus, we just wanted to hang out with one another without anyone else around. After Jenna and I had knocked boots, she rolled off the bed and started putting her clothes on. She then grabbed up her little green tennis shoes, which I'd hardly ever seen her wear, and announced that she wanted me to show her the woods.

Jenna told me that she was tired of watching Deena running around with me and hiking through the forest, shooting the gun, and so on. Deena and I only hung out like that because Deena was a country girl and Jenna... well... wasn't. As a matter of fact, ever since I let Jenna start dancing again it was rare to see her, even out here in the woods, without her four inch stiletto heels on. She would go clicking around on the hardwood floors bouncing around those high-dollar, surgical saline sacks that I'd bought her.

So to say that I was pleased and enthusiastic to see this side of my wife resurface would be an understatement. "Hell, yeah, Jenna! Let's go! You'll love it. It's beautiful out there. Besides, I need to show you how we'd have to go if we ever had to leave here on foot."

She smiled and jumped up, squeaking her sneakers against the polished wood floor. "I want to see it all, everything you showed her," Jenna announced enthusiastically, referring to Deena.

Mr. Big had picked up on the mood and was prancing around in a circle, watching us. As I put my clothes on, my heart felt light for the first time in weeks. It was good to see Jenna excited about something other than a push-up bra or a line of dope.

I snatched up my rifle and we headed out of the door with Mr. Big trucking right along beside us. It was a very beautiful morning; the smells, sounds and even the way the sun feels coming down on you, are all very acute, unique and special when you're out and the country by yourself. I was feeling all that and happy that Jenna, Mr. Big and me were sharing a moment, when I suddenly got that sense that I was being watched again.

I scanned the trees through the sites in my rifle. *Was that a guy up in that tree?* I tried to scope in on what I thought I was seeing, but I was just out of range. I couldn't get a clear shot or line of sight. Surely it wasn't, but what it looked like was a guy in a harness trying to get down out of sight when I raised my rifle - *hummmm...*

It was probably the wind, and maybe the reflection of the leaves. They were changing colors at that time of year and often played tricks on your sight. "It could be a lot of things other than what I thought I saw," I told Jenna. However, I guided us over in that direction, trying to keep an eye on the base of that tree; hoping to see anyone running away from it as we ambled around to it.

We were enjoying ourselves walking through the woods together. Watching Mr. Big discover different things he wasn't used to made us laugh and my heart smile. He was always a little braver and more curious when he was with me, but when he disturbed some ground hornets he came running back for me to carry him past the angry little creatures.

When we made it over by the tree I thought I'd seen the guy hanging from, there was nothing out of place. I decided that it must have been my imagination after all. Relaxing, we continued on up the wooded hills to the top of the sheer rock cliff that overlooked the house.

To my delight, Jenna was getting into it. When we got up to the top, I showed her where we could stand and look straight down on our place. From there we were able to see the whole front yard, as well as the car out back. Jenna was just telling me how cool it was to look down from that angle when I noticed the fresh boot print in the sod next to our feet.

"Watch your step! Jenna, look at that." I squatted down to show her, keeping her from stepping on any other signs of our mysterious interloper. There was no doubt... it was a clear print made by the heel of a cowboy boot and I could tell that it had been made fairly recently. Hell, it had rained a waterfall the night before last; setting off our Halloween skull alarm all night long, so this was very fresh. I followed the tracks as far as I could and finally lost them as we got to a place that our quarry could take to traveling on the spore-concealing rocks.

Carrying Mr. Big, we weaved our way down a couple of cutback plateaus and followed a game trail until we came out behind our temporary, little home. I told Jenna she needed to pay attention to that spot, pointing out an old truck tire that we were next to. "This is the way that we will take if we ever have to leave here on foot."

She shooed a bee away from her face. "Whose tracks do you think those were, Jimmy?" She stared up at me with worry creasing the corners of her eyes.

"I don't know, honey. Could be anybody. They don't necessarily mean it is the police, but I want you prepared nevertheless."

Taking Mr. Big, Jenna went into the house to make lunch, while I walked around to the front yard and looked up at the ridge where we'd just stood. I scanned the cliff and trees with my rifle; threatening and warning anyone who would be foolish enough to be playing cat and mouse games with me. I even took a few shots at cans and bottles that were laying out in the trees.

Not getting any response and feeling a little foolish, but still sensing something... I finally shook it and set my gun down against the trunk of the big Cyprus. Then I went back to raking more of the trash into the fire pit to be burned. All the while, pins and needles climbed up my spine.

CHAPTER THIRTY-FIVE

SURROUNDED

Unknown to me, I was slap-bang in a sniper's crosshairs, who was just waiting for orders to take me down. That is what I was told by the police later. According to them, a couple of F.B.I. agents had been instructed by their informant to follow the *'electric lines'* to the cabin where I was stowed. However, when they spotted me, they couldn't be sure if it was me or not. Nevertheless, they started setting up a perimeter.

I *had* been feeling their presence and, every so often inadvertently pointing my gun directly at them, only just escaping the order to have a .50 caliber round turn my skull and brains into so much Swiss cheese. Doubting myself the whole time. Was it the paranoia of ife on the lam? Was it the drugs? At least my unpredictability had kept them at a distance, but it almost got me killed as well. What saved my life was their inability to make a positive identification.

Anyway, what really went on across their side of the law line, I couldn't say. Whether I, "almost stepped on them," as they said, or not, I don't know.

What I do know is that I got a phone call from Della around mid afternoon. Since Philip had gone to jail a couple of months earlier she'd been keeping in close contact with Jenna and me. She was one of the few who had driven Jenna down Barnsdall Road to try and find me after the bike accident. Della was screaming for me to get the hell out of there! Deena had called her, not having the number to my phone memorized, and told her that when she was coming back out to the cabin, all the entrances were being blocked off. We were being surrounded!

I told Della to give Deena the phone number and hung up. Then I immediately picked up my rifle and stepped around the side of the house.

At the side door I hollered for Jenna. "Come on, we have to get out of here – *Now!* Della just called and said that the police were blocking off the entrances to this tract of land!"

She could see the seriousness of the situation on my face. Standing there holding Mr. Big. she held him a little closer and asked me whether she should bring him or not?

My first response was: "Yes", but then visions of that little pack of wolves and that solitary mountain lion came to mind. I didn't know how close the police were to getting us, but if they were at the gates then they would be in the woods as well. Afraid that if they did fall upon us out in the forest, Mr. Big might get kicked to the side in the arrest and have to fend for himself out in the wild, I couldn't risk it. "No... on second thought leave him here, just grab your tennis shoes and let's go!"

Jenna put Mr. Big back on the couch. Then she grabbed her shoes and came hopping out putting them on. I closed the door to protect Mr. Big and we moved toward that old truck tire that I'd shown Jenna earlier that day. It seemed no sooner than we'd got into the tree-line than gunfire erupted to our northeast. There didn't seem to be anything hitting close to us, so I held my fire and moved away from it. I was fully aware that we may be being herded in the direction that someone wanted us to go, but I had no ideas of how to avoid the suspected rat-run. Then again, they may think they have me somewhere else on this mountain, I reasoned. Regardless, we remained low, with me directing Jenna to stay in my footprints.

My phone started vibrating and it was Deena on the line. "Jimmy, where are you?"

"We're running through the woods. Where do you think we are?" I panted into the phone.

"Well, listen. Turn west away from the gunfire. I've been around this whole area three times and they are everywhere except to the west. I'll drive in as far as I can and pick you up."

Jenna was stumbling along behind me and doing pretty well, actually, considering that she was so scared she was crying. "Okay - talk to Jenna." I handed the phone to my wife, while telling her: "Keep her on the line, honey, and tell me what she says while I work our way out of here."

Jenna sniffled and took the phone. "Deena, I am soooo scared," she cried as soon as she got it. I felt sorry for her, but I was also very proud of her. She stayed right behind me, following in my footsteps and making little more noise than I was. I was moving as quickly and quietly as I could, avoiding twigs and dry leaves and keeping us on the soft, grassy spots or hard rocks that broke the surface of the ground.

Adrenaline coursed through my veins in a tidal wave and every one of my senses crackled with acute, animal vigilance. Nevertheless, I remained calm. With my mind now in business mode, my senses seemed to reach out for miles. I could hear, see, feel, and smell my surroundings almost as if I was in a Zen state. Panic and confusion were... somewhere.. far away locked behind a solid door of determination. I calmed Jenna and we moved through the woods.

I buckled down to the job of finding our way out and away from that sporadic gunfire. *What the hell was that, anyway?* There was no way that they had us in sight and there was certainly no reason for me to shoot back and give our location away. Instead, we just quickly and stealthily trekked our way west.

Finally, I came out next to a gravel service road that headed due west. Looking around a tree and up the road I could see the silhouette of a vehicle parked a mile or so away at the top of the grade. It was just sitting and watching.

Ducking back behind the tree I grabbed the phone from Jenna. "Are you on the service road that runs west next to the high power lines?" I asked Deena.

"Yes," she replied.

I studied it for other vehicles as best I could from my limited vantage point. "Are you the only ones on the road?"

"I don't know," Deena admitted. I glanced at Jenna. Her eyes were as wide as saucers. She was shaking, but holding it together.

"Come on down and I'll watch to see," I instructed Deena. Then I reached out and squeezed Jenna's hand. "We're almost there, honey," I reassured her.

She gave me a weak, but brave little smile in return. "I'll be alright," she said, brushing a cob web she'd walked through off of her arm.

Jenna and I worked our way north to the top of a cliff. It looked down on the road where it passed through the bottom of the valley. As Deena's truck came into view I could see her clearly through my rifle's scope.

"We're on the south side, by the wires," I said into the phone, intentionally giving her the wrong direction. Just in case someone was watching them.

"I don't see you."

"Is there any sign of the police out there?" I went on, scanning as much of the area as I could.

"No, Jimmy." I could see her and Aaron craning their necks looking for us to the south.

"Okay. well, we're actually over here on the top of the cliff. Look over your left shoulder." Tired of holding the rifle up with one arm so I could talk in the phone, I concluded: "Just drive around the curve real slow and we'll meet you there and get the hell out of here." Jenna was now gripping my arm as if she was afraid to let go of me. "Are you Okay?" I asked her.

She looked up and nodded, but held on a little tighter. I gave her a hug.

"Oh... now I see you!" Deena exclaimed. "Okay, we'll be there in a minute," she said. I watched her truck roll out of sight toward our rendezvous point. Jenna and I hurried to meet them.

I'm not going to lie, when we first met that girl I was a little unsure as to whether I could trust her or not. But when she rolled around those hills. guiding us, and then penetrating the enemy lines to pull us out, she became my little sister for life.

Deena and Aaron met us around the corner where there was a blind spot that could not be seen from anywhere else on the road. There Jenna and I climbed in staying low in the backseat of the big truck. Deena drove west out to Old Prue Road; passing right by a suspiciously governmental-looking car that was sitting at the mouth of the turn-off. Then we turned south and headed to Highway 64.

On our way back into Sand Springs I heard Deena and Aaron both gasp. "Man, look at all those tinted windows!" Aaron stated in shock.

I leaned up. We were passing *'spot one'*. The Phillips 66 station was swarming with parked vehicles; mostly S.U.V.s with blacked-out windows. We had just driven by the Marshall's staging area. Seeing the magnitude of the operation that was mounted against me drove home the gravity of the consequences I would face if I was caught. How many more times we'd be able to slip through the net, I didn't know. But, losing that cabin was going to hurt. Someone had given us up. Someone that I *knew*, and I was mad... Not to mention, worried about Mr. Big.

CHAPTER THIRTY-SIX
MR. BIG

I had Deena take us over to Ray and Della's house and drop us off. Ray was Della's current boyfriend. I didn't know how Phillip would feel about him, but I couldn't begrudge Ray. After all, what was going on was more Della's doing than his. He knew me from the joint as well. Anyway, Ray was about as average as a guy could get: five foot nine and one hundred and eighty-five pounds, brown over brown. He probably couldn't even point himself out in a crowd.

Over the next couple days we stayed held up there with our heads low, listening to reports of how the police were going door to door to all the remote homes out by our, now abandoned, hideout. They were showing pictures of Jenna and me around and asking whether anyone knew of our whereabouts.

With all of that police activity going on out and around the area, no-one wanted to go and get Mr. Big. I was getting increasingly worried about him. Jenna was sure that he was scared to death. I was too, for that matter; not to mention that he would soon be running low on food and water. I loved that little guy. I also knew that he lived for us and, besides being scared, he was lonely and wondering whether we had abandoned him. So, going into the third night, I announced that I was going to put my camouflage gear on and go into the woods to get my tiny friend.

"You can't," Ray said. "They are going to be waiting for you for certain. They know you left him out there and will be coming for him if he's even still there."

Well that did it. Not knowing if he was Okay, or even still at the cabin, was even worse. "I don't care anymore. I'm not leaving him for one more night. If he's there, he's feeling lost and alone. If he isn't, I will find him.

He will be in a shelter somewhere that I can bust him out of," I vowed, slamming my fist on the table for emphasis. Then I cursed myself silently once more for leaving him in the first place.

Jenna, holding on to my arm, looked up at me with pain in her eyes. "Yeah, Jimmy. You can't leave him there any longer. What if one of those animals got into the house, or the cops left the door open?"

"You're right. I'm going, Ray. No matter what! Let me get dressed and y'all can drop me off a few miles out. I will hike in the rest of the way."

"Okay, Okay," Ray said, throwing his hands up in surrender. "Let's get someone else to go. Someone with a license and maybe they can pull your car out of there while they're at it."

"Someone needs to drop their balls then! It's going to be getting dark again soon." My level of determination was obvious in the set of my jaw and left no further room for debate.

It didn't take a whole hour with Ray, Jenna and me calling around for us to find a young 'prospect' named Kevin who was willing to go after Mr. Big and my car. No-one wanted to see me go back down to the cabin myself. Of course, it may have helped that I told him he could have the gram or two of *'pure'* meth, which was floating in the bottom of a Coleman gas off jar - hidden in the garage.

Jenna rounded up Valerie-Danielle. The same Valerie that Shawn from the Walmart used to see – Dale's daughter. The little, round-faced, blonde picked Kevin up in her raggedy, Ford pick-up and brought the skinny tow-headed boy over to Ray and Della's. I gave them the whole rundown of how to get out there and what to watch for as well as explaining a few other things I needed Kevin to do, since he would be there anyway. I then gave Kevin my car keys and watched him and Valerie drive off.

I waited about thirty or forty minutes before I called. If, for some reason, they didn't answer, Jenna and I were going to have to pack up and leave Della and Ray's too. Not that young Kevin nor Valerie would necessarily give up our location, but I wasn't going to take any chances of being trapped again. Valerie answered right as they were pulling up to the front of the remote little house. I asked her if they had seen anyone who looked like the law on their way out.

"No, Jimmy, but we can see the door to the cabin has been bashed in," Val replied.

"Well, they're gone now. Just stay on the phone and tell Kevin to go in and see if Mr. Big is in there."

"He's going in now," she reported.

"Mr. Big! Mr. Big! Mr. Big!" I could hear Kevin and Val both yelling...

A couple of minutes later, Val came back on. "I don't think he's here, Jimmy. Here's Kevin," she said, handing the phone to him.

My chest was full and tight. I held my breath as I prepared for the worst. Kevin came on: "Brother, he's not here." I shook my head at Jenna, who was waiting almost on her tippy-toes. She crumbled into a ball on the bed and started crying. I felt bad enough to cry too, but I couldn't. Even though my stomach was wrenching itself into tight, hard knots of tension, and burning as if my intestines were suddenly pumped full of acid, I continued listening to Kevin. "The police were definitely here. They tore up the place and left a warrant pinned to the coffee table with a little lock-blade that I guess you had laying on top of it. They also flattened two of your car tires with a knife - straight through the white walls."

"Fucking assholes," I grumbled. Still choked up and heartbroken about Mr. Big I asked: "Are you sure my little dude is not out there? Did you look real good?"

"Yes, brother, we looked and we yelled for him. He would have came out if he was here."

I felt so bad that I was finding it hard to think and my heart resembled a woodpecker rapping against my ribs. I had made a bad call in leaving him. Everything was made even worse by the plaintive, moaning sobs of Jenna in the background. My mind was desperately grabbing on to the hope of finding him in a shelter somewhere, but right then I had to clench down on my feelings and get back to business. I hated myself at that moment.

"Listen, get that jar out of the garage and then I need you to go get a stool and open the attic. Get that bottle of stuff out of there and throw it all, except for *your* jar, in the trash pit. It's got fingerprints all over it. *Do not* try driving with it," I ordered him.

I had Kevin give the phone back to Valerie. I was going to keep them on an open line until they were all the way free of that place. A few minutes went by and I was discussing with Ray what animal shelters the cops might have taken Mr. Big to, not willing to consider the alternative. My stomach had just tightened itself down into a softball sized chunk of solid gristle. All of a sudden, I heard Valerie yelling into the phone. "He's here! He's here! I think he's found him! Yeah - I see him! Kevin's got him!"

"What? Are you sure?" I demanded with hope rising, but still afraid to drop my emotional guard. Valerie said that she was, so I said a silent thank-you for the prayer that had just been answered. To the rest of the house I yelled: "They have him! They've got Mr. Big!"

Kevin got on the line and confirmed that he had him. "He was just hiding. He came out hopping up and down on the leg of the chair I was standing on when I was looking in the attic."

"Well, just come on and bring him home." I was so happy that I just hung the phone up; forgetting all about staying on the line with them until they got clear.

As it turned out, though, they made it back just fine. They cut it close coming out of the entrance, where they saw a County cruiser pass by right before they were visible. Kevin said he jumped out and hid the jar behind a tree before they pulled out onto the highway. From then on, they said they didn't see anyone else.

The house erupted in joy when they arrived. Mr. Big came running into the house prancing on three legs and holding up his left like he did when he was really happy. It was wonderful to see him and for the first time in days I felt the band around my heart loosen.

Jenna was hugging Mr. Big to her chest with tears of happiness and relief running down her face. "I'm so happy! This was just like a made for T.V. movie," she said.

I laughed and, squeezing her, I took my little guy. "Yeah, well I'm just glad it was a happy ending." Mr. Big was licking the hand that I was holding him in and making a spirited attempt to lick my face when he could. It was obvious that he was glad to be back with his mom and dad. Anyone who doesn't think that dogs have feelings have never loved one.

They certainly never knew Mr. Big.

CHAPTER THIRTY-SEVEN
THE HILL

We hung out for almost a week at Ray and Della's. However, they were meth cooks too, and they were doing their chemistry right in their house in the middle of town. Not to mention, they didn't live there alone. James *'the chef'* lived there as well, so even though it was a two-bedroom house it was still kind-of tight.

But, that was the least of our problems. The main thing was that I wasn't making any money there. This was their setup, not mine. They did supply our increasing drug habit, but man cannot live on drugs alone. My money dwindled and, now without a vehicle, our world and avenues of escaping the closing dragnet dwindled as well. At the same time whilst sitting in a house, which had all the ventilation blocked off so the neighbors, hopefully, wouldn't smell the toxic fumes that manufacturing methamphetamine puts off, had us all higher than giraffe pussy. This sends a wanted fugitive's paranoia level through the roof and not just mine. By the end of the week, we all thought the tree-trimming crew a couple of doors down were a drug task force stakeout team.

I stretched my neck, which had developed a crick. "Ray, we need to get out of here. I don't care where, but you're taking us somewhere - a motel, I don't care. Right now," I stated flatly as we watched the tree-trimming crew drive off for the day.

All of our nerves had been on high alert ever since Ray had cracked the blinds that morning and whispered: "That crew looks suspicious. I think it's the Feds." That's all it took and we held our breath the rest of the day. Knowing we couldn't leave and be stopped, we waited for the raid - by the tree trimmers - that never came.

Ray said nothing, just standing there looking sheepish. Hell, we all were, myself included, and I was mad about it. "I can't handle this shit! I'm way too high-strung and way too wanted to be holed up in a methamphetamine factory right in the middle of suburbia. Let's go..." I repeated.

Jenna started packing up.

"Where do you want to go?" Ray asked.

"We'll go to the Executive Suites motel. It's got rooms that I can rent for three days for a hundred dollars or so. Time enough to get my wits back together." I was very aware as I said it that it would be the end of our money as well as knowing that we would now be on foot. Desperation was creeping in.

We loaded up and Della and Ray drove us to the motel. The Executive Suites motel was a two and three story affair. Its top two balconies wound their way around the front of the long, multi-sectioned building. Built like a short stairway that was laying on its side, each section of the motel stepped back a little further out of sight. We were in the middle on the second floor just out of view of the office. Della put the room in her name for us.

Jenna and Della said their goodbyes. I shook hands with Ray even though I had ruffled his feathers by prying him out of his house, but at that point I really didn't give a fuck. Jenna, Mr. Big and me hung out in the motel, finally feeling that we were off the grid. However, after the first night, I realized this particular motel might not have been the best choice. It was hooker central; with girls in high heels and mini-skirts that showed their panties and tops stretched tightly over breasts barely contained by their push-up bras coming and going all hours of the night. Not to mention, their pimps hanging out on the rails trying to look hard. The motel was bound to be watched closely by the cops. But, if we weren't out and about at night we probably wouldn't be spotted in the day time. A place like that you just have to hope that nothing happens in any of the rooms near you, because once something does the cops roust everyone in the vicinity checking names and taking statements.

We were officially broke now. With just a few dollars left, we spent as little as we could get by with. What we had, we would parlay into legitimate purchases, while Jenna and I would shoplift the bulk of what we needed. We hung out at the motel for a couple of days, just the two of us, recuperating and making trips over to the strip mall's grocery store across the street to keep us in food, but things were getting tight. I needed to do something quick.

I called Deena. She and Aaron came and spent the last night at the motel with us. I told Deena how thin our money was getting and I needed her to drive me back out to Barnsdall. I had decided to go back for the dope I'd left hidden on the hillside the month before. At this point, I *'needed'* too. I reasoned that it should be dried out by now and even if it hadn't, I could figure out how to dehydrate it. It would still be in the baggies. Shit, there had to be a good chunk of it that was still salvageable. At least I hoped there was...

She was willing to help, but strapped for cash and gas as well. So, the next morning I took her and her truck on a gas run and filled up her tanks. At this day and age it's hard to find a station that will turn their pumps on without you first pre-paying. Thankfully there are still a few. Then we went back and loaded up Jenna, Aaron and Mr. Big.

We made a quick detour to the La Quinta Inn. We all went in, acting like we had rooms there and stocked up on their Continental breakfast; carrying off as much as we could for later without giving ourselves away. Times were obviously getting tougher.

Next we drove to Barnsdall and followed the little two-lane highway out to where I had wrecked my bike. We found the road I'd spotted by the Google Maps at Trudy's, which paralleled the hunter's cabin I'd stayed in. It sat at the top of the ridge where I had left the drugs and was the only stable landmark I could spot via the satellite.

We went down that back road an extra half a mile and found a place next to an abandoned pump jack to leave the truck and the girls. Aaron and I took to the woods, hiking back in the direction of the little lodge on the hill. My lungs showed relief at sucking in the fresh air of the wild once again as opposed to the stale atmosphere of motel rooms and meth labs. I could smell the flora and it smelled good. We had to climb a tree to get our bearings a couple of times, because we were having to cross and move up one of those deep ravines that chop up the northern part of the State.

We found it in short order. Coming up on the shack from the north, we stopped there before I took Aaron to canvas the hillside. Aaron was impressed with the location of the hidden hunter's lodge. As for myself, I was studying the inside of the cabin.

It had been trashed, to some degree, before I'd got there five or six weeks earlier, but the interior was trampled now. It wasn't vandalized and it wasn't the kind of disturbance you would get from looking for something small. The room had been searched. Everything that a person could have been hiding behind or under was thrown to the side. The cot had its torn up mattress and blanket thrown over. There was a tin locker, the kind you might find in a school hallway, that was pulled away from the wall and thrown to the floor as well. *The cops had managed to track me here after all. When?* I wondered.

"Come on, Aaron. Let's go check the side of the hill. I've got a feeling we may be too late." I hadn't taken great pains to hide the sack in the first place. If they had followed my trail to this shack, then they probably found where I had lain down also. Aaron and me climbed over the side of the hill and every flat little plateau that led up to the ridge. We searched everything; moving rocks, leaves and branches, but there was no sign of it. Although, there were plenty of signs of my hunters. They had left their marks; broken branches and leaves that could be seen even after the rains.

After two hours I called a halt to the search. "Alright, let's go… If it was here, we would have found it. If they were tracking me with a dog then he probably sniffed it out from under that rock that was on it. Even without a dog they may have been able to follow my trail to it. But regardless, it's gone."

Aaron, although really hoping we would find it, mainly because he knew I would have broken him and Deena off some, was tired of climbing all over the hill as well. He nodded his agreement and we headed back to the truck, Mr. Big, and the girls. Damn it - I was getting frustrated!

"It wasn't there," I grumbled as I walked up.

"It was a long shot anyway, Jimmy. You said so yourself," Deena pointed out, flipping a cigarette butt to the ground.

"I know, but we needed it now," I replied, walking over and snuffing the smoldering snipe out with the toe of my boot.

"What are we going to do, Jimmy?" Jenna asked while wiping the sweat off her forehead from the unseasonably warm autumn day. She was peering intently at me with a concerned look in her eyes.

"I don't know for sure, but I blame our present hardships on the rat or rats who caused us to lose our cabin, and they are going to pay up before I get caught or killed." To Deena I said: "We're done here. Let's go back to town."

Things were getting harder now. The cops seemed to be closing in on me. Everywhere, not just out in the country. Even in town they had shown up several places that Jenna and I had stayed at for a night or two just shortly after we had left. They had been to Stephanie's house several more times while we were out of town. I was keeping a mental list of the people who knew of my whereabouts, or at least thought they did, before the police would show up. I was absolutely sure I had more than one so-called friend working against me. My world was closing in, like a fish in a watering hole that's drying out. To make matters worse, they were threatening everyone who helped me. If I didn't leave the State, there was no doubt that I would be trapped soon.

I liked Deena and so did Jenna. She was a little soldier. But, I could feel the jaws of the bear-trap getting tighter and, for whatever reason, I seemed to be stuck within its jagged, grasping fangs. All the more reason… I told her that we needed to part ways. Whoever was with us would also be subject to arrest. Especially Deena, if they recognized her as the one who spoiled their big operation to get me out at the cabin. The girl didn't really have anything invested, she was just trying to help and there was no reason for her to go down with us.

I had her drop us off a couple of blocks from Stephanie's. "You need to go ahead and get clear of this now. As it is, the cops don't know anything about you. Stay with us and you will probably end up in jail," I told her.

"Yeah I know you're right, big brother, but its been a helluv an adventure. Don't push me too far away, I'll be here if you need me." Then she leaned out of her truck and kissed me. I stepped back with a warm feeling for her and watched as she drove away.

CHAPTER THIRTY-EIGHT
MARTY & ANGIE

Stephanie's was the last place that I needed to be, but when it comes to trust, she's the one that I can truly count on. We circled around and came in the back way. It was dark by now and there wasn't any cops around, but you never knew who was watching. A neighbor had told Stephanie the Feds had asked the surrounding people to call them if they saw anyone around matching mine or Jenna's descriptions.

Maryjo was there. She'd gotten out of jail three days after the Walmart ordeal. When I came through the back door she came running up to me. "Jimmy - Jimmy, where have you been? I've been trying to find you for days! One of your bro's, Danny, and his wife Lisa, have a place to hide you out!" I noticed a couple people in the kitchen smoking meth from a round, glass beaker. They didn't seem to take any notice of me, so we went in, sat and talked about it for a few minutes. Danny's place was about sixty miles out of Tulsa, a couple of miles south of Cleveland, Oklahoma... "They have a nice, big four-bedroom house that they are remodeling and plenty of land. You could steal a trailer and put it out there, they said. Or you can stay with them. Whatever you want. All we have to do is get you out there."

"Sixty miles isn't far, but it's a little more than a casual drive and I don't think pulling my car out of those woods yet is a good idea. That is, if the police didn't do more than flatten the tires. Who are we going to get to drive us?"

"Anyone but Teddy," Maryjo said. "I don't think we should tell him where you are at any more." Her tone implied what she didn't say.

Now I don't like Teddy Johnson and it wasn't just because he married my ex-wife. He was, and is, a low-life piece of shit. But he was a 'Brother' and just because I don't like someone doesn't mean that I will put, or even let someone else, put a rat jacket on them without some evidence to back it up.

"Why, Maryjo? Tell me why, or are you just mad at him right now?" My voice carried a hint of disdain in it; hating the way, women especially, will throw such serious accusations around for the most petty reasons.

Mr. Big had started a fight with one of Maryjo's Dalmatians and so he ran and jumped up in my lap.

"No, Jimmy. It's not because I'm mad at him. I am mad at him, but that's not the reason," Maryjo insisted.

"You still haven't told me why I should think that he would tell on me, Maryjo." I was getting agitated and I shoved one of her dogs away who was harassing Mr. Big.

"Puppers! Leave Mr. Big alone," she yelled at her dog. Then, looking back at me: "Because... he's been saying things like - I just wish Jimmy would get caught already. He is bringing heat on all of us - amongst other things."

"Yeah, well, that is a bitch-ass thing to say. He's always been weak, you know that. But, that doesn't mean that he is a rat. It just makes him a bigger piece of shit than I already knew he was," I said, although I was starting to wonder whether she knew more than she was telling me.

"Well, Jimmy. I'm telling you, you can't trust him!"

"Okay, Maryjo. If you know something more, then you need to tell me, *now!*" I demanded.

"Well, do you remember our friend Jerry Stephenson? The guy the Feds got for all those bank burglaries?" Maryjo asked.

I said nothing. Just stared at her... waiting.

"Teddy made me swear that I would never tell anyone, but you're my kids' father. Anyway, when he was in jail last summer the Feds made a deal with him to drop his charges and let him out of jail if he would assist them in their investigation of Jerry."

"What!? Why didn't you tell me this a month ago?" I jumped up, depositing Mr. Big onto the couch in a fury ball of bewilderment. His ears turned south. "How could you keep a secret like that from anyone, least of all me? This whole time I've been running around hiding and he was right there in the shadows!" I looked at her, furious for a moment as I paced back and forth.

The people in the kitchen decided to leave. Maryjo waited until the door shut behind them. "Well, he told me that he wasn't really going to go through with it. He just told the Feds what they wanted to hear to get out of jail. I believed him, but now I'm not so sure…"

"Jesus Christ, Maryjo! Of course he's going to tell you that. Hell fucking *'yes'* he's a rat. Do you think that the F.B.I. is so stupid that they would drop the charges to let a seasoned, patch-wearing con out of jail on just his word that he would tell them something when he found out, if he hadn't already been telling them stuff? Damn. Maryjo, you cannot be that dumb!"

"Well, at least, I'm telling you *now*, Jimmy," Maryjo countered, whilst tossing her long, dark hair over her shoulder and lighting a cigarette. Agitation was present in her every movement.

"Yeah, and you've convinced me, so letting him know anything is out of the question. Even after you're done being mad at him, he's a rat for sure! I'll have to deal with him later. What are we going to do until we can get out to Danny's?"

"Well, I've got that figured out too," Maryjo went on. "If you're done putting me down, that is?"

"Let's hear it, honey. You know I don't doubt you or think you're dumb… just blind sometimes."

"Okay, well I've got some really good friends - Angie and Marty, that don't live very far from here. You and Jenna met Angie at Dale's a while back. She's the dark-haired girl - thin like me, that said she'd grown up hearing about you."

Jenna picked Mr. Big up, scratching him between his ears. "I remember her. She offered me a ride once. I think she's alright," she interjected.

Maryjo went on: "Well, anyway, you can stay there until we can get you a ride out of town. They're good people, Jimmy. No-one would know where you're at or where you're going except us."

"Yeah, and whoever we have drive us out there," I added.

"Maybe we can get Danny and Lisa to come get you," she hypothesized.

"That would be the best option. It's a good plan, Maryjo. Just don't take too long to get a hold of Danny, or get us another ride. I don't want to burden those people any more than necessary," I told her. I reached down and patted Puppers on the head to let him know that I wasn't mad at him.

Stephanie borrowed a car and drove us over to Marty and Angie's house, which, as it turned out, was only a couple of miles away.

We pulled up to a quaint, low-built, white, one-bedroom home with blue trim. It had a well cared-for lawn with a white picket fence around it, looking like any other all-American home.

Marty and Angie welcomed us like we were part of the family; making as much room for us as they could in the little house. Marty was only a little bit older than me, but he was already almost completely grey-headed. He'd lived a relatively easy life, never having to do anything harder than County time, so he was a little soft around the core. He and Angie were cool as an Albertsons' produce aisle, though, and I liked them both right away. They knew who I was, but I told them our aliases of Dirk and Julie Zimmerman anyway; assuring them that if by some chance the cops found me there, I would claim that this was the only name that they knew me by. I told them to do the same to keep themselves from being culpable of harboring a fugitive. However, I did warn them, if that happened I wouldn't be taken down easily.

Two days later I hit the evening News. Stephanie called: "Turn on Channel 5, hurry!"

We watched and listened as a couple of my worst mug-shots graced the television screen. The news castor was saying: "…believed to be armed and very dangerous, law enforcement officials say. Again - James 'Jimmy' Maxwell is just out as the F.B.I.'s most wanted *fugitive of the hour.*' He is wanted for possession of firearms, parole violations and has racked up a number of other State felonies. Maxwell is most likely carrying a gun and has been known to use aliases. He is also, apparently, a ladies' man. Reports say that there are quite a few women who seem to be hiding and aiding Maxwell in his attempt at evading capture. The Federal Marshal's Office wants to send a warning to anyone helping Maxwell that they will be prosecuted. Again - he is armed and very dangerous. There is a sizable reward for any information leading to his arrest."

As the news cast moved on to other matters, I stood there shaking my head. "What the fuck did I do that makes them want me so bad? Is it simply because I don't want to get caught?"

No-one said anything.

"Shit... Now if somehow the cops get wind I'm here, you guys won't be able to claim you didn't know who I was," I told Marty and Angie. They were sitting there watching the News with us. Marty was looking a little more nervous, but he patted me on the back and assured me that I was safe there. I picked up my phone and called Maryjo. My world really was getting smaller now. I wasn't a fish in a shrinking watering hole, I was a fish in a puddle. Maryjo answered on the third ring. "Did you see the News?" I asked her.

"I caught the last of it. Stephanie called."

"Listen, we need to get out of here. Tomorrow at the latest. It will have been three days we've been held up in these people's house and now, with that news cast, they don't even have any deniability of who I am. Hell, it will be on the News for the next week!"

"Okay, Jimmy. I'll think of something and see you tomorrow."

"Alright, Maryjo, just be here," I said and hung up.

The next day a truck pulled up in the driveway. I barely caught a glimpse of the white Ford as it passed by the window. I didn't recognize it, but the next thing I knew, Maryjo came popping in the door. "I told you I'd come," she said with a self-satisfied grin on her face.

"You sure did. I'm glad, because I hate to put these folks at risk even one more day," I admitted. "So, who have you got to drive us out there? Hopefully it's someone who doesn't know us or watch the News. The less people know the better."

"Well..." she stammered. "Teddy's driving us."

"What? Are you flipping out of your mind!" I exploded, leaping to my feet. "He's the one out in the truck right now?" She did not even have time to answer, before I went off again. "Maryjo... you spent over an hour trying to convince me that Teddy Johnson was a rat... and you succeeded! Undoubtedly, he is a rat. So why would you bring him to where I'm at; endangering me and your friends? And now... you expect me to let him take us to the last place we have to hide? I take it back, you are dumb, dumb as shit!"

"Well, you said you wanted out of here. I was just trying to help," she pouted.

I looked at her, then around the room at Marty and Angie. I was stupefied. I looked at Jenna and she was even at a loss for words. Finally I looked down at Mr. Big, "What is wrong with her, little buddy? Is she serious?" To Maryjo I said: "Get him and get the fuck out of here. I'll have to find somewhere else to go now! Thanks for your help."

"I didn't tell him where we were going yet," she said as I walked over and shooed her out the door. "I'm sorry!" was her parting words as the screen door slammed back on its springs.

Next we heard the truck spin its wheels backing out of the driveway, then burn off down the street in a cloud of classic getaway dust. *'I'm going to get that son of a bitch,'* I told myself. It was really my responsibility. Him being a patch-holder and me now knowing what I knew about him. I put it on my *'things-to-do'* list before the end came.

Night fell like a shroud on the third day at Angie and Marty's and now there was no way I could relax. The fact that Teddy was a rat didn't necessarily mean that he would just pick up the phone and run to tell the cops where I was at, but it was a ticking time-bomb and there was no way of knowing whether there was ten seconds or ten days left on the timer. So I tossed and turned, knowing that my world could explode into confusion at any moment.

At 3:30 a.m. I went back and rousted Angie and Marty out of bed. "I'm just going to have to trust you guys. With Teddy knowing I'm here, I predict that the cops will show up in the next few days. I don't want to be here if – when - they do, and you don't want me here then either. I don't mean to be rude... but I need you to get up and drive us out to our safe house before the sun comes up."

"We understand, Jimmy. We'll be happy to take you out there. We would have offered before, but we figured you didn't know us well enough to want us to know where you were going to be," Marty admitted, still rubbing sleep from his eyes.

"Well, things are different now and, at the moment, you are the only two people I *do* trust. That piece of shit knows where I'm at and I believe the cops will come. If I'm still here, you won't be able to claim ignorance of who I am. But if I'm gone, you can say that I was here under another name. When I came out on the News, I either got paranoid and left or you asked me to leave. And, we will *know* that it was Teddy."

They hurried and got dressed as Jenna and me packed our ever-dwindling possessions in a backpack. I handed Jenna her purse, picked up Mr. Big and headed out into the night.

We were rousted from our refuge once again…

It was dawn by the time we turned in at the gate and drove down the thirty-yard drive to Danny and Lisa's house.

The house was actually owned by Danny's godparents. They let him and his wife stay out there *'rent free'*, under the guise of live-in remodelers. From the outside it was a beautiful place, not bad on the inside either, just unfinished. But, we didn't know that driving down to it. It was a two-tone, grey and brown, two-story house with gables at each end of the roof. It had a big set of windows under the peaked gable facing us and I assumed the same under the one facing out north. There was a fenced in pen built off the back of the house, which housed three smiling and barking, pit-Rottweiler mixes. They made a great alarm system.

But what I liked most was the beautiful, thick tract of trees that surrounded the property. It started on the east side of the gate then swept down, around, and back up the front to completely encircle the house and its quarter-acre clearing. The wood-line grew all the way across to the west side of the gate that we'd just driven through; effectively shielding the sight side of the house from the road as well as their not-so-near neighbors, unless they were standing right in the entrance.

As we pulled down into the big, round clearing to the front of the house, Danny and Lisa heard and came out to greet us. We parked next to their fairly-new, silver Pontiac… also the godparents'. "Hey, brother," Danny smiled as we walked up. We bear-hugged and patted each other on the back. "Maryjo said that you had changed your mind about coming out?"

"Yeah, well, let's not tell her any different, Okay?"

We introduced our wives to each other. Danny was about five foot nine, dark-headed and kind-of stocky. He was a bit braggy and thought he was a little tougher than he was, but hell who doesn't? I tend to bring that out in people, although the more someone tells me about how down and tough they are, the less impressed I am. But, overall, he was a good dude. His wife Lisa was a pretty, petite Asian girl with long, dark hair. Sharing the Asian heritage was probably the reason that Maryjo liked her. I may have thought more about her, but I really don't think too much about what my friends' wives look like. I don't mess with their women, so I don't *'check them out'* like that.

"Who have you got in the car, bro?" Danny asked.

I told him.

"Can you trust them?"

"I think so... I'm gambling on it. I didn't have much choice. I'll fill you in later," I told him. Then I walked back over to where Angie and Marty were waiting in their car.

"Thanks a lot, y'all. I'm sorry I got you out of bed. I'll be alright out here. Remember what I said about if the Law shows up. They know that getting up and splitting at the drop of a hat is my M.O., so they should believe you. Anyway, maybe they won't come at all. I hope they don't, but let me know if they do." Then I shook Marty's hand and waved to Angie.

As I watched them pull up the driveway and out of the gate, I hoped I hadn't been wrong about them, because now my gamble included Danny and Lisa in the stakes; by no choice of their own.

A couple of days later I got word that the task force had hit their house that same day. They'd raided Stephanie's first and pulled up Teddy who was there. Stephanie said the Marshals who had Ted hemmed up all of a sudden packed up and left, leaving Teddy behind. The next thing they heard was that the fugitive team had shown up over at Angie and Marty's.

I was told that Marty and Angie stuck to their guns and their story. Of course I was worried, but I was done running for a minute and I really didn't have anywhere else to go right then. However, time proved them to be good people, in the few weeks that I was in an out of Danny and Lisa's, theirs was the only place the Law never looked. The tally for Teddy was getting higher and higher.

CHAPTER THIRTY-NINE

THE LAKE HOUSE

We relaxed at Danny and Lisa's; hunting, hiking and shooting firearms. Danny had a couple of shotguns and an SKS that he gave me, which I toted all over the wooded hills that surrounded his house. It was quite a bit louder and harder to hide than my rifle, and ammunition was scarce for it. When we'd go into town I would still stick with my lighter .22 semi-auto. I'd cut the buttstock off and the barrel down to make it easier to conceal knowing that, sooner or later, I was going to have to make a trip back to Tulsa and deal with the vermin that had been making life so hard for Jenna and me.

I'd been telling Danny about how things had been going. We talked about the cabin in the woods; how we'd got surrounded and discussed who I thought the informant could have been in that circumstance. I had five suspects in mind, with Tuck and Billy right at the top of the list. I also enlightened him about Teddy and that he had turned out to be working for the Feds all along. I told him that I would need to deal with them all before I left and that, if I played my cards right, I'd pick up some traveling money in the process.

"Brother, you need to let that shit go and just leave the State," he said concernedly.

Danny and I were standing in front of his house. I watched the tall grass sway with the Autumn breeze as it blew pleasantly down through the clearing. I thought about the *'feel'* and *'smell'* of freedom. I knew he was right. "How am I supposed to do that without any money? No... I'm not going to let those snitching pieces of crap get away from me that easy," I told him, pushing logic aside in favor of principal.

Danny lit a cigarette and regarded me through a cloud of exhaled smoke. "Hell, you're not even sure who it was that gave you up at the cabin," he said.

"Well, ten people knew I was there and five of them I can cross off of the list. Two of them helped me to get out. Three more I can discount for other reasons. The other five - the rat is one of them. We'll start with the most likely and work our way down the list."

Danny shot me a questioning look.

"I won't kill them. I promise. I'll just fuck them up and take whatever cash they have to help me get out of the State. So what if I get some of the wrong ones? The whole five are pieces of shit, anyway, and I'll get my man in the process. The rat is counting on the fact that I can't be sure. I just can't let it go down like that," I concluded with a disgusted shake of my head.

"Okay, bro. I understand." He brushed a grasshopper off his arm that had jumped out of the grass and went on: "But you have a lot at stake. Have you ever see the movie *'Heat'* with Robert DeNiro? He'd have gotten away if he hadn't gone back."

I didn't say anything.

"Well, give me the list and I'll find out where those ones are that you don't know about and try to locate Teddy for you. You and Jenna can go stay at mom and dad's lake-house for a couple of days; fish and think things through," Danny concluded.

"Sounds good to me," I agreed.

We went out to Danny's mom and dad's - his godparents he called them. Buck and Susan Oakhearst were not really any kin to Danny and I don't know why they looked after him the way they did, but they did. His dad instantly became Uncle Buck to me as well. They were an older, good looking-couple with lots of toys and money that they had made in the dental industry. They lived in Ponca City, which is another fifty miles northwest of Cleveland, Oklahoma. There we got the keys and a note from Buck granting Dirk Zimmerman and his wife permission to stay at the small lake-house that they owned on the shore of Lake Ponca. From there we drove out to have a look.

Lake Ponca is remotely attached to Ponca City. I could tell once we were dropped off out there that we were going to be on our own. Just what we needed, well – what *I* needed... I'd made a mistake by running and by now I knew it. The thing about doing stupid shit is, even after you see it, you can't take it back. I kept those thoughts to myself, but wished every day that I could. I felt as if I was hanging from a thousand-foot ledge by my fingertips and I was watching them give out one at a time. The clock was running out. I needed to think and the lake-house was a perfect place for thinking.

The side of the lake that we approached from was lined with lake houses; all with their own private little docks and barbecue grills. Some were nice, two-story, elaborate affairs and some, like Uncle Buck's, were just square, little wooden sheds while others were no more than four poles that supported a roof over a picnic table. But, just having property out there was a sure sign of success, regardless of the size of the structure. Buck's was small but pleasant. It sat right on the water's edge with a sturdy, fenced-in porch and its own little wooden dock.

At this time of year, breaking into November, we had the place to ourselves, the whole lake it appeared. Although the days were still warm enough for the trees to have their leaves, the water was cold and people didn't want to get out on it, even in boats. Not just for recreation, anyhow. We saw no-one as we wound our way around the wooded back road that accessed the continuous row of small waterfront properties. The way I liked it. This was going to be peaceful, I thought.

Once we arrived at Uncle Buck's landing, Danny showed me where to unlock the utility box on the electric pole. We turned the power on. Then we walked down the side of the hill to the gate that accessed the porch and front... well, *only*, door. I was carrying Mr. Big until I saw what we were going to be dealing with, while he squirmed around anxiously in my hand. The porch/dock looked solid enough. There were no holes in it that my little man would fall through. However, it was fenced in by a three-foot tall chain-link mesh that needed a couple of places repaired before I would trust it to contain my curious, little pooch safely. The front door, and the wall next to it, had a fist-sized hole about waist high where a big logging chain was draped though them and fastened with a large padlock to keep people out. The porch was empty, with all its patio furniture stowed away inside. The only thing on it was a big, yellow, six-by-four foot rubber inflated raft. It was the kind that just has straps across the bottom instead of a full floor, so your legs can hang down into the water.

"They had someone break in here earlier this year," Danny informed us. "The only thing missing was a fishing pole and whoever it was left this raft. Dad thinks it was a pretty fair trade, haha. Anyway, that's why the big chain."

Danny unlocked it and we went in. The inside was crowded from the plastic tables and chairs that went on the porch, but once we pulled them out it was accommodating enough. What was left in the small, rectangular shack was two metal frames with cushions that served as couches, which could be pulled out and flattened into a couple of double-beds. There was a radio on a shelf and five or six fishing poles leaned up in the corner.

"Well, at least they left *some* fishing poles," I directed at Danny.

"Yeah, they just took one," he said, with a bemused grin. "That was one conscientious thief."

In the corner on the other side of the little hut was a round kitchen table with four chairs. Right by it, sharing the north wall, was a small square framed alcove that was no bigger than a travel-trailer's bathroom. It served as a kitchenette, with a few drawers under a sink-less counter. Above the counter was a window, the kind that slides - sideways. Of course the thing that I noticed first was that it was too small for me to get out of if the need arose.

Directly across from the counter was a refrigerator, which had little reminder notes stuck to it with magnets that looked like Disney characters. The space was barely big enough to open the refrigerator door without it touching the counter on its swing.

The whole lodge was smaller than a one-car garage. It was still cool, especially in the summer months. I could see the whole front side could be unlatched from the bottom and stood on poles out on the porch, making the wall an awning of sorts.

"Nice... this will be great," I said, setting a grocery sack down on the kitchen table that I had in one hand and Mr. Big down on the daybed with the other.

"Yeah," Jenna agreed, setting the other grocery sack down. "Just don't forget I'm running low on cigarettes."

We hadn't stopped at the store. Uncle Buck and his wife had loaded us down with food out of their own cupboards. Lisa gave Jenna the rest of her pack. Then Danny said they would try and come back and check on us the next day "...two days at the longest. I wish we would have picked you guys up another phone, but they don't work worth a damn out here, anyway."

"Don't worry about us. We'll be alright… we need to be off the grid for a little while. See you in a couple of days." I shook his hand and watched him and his wife walk out the gate and start up the hill. "So what do you think, Jenna?" I asked as I turned to her. "Those two and their parents - who don't even know who we are – are the only people on the planet that know where we're at right now. I think that we can finally relax. Don't you?"

"I think… I want you to teach me how to fish!" Jenna beamed at me whilst she bounced from foot to foot like a kid at Christmas.

"You got it! We may have to dig up some worms, though. Those lures aren't going to work worth a damn out in that calm dark water," I told her.

Lake Ponca was a good-looking lake; surrounded by trees set in amongst a bowl of rolling hills that ran right into town. It was a big lake and stretched out of sight toward the north. I could see the southern end, a good two miles away, and it was at least a half a mile across. Calm, dark and cold - just the way fish like it!

We settled in and got our food stored, then I fixed the holes in the chain-link fence around the porch. I didn't know what was out here and I didn't want Mr. Big finding something under one of these docks that might drag him into the water, or carry him off. But, try as I might to close up the holes, he would keep popping up next to us while we were digging and turning over rocks to find worms. I gave up and just made sure to keep a close eye on him.

Turns out, Jenna loved to fish, and we were at it late into the first night. We were trying to dig up more worms when I heard Jenna whisper to me under her breath: "Don't freak out when you see the cop standing at the top of the hill."

I glanced at her. Then I heard someone say: "Hey, what are you folks doing down there?"

I stood up and looked at him. He might have been a County cop, but more likely a game warden. He was older than me, slightly balding and fifty pounds overweight. My mind was automatically assessing him and my chances of getting away on foot in that first look.

"Teaching her to fish." I laughed. "I got her started and now she doesn't want to stop."

"Yeah," Jenna confirmed. "I love it! We were just digging for more worms."

"Where's your car?" the County man scratched his head as he asked the obvious question.

"Uncle Buck dropped us off out here. He is letting us stay in his boat-house a couple of days as kind of a *'marital get away'* - if you know what I mean." I smiled, holding my hands up in mock surrender. "But all she wants to do is fish!" I laughed again.

He stood there for a few minutes then kind-of shook his head and laughed himself. "Well, I just had to check. I hope y'all don't have any problems out here, because it's a ways to town."

"We'll be alright. Buck and Susan will be out here tomorrow to see if we need anything," I assured him.

"Okay then, you two have a good night," he waved as he walked off.

"You too, Officer," I replied as I went back to digging in the soil. I wondered if he would come back when he had thought more about it. He never did.

We went on fishing and had a good and peaceful time for two days and nights; never catching a single fish! We used worms, we used lures and even spiders as bait, all to no avail. But we did have a good time trying.

In the middle of the second full day, Jenna announced that she was out of cigarettes. Our food was starting to get low as well. I kept expecting Danny and Lisa to show up at any time. Danny had said that cellphones didn't work that well out there, but I was still kicking myself for not taking the time to get one.

Finally, we decided to walk to the store. I left my gun and Mr. Big in the boathouse and chained the door shut. I hung a note on the lock, then Jenna and me took off walking. Shit - it was a long way just to get off of the lake's access road. It must have been a couple of miles' hike with us never seeing a soul.

The only sign of life we did see was a large, tan, mountain lion that we walked up on sitting out in the middle of the road. He watched us while he flicked his long tail. "Look how big that cat is!" Jenna gasped.

Hell, he was still twenty yards from us and I could tell his head would come up to my waist. "That ain't no cat, honey," I cautioned her. I pulled my knife from my pocket and put myself between her and the animal. The mountain lion's ears twitched at the sound of the three-inch blade snapping open and I couldn't help but think that this was one knife fight I was sure to lose. But he just looked at us; following us with his head and swishing his tail again, as we walked on by. I breathed a sigh of relief when I had Jenna clear of the danger. However, I was acutely aware of the fact that we were going to have to walk through this same stretch of road on our way back.

We kept going. It was still another mile and a half to get to the nearest store. Half way into it, we heard Danny and Lisa honking their horn at as they drove up behind us. They had got our note and came looking for us. I was damn glad to see them. We climbed in and they drove us back to the lake-house. They had stuck a couple of packs of Marlboro 100's in the chain for Jenna and put a sack of McDonald's burgers and fries on the plastic patio table we'd sat on the porch; just in case they missed us.

Danny pulled me to the side as I scarfed down a burger. "I found everyone except Teddy." He looked at me with an *I'm down for what ever you decide*' stare and went on: "Do you want to stay out here a little longer or do you want to go handle this?"

I stared back and to Jenna I said: "Let's get our stuff together. We're going to pay a visit to Tulsa."

CHAPTER FORTY
TAKING OUT THE TRASH

The idea was to drop the women off at Danny's place before we went to Tulsa, but they weren't having it. If we were going to town, they were going with us. What the hell, I thought. What I had in mind should be easy-peasy, anyway. So, off to Tulsa we went.

When we got to town, we chased down a few patch-holders and friends trying to get a lead on Teddy, but no-one knew where he was. We stopped at a gas station where Danny and me had a conversation and he gave me the run-down of where the other potential snitches were. "Tuck and his wife/prostitute live off of 21st and Sheridan in a middle, bottom-floor apartment. Devin that dike girl and Bud live together in a house off of Charles Page Boulevard. Bud's a weirdo - probably a child molester. He has four different boys that live with him; all runaways between twelve and sixteen. They're not too far from where Della and Ray just moved too."

"I always did get a weird vibe from that guy," I said. "When did Ray and Della move?"

"I don't know when, but I'll show you where later," Danny said. "The other guy Steve'o; he's on the west side also, but on the south side of the river. And I guess you know where Billy is," he finished.

"Good job. This might be too much for the girls. Maybe we should drop them off at Della's after we hit Tuck's. But we need to go ahead and get him before we do anything, since he isn't far from where we're at now. We can get Bob on our way to Sand Springs and nail Billy's ass to the wall on our way back out of town. I will worry about Steve'o later. He's really low on the suspect list, anyway," I said.

"Whatever you wanna do, Jimmy," Danny shrugged. "It's your call."

So with that plan in mind we headed for Tuck's.

The apartments that Tuck, his wife and his twenty-five year old son lived in, who was also a meth cook, was just one long, two-story building that sat a block off of 21st Street, behind the Hibdon's tire store. Its apartments were built back to back in the single building. So both sides were spaced along with little alcoves that serviced the stairwells to the upper floor units. The entryways to the ground floor rentals were accessed by stepping in the alcove under the stairs, where there was a door on either side.

It was a raggedy area, with no trees and only a few bushes. There was an old 442 Oldsmobile sitting on blocks in the parking lot next to an over-flowing trash dumpster that stank of rotting meat. We parked on the end where there wasn't any doors, stairs nor alcoves. The only thing we had to watch out for were just a few windows. It was night-time and in this part of town and in this complex, everyone valued their privacy. So, all the windows were covered with either thick curtains or tinfoil.

When we stopped I reached under the seat for my gun. That was the first time the girls realized that we were up to no good. "What are you doing, Jimmy?" Jenna asked nervously.

"Just sit tight. We'll be right back. I'm going to get us some traveling money."

"Are you crazy? You're the one that said we needed to lay low and not make people any more afraid of you than they already are. You said scared people are dangerous people. This is just going to make them up the ante on you," Jenna cried.

She was right. I had told her that and it was true. The more afraid people became of me, the more they wanted me off of the streets. Fear was a double-edged sword. It may hold your enemy in check, but in their hearts they will always have a knife at your back, and if you become vulnerable enough you will find it sticking in your ribs. I was very vulnerable; walking a tightrope of freedom that was little more than a thread; with people cutting at both ends, while others were anonymously throwing stones at me to bring me down. By upping the fear-factor I was just adding fuel to the fire. But... I was mad now. More accurately, I was sensing defeat and hopelessness is not a corner you want to push me into. Short of being able to win the game, I had decided to at-least take out as many of my opponent's pieces as I could in a self-sacrificing tantrum of destruction; like the guy who jumps up and knocks the whole chessboard over, because he sees no way to win. I was frustrated to the point of desperation.

"I'm not going to let these bastards get away with selling us out. We've got no place of our own because of them." I could feel the flames of anger heating up in my guts.

"You don't even know for sure who did it."

"That's why we're getting *all* of them," I stated. "I'm not going to let the snake get away with doin' us like that. Especially by counting on me being such a good guy that I wouldn't risk getting the wrong person to get to him. They are all backstabbing cut-throats, anyway." She opened her mouth to protest more, but I cut her off. "It is what it is. Now shut up, I'll be back in a minute."

Then I got out and closed the door. I could see the tears in her eyes and hear her muffled voice as she yelled at me through the glass. Bringing them along was definitely a mistake, I realized. I could tell Danny wasn't getting much more support, but at least Lisa was quieter about her objections.

He shut his door and we walked around the side of the apartment building. Tuck's was the second set of doorways from our end, along the west wall. I was holding my gun down to my side with a T-shirt wrapped around it, as if the shirt was all that I held. I could feel my pulse quicken as my adrenaline kicked in.

Walking up it was hard to tell what color the building was painted. In the cold darkness it just seemed drab and grey. Once we stepped around into the light under the stairs, I could see that the building was overall tan and the trim and doors a deeper brown. There was trash under the bottom couple of stairs; a crushed Pepsi can and miscellaneous empty food wrappers that gave off the smell of decay. There was a round, three-legged grill with one of the wheels broken off, and right by the far door was a soiled diaper that had been kicked in the corner. *Nice...* I thought.

"That's the one," Danny said, pointing at the door on the left. I looked the door over. It looked solid and heavy. There were chips in the wood and paint around both the door and frame. I could see that the trim had been blue in a previous life and yellow in another. It had a big, round, brass keyhole three quarters of the way up, which represented its dead bolt. The door handle itself looked sturdy and had a keyhole in the center of it as well. My guess was that they were both locked, with maybe even a chain lock and/or a propped-up bar inside under the door handle. They were known to have money and drugs here. Tuck most likely stayed prepared to either be raided or robbed.

It wouldn't matter. With the two of us on it, the door was coming open. Not wasting any time I shook the T-shirt off of my chopped-down rifle. I felt the familiar rush of blood come on that gives you the excited, butterfly sensation in your stomach before doing something dangerous. Knowing that there was the real possibility of being shot down coming through the door, I set my mind to it, stepped back and nodded at Danny. We both planted an alternating foot, my right and his left, in the center of the big brown wooden barrier. Crunch, went the door frame.

Where the locks had been engaged, the door and the wood around it just split and splintered. There was something else keeping it from coming all the way open, but another boot to it and we were in before the splinters stopped splintering.

When we entered we burst right into the living room of a small, compact apartment. The living room was laid out to our left, with the hallway to the bath and bedrooms directly ahead. To the right was the kitchen. A startled Tuck was against the far wall of the living room gawking from an easy-chair that normally sat with its back lined up with the hallway. Tuck wasn't sitting very easy in his easy-chair now. He'd spun around so hard that the chair's backrest gouged a groove in the sheetrock behind him. His back was against the wall and he was trying to get as far away from the explosion of his front door as possible. I came in with my gun raised. Danny cut across me to get to Tuck and knocked him and the chair the rest of the way over.

I heard someone screaming in the kitchen and moved my gun to cover that room. It was Tuck's wife and *'working girl'*. She screamed again and dived for the floor as I swung the firearm towards her. Her long, skinny arms and legs seemed to be moving in all directions at once as she scrambled behind the table and chair legs; frantically trying to put them between herself and the trajectory of my locked-on barrel.

Hearing the crashing of the door and the screams from the kitchen, the son, I presumed, came rushing out of one of the bedrooms into the hallway. "Down on the fucking ground," I snarled at a tall, gangly kid who had left over acne scars on his face and neck. He got down to comply immediately and lay on his stomach with his hands over his head.

"What do you want, Jimmy?" Tuck cried anxiously as I turned my attention and my barrel back on him.

"I want to kill your ratty ass... is what I want. But I'll just have to settle for whatever you've got in your pockets and a couple of your teeth," I said and I pulled a pair of pliers out of my back pocket. My voice was sounding like death, full of the anger and frustration that had been building since Jenna and I were rousted from our remote cabin on Cook Mountain.

Tuck's wife started crying and wailing. "Please don't kill him!" she begged me. To Tuck she yelled: "What did you do? Please, Sir, whatever he did, please don't kill him!" she continued pleading with me.

I ignored her and glared at Tuck. "You piece of shit, my world has gotten real small because of you!" I stepped up and put the barrel of a gun to his forehead. "I'm real tempted here," I told Danny.

"No! Don't kill him. Take whatever you want," his wife screamed from underneath the kitchen table.

"Tell me why I shouldn't, Tu-ck'a," I snapped with a click on the end of Tuck and staring down at him over the top of the rifle.

"Because I didn't turn you in, Jimmy. I swear it." He looked me straight in the eyes without even looking at the barrel of the gun, which was pointed right at the bridge of his nose. "I swear - I am *not* the one that did that," he repeated.

"Then why didn't you send my money and cut that day?" I asked, pressing the gun barrel against his forehead.

"I did. I gave it to Billy that morning," he stated, still maintaining eye contact, except for when he squeezed them shut, because I pressed the gun harder into the flesh of his skull. "I swear I didn't rat you out."

I realized then that the son of a bitch was telling the truth. At least the part about not dropping the dime on me. I stepped back. "Shut up in there," I yelled at the blubbering woman who was still hiding under the dinner table. "He's going to be alright." To Danny I directed: "Check his pockets... he may not have told on me, but he still owes me money. Take that phone too. I'm going to need it for a couple days."

Danny rolled Tuck over and pulled his wallet out of his back pocket. When he flipped it open he came up with a handful of bills. Then Danny handed the money and the phone to me. "Do you want me to check the son, too?" The boy had just been laying there the whole time.

"No, leave him."

Tuck's old lady whimpered: "Thank you, Sir, for not killing him… there's money in my purse."

"I don't want your money. You don't owe me. He does," I told her. "You can quit crying now, he's off the hook. He ain't the rat." I turned my attention to Tuck. "You may be telling the truth about the dope too. You will have to settle up with Billy about that yourself. But you will have to beat me to him." I jerked my head toward the door and told Danny that we were done there.

He backed away from Tuck, went around me and out the door. I kept the room covered as I stepped backwards out right behind him. He was already moving around the front as I was wrapping the T-shirt back around the gun. Then, walking quickly, but nonchalantly, I followed Danny back to the car. We were starting to hear police sirens coming from the north and east; indicating that they were converging on where we were.

We hurried into the car. Danny started it and pulled out onto 21st Street as fast and calmly as he could; wanting to blend in with the evening traffic before the cops started showing up. We made it onto the road smoothly enough, but our wives were livid. "Are you crazy, Jimmy!" Jenna yelled at me again. Then she repeated everything she had said to me before I'd left.

"Hush up, we needed to do this," I grumbled, handing her the phone. "Be careful who you call, because if the cops do get involved they will be able to see what numbers we've called with it." Then I thumbed through and counted the money. I could hear Lisa and Danny also arguing quietly up in the front seat. *This was not going to work,* I thought. *The women shouldn't have been with us in the first place. It was my fault.*

There was four hundred and fifty dollars in the folded-over wad of money that Danny had taken from Tuck's wallet. I handed Danny two one hundred dollar bills over the front seat and told him we should drop the girls off at Della's place before we hit the next one. Danny was trying to tell me that he wasn't going to take the money - that I needed it - but he could not get the words out, before both women let us have it.

"*The next one!?*" they both yelled at once.

"Oh hell no… Jimmy! I could end up going down with you! Don't you care?" Jenna wailed while giving me a look designed to transmit the maximum dose of raw guilt possible.

Lisa was telling Danny up in the front seat: "Yeah, we can get in a lot of trouble too, honey."

Jenna had Mr. Big clutched in her arms. He reached out and licked my hand letting me know that he, at least, understood. Jenna's attitude was starting to grate on my nerves. Wasn't she a big part of the reason I was in this position in the first place? 'Romeo and Juliet...' wasn't it? I told Jenna: "Of course I care. We tried to leave you at Danny's place, but you all wouldn't have it, remember? I don't like this any more than you do, but it's something that needs to be done and we needed our money. We'll drop you off at Della's," I finished as Danny announced that we were almost there.

"No you're not. I'm going with you. You're going to get caught and you're going to leave me again!" Jenna cried. I was sitting there watching as tears rolled down her face and thinking that she was right. The end was coming - one way or another - and there was no way, it seemed, to stop it. I felt like I was a train stuck on a track with no way to turn left nor right.

There was a similar conversation going on up in the front seat as we pulled into Ray and Della's new place. Danny and I got out of the car. Then, a little sadly, he said: "I don't know about this, Jimmy. The girls, I mean. I don't know if Lisa would wait for me if I went to jail."

I was listening to him, but watching Jenna, still sobbing, through the back window of the car. The hard truth was, that no matter what was said, or how this started, I could only blame myself. I needed to make sure that Jenna and the others didn't get caught in the fallout.

"Don't worry about it, Bro. You all have a pretty good life out there. I shouldn't be dragging people into my drama, anyway. Go on... I'll take care of this stuff myself."

"Are you sure, Jimmy? Because I'll stay. I've got your back. Better yet... you should come with me."

"I'm sure, Brother. I've got yours too."

He answered by shoving the bills back in my hand. "You're going to need this more than me."

I turned and looked at Della standing on the porch. I was asking myself: why was I still in Oklahoma let-alone Tulsa? At about the time that she mouthed the same question to me from the porch.

I heard Danny telling Jenna that I had decided to stay and that they were leaving. I saw Lisa squeeze his arm in relief. At least they were out of this, I thought.

As Jenna was getting out, Danny stepped back and asked me one more time while he was popping the trunk: "Are you sure about this, Brother? You really should come with me." He had true concern and compassion on his face.

"I'm sure. You guys take care," I said. Then I pulled my backpack and a sack of mine and Jenna's stuff we'd taken to the lake out of the trunk. After I retrieved my rifle from under the back seat, I watched as Danny and Lisa got into their silver Pontiac and drove off. "You probably should have went with them," I told Jenna.

"No, Jimmy. You're not leaving me," she said.

"Time is short now and I feel... *doom* coming. And I am at a loss to stop it," I could feel the sadness in my eyes.

"All the more reason to stay with you," she went on.

Sometimes she still surprised me...

CHAPTER FORTY-ONE

DOWNWARD SPIRAL

As we walked up the short sidewalk that led up to Della's new digs, I took in the quaint little place; light blue trim on pale yellow paint, the yard was clean and the grass was cut to lend the air that just-mown aroma. It even looked like it had been roofed recently. For a drug addict, Della always seemed to maintain a semblance of class. We climbed the three steps to her small porch and Della repeated - out loud this time: "What are you doing still here? You should be long gone!"

"Yeah, I know. I have a couple of things to finish first," I said. *'Including getting my car out of the woods'* I reminded myself. I was tired of being dropped off places.

"Well, you're crazy; the heat has been turned up around here since you've been away." She was standing there in jeans and a T-shirt with a worried look in her green eyes.

"It's really going to get turned up around here if Jimmy has anything to do with it," Jenna spouted off. She gave me a sidelong glance before *'huffing'* and tossing her long, brown hair over her shoulder. Then she went on, telling Della, just what I'd been doing.

I didn't really care at this point. I was intent on setting some examples, anyway. "Yeah, and next on my list is Bud and that little bitch that lives with him. She told on Deena's boyfriend last year and she's why he's doing time now. That puts her pretty high on the list of suspects and we've already talked about what I think about Bud." Looking directly at Della I went on: "Danny told me that you told him where they lived? I need you to show me too, Okay?"

"Well, it was really Kevin; the young kid that went out and got Mr. Big for you, who knows - *he* told Danny. Kevin used to live with Bud, but he saw some weird shit going on over there and left. He's been staying with us. As a matter of fact, he's in the house right now."

Cool. Maybe my luck was changing, I hoped. I went on inside. Ray was geetered out on meth and hiding in his bedroom. Kevin was in the living room. I told him what I suspected and that I needed him to show me where Bud lived. Jenna was steadily complaining, about my intentions in the background; trying to convince the bony youngster that he shouldn't help me - *'for my own good'*. Ignoring her, Kevin nodded his blond head and agreed to show me, but allowed he needed to go do something first. While he went to go handle his business, we settled in, letting Della wash our clothes and feed us.

I looked around Della and Ray's new place. "It's a lot smaller than you're last house, but it seems nice," I told her.

"Yeah, I like it. It's easier to keep up with," she said, lighting a cigarette and smiling a sweet smile at Jenna through the smoke she exhaled.

I kicked back on the couch and waited on Kevin. I fell asleep listening to the murmuring sounds of Jenna and Della's voices talking into the night.

Della and Jenna were good friends. They even had a little side affair going on. That was Okay by me, but I still saw Della as my friend Phillip's ol'lady, so, as much as Della and Jenna wanted me to, I wouldn't participate. That's just one of the rules I live by. Including anyone else was out of the question as well. Not that either of them wanted to anyway. I left them alone. They were up late into the night.

I woke as the sun was coming up, sweating and breathing hard from the dream - nightmare, I'd been having. I was trapped and suffocating... falling? Mr. Big was stretched out beside me, almost under me. I don't know how he survived sometimes. He had to have a collapsible body or something. I saw his little feet moving and wondered if he was dreaming too. Probably of riding with me on my Harley – his head hanging out the collar of my leather coat and his face in the wind. I smiled. I was envious, sure that his dreams were better than mine.

I heard movement in the kitchen so I got up. Della was still awake. She had our laundry folded neatly in a chair and was now in the process of washing her dishes. "Did Kevin ever come back?" I asked her.

"No, Jimmy. He never did."

"Where's Jenna?"

"She's passed out in the spare room," Della said with a little self-satisfied smile. I noticed that her sandy-blonde hair had grown past her shoulders since I'd first met her and it was a little mussed up from the night before. "You know Phillip wouldn't mind if you joined Jenna and me, Jimmy. After all, I am with someone else now."

"Maybe not, and I would love rolling around with you two, but I would mind if the shoe were on the other foot. Friendship is a two-way street," I pointed out. "Anyway, I'm going to let her sleep in. I need you to take me over to someone's house. If *you* don't... *mind.*" I smiled at her over my corny little word play.

Della grinned back and sighed with a twinkle in her eyes. "Well, it's a shame..." Then she said: "Sure, honey. Whatever you need," wiping her hands on a dish towel. "Now?"

I just nodded.

We rolled out of there quietly with Della driving me in Ray's little, yellow Malibu, because Ray had torn the transmission out of her truck. I left Mr. Big and our stuff with Jenna. The only thing that I took was my gun. I had her drop me off a block from Rob's place. Not that I didn't trust her, but if a person didn't need to know where I was at then there was no reason to advertise it. Not to mention that it would have been impolite to show her where someone else lived whom she didn't know. I got out around the corner and I walked the block to Rob's; keeping my gun concealed as I did so.

Rob was there and I told him we needed to cook up a batch. The little money I had wasn't going to last and we needed to re-up whilst we could. The rest of the day, the two of us went about gathering the things that we needed and proceeded with the manufacturing of Methamphetamine. When you're involved in an operation like this, time will slip right by you. It wasn't until the sun was going down that I realized Jenna wouldn't know where I was and would be worried. I picked up the phone and called Della. "Put Jenna on," I said when she answered.

"Sorry, Jimmy, she's not here. She got to thinking that you left her. She said she needed to make some money, so she made us take her to the *'Doll House'* and drop her off.

"The *Doll House*? Are you freaking kidding me? Why would you take her to a place like that?!" I yelled into the phone. "The Doll House is nothing like what she is used to! That's no strip joint, that's a whorehouse!"

"Jimmy, I tried to talk her out of it, but that's what she wanted. So we took her."

I'm going to kill her, I thought to myself. "Where is Mr. Big?"

"He's here. She just took a bag of her stuff and left everything else. I told her you just had some things you needed to do and that you'd be back, but…" Della let her words trail off.

"Fuck, I'll come get Mr. Big later," I fumed.

"You need to know the laws been acting real funny around here, I swear they are following us," Della warned. "For real."

"Then have James take Mr. Big to your old house and I'll pick him up over there. I'll call you guys later."

As soon as I hung up I called the Doll House.

"Doll House," the girl tending the bar - and the girls - purred.

"Put Jenna Maxwell on. She just went to work there today…"

"Jenna, uumm… oh, she can't. She's just fixing to take a customer back for a lap dance," the girl told me.

With my hands squeezing the phone until it almost broke, I growled into it: "I don't know if you know me or not… but, my name is Jimmy Maxwell. If you don't know me, you need to call your boss Katrina, because she does." Katrina, Trina for short, used to live with me and Maryjo back in the late Eighties. She saw me take a whole house hostage until I'd got the money back that the people had stolen from her for turning tricks. She *knew* that I could be extremely dangerous. "I'm telling you, you do not want me coming down there. If my wife goes back into the dark room I will come down and tear that place to the ground. She has no idea what's expected of her back there."

"Just hold up, Jimmy. I know you… I was here when you backed up our bouncer Digger. When those black gangbangers came in here starting trouble last summer. Don't worry. I'll stop her. Just give me a minute," she said.

A few minutes later Jenna got on the phone. "Why is everybody freaking out around here?" she asked.

Not for the first time since I'd been out, I wondered if I had just manufactured all the good things that I thought about Jenna in my head. "Because they don't want me storming up in there shooting up the place – over *you!* What the fuck are you doing there? That isn't the kind of place that you are used too. They don't have a 'NO TOUCHING' policy, quite the opposite! What do you think you're doing?"

"I'm just figuring that out, Jimmy. I didn't know what to do. I thought you had left me."

"Jesus Christ, I'm trying to get shit together, then get our car so we can get out of here. I was trying to leave you somewhere that I wouldn't have to worry about you. Now get your stuff! I'm coming to get you."

"Will you call Katrina and tell her. She told me she wanted me to be reliable when she hired me," Jenna whined.

"Kat hired you! She should have known better than that... don't worry about it, just be ready!" I hung up on her then called Trina. "What are you doing putting my old lady out there like that?" As I said before, Trina knew my anger first-hand. "That's my wife you put to work. She doesn't even know what's going on there!" Then I told her what I had told her bartender on the phone.

"Jimmy, I didn't know. She sure acted like she knew what she was getting into to me. I assumed that you didn't mind or she wouldn't have even been there to see me."

"Well I do mind."

"I understand. Don't worry, they will sit her down in a chair and make sure that she sits there until you come and pick her up. Okay?" Katrina assured me.

"Thanks, darlin'. I know it really isn't your fault... it's hers. Take care." I told her, then hung up. I took Rob's truck, damn near against his will, and went and picked up Jenna right *'in the middle'* of our dope cook. "What is wrong with you, Jenna?" I grumbled on our way back. "You're losing it or something?"

"No... you're losing it. I'm just getting ready for when you're gone," she pouted. She crossed her arms and stared out of the window.

"And this is how you intend to maintain when I'm gone?!" I asked her.

She was right, I was losing something. I wasn't sure what, but it was... *something.*

Jenna turned and glared at me. "No. I'm going to get shot, or go to jail with you and you know it." She was high and barely making sense, but she had a point.

I had been worrying about that eventuality ever since this thing began. It had really hit home seeing the warning on the News about my female accomplices. But now her moral and mental states were really getting accosted. They were being eaten alive by the little, drug-addict demon that was putting down roots inside of her soul.

"Jenna, I need to send you away from me for a while. You need to go to Guymon and stay with mom. I will get something together and slip through all this. Then I will come and get you. I don't want you getting hurt or have to go to jail if they catch me," I told her.

She looked at me with tears welling up in her eyes. "I know you're right. Something's going to happen soon, isn't it?"

"Yes, Jenna. But maybe we can still pull through this. I'm sending you over to Stephanie's house. She'll take care of you until I can get you to Guymon."

"What about Mr. Big?"

"I'll get him and bring him to you. You can take him with you until this is all over with."

With that I made arrangements and had Jenna taken to Stephanie's. I jumped back in Rob's truck after all our business was done and picked up Mr. Big. Rob took off shortly after. I think he may have been getting nervous, thinking I might just decide to keep his truck.

I needed to stop this downward spiral. I needed my car and I needed to get my business done with at least Billy and Teddy.

Most of all, I needed to get Jenna, Mr. Big and myself... out of this town.

CHAPTER FORTY-TWO
GETTING THE BUICK BACK

I sat around Rob's place with Joe and Dan, a couple of Rob's friends who hung out there together. Joe was a tall, slender, blond-headed guy in his early forties and was as gay as men's figure skating. Dan was shorter and stockier than Joe with dark hair. I don't know whether he was gay or not. He claimed to be straight and after what happened the next day, he probably was. Didn't make much difference to me, either way. I paid them very little attention. However, I was going to need a ride to get my car and Dan had a Jeep.

I'd called Dale and Maryjo, letting them know I was going to need them to bring me a couple of tires out to the cabin in the woods the next day, "Five hole fifteen inch, or something universal," I said specifically. It was time to go out there and get my car. The plan was to have someone drop me a couple of miles off, so I could hike in the back way and look over the place for traps. Dale said he would bring me what I needed after I declared it safe and help me get out of there un-accosted by the Law.

Dan agreed to give me a ride the next morning. He didn't know anything about the cabin, or why I wanted him to drop me in the middle of nowhere, and I kept it that way. I warned him not to tell anyone who might ask where he took me. I was going to be trapped out there and I needed as much anonymity as possible.

I was carrying the phone from the robbery, but I'd learned the police *had* been called out to Tucks and, supposedly, they'd made statements implicating me. I didn't know what Tuck had actually told law enforcement, but if he had given me up, they would be all over the phone I had taken. Therefore, I used it very sparingly.

Jenna called me on it while Dan was driving me out to Old Prue Road, on my way to get our car. I was very vague about where I was and what I was doing, just in case there was some way for the police to be listening in on the line. In turn, she caught on and was very vague about where she was and what she was doing. The best I could do without giving up too many clues to my destination was to tell her in descriptive terms who I was with. I could tell that she wasn't very satisfied with my *'cryptic'* elucidation, but I assured her I was doing what needed to be done and hung up.

I directed Dan to take me in the way Deena had brought Jenna and I out weeks before. A quarter of a mile short of where she had picked us up I ducked out of the truck and sprinted up into the trees with Mr. Big in my shirt.

I had only taken a few steps out of the full view of the road when I heard another vehicle pull up. What the hell? I froze! There were now more trees between me and the gravel lane, so all I could see when I looked was the top of a grey S.U.V.. It had stopped then slowly backed up. It moved back and forth in the exact spot I had just jumped out of Dan's Jeep.

My mind scrambled to make sense of it. *Could the cops somehow already be on me? Could they be on Rob and his clan? Maybe they were watching the surrounding roads, thought they saw something and are just investigating why the Jeep came down the road and retreated the way that it did? Or, could it be just someone randomly driving down the road who saw me and was wondering why someone would run into the woods and not come back out?* I didn't know. I didn't see anyone, but once I was out of the Jeep I wasn't looking. I just ran for cover with my head down.

Regardless, it was *'something'* and I needed to be wary. Even though many weeks had passed, the marshals were aware that my car and all my property was still out here. It was a very hot spot to be. I knew the police would be counting on me coming to get my things sooner or later, which is why once I had retrieved Mr. Big I'd left all our stuff out here for so long. It wasn't just me. Everybody left this place alone. This was a bold move I was making, but it had to be done and surprise was my only ally. Now I wasn't even sure I had that.

The morning was quiet and there wasn't any gunfire popping and cracking through the hills this time. The air was brisk and smelled fresh; the way only a country morning could. The sun was up, but laying low in the east. There was still dew on the ground and on the west side of the trees. Mr. Big and me cut directly for the cabin. The only thing separating us from it was the deep ravine that ran from the north down the cabin's western side. That gorge was what isolated the cabin from the other roads and neighboring properties; leaving the winding pass that came in from the Shell Creek Road its only vehicular access.

The sound carried incredibly well through the quiet and cool ravine. I could hear dump trucks and men at work echoing down its long, steep walls from the local landfill. I knew it was several miles away, but it sounded like just a few hundred yards. With the man-made sounds confusing my senses, I had to be extra careful. Closing my eyes, I concentrated on listening… taking a moment to separate the distant, amplified sounds from what was truly near by. I needed to make sure that all was well before I called Dale in with the tires.

I worked my way through the woods and came in straight across from the cabin. Separated by only a hundred yards of scraggly trees and the ravine, I climbed up another tall Cyprus, so I could put my eyes on the place and the surrounding area. Once up in its branches, I could see the scat of a big cat… probably the same one I'd spotted running down into this cut of land before. I tucked Mr. Big a little tighter down into my shirt. Looking through my compact, camouflaged binoculars – I'd long since removed the scope from my rifle – I surveyed the cabin, the access road and the cliff above it.

I didn't see anything indicating that there had been any *recent* activity around. I did, however, notice that every branch and twig laying on the ground had been stepped on, or broken, as far as I could see in every direction. The sign was old; the police must have canvassed this whole area. My ears were still playing tricks with me. However, I'd already separated the background from the foreground sounds the best I could and assumed that most of what I was hearing was related to the dump and had nothing to do with me. Still… there was that grey S.U.V. out on the road to consider.

Anyway, I had a job to do and couldn't stay in the tree all day. We made our way as stealthily as possible across the tree-choked gully. The woodline ended up a half a dozen feet from the door of the cabin's converted garage. While we were still under cover I stopped and listened for noises that would betray anyone in the house already. Hearing nothing new, I stepped smoothly across the six feet of open ground into the side door.

Once inside I was immediately aware that, if I'd been seen, I was now trapped. I continued listening as I moved beyond the threshold. It was quiet the way abandoned houses are. The garage-turned-rec-room looked the same as it had before, except the window had been uncovered. The air was still enough to see dust motes floating in the diffuse sunbeams that shined in through the dirty window's cracked panes.

I continued on into the kitchen of the house. Everything looked the same in there, but I could tell by the absence of sound from the refrigerator that the power was now off. In the living room I noticed the Coleman heater Billy had loaned me was gone. *Interesting,* I thought. *Everybody else was afraid to come near this place, knowing it was being watched, but not Billy, huh?*

The rest of the living room was in disarray. The daybed was pulled out to reveal the grate to the floor furnace. In the corner was a toppled-over chair and end table. The front door was dented and beaten in, but closed. Surprisingly, the coffee table with all of its clutter on top of it was still intact. Right in the center of it was the *'shake-n-bake'* bottle with all of its used contents in it; the one I had told Kevin to get out of the house and throw into the refuse pile.

The list of people who needed punishment was growing longer as my time to deal with them - I sensed - was getting shorter. The sad thing was, I knew that little things like this would probably go un-chastised, unless I just happen to run into him again. Time was running out and I was going to have to prioritize. The minor annoyances were going to have to be ignored and the concentration I could spare from trying to stay free and get out of town had to go to the top two hits on the list.

Teddy Johnson was number one. I had proof he was working with the Feds. He was a dirty Brother and *my* responsibility. Billy Ray was next. There were a half-dozen clues that pointed toward Billy as the one who had ratted me out at the cabin, even before I had learned that he'd stiffed me on my cut of the drugs that day. Probably expecting me to be apprehended before he needed to pay me. That just solidified it, putting him at the top of the list of snakes right next to Teddy, who I needed to pay a visit to before I left town. They had directly tried to cross me out and they were probably the only two I was going to have time for.

The net was closing. I knew all the rats were out in full force working overtime against me; knowing that after I knocked over Tuck's house, they could be next on the list. It was a race, I knew down in my heart, I was destined to lose. Unless I just got in my car and left. Maybe that's what I should do. Just get the car, go pick up Jenna and Mr. Big, then the three of us just make a run for the border. It was something to think about, I guess.

I scratched my head. *How had I fallen so far?* I'd vowed never to be back in this world of cutthroat, back-stabbing junkies. Yet here I was, up to my neck in the muck. I hated that I had let my world digress back to this… I hated what I had become.

Anyway, I moved across the living room and down the hallway. Deena's room was mostly cleared out, which didn't surprise me. If Billy had been allowed back in here he would have tried to pick up Deena's things too, strictly for brownie points. I'm sure that if he wouldn't have been supervised he probably would have cleaned me and Jenna's things out as well, but not with the intent of returning them. As it was, other than our stuff being moved around during the search, all of our belongings were still there.

I froze. I heard two men talking. Mr. Big is such a good dog, he knew just from the tension in my body when it was Okay to bark and when it wasn't. We both stayed absolutely quiet while I listened. They were right outside the house and moving. However, the men were not taking pains to conceal their voices and were conversing in casual tones. *Would they be doing that if they had any idea I was in here or close enough to hear them? Were they cops? Where they hunters? Or, were they just neighbors who after all the "to-do" out here, were asked to keep an eye on the place?*

Mr. Big and I sat stone still, ready to confront and take the men by surprise when they entered the woodland home. Even in the cool morning air I felt beads of sweat running down my forehead. My only movement was to smooth the hackles down that had risen on Mr. Big's neck, to reassure him that silence and patience was what was required at the moment. The voices moved on. We were in the middle of a remote woods! What the hell was that, I wondered? Regardless, I now knew, no one was aware of my presence in the house. However, that could change in an instant.

Unsure of what was going on, I realized I needed to be looking from outside the situation in, rather than from the inside out. I grabbed a backpack from Deena's closet, one of the few remnants left of her things and stuffed it full of supplies, extra clothes and so on. Putting Mr. Big in last, I cinched the drawstrings up so that his body was inside with just his head sticking out the top. I then slipped on some camo gear that I'd kept out there over my clothes. When I was fairly camouflaged, I mounted the backpack and Mr. Big up on my shoulders. Then I slipped out the side door and around the back of the shack.

I stopped to inspect my car. It was where I'd left it, still locked up tight. Sure enough my front two tires had each suffered a knife blade through the white walls... irreparable damage. Smart move on the police's part - illegal, but smart. I felt under the bumpers and the fender wells to make sure a tracking device hadn't been attached under there. After looking everything over, I moved back off into the trees thinking I was lucky the Regal's windows were still intact. As long as no one had been able to get under the hood, I was reasonably confident that the engine hadn't been damaged. Once back into the woods, I stealthied my way in a big circle around the cabin looking for signs of the men I'd heard, or anything that would cause me to delay calling Dale and Maryjo in.

I didn't spot the men, but as I was coming up the back side of the mountain I heard one yell something to the other. They were down in the bottom of the arroyo where I had just ascended from, looking for something. I let off six or seven rapid-fire gunshots. From where I was, it would be hard to pinpoint, because the echoes out there play havoc on a person's auditory senses. It wouldn't mean much; in the country gunfire happens all the time, but it would give whoever it was something to think about.

If they were hunting me, I figured them to have to at least investigate the shots. I found a concealed spot behind a fallen, termite-eaten log, then, Mr. Big and me hunkered down; laying in the cut to see just who and what was roaming around out here in these woods. Even though the tension was tight as a guitar string, I couldn't help but admire the beauty of these woods. The greens, yellows and browns of the leaves; the sounds of the birds in the trees, even the smell of the decaying log that I was laying against, gave me a sense of appreciation for the freedom that I was so tentatively holding on to. My mind cleared while I waited. Finally, I felt that whoever it was probably wasn't really wanting to find us and had given up.

I made one more circuit, reconnoitering the whole area. Then I moved Mr. Big and me to a spot that was set back in the woods enough to survey the area at the top of the cliff that overlooked the cabin. If anyone was watching the place that would be an irresistible location to do it from. Staking it out, I tethered Mr. Big with a bootlace in case I dozed off.

It was peaceful and it got very quiet now that we were out of the ravine and the sounds of the distant dump couldn't reach us. The hunters, cops, neighbors, whoever they were, seemed to have disappeared as well. With nothing showing itself, visibly or audibly for some time, I did fall asleep for a couple of hours. When I woke up, I tried to call Dale. I say *'tried'*, because I wasn't getting any signal on the Cricket service that Tuck had on his phone. Damn it!

I returned my little dude to the backpack, letting him ride in it like an Indian baby in a papoose and headed across the wooded hills, closer to town and a cellphone tower. Now that I'd finally deemed it safe, I abandoned the dense forest for the dirt road to make better time. As I traveled, I checked the wheel ruts for recent activity. The road was smooth and sandy; read easily in the places where the ground was flat and covered over by the treetops. The tire tracks I could see were several days old. Whoever had been out here around the cabin had hiked in from another direction; probably watchful neighbors, or maybe random cops, just nosing around. Whichever they were, they obviously didn't want any part of gunfire, especially if it was coming from me. Everyone knew I was desperate and they were well aware that made me highly dangerous. Even if the gunfire was a careless hunter, or some kid out in the hills just shooting up shit, it stands to reason that people out snooping around where they shouldn't be could get shot *'accidentally'*.

All of a sudden my vision fell on a fresh boot print. It overlay an older tire track in the thin layer of soft sand; as clear as a plaster cast and headed in the direction I was coming from. With my heart beating double-time, I moved back off into the woods and squatted down. Peering through my binoculars, I examined every thicket and leafy shadow on the ground and in the trees, for the man who made that track. Not seeing anything or hearing any sound, I stepped back onto the road looking for more clues. My mind searched for answers to the riddle. The boot print was of a standard paratrooper sole, the same kind almost every cop and every hunter in the country wore. The prints came in, suddenly stopped, turned and went back out the same way they'd entered - very fresh! I wanted to keep following them untill they turned off or came to some other readable conclusion, but I would be walking straight into an ambush if he'd jumped off the road and was waiting. With that in mind, I went back to paralleling the road through the forest. Occasionally I'd fire a few rounds into the trees, knowing the echoes were ricocheting through the hills.

Finally I came to a clearing where I could see the grass pushed down from an A.T.V. four-wheeler. It had come and gone. I was scaring people off, but I still didn't know whom. If it was the cops, and they had any reasonable reason to conclude that it was me out in these woods and not, like I said, some hunter or a kid out here shooting at squirrels, they would pull back and surround the place again, while they waited to get a warrant. This was still private property. For that matter, the fresh track could belong to one of the Burns' who owned the land. They owned several A.T.V.s also and were aware that a wanted outlaw had commandeered this little part of their property. Maybe they were curious and I scared them off too. Out of everything, that was the most likely. Either way, I needed to be careful pulling my car out onto the open road.

I found what I was looking for; a tall deer-stand that sat up in a tree at one of the highest places on the mountain. It was rusted and had been there a while, but it was still functional. I'd spotted it when I first came out here and was exploring these hills.

Taking Mr. Big out of my backpack, I sat it down against the base of the tree and stuck him in my shirt. Even with a gun in hand, I wasn't going to leave my little man staked out at the bottom while I was up it making a phone call. There were far too many dangers to leave him unguarded, even for a few moments. He was already used to riding in my shirt like that, so together we went up the tree-stand stairs.

We settled on the deer-blinds bench seat, which was equipped with weather beaten arm rests and still even had a couple of its warped, wooden floorboards intact. Mr. Big struggled to get his head out of the neck of my shirt, the way he did when he rode with me on my Harley. He wanted to see too. Stretching his head up, he licked my chin a couple of times. "I know, I know, little buddy, we need to get down to business. It's going to start getting cold soon," I told him.

Flipping the phone open, I dialed the number Maryjo had given me. She answered right away. "Where are you?" she asked.

"At the moment I'm up a tree. Come on... just keep your eyes open on your way out," I told her.

"We're ready. Dale just went to get some gas. He's been waiting on you to call all day!"

"My reception is bad. Where I'm at, right now, is the only place I can call from on this weak-ass phone, and when I'm off with you I probably won't be able to call again. Besides, I don't want the cops to be able to see my signal bouncing off of one of the cell towers out here. They know about the cabin. It wouldn't take a rocket scientist to figure out I was out here getting my shit. Just... come on, I'll watch your back trail as you drive in."

"Okay, Jimmy. We'll be there soon," Maryjo promised and hung up.

It was late afternoon and the temperature was already dropping this high up. I climbed down and found a spot where I could see the road through the trees and waited.

It took well over an hour before I heard the sounds of a fairly large vehicle coming along the lonely, dirt road. Not wanting to step out under the assumption it was Dale and Maryjo, just to end up face to face with a County S.U.V. who may have finally decided to roll in to have a look, I stayed in the trees and watched as a red Bronco drove by with Dale, Maryjo, and Bear - Dale's huge black dog, sitting in the back seat. There was a young, clean-cut kid driving and a long-haired, heavily-bearded man sitting in the passenger seat. The passenger was a thin, tall man who wore a black duster and a black, beat-up, old hat; the same kind Jed Clampett in *The Beverly Hillbilly's'* wore, giving him the appearance of a man who belonged up in these hills. I'd never met him, but I knew him to be Frank Burns. He was the brother of the man who owned the cabin I'd appropriated as my hideout. He himself lived a couple of miles to the east on the same tract of land. *They must've recruited Frank to guide them in,* I thought to myself. As they passed on by, I continued to watch the trail for a few minutes to see if anyone followed them.

Cutting straight across the top of the mountain, I jogged the mile or so back to the cabin. I wasn't far behind them since they had to weave their way down that treacherous, rain eroded road to get to the bottom.

I watched them unobserved from the top of the cliff for a few moments. They were looking around, confused by my absence. When I was sure they hadn't been tailed out there, I descended from the rocky precipice. Frank was standing on the porch looking at the fire-pit, appreciating how much of the property I'd cleaned up, when I walked up and stuck my gun in his back. "Who are you?" I demanded.

Startled, he stiffened, then slowly raised his hands. At a jab from the barrel of my rifle, he looked over his shoulder. "I - I - I'm Frank. I'm Bill's brother and I live over off 177th. Dale needed a guide down here, that's all. Are you Jimmy?" he stammered.

"Maybe. Have the cops been to see you?"

"Who haven't they been to see? They've been all over this mountain showing pictures of you and your wife to everyone who lives within five miles. They say there's a ten-thousand dollar reward for you," he answered.

I let him lower his hands, but kept him covered. "Have you been out snooping around here on your A.T.V. in the last couple of days?"

I knew the answer before he even said: "No." Because he was wearing cowboy boots... not combat boots. The imprint left behind couldn't be more different.

"Damn it," I said. Lowering my gun, I went on in the house to look for Dale. I could feel the hairs rising on the back of my neck. I didn't realize how much I had assumed that track was probably left by him or one of his family until now. We needed to hurry and get this done and get out of here.

Behind me I heard Frank say: "Thanks for cleaning up the yard like that."

I said nothing, but kept right on walking down the hallway. Dale, Maryjo and the youngster who'd been driving were all standing in my back room looking at each other like they couldn't figure out where I could be.

"There you are - and Mr. Big too! Let me have him." Maryjo walked over and gave me a quick hug before taking the little guy from the backpack.

"Damn, Brother. We were getting worried," Dale said. Dale looked like a short, over-weight Jack Nicholson; crazy hair, eyebrows and all.

"Who's this?" I demanded, indicating the blond kid with the barrel of my gun. He was so fresh and clean-cut that he instantly stood out as suspicious in my hypersensitive state of mind.

"Oh... this is Dylan. He's alright. He volunteered to help us. He's the one who got the tires for you," Dale went on.

"Jimmy, ease up. Everybody isn't out to get you," Maryjo spouted off. She went on to tell me Mr. Big was infested with fleas. She picked one off of him and crushed it between her finger and thumb nails.

"You haven't been living in my world, Maryjo." My car was sitting right under the bedroom's window, so I turned to Dale and said: "Hand mine and Jenna's stuff to me through there," pointing at it. "Then I'll pull around front to change the tires. We need to hurry... there was some activity out here earlier and Frank assures me it wasn't him or his clan. Maryjo will probably have to drive it out."

"Let's do it," Dale said, clapping his hands together. "That's what we're here for. Damn, Jim, this is a nice place for a hideout. Do you know who dropped the dime on you yet? It's all over town that you're going after them."

"Billy Ray would be my guess," I replied.

Maryjo jumped in: "I don't blame you for being mad, Jimmy. This place is nice. You pretty-much had to be told on for the cops to find you way out here. But Billy Ray brought you to this place, didn't he? Are you sure it's him?"

"Not as sure about him being a rat as I am that your current husband is, but yeah! If Tuck was telling the truth, and I think he was, then Billy had the most opportunity and the most motive," I told her.

We had left Dale and Dylan in the bedroom and walked around to the back yard, so I could load the car with the stuff they handed out to me. "You know, people are saying Tuck fingered you to the cops for robbing him, don't you? He's not Mr. Squeaky-Clean," Maryjo informed me.

"I heard rumors. It doesn't surprise me. Nothing does any more. Who said that he fingered me, anyway?" I asked, absentmindedly admiring how pretty she still was.

While I was taking the first load of clothes Dale handed me through the window, I noticed Dylan inside texting on his phone. "Hey, what the fuck are you doing? Don't be making any phone calls and don't be texting anybody while you are around me," I growled at him. "I am on my last nerve and you don't want to see what happens when that snaps!" At that point, I was so high-strung and paranoid that I thought everyone and every action, out of my immediate control was, or could be, potentially out to set me up. It was a very miserable way to live, but also made me very volatile.

"Put the phone up Dylan - now." Maryjo warned him with her eyes as well as with her words. Then to me she said: "He's really Okay. He's not telling anybody where you're at, Jimmy."

"Yeah, I was just texting my girlfriend," Dylan said, at the same time trying to show me his phone to cosign Maryjo's statement.

"Well do it when I'm not around..." I gave him a look that told him I wasn't going to warn him again. "We need to get this stuff loaded and get this car fixed, so we can leave," I finished.

Months later, he told me that he was telling his girlfriend he thought I was going to shoot him if he didn't get off of the phone with her. I asked what she'd said. He said she told him: "Then get off the phone!" He ended up being a pretty good kid. Dumb, but good.

We finished loading everything; packing the trunk and back seat with what Jenna and me had left. Taking a mental inventory of the pathetic remnants of our lives, I couldn't help but think of all we'd lost. Not for the first time, I was almost crushed by the weight and ignorance of my decision to run when I did, and once again, I had to just accept it. What was done was done and I had to live in the moment with what was *not* what I wished it could be. Dale and Dylan joined us outside, while Frank wandered the property around his brother's house looking things over.

The Buick started right up and I pulled it around to the front of the house slowly; trying not to warp the aluminum mags that my car was now rolling on. I found a smooth, flat spot and parked.

Not wasting time, I started jacking up the front of the car. I looked at Dylan and told him to grab the tires that he had brought, but all he did was stand there and look at me stupidly. "What the hell is wrong with him?" I inquired suspiciously of Dale.

Dylan... too scared to even look at me, looked at Dale. I could smell fear oozing from his pores, when he mumbled: "I thought you said six bolts. This car has five."

"No fucking way," I swore under my breath. I walked over to his S.U.V. and looked in the back. Sure enough, this shit-head had brought wheels and tires that would fit on his God-forsaken Bronco, not my Buick Regal. I probably should have shot that kid right then and there just to do the world a favor and rid it of one more idiot. But, instead, I just hung my head in defeat. I could feel the forces that were guiding my destiny, hard at work tightening the vice, driving me deeper into the jaws of doom.

312

"Damn it, Brother, I'm sorry. I told him what to get and he said that he got them. I never even looked," Dale said, arching one of his brows defensively.

I looked at the sky... *Why me? What did I ever do to you?* I asked God silently. No response... but I felt my world getting just a little bit smaller.

Standing there looking at Dale, Dylan and my car in disbelief, I rubbed my forehead while I thought for a minute. Then I mentally got a grip and shook it off. There was no time for self-pity. I was reaping what I'd sown from the threads of my own stubbornness and I knew it. "Alright..." I said. "We're going to put the front of the car up on those cinder blocks and load the wheels in Dylan's Bronco. We'll take my wheels to town, put some used rubber on my mags and come back out here tomorrow. You are going to be available tomorrow... if I don't kill you today, aren't you, Dylan?" Knowing full-well that by tomorrow this place could be overrun with cops again.

"S-sh-sure, whatever you need. I'm so sorry," he stammered. The weird thing was, out of all the hardcore criminals and junkies I'd been dealing with the last few months, this kid, as scared as he was, seemed to be actually saying he was sorry for having let me down and not out of his fear of me. I found myself liking him.

"Yeah, well... it's getting dark now. Let's just get out of here," I said. Then I reached down and scratched Bear between the ears of his huge head. I told Maryjo, who was still picking fleas off of Mr. Big, to round Frank up. It was time to leave. I don't know how she did it, but given a bit of time, Maryjo could de-flea a dog one flea at a time.

We carefully found our way in the waning light back up the mountain. Once we made it to the edge of the woods we could see more traffic on the two-lane blacktop than usual. Telling them I would meet them at Franks, I got out and took a short-cut through the woods, while Dylan pulled out onto the road. Maryjo told me later, they'd felt scrutinized by three or four suspicious S.U.V.s that passed by them, but made it to Burn's place without being stopped.

It was full on dark by the time I caught up with them. I told Frank that time would tell whether he was one of the good guys or not. He assured me that he was and thanked me again for cleaning up his brother's property. Without any more preamble, we headed back to Dale's.

CHAPTER FORTY-THREE
THE CLOUDS GETTING DARKER

Dale lived on Ridge Drive in the hills of Sand Springs. He was at the bottom of a valley between two steep, rolling, wooded rises that were climbing up and coming together at the top of a small mountain. It would have been picturesque if homes hadn't been built all over them. He lived in a white cookie-cutter house with brown trim that was built on an acre and a half strip of land, which ran straight back and up the slope.

As we pulled up to it, there was the familiar sight of Rebecca's beat-up travel trailer. She was the female meth cook I mentioned earlier. It didn't run at the moment and was stranded out front of Dale's house. The R.V. sat right beside the three-and-a-half foot high, chain-link property fence, which circled his whole lot except where the driveway gates would have been - if they hadn't been missing. The yard wasn't bad. It was green and grassy, a little overgrown like everything up in these hills. The only real eyesore was the foot-wide trench that ran around from the driveway to the back yard with dirt piled on both sides. A left-over mess from an on going plumbing problem that should have been fixed long before.

Once at Dale's we unloaded my wheels, and Bear, which was like watching a horse exit his trailer. Then Dylan left and Maryjo went to her room with Mr. Big.

Dale's house was built like a shoebox and even though it had three bedrooms it was not much bigger than one. It faced east and the living-room sat in the north corner. It was all of about twenty feet to the other wall, where there was a back door that led to the rest of the overgrown, narrowing lot Dale owned.

It had a hallway that split the rest of the house, more or less, down the middle. On the right side was a floor-to-ceiling island wall divider, separating the passage-way from the kitchen. Further along was a small, but full bath and spare room that Maryjo lived in when she was there. The left wall housed the room of Dale's daughter, Valerie-Daniel, first, then Dale's. None of the rooms were very big, but it still never ceased to amaze me how much could fit into that little house.

I sat out in the living room with Dale. "I'll probably never make it back out there to get my car and get out of here," I told him. He was taking a hit off his glass pipe, which he always smoked with too much flame - no matter how many people tried to tell him not too. I could feel the darkness wrapping itself around me like the tentacles of a giant squid that was dragging me down to the deep, crushing, black depths of the ocean. I was drowning. "It's almost over," I confided in him. "I just don't know how it's going to end."

"What do you mean? Sure you will," Dale said, nodding his head toward the charred glass beaker in his hand; silently offering me a hit of speed.

I waved it off. That was the last thing I needed. "I had a dream the other night. Everywhere I stepped... everywhere there was a direction for me to go, I was either cut off, or there was a trap. I slid through, over and around, most of them, but as soon as I thought I was going to make it, everything but the spot I was standing on fell away; down into a bottomless abyss. I was trapped, and then that spot started crumbling as well." I breathed out a sigh and closed my eyes. I rubbed my forehead between my fingers and thumb, *how could I have been such a fool to let it come to this*, I thought to myself; wishing that I could go back in time and turn right instead of left at that liquor store. Or even just turned myself in back when everyone was saying I should.

"It was just a dream you had, because you were feeling trapped and chased. It doesn't mean it's got to end that way," Dale offered, trying to reassure me.

Squinting my eyes tighter, I gathered myself to a point of focus. Right or wrong, it didn't matter now. I shut the past out of my mind... it was what it was - but damn. When I opened my eyes, I tightened my jaw and stared at Dale with determined resolution. "Well, all I know is that I'm not going to let Teddy slip by. I'm down to that. I'm going to sit here, hiding in the spare room until he comes back and then I'm going to take him. He will come if he doesn't know that I'm here," I finished.

"Okay, Jimmy, but Valerie still clings to Teddy sometimes. She's my only daughter and the last time there was a hit out on a brother she was on the back of his motorcycle when it went down. She broke five bones and almost died. Just promise me you will keep her out of the line of fire this time," Dale pleaded.

"Sure, Dale. I love Valerie too and I'm sorry about the last time. They should have waited until he was alone. Don't worry, but do me a favor and don't tell Maryjo what I'm doing." I hugged Dale as Maryjo came out of her room, he grabbed his coat and walked, kind of sadly, out into the backyard with her. I think that my downer mood infected him too. So much for Dale not believing in my dream, I thought.

I headed back to the spare bedroom, where I knew the floor access under the house was located and started working on a little hiding place I had back there in case the Law decided to raid Dale's house while I was waiting. I didn't tell Dale that I intended to shoot Teddy down in his front yard when he showed up, but that's what I was going to do. My life was forfeit, anyway. The best thing I could do, I told myself, was to rid the world of one of the lowest forms of life on the planet. A trusted - by many, patch-wearing, fraud and government snitch, on my way out.

Back in the guest room, I moved a box of Maryjo's shoes and clothes off of the patch of carpet that covered the floor boards in the closet. When it was cleared off I pulled the carpet back to reveal a rectangular, wooden trap door. It was the access portal to the two-foot crawl space that was under Dale's house. I would work on it, from time to time, when I was there and had a shallow hole dug out in the ground that I could drop into if needs be. It was equipped with a couple of nails in the floor joists. One had a flashlight hanging from it, while the other was for my gun. It was tight and still had a lot of room for improvement, but apart from the spiders, it wasn't bad. Once in there with the carpet laid back down and a box, maybe even a couple pairs of shoes, thrown on top of it, it was completely invisible to anyone unaware of its existence.

The spiders were bad, though, and it was all the wicked ones like Brown Recluses, also known as Fiddle Backs and Black Widows. The one time I was in there with the hole buttoned up, I could see dozens of them hanging and crawling on every floor joist. I'm not a big fan of spiders even in the light, but in the dark I am almost phobic. I watched them watching me in the waning beam of the flashlight; praying that the light would not fail me. Laying there feeling as if there were tiny, venomous creatures crawling all over me, I wrapped my will tightly around my fear; forcing myself into a calm place in my mind. With the balance teetering solely on the difference between, light and darkness, I could feel panic waiting like a wolf at the door for any crack to open so that it could slip through and devour me. By sheer grit I ignored those thoughts… You would be surprised at what you can endure, when the police are knocking on the door.

Anyway, this day the police were not at the door, but I did hear Valerie-Daniel and Regina, one of her friends, come in. Valerie was a thick, shapely girl. As I said before, she had a pretty, round face framed by short, blonde hair. Regina was a short, dark-headed girl; cute in a average sort of way. Her boyfriend, Bubba, was a cover-up - what we call an excommunicated brother, because his tattoo identifying him as a member in good standing had either been covered up with another tattoo, or burned off. Bubba's and Regina's apartment in Sandy Park was the last known whereabouts of Teddy Johnson and Valerie, even though he was still married to Maryjo, was Teddy's *'sometimes'* girlfriend, so it was a good bet, he wasn't far away. I sat and listened for sounds of him as the girls walked into Valerie's bedroom. I couldn't hear anyone else in the house. Maryjo and Dale must've taken a walk. Stepping across the three-foot wide hallway quietly, I propped my gun against the wall out of sight and waited until they noticed me.

Valerie, facing the door, saw me when she raised her eyes from the open jewelry box they were looking at on her bed. "Whoa! Hey, Uncle Jack, where did you come from? I didn't know that you were here." She'd been calling me that ever since I started running from the Feds months back.

"Hi, Jimmy," Regina said, seeing me also.

"Hi, Gina." Then looking at Val: "Is Teddy out in the car or around somewhere?"

"No… Uncle Jack, he's not. Why, what's up?" Valerie put the brooch she was showing Regina back in the box and shut the lid.

"It's nothing." I stood there and spoke to them both for a few minutes. Then I told them not to tell anyone, stressing Teddy or Regina's old man, or *'anyone'*, that they'd seen me over there. They assured me that they wouldn't. Looking at Valerie and remembering my promise to Dale, I told her to come talk to me before she left. I turned, taking my gun with me, and stepped back into the room across the hall.

A little while later Valerie came over. The room was piled high with Maryjo's things right inside of the door, causing Valerie to have to walk around them to see me. I was standing in the hole in the closet with my gun against the wall and a shovel in my hand. She sat down on the end of the bed. "I remember that hole in the floor from when I was a kid."

"Yeah, there's a lot of potential for a safe room down here. As long as no one knows about it... *right?*"

"You know I'm your biggest fan, Uncle Jack. I don't want you to get caught. I'll never tell anybody, I promise. Dad and Maryjo are probably the only other people who know about that hole," she said.

In most instances, I knew that I could trust Valerie. But I wasn't so sure if I could on the subject of Teddy. At one time she had claimed to love him, though that was years back. However, she was young, in her early thirties, and blonde; and I knew they still had an occasional triste. I wasn't sure where her loyalty to me ended and her loyalty to him began. If Teddy found out that I knew he was dirty, he would avoid me like Maryjo avoids rehab and work overtime with the Feds to get me off the street. But, a promise is a promise.

I knocked a granddaddy long-legs off my arm then climbed out of the hole and squatted down on my haunches, where I could look at her eye to eye. "Do you love Teddy?" I asked, just cutting to the chase.

"Uhhhh... well," she squirmed uncomfortably. "No... I used to think I did a long time ago. Why do you ask?"

"Do you know where he is?"

"No."

"Do me a favor and stay away from him for the next few days," I said. I moved around to sit beside her on the bed.

"Why? Are you after him for something, Uncle Jack?" she asked, shifting around so that she could see me better.

"I'm just saying that you should stay away from him. I want you to promise me that you will."

"Okay, I promise that I will, but tell me is there something that I need to know."

"You need to know to stay away from him. He's a rat and bad things happen to rats. I just don't want you to get caught in the crossfire again. I love you and I assured your dad that I would keep you out of it. I also need you to be quiet about this whole thing. If you betray me it will change things between us - *forever*," I told her.

She could see the sincerity in my eyes and swore to me that she wouldn't.

She was inquisitive and I told her what Maryjo had told me. About Teddy's and the Federal marshals' arrangement for him to get out of jail and his subsequent relationship with them. How all the houses had been raided, right up to Marty and Angie's; whose was hit less than twenty-four hours after he found out that I was there. I knew the more that I talked the more serious she would know the consequences for Teddy were going to be. Being a man, I automatically assumed, that learning things like what I was telling her about Ted, especially from someone like me, would instantly cut all cords of loyalty and concern she had for him. As intelligent as I can be, I am still very naive sometimes.

Naturally, she agreed he was a low-life and promised to stay clear of him. She swore not to say anything to anyone about where I was, or what I told her. Valerie thanked me for trusting her enough to give her the heads up. She then gave me a hug and a kiss on the cheek before she left… and went straight over and warned Teddy that I was after him and why.

Maryjo and Dale came back from walking to the store. Maryjo was still carrying Mr. Big around, now tucked inside her jacket. I got tired of digging in the dirt and took a shower. I had tried using a different phone to call Jenna several times without results. Finally, I turned Tuck's hot-ass phone on. It was off, because I knew I would be stuck at Dale's for the night and I didn't want any cellphone towers pinging off it alerting the police to my general whereabouts. Hell, I didn't know what the cops could or couldn't do. Technology had moved by leaps and bounds while I had been in prison the last time. I figured the police, even the F.B.I., probably couldn't do what they did in the movies, but I had no clue where technologies reality ended and science fiction began. So, I tried to err on the side of caution.

Jenna called me as soon as I turned it on.

"Hey," I said, happy to hear from her and looking forward to telling her that I almost had our car back.

Drunk and higher than lady Liberty's torch she just started screaming out of control at me. "You mother-frucker, I hate you! I'm here with Dan and I'm going to fuck him! You two-timing bastard!"

"What are you talking about—" I was trying to ask her.

But suddenly Dan grabbed the phone out of Jenna's hand. "Hey, Jimmy. Don't believe that. She's just mad and talking smack!"

I could hear Jenna in the background. "Nooo... I'm not lying... I'm going to fuck him!" Her speech was slurred as she hollered several other drunken, derogatory insults at me over Dan's shoulder.

I felt my head turn red with anger and I snarled into the phone at Dan: "What the hell is she doing with you, anyway? She's supposed to be laying low at Stephanie's. How did she get so fucked up?"

"She made me come pick her up. Don't believe what she saying," Dan pleaded.

About that time, she grabbed the phone and yelled into it: "I'm getting ready to go into a bar and you won't be able to find me."

"Hold up, what has happened?" I asked, bewildered. "Why are you mad? What do you think that I've been doing all day?"

"You sent me away, so you can have threesomes and stick your big dick in every bitch you can before you go to jail. That's why you told them not to tell me where you were at," she screamed at me.

"What? I'm not going to say where I've been on this phone, but I have been doing stuff that needed to be done – for *us*. The only one I've been with is Mr. Big."

"*Liar!*" she screeched into the phone, then hung up. I tried calling back and got no answer.

An hour later... I got Dan back on the phone. "Where is she at?" I demanded of him.

"She had me drop her off at some club."

"Well, go get her!" I yelled into the mouthpiece. "You don't leave a woman that wasted alone, you dumb fuck! You are going to regret ever meeting either one of us. Go get her – now!" I slammed my phone shut. Giving up all thoughts of Teddy, I tried to think of how I was going to get to my wife.

How did she get so messed up, anyway, and where is she getting this threesome shit from? I questioned the night. Dan, Rob and Joe, all three, knew basically where I was and Rob, at least, knew what I was doing. *Wouldn't they have went ahead and told her when she started getting these crazy thoughts in her head?*

I thought about how to get across town. Dan said he was at Rob's, which was on the north side of Tulsa, and there's no telling where this club was. It was too far to walk and even if it hadn't been so far, there was no way I could be out in the open at that time of night. Any cop who saw me would try to stop me just to see why I was moving around on foot so late. Not to mention the temperature had dropped with the sun.

I threatened Dan on the phone a few more times and made him tell me that he would come and get me, which he never did. I called Stephanie and made her promise to come get me, but she never made it either.

Frustrated, I went out to Rebecca's empty travel trailer and laid down. Maryjo and I talked a little bit when she brought Mr. Big out to me. She tried to tell me then, that maybe Jenna never was what I'd thought she was in the first place. That, maybe, I should just move on without her. I would have a better chance of staying free, she said. I knew that she was probably right, but the only reason I'd ran in the first place was because I didn't want to abandon her. I laid there and thought about the girl that had got away, the one that I met at the Halloween party so many years back. Our two week long love affair had felt... so right. She wasn't like anyone else - not like this. Closing my eyes, I pictured her beautiful face and mischievous smile. I just knew that somewhere my life had taken the wrong fork in the road. I shook it off - I hadn't thought of Karyn in a while. However, at times like this, I still wondered to myself: *'what if?'*. Well, that was long ago and long gone... and I still loved Jenna, didn't I? Sometime in the night, waiting for a ride, worried for Jenna's safety, I fell asleep; but I dreamed of Karyn.

The next morning I woke up with the phone still in my hand, fully dressed waiting on rides that never came. I hadn't been up forty-five minutes and was on my second cup of coffee when young Dylan showed up. "Change of plans," I informed him. "I need you to take me somewhere else this-morning." After leaving instructions for Dale to get my tires fixed, I had Dylan take me straight to Rob's and drop me off.

Rob's wife let me in. I walked back past their big, beautiful, grey pit bull carrying Mr. Big, so he wouldn't become a morning snack, to find Rob back in his little *'dope den'*. That's what he called the little room he'd furnished with a couple of raggedy couches, a T.V., stereo and D.V.D.

player. It was also where his wife had restricted him to keep all his drug paraphernalia and so on; including his drug-addict friends. I asked him if he'd seen Jenna and if he knew what the hell had gotten into her.

"I don't know, brother, but I know she's alright. We had to go get her last night. By the time we got there she was running down the street carrying those damned high-heeled shoes in her hand. I don't know why she was running, but she was Okay. She's been real high," he told me.

"And where the fuck did she get the dope?"

"Well, I'm going to be honest, she got me a box of pills and I gave her a half gram like I do everybody. But that's not how she got so high. She was running around with Dan most of the day yesterday. They were already pretty wasted."

I lent forward in a threatening gesture. "You what? You don't give my o'lady dope! I wouldn't give a fuck if she had green money in her hand, do you understand me? I like you, Rob, but you don't want to find yourself on the wrong side of me," I warned him, pinning him to the couch with my stare. Down inside I was starting to feel like shooting everybody.

The intensity of my glare made him fidgety. "I'm sorry, bro, I didn't know. Like I said, she had some already."

"Yeah, well… I'm going to have a talk with Dan about that when I see him. Where is she now?"

"She should be over at Joey's." As soon as I leaned back, Rob got up; deciding we needed a cup of coffee and some dope.

I called over to Joey's on the landline. Joe answered. "Put Jenna on," I gritted.

"Jimmy," she said when she came on. "Where are you? I got so fucked up last night and I messed up… I was so mad at you Dan told me that you had him drop you off at some girl's house and that you told him not to tell me where. He said that you were going to have a threesome with her and some other girl. I messed up, Jimmy. When I realized what I'd done, I gave the rest of the dope I got from Rob to Joey here and I told him I didn't want it any more!"

"Dan told you that, did he? And I suppose you let him get in your pants because of it?" I said in my softest, deadliest, voice.

"No, but he tried," she lied.

Now that I could talk freely on the phone, I told her what I'd actually been doing. "I'm sorry, Jimmy. Forgive me. Please just come and get me," she pleaded.

"I'll be over there to get you as soon as I can." I hung up thinking of how stupid she was to fall for that trick and how stupid Dan was for pulling it. I was disgusted with my whole life at that moment.

I got high and, two hours later, I had Rob take me over to Joe's house to collect Jenna. When we pulled past the gate, I saw that Dan's Jeep wasn't there. Damn - another piece of shit that was going to slip through un-checked for his crimes against me. God... I thought, if there really was one, that's how I felt at the time, anyway, seems to be working overtime on the behalf of the rats, pedophiles and snakes in general. *A good motherfucker doesn't stand a chance,* was what I was thinking to myself as I walked up to the door.

My gun was still in Rob's truck along with Mr. Big and that's probably what saved Dan's life, because no sooner than I started to knock Dan opened the door. "Hi, Jimmy..."

I don't know what else he was going to say. Before he could say anything more, I hit him in the mouth. He fell backward, knocking a coat rack over and a picture off of the wall. I stepped into the house after him, pounding him into the corner. Using my hands like slugs from a Gatling gun, I beat him down until he had curled himself into a tight ball, making himself into the smallest target he could... I stomped him some more. He was screaming for help, while he was trying to cover himself with his arms and knees and crawl into the corner... I could smell the rank stink of urine as he pissed himself, *ugh!* Maybe he was gay after all - at least this part of him was a girl. "What did I do!? What did I do!?" Dan implored me through busted, bloody lips. He screamed and begged so much that I finally stopped. It was unnerving. After all, who does that?

Jenna was snidely popping off to Dan from behind me: "I told you... I told you what would happen, if you kept on."

Turning on her I spat: "Shut up! I can't believe you let this shmuck play you like a trick and in the process play me like a chump as well!" I pushed her back on the couch and took her clear, plastic, toeless, four inch high heels off of her feet. "The higher your heels are, the lower your I.Q. is. No more Starr! That dip shit bimbo is dead!" I thundered as I was breaking the heels off of her shoes. *'Starr'* was her ditzy, big-titted alter

AMERICAN OUTLAW ~ PRICE OF PRIDE

ego's name that she danced by, and was even dumber than Jenna – however that works? I finished by telling her to get her purse and get in the truck. To Rob I growled: "I should kick your ass, too. You're lucky I don't take your fucking truck for giving her dope in the first place. Drive us to a motel!" I thought I liked Rob, but at this point I wasn't asking him, I was telling him… and I was an inch from taking his wheels.

I kicked Dan one more time, eliciting another girlish scream from him, before we headed out to the truck. We didn't talk as Rob drove us across to the west side of Tulsa - back to the *Gateway Motel*. The 'WE HAVE PORN' sign was still blinking on and off the way it had the last time that we were there. I told Rob to pick us up the next day before checkout time.

CHAPTER FORTY-FOUR
NOWHERE TO RUN

We checked into the one-story, rundown motel. Our room, number four, faced the turnpike and was the closest and most exposed sublet to the highway. Not by choice, that's just what was left. There was a McDonalds and a Quick Trip convenience store on the far side of the asphalt artery, but they may as well have been in a foreign country, because we were completely cut off from them by the fences that ran along both sides of the eight-lane Turnpike. The *'Gateway Motel'* wasn't that easily accessible to begin with. There was only a one-way service-road to it and it was a mile in either direction before reaching an underpass to get to the other side. Rob had registered us into the room in his name. He split once we were nice and tucked in, with me reminding him to pick us up *before* checkout time the next morning.

As soon as he left, Jenna and I resumed our fight about Dan. She was still screwed-up and was trying to stand on the lame story that Dan's bitch-ass had used to drive a wedge between us in the first place. Every time she mentioned it, I got angrier. At that point I wished that I *had* been off screwing someone, instead of crawling through the woods all day! It infuriated me how she had let that insignificant piece of shit manipulate us, just to get into her pants, which I was sure did happen, regardless of her vehement denials.

In the end, she finally got Maryjo on the phone, who verified that she and Dale had, in fact, picked me and my Buick's tires up from the cabin, where I'd been stuck all day... by myself. It occurred to me that by calling Dale's home phone from the motel it had left an electronic trail to us, but I was so tired of fighting I just ignored it. Disgusted, I took a shower and went to bed.

The next morning I got up, feeling fairly safe, and confident for the first time in a while. Whether I was going to stay with Jenna or not was up in the air, but I was real close to having our car back and no matter what happened next, I would be mobile again. Soon, I could take care of my business... then Tulsa and everyone looking for me, and maybe even Jenna, would be in my rearview mirror. So much for Romeo and Juliet...

I looked out of the window as I got a hold of Rob. I didn't notice anything out of place. Rob said he had a couple of things to do, but would be there soon. Feeling at ease, Mr. Big and me walked to the small grocery store just down the access road and picked up something to eat for breakfast.

When we got back, Jenna and I talked. She was getting her head back together, but something was different about her. There was something different about the atmosphere altogether. When you've been on the run for a while, you start to sense things. Of course, there's rarely any tangible evidence to support your heebie-jeebies and are often left doubting whether your feelings are substantiated or not. However, when the hairs on my arms are standing up I've learned to take notice of them. I really couldn't put my finger on the problem, but wanting to hurry up and get out of there, I got on the phone and called Rob again. This time the phone only rang and rang. I looked at my watch. I had an hour left before check out time. I kept trying with no results.

I'd gotten rid of Tuck's phone the night before, finally, realizing how foolish it was to hang on to it. All we had was the motel's and, the last thing I wanted to do, was start making calls from its landline, but the clock was ticking and Rob was not answering. The Camel Jockey's who run these little low-rent motels are quick to call the cops for just about anything, so when check-out time got there, I called the office and told them we were waiting on our ride and would be out shortly. They, naturally, threatened us with calling the police.

I went ahead and rang Dale's. When he answered, I told him I had a bad feeling and I needed to get out of there. He said he would send Dylan to come get us and bring me some more money.

I looked out the window again... now I was seeing strangeness in every activity. I squinted my eyes trying to focus on what I thought I was seeing.

"Jenna, is that a guy across the turnpike looking through binoculars at our room?"

She hurried to come look. "I don't know... maybe." Jesus, *I'm bugging out*, I thought. But, *something* wasn't right. I wished that I still had my binoculars or my scope. I couldn't see well enough to be sure about anything.

I considered walking out of there, but even though I'd cut my rifle down it was still not completely concealable. I *knew* that the end was coming, in one way or the other, and discarding it this close to the finish line was not an option.

The phone rang; it was Rob. "I'm on my way. I'll be there in fifteen minutes. Don't go anywhere."

"We're well past checkout time... where've you been?" I asked him. I was holding my anger back, wanting to find out what he had to say before he realized how mad I was.

"We got pulled over," he went on. "But everything is Okay. We'll be right there."

"They missed your mobile meth lab?" I asked, holding my voice steady.

"Yeah, bro. They didn't even search us. We'll be there in a minute," he finished. I could feel my chest tighten.

When I hung up I started grabbing stuff. "Get your shit, Jenna. We're getting out of here!" Then I picked up the phone again and dialed Maryjo. When she didn't answer I left her a voicemail, telling her when she didn't find us there, that she would need to look on the back roads because we had to leave on foot.

"What's wrong," Jenna was asking. She was picking up on my agitation and was now bouncing around nervously from foot to foot. "Aren't we waiting for Rob or M.J.?"

"No! Now let's roll," I said, herding her and Mr. Big towards the door. Every hair on my neck was standing up on end. I knew that Rob didn't have a license or an up-to-date inspection sticker on his truck; more than enough to warrant being searched, and he rolled with a mobile Methamphetamine lab everywhere he went. No wonder I couldn't get him on the phone for two hours.

Dylan and Maryjo were pulling up in his red Jeep when Jenna and I came out of the room. "Don't get out," I shouted at Dylan and M.J., stopping them as they were opening their doors. I was carrying my rifle under a blanket in one arm and Mr. Big in the other. My fingers were crossed, hoping that I wasn't going to have to fight our way out of there, while Jenna and I rushed to get in. My nerves were strung every bit as tight as they had been out in the woods, when I'd obviously been surrounded. I didn't have any more reason to '*know*' this was the case now than I did then. However, I was learning I was right more often than not, so when we came out of there I was prepared for anything.

"Why? What's wrong?" they both exclaimed at the same time.

"Something's not right. If the cops are not already here they will be soon," I said, pushing Jenna into the back seat ahead of me. I climbed in with my gun in my lap, scanning the access road and nearby cars for signs of a trap. My nerves were contagious. I could see Dylan swiveling his blond head to see everything that he could see as he was pulling out of the parking lot. We took a couple of right turns onto back roads and once we had a little space between us and the motel, not having seen any signs of pursuit, I relaxed a little bit.

"What was all that about?" Maryjo asked. She was handing me a wad of money that Dale had sent. I told her about the situation with Rob and my conversation with him right before they'd got there. Maybe I was wrong, I thought, but I've been in the mix long enough to know when something is off.

When we were a few miles away from the motel, I told Dylan to pull into an Arby's coming up. "I guess we got out of there in time. I didn't see anyone following us," I commented. Still looking, but not seeing anything suspicious, I took a breath and geared down. When we got out at the Arby's I shoved my blanket-wrapped rifle under the Jeep's backseat before going in. Jenna smuggled Mr. Big inside her purse and I bought everyone lunch. Before we got all the way through the meal my nerves started up again. *Dammit! I was getting tired of this shit.*

I was seeing dark-tinted windows in every vehicle that went by now. *What the hell?* I was sure I was just trippin', but I'd rather be safe than sorry, I thought. "Alright, y'all, let's pack it up. I need to get back out to the woods with the tires Dale got for me. I'm going to take care of a couple of things and get the fuck out of this town before I lose my freaking mind. I'm seeing Feds in every S.U.V.," I told Maryjo and Dylan disgustedly, while we were loading back up into the Jeep. My skin was crawling, as if I was laying in an ant den and I was mad about it, counting myself as one of those damn fool tweekers who thinks every light in the sky is a helicopter looking specifically for them. Not that I didn't feel that way, too, sometimes, but the difference was they really *were* after me like that. But now, with no evidence to support my concerns, I chastised myself. It appeared that I could no longer distinguish between the lines of reality and the lines of just simple psychosis. Feeling foolish, I cursed under my breath about what an idiot I was.

Maryjo, overhearing me, interrupted my thoughts. "I wouldn't be so sure about that, Jimmy." She was jumping from side to side in her seat, looking everywhere at once. "You may be on to something. I'm seeing them too!"

Dylan was held up in traffic while he was trying to merge from the access road to the highway. "Yeah, about four cars back, check that car out," he said, looking in his mirror. I Looked back. I could clearly see the spotlight on the side of the grey, blacked out, unmarked cop car. He was sitting out of the line of traffic in a way that gave him a clear line of sight of our Jeep.

"Don't panic, Dylan," I pacified. "It's almost too obvious. Just drive normally and we'll keep an eye on it. Stay in the far lane, so if I have to jump out, I can cross the opposing traffic and climb the highway fence on the other side."

He did as I told him.

It looked as if the cop car was following us for a minute, then we lost sight of him. I had Dylan take an upcoming exit. We didn't see the grey car any more, but we did see three other, darkly-tinted, windowed vehicles quickly switch lanes in order to take the same exit that we had just turned into. I was done doubting myself, and everyone else in the Jeep knew something was going on too.

I directed Dylan to start taking evasive maneuvers whilst we still had a line of traffic between us and the pursuers whom we could see. "Turn into the McDonald's parking lot and go out the back exit," I snapped at Dylan. He cut someone off and turned into it. The surveillance team who'd been trying to shadow us had to break cover to keep from losing us. They were now aware they'd been spotted, so even though we were in a densely-populated area the cops made their move. There were a lot more than we'd seen. I found out later that the grey car we first noticed wasn't even supposed to be in on the chase, but heard the radio chatter and jumped in behind us before they could call him off.

Now in full flight we shot down two more side streets, with Dylan's Jeep cutting out every time he jammed his foot on the gas. I knew I would never be able to outrun them in that piece of junk. There was a line of cop cars coming up on us from behind and I could see red and blue flashers turning the corner ahead at the end of the residential street that we were on.

"Hit the gas!" Maryjo and Jenna both yelled at Dylan. Jenna was clutching Mr. Big close to her chest.

"No! Stop!" I said, overriding the women. There was nowhere to go, anyway. I reached under the seat for my gun. Whether I was going to shoot it out with the militia behind me or not, I didn't know, but I didn't want to leave it behind for someone else to have to deal with. Besides, honestly, I was tired of running and I was tired of doing time. Part of me was ready to just go down in a blaze of glory. Regardless, I needed to take the fight away from the sight of my ex-wives and my little half-pint partner. I only had a split second to do anything. The blanket the gun was wrapped in, got caught in the springs I'd stuck it between under the Jeep's backseat, it was stuck tight. Fuck! Slamming on their brakes, the oncoming cavalcade had caught up.

Having no more time to waste on the rifle, not if I wanted any chance at all of moving away from the Jeep, I opened my door as the Federal Marshalls were just coming to a stop. They froze in their places, unsure of whether or not I was going to come out with a gun and open fire. I took one last drink of my soda then broke and ran. There were cops everywhere. I ran straight into three, who were coming up fast and aiming their pistols at me. They were alternately ordering me to stop, freeze and put my hands in the air, but I ignored them. A black cop and two white officers were closest to me. I snarled and growled at the policemen, before turning and running inbetween two houses. Seeing I didn't have my weapon, they holstered theirs and ran after me.

Even though, I'd been immersed in the drug world pretty heavily since I'd been on the run, I was still healthy and I had full intentions of outrunning them. However, when I made it into the backyard of the house I was sprinting around I saw that, in order to get out of the property, I would have to scale a seven-foot tall, chain-link fence. I immediately realized that there was no way I could get over the top without being grabbed from behind and slammed to the ground. A couple of my foot pursuers were within mere steps of me. Not one to go down without a fight, I jammed on my brakes and turned, throwing up my fists. I clotheslined two of the officers running up on me. The three of us were just hitting the ground when the next one showed up. As we rolled and fought, the officer arriving last pretty-much had free reign to punch and kick me, except when I could twist one of the other officers I was fighting with on the ground into the path of the incoming blows. One of the cops pulled his mace, so locking my hand onto his, I squeezed until the can crushed and I was able to force it from his grasp. I then gave my closest adversaries a short blast of its contents before the damaged can malfunctioned. We struggled, hitting and punching each other, but it was all too soon when the men I was fighting with gained control of me and I was left vulnerable to the continuous strikes of the angry officers. My last act of defiance was refusing to allow them to bend one of my arms behind my back to be cuffed. Eventually, even that became futile and, in the end, I was laying there under a pile of Fugitive Task Force members; handcuffed, with my face being mashed into the muddy grass by someone's Tech-Nine combat boot. I had a new black eye, a cracked rib and the coppery smell of caking blood in my nostrils.

First, the paramedic dealt with the injuries officer Spradlin sustained from the struggle, while I waited, chained up, face down and defeated. After Spradlin went on to the hospital, the E.M.T. checked me out. The fugitive team sat me on the curb next to the ambulance with my shirt pulled up, while officer after officer retrieved their cameras and took pictures of the large A.B. patch on my back. They showed them off as if they had just bagged a twelve-point buck.

From where I was, I could see Dylan, M.J., who was holding Mr. Big, and Jenna lined up on the back bumper of the Jeep. Pretty soon, one of the officers attending me said they'd found my gun, which 'someone' had thrown towards the bushes while everyone was chasing me. The officers told me how they had me surrounded several times out in the woods and nicknamed me 'Bigfoot' because I was so elusive. This was where I learned that, for a moment, I'd been lined up in a sniper's sights waiting for the order to fire, because at the same time, unknown to me, I was aiming my rifle directly at them. As I've said, the only thing to save me was that I was on private property and that they couldn't make a positive I.D.. Then I was loaded up in one of their S.U.V.'s, and after a brief stop at the emergency room to x-ray my ribs, taken to the Tulsa County Jail.

I got a hold of Jenna, who told me they had all been interrogated, but in the end, had been released. Angry and disgusted over my capture, I beat a guy off of the jail's payphone. The man's overly-loud and obnoxious voice pushed my overstressed brain over the limit. I soon found myself in an isolation cell in the jail's internal lockup unit; seething with hate and despair. I had never intended to be taken alive. I was so sick and tired of prison and now I was going back, I knew - for a very long time.

I was charged with assault on the officers during the arrest and two counts of possession of a firearm under the Armed Career Criminal Act. What else I would have to face I didn't know yet. For the first time in my life I contemplated suicide.

Part III

Chapter Forty-Five

Jail

Back in the interview, I leant back in my seat as Sara held up her hand to stop me. The rest of the production crew scrambled to do their jobs the same why they had been throughout a couple short pauses in my story. "I don't want to interrupt you, but I find it hard to believe that you would just consider giving up that way," Sara stared at me through her sparkling, blue eyes. I could see concern and compassion in them. "You know that there is always hope."

"I know. I was just tired, tired of '*this*' life. It's hard to face seeing nothing in your future except prison bars when you feel like you were meant for more." I shifted uncomfortably in my leg-shackles and belly-chain. "Don't worry. I'm not suicidal, but people on the outside forget that life on the inside isn't really life at all. Death Penalty cases get all the notoriety because it's a moral issue to take a life, regardless of how heinous the crime, while thousands of people all over this country are having years, decades, even their lives stripped away from them for non-violent drug-related offences, firearms charges or mistakes they've made in their youth."

"Yes, well your State is especially notorious for excessive time for low-ball crimes," she said, offering me another bottle of water. Brad had finished changing tapes and was leaning forward, listening.

"Not only Oklahoma, the Federal government with its impersonal sentencing guidelines and no reprieve. Somewhere along the way, it has become '*Okay*' to take ten, twenty, even thirty years from a man for hardly more than a few bad habits and his past." I looked over and saw that the guards in charge of me had found themselves some chairs and were now sitting down, watching and listening as well. "Anyway, life in jail has become a slow and tortuous death sentence to me, which '*sometimes*', I'd just rather be done with. I am far from the only one who has feelings like that,"

I finished, aware that I'd just revealed a side of the big, hardened convict/outlaw that they hadn't expected to see.

Tracy, Sam and Tim, all having tended to their individual responsibilities, had stepped back. By now, Sam the sound man was having me snap the clapperboard together for him when we were ready, which I did from a signal by Brad, and we were rolling again.

"Okay," Sara said. "Well, that was in 2010. We see that you obviously made it out since then. Would you continue the story and explain your feelings after your capture? Tell us what brought you, and your son, to this place in your lives?" She took one last drink of her water and I admired her long, slim fingers as she tightened the cap back on the bottle. I placed my own, with its secured lid, down on the floor beside me and continued:

Sitting in that cell after I'd been arrested, I literally felt crushed. I replayed the chain of events that had led me back to where I was; where, just eight months before, I never thought I would ever be again. It was hard for me to accept that I was solely responsible for the systematic dismantling of my life. As intelligent as I believed I was, I'd made one self-destructive, destiny-altering decision after another. It was as if I had sabotaged myself. I thought back to when my plans for my future were so focused and clear-cut. I tried to lay the blame for my fall from grace on Jenna and a hundred other things, but in the end, I knew, I alone was to blame for what I did, or didn't, do.

I examined my collapse. It began with ego. Humble as I pretended to be, I can remember being aware of my pride rampaging like a raging river through my veins; a hidden, devastating force surging just under the surface. I heard the words *somewhere* "that pride goeth before the fall," and knowing the truth in those words, I also remember, arrogantly, ignoring them. Self-aware and honest enough to realize that my downfall was of my own making, long before I ever started on the run, served only to drive me deeper into a state of depression...

I still couldn't wrap my brain around what possessed me to get in a wreck behind Stan back in Oklahoma City in the first place, but I understood why I made so many stupid decisions *after* I got into trouble. I knew where my panic stemmed from. My last sentence had suffocated me. I felt cheated and used by the justice system and the politics of the times. I'd gone in with that forty-five year sentence for possession of a minuscule amount of an illegal drug. By the time I got out, the 'Powers That Be' had changed their insanely hardcore stance on drugs; mostly due to the public's outcry over the cost of prison overcrowding, not out of any sense of compassion, mind you. The result was a shift to a more rehabilitative mindset and the creation of an entity called 'Drug Court'. Now, people caught with a lot more drugs than me and who'd done a lot more dirt to get them were remanded to the custody of the Courts to do their time on the streets. I was stunned. My children had grown up without me. I'd been in prison from the time that they were babies. I had become a feared, violent criminal who could barely function in society… and I got out to find that if my crime had only happened a few years later, I would not have even gone to prison! My life was changed, I was changed - as strong as I was in some ways, I was devastated. I had come to despise, loathe and hate the cage and the system.

I ran… and I ran hard… right into the wall I knew was waiting for me.

While I was in that cell, I got deeply spiritual, which remains with me still today in spite of a few more bad decisions I've made since then. I was alone and inventoried all the rights and wrongs of my life. Some were hard to face. I believed I was a good person under it all and that there was something *good* that I was meant for. At some point, I pushed the darkness and despair out of my head. Well, I don't know if I can actually say I ever really accomplished that. However, I did determine that I wasn't a quitter and after a long, heartfelt talk with God decided that my productive time on this earth was not yet over. I saw in my future that, no-matter-what, I would not spend the rest of my life in prison either.

So… I fought – *hard*, for over a year, through every Court and every hearing; shedding a few other legal cases that they tried to rack up against me in the process. In the end, the charges I faced in Court were assaulting the police officers during my arrest, possession of a firearm and, of course, that First Degree Burglary I had for chasing Joe into his house. The real fight, and the reason I ran in the first place, was from my past: my past crimes, the ones I had, in some cases unfairly, already paid for with decades of my life. In accordance with my past, my Federal firearms charge qualified me as an Armed Career Criminal that would start at fifteen years flat; a devastating sentence for a forty-seven year-old man, even on the lowest possible terms, and they were talking thirty if I took them to trial.

My past record increased my State penalties as well; making each of my Court battles literally a fight for my life.

I didn't back down. I took my cases all the way to trial, fighting like a drowning man wearing lead shoes. They paraded the witnesses up on the stand. The Barnsdall officer and his wife were first. Then came Trudy and many of the Fugitive Task Force team who had been after me. That's where I learned more about the officers during the hunt. They even tried to force my ex-wives and my friends to testify against me. In the end, even though many of the government's witnesses recanted, or downright testified in my behalf, I still lost...

Thanks to a fair judge who saw something in me, the government didn't get to take the rest of my life. With his hands tied, Judge Payne sentenced me to seventeen years... the lower end of the guidelines, not for the crime, but for the enhancement statue. Although my fate could have been far worse, it would still take fifteen calendar years to do it! After all the time I had done, over what people were now getting probation for, I felt very cheated and defeated. The other sentences I received were a State twelve for fighting with police officers and seven for the fiasco of going after Joe. I would get good time for those. The consuming and life-altering sentence was the Federal one, which would make me nearly sixty years old by the time I got out. Some may think I should be happy with what I had, but would you be? It *was* better than getting out at seventy or eighty, or not at all. However, I'd already started the evolution from being a man who could accept prison as his home into one who couldn't. I needed to accomplish something with my life besides being a *'good convict'* or I would implode and die of a broken spirit or broken mind. I prayed for one more chance.

I had been down for little more than a year and was holding down a cell in a private prison at Cushing, Oklahoma, where they send most gang members to now, when I learned that my son, Brandon, had a terrible accident and ran over a lady whilst trying to steal her car. I heard that he was in the County jail facing a second-degree murder case; the very thing I'd told my son could happen if he didn't get away from the drugs and the crowd that he was hanging out with. As unbelievable as it was, it was a reality that couldn't be undone. My heart broke for my son, the lady and her family. On top of that, he was in lock-up at the jail, Brandon had ran into Billy Ray, whereupon he hospitalized the rodent for his crimes against our clan. I blamed myself and my despair was multiplied.

Mine and Jenna's relationship had been rocky ever since my capture, and it only got worse after I went to prison. We tried to work things out, but she was now a full-blown addict. I called in favors to get her into treatment. She went, but thumbed her nose at it and everyone who tried to help her. I held on out of *'love'* and a guilty sense of responsibility for my part in her struggles, but the monkey on her back grew too ferocious. Finally, I gave up and she chose to pursue that life. I made her take Mr. Big to my mother's. He deserved a comfortable retirement after all he'd been through.

Our relationship officially ended when she took up with Buddy. That's right… my albino right hand man. I've learned that often in life loyalty only goes as far as the dope sack, or is only as long as your girl's skirt. Meaning, the skimpier the clothes she wears the less loyalty you can expect from your friends; two of the things that many men have traded their honor, self respect, patches and even lives for, a thousand times over. It drove me mad! I called in every marker owed to me and pulled every string that I could; succeeding only in driving them apart and into hiding. I vowed to be free in order to end Buddy's miserable life. My spiritualism took a big hit when my prayers turned from good and wholesome requests of God to hateful pleas for vengeance. With my new Christian, passive attitude fully shattered, I fell back into drugs. I used them to fund my new plan, my plan to escape. I wanted revenge!

I found out that, if I could get my parole revocation running concurrent with the sentence I was doing, I would qualify for minimum security. Every waking thought went towards that goal. I focused on flying under the radar. I refused the leadership mantel of the Brotherhood, which I had become disenchanted with on the streets and which would distract me from my purpose. When I had the money, I sought out an attorney to help get my cases lined up, so I would be eligible for a transfer.

I had no real hope of success with my plans and schemes built on such negativity. However, despite that, things did begin to turn in my favor. In the meanwhile, the hate consumed me to the point where I had to come to terms with it or lose my mind. I searched my soul and pushed myself through it with God's help; finally realizing my anger was hurting *me* more than them. It was pointless and was only serving to suffocate me even more. Jenna had done enough to me and, frankly, I had done enough to her. She didn't deserve my hate nor any emotion from me at all. All of a sudden, my fury popped like a soap bubble... and was gone. It was funny, all that energy to drive Jenna and Buddy apart and now it didn't even matter. By the time that I reached the end of my struggle to get to lower security and was finally able to request a transfer, my motivation for wanting to break free so badly had changed. What I was left with was simply my desire to be free... to *spite* everyone else. I thought it was unlikely Regional would approve the move, anyway.

Perhaps I should have reconsidered, but I'd been yearning to be free for so long, and had so many years left to go, that running was in my D.N.A.. Even though I'd messed it up so many times before, I thought that maybe without all the distractions, and if I was living as a law-abiding citizen, I could steal a few quality years now and finish my time when I was older. I slammed the brakes down and quit doing and dealing drugs. I made a deal with myself to never commit another crime, except for escape, of course, and decided to go for it. With no hate, drugs nor Jenna in the picture, I believed I could pull it off. It seemed as if no sooner than I had made up my mind, than the powers who were in control of my life informed me to pack my things. I was told I was going to minimum. I thought this must be the answer to my prayers.

As I was riding in the backseat of a white, Oklahoma Department of Corrections transport van; black boxed and chained so tight that my wrists and ankles ached, my mind raced along with the scenery that flashed by my windows. It was late January, the spring was going to come early this year, the trees and fields we were passing were already turning green. I laughed out loud, thinking that I soon would be free again. I couldn't wait to once again feel the air rushing against my face as I rode down one of these tree-lined, two-laned, winding strips of asphalt on my Harley.

A black guy named Brown, who was sat next to me and chained just as tightly, and miserably, as I was, looked over at me as if I was crazy. "What's so funny, Maxwell?"

I just kept looking out the window. "You'll see," I smiled to myself. "You'll see..."

CHAPTER FORTY-SIX
MAKING A BREAK FOR IT

We didn't arrive at the prison, which sat three miles northeast of Vinita, Oklahoma, until after dark. I couldn't see it very well, but I could see that half of the prison was behind a concertina wire-topped fence and half of the prison wasn't. We were informed that our housing unit would be *behind* the razor wire. I was still in shock that I was even there, and knew at any moment I would be told a mistake had been made and be re-shackled before I ever had another chance at it. We were being unloaded and unchained in an unsecured building before we were to be marched through the gates. I toyed with the thought of making a run for it right from the van. This was a stroke of luck in the first place and it probably would be my only chance to be free in the next ten calendar years. It had to be considered.

However, running before I was ready was far too reckless for all the same reasons. My one opportunity couldn't be squandered. I just had to hope the mistake wasn't caught before I was able to make my move. I decided to at least *act* like I belonged there and settled into that frame of mind as the officers removed our restraints then marched us through the gates to the secure part of the prison. I couldn't help but feel my hope sink a little with every step.

All five of us who came in on our transport were assigned areas throughout the dormitory part of the cell house. Brown and I got shuffled off to a twelve-man tank. There, we found a couple of guys who had come a week or two before us from Cushing and they gave us the rundown on how the place operated.

I learned, to my relief, that no matter what other restrictions I might run into, the mess hall was on the other side of the fence. Short of being put in the S.H.U., I would be allowed out from behind the razor wire at least three times a day to eat; morning, noon and night. With that knowledge, I relaxed and went to sleep waiting to see what would happen next.

I woke up to find the chow hall and the gates were open before sunrise. I was getting happier by the minute. I also found a half-dozen Brothers waiting to welcome me. Two of them I'd known for a couple of decades. I'm a man that tries to keep his plans to himself, even when dealing with bros. It's just my policy. I'm a firm believer that if someone doesn't need to know something, then they don't need to know... secrets are hard to keep in prison. However, I had questions and I needed help and advice from someone *'in the know'*. I was happy to see Stig and Tommy Lewis were there.

Until I had a chance to talk to them alone, I just kept my thoughts to myself as the Brothers welcomed me with hugs, handshakes and offers of drugs, tobacco and commissary. All of which I declined. My only open request was for a cellphone. I'd left my other one back at Cushing with the bro who was collecting in the money that was still owed to me on that yard. Cellphones had gotten pretty popular in the State prisons while I'd been doing Federal time. My friends immediately started trying to locate one for me. I had to secure a phone, because I didn't want to try and coordinate my escape without one.

Phones are not easily concealed in an open dormitory, with all the prying eyes and ears, so they weren't as readily available as I'd hoped and it took me a week to get my own. I spent that week looking over the grounds. I knew the staff was keeping an eye on me, so I tried not to be seen with Tommy nor Stig too much. However, when we could do so without attracting too much notice, we would walk around the complex together. Tommy and Stig took turns pointing out cameras, fences and explaining the guard's routines as best they could.

Stig was a couple of inches taller than me, dark-headed and as strong as a John Deere tractor. He worked on a farm crew. The State's property covered an additional eighty acres besides the prison compound itself, where the crews on the farm raised cattle and cut cordwood amongst other things. My bro tried to convince me that I should wait, get on his crew and make my run from out there. He thought it might take a month or so, because they didn't do much hiring in the winter, but he was sure he could get me on. He was hard-working and well-liked. He told me they were always looking for more like him. Stig was right; making the break from the farm would definitely be my best chance of success. With the shortage of fences, the prison proper was ringed with an extensive camera system, which extended a hundred yards in every direction. However, my friend was doing a *lot* of time and doing it right. I really didn't want to get him off into something that would reflect badly on him.

"Don't worry about me, brother. You won't have another chance like this. You can make a quiet, smooth exit from out there," he tried to reassure me when I expressed my concerns for him. I was even more resistant to the idea after I talked to his boss, just an old country boy who was willing to agree to hire me on Stig's word and my handshake. No matter what my bro said, I knew they would never look at him the same way after I left, and he'd probably lose his job. He loved being able to go out and ride horses all day. It takes a good friend to give up something that they really enjoy for you… likewise, a true friend wouldn't take it. I decided that I couldn't wait that long, anyway.

Tommy wanted to be just as helpful. He was old as the sun and looked like Yoda from *Star Wars*, minus the ears. My friend had retired his patch a couple years before, but was still just as good and trustworthy as they came. I told him he didn't want to be seen walking around looking into the fields too much with me, either. Once I was gone, it would be only too obvious what I'd been about… and just like Stiggy… he didn't care.

I walked around the perimeter countless times with them, and by myself, marking the cameras and the lay of the land. I had three open directions I could go. The drawbacks were that it was surrounded by fields as far as the eye could see; with all of them covered by the surveillance system.

My only other alternative was south. N.E.O.C.C. was built off of an old, abandoned mental institution whose vacant buildings and extensive complex sat as quiet and dark as a ghost-town just on the other side of the visiting yard. There were cameras on the prison and visiting grounds, but I suspected that the surveillance ended at the institution's property line. Instead, that direction had several different-sized fences still remaining from its days as the State's insane asylum. For that reason, even though the turnpike was only a couple more miles further south, it made it the most unlikely direction for an escaping inmate to choose.

As I thought it over my daughter, Stephanie, enlisted the help of Ferret Peterson, a Brother who was on the streets at the time. They drove up from Tulsa together, scoping out a place to pick me up from once I'd made it off prison property. Stephanie wanted to *make sure* I got away. Of course, that involved them sitting on some side road waiting for me to show up with who knows what on my trail. It was a risk I didn't want my daughter to take. She'd already done enough for me. She stabbed Teddy not long after I'd gotten caught, putting him in the hospital and barely avoiding prosecution herself over it. Brothers had gone after him *twice* more for ratting me out the first time and yet he was still slithering around Tulsa like the snake he was. I knew my time there at the minimum was limited until he heard about it. He would know I was coming out and he'd assume I was coming for him. It was just a matter of time before he learned where I was and called his Federal agent pals and convinced them not to let me have the chance. He didn't know I'd had a reckoning with myself and just wanted to be free and as far away from Oklahoma, and everyone in it, as possible.

I still had a couple of grand coming that one of my Brothers was supposed to collect for me back at Cushing and filter to my bank account. That and what I already had would fund my initial run. I also had a Spanish friend whose parents made driver's licenses for illegals. I'd made arrangements to have them make one for me on my way out of the State. I had a plan to go out west and lay low for awhile.

What I didn't want to do was leave a wake of legal problems for the people who were determined to help me. With that in mind, I got a hold of Ferret and told him I wasn't willing to let Stephanie risk herself any further, nor him either for that matter. I'd find my own way out and give him a call when I was somewhere relatively safe. He could then pick me up and help me from there. The bro agreed to be on call, whenever and wherever.

That decision made it a little bit harder, but it did narrow down which direction I intended to leave the institution from. I would go straight for the turnpike. My ride would never have to go through the town of Vinita nor travel on any of the backroads where their presence would raise eyebrows. From that point on, I just watched and waited for the right combination of humidity and fluctuating temperatures to produce a nice bank of morning fog.

I didn't have long to wait. I woke up on the morning of February the thirteenth to look out of the window and find that I could barely see the fence twenty yards away. It was time!

All of a sudden, my brain switched gears. I went from hoping and wishing for this moment to present itself... to it being here! My pulse quickened and my mind sharpened as the neurons in my brain lit up like a string of Christmas tree lights. I paused for one split second, wondering, if this was the right thing to do or not. I'd been thinking about breaking out for so long that I just marked it as nerves and bottled the thought up and stuck it on the shelf.

Josh, a youngster who said he knew my kids on the streets, slept near me. I trusted him about as much as I could trust anybody I'd just met. "Josh. Get up, you're going to breakfast with me," I told him.

"Huh..." he said sleepily. "Is it raining?" He was squinting through watery, hazel eyes towards the window.

"No, it's just foggy. Now get up - I'm not asking," I ordered.

"Alright, I'm coming," the skinny, ginger haired twenty year old said, sitting up wiping his eyes. He hadn't been in for very long and still had his A&R buzzcut going on. He was a good kid and I liked him.

"Get the fuck up!" I snapped. "I mean it, I'm in a hurry and I need your help." With that, Josh jumped down from his rack and quickly got dressed. I don't know if it showed or not, but I was beginning to vibrate from the adrenaline starting to flow. My mind raced in dozens of directions, trying to put in order what was about to happen. Not to mention, fend off the fear of failure that tried to creep into my soul along with the nagging thought that this was probably not the answer God had in mind to my prayers. Each negative and distracting thought was bottled, corked and shelved immediately along with the rest of my doubts. I had a growing wine cellar of bottled up rational thoughts in my mind. In retrospect, I probably should have sipped on a few of them just to see what they tasted like.

I looked at Josh. Regardless of the chaotic thoughts flashing through my mind, he seemed completely oblivious to my heightened state. As he pulled his coat on to follow me out of the dorm he asked: "What do you need me for, big brother?"

"I'll tell you in a minute," I replied, leading us out of the building. As we headed out the door I could see the fog was just as thick as it looked from the window... and the gates were open. I could feel the skin on the back of my neck tingle as I realized that if things went right, I could be a thousand miles from where I stood in a couple of days, starting another life. It's an incredible feeling to go from not having any hopes of liberation for at least ten years to thinking that you may have it by the end of the day!

Once outside of the wire we headed across the compound toward the mess hall. On the way I told Josh when he got back to the dorm to switch mattresses and bedding with me. I had already thrown my dirty clothes bag into the laundry room with everyone else's. There was nothing except the bedroll that had a scent the dogs could follow on it. "Huh? What for?" Josh asked. "Where are you going?"

"You'll see," I said. I fell a little behind him as we were nearing another gate, where we either turned towards the chow hall or continued on to the visiting yard. I didn't tell him what I was doing, because, if at the last second I had to abort my mission, I didn't want to have someone else, especially some youngster I barely knew, knowing what I was up to. I liked him, but people talk and you can't un-ring a bell once it's rung.

When we got to the intersecting sidewalk I stopped, letting Josh walk on through the gate. I peered into the dark, predawn fog covering the visiting yard, visualizing my path through the balls of fuzzy flood lights that were working hard to penetrate the haze. I knew where the cameras were. The main one sat on a twenty-two foot tower and looked directly over the ground I would have to traverse. My plan was to go directly for that camera. There were others, but they were spaced for overlapping coverage and I doubted that they were actually covering each other. Regardless, the fog cut even night-vision-equipped surveillance down to what was immediately in front of it. I would still be exposed for two separate, thirty-yard stretches before I could reach the ghost town at the other end of the property, but no escape is without risk and I would take what I calculated to be the best chance of getting lucky. All that went through my mind in a moment. It was do or die time - maybe both.

A couple of guys had walked past on their way back from eating. I waited until they were out of earshot, then quietly hollered at Josh. He'd been walking with his head down and hadn't noticed me stop. He was fifteen feet ahead of me when he looked back. Now my heart was pounding and my face was flushed enough that he could see something was up. Before he could voice an inquiry, I told him to look around the corner. "Is anyone else coming?" I asked.

"No… What's goi-" he was saying when I cut him off.

"I'm trusting you. Don't forget to switch my bedroll out." With that I gave him a two-fingered, loose salute, smiled a shit-eating grin, then turned and ran straight at the camera tower.

My nerves had been bucking against the restraining reins holding my hope and excitement in check, but when I stepped off into the dark and made my move the yoke broke and I felt like a wild stallion who has just broken free from his harness. I was almost out of control. My legs ran with a life of their own as fast as they could carry me. I sprinted through the first fuzzy ball of light, knowing that if someone was watching that particular camera, at that particular moment, then my chances of success would drop to less than zero. I was also well-aware as I crossed under the tower that I had passed *'the point of no return'*. In a near panic I lost all thought except to run. I climbed the fence at the other side of the visiting yard and dropped into the old asylum's grounds. Swallowed up into the darkness, I ran past the even darker shadows of the abandoned buildings. I imagined that I could faintly hear the ghosts of the insane laughing from behind the broken windows as they watched me run past. By the time I got to the second fence my heart was bursting and my boots felt as if they were full of lead. I stopped long enough to listen and gain control of my panic. I heard nothing, but my own labored breathing in the thick air. I climbed over the fence. The fog wasn't as bad amongst all the buildings, but it was still dark. Jogging, I followed the faint glow of the moon. My heart was still hammering away, but I had gotten control of myself. At this point, it was what it was; I was here, I was doing this, so there was nothing else to think about except making it across the turnpike before sunrise.

Once I passed through the quarter-mile wide complex of buildings, which I never would have guessed to be that extensive from the outside, I came upon a couple of additional fences that I would have to clamber over before I could exit the asylum's grounds. Incidentally, putting me back on prison property, not far from the warden's house, no less. It was part of the *'farm'* and extended the rest of the way to the turnpike. I climbed the first, higher fence and ran up and crouched beside the next five-foot, chain-link barrier, which ran along the prison's access road. The only cover was a couple of bushes and I had to be careful, because anything on it would be coming from, or going to, the penal colony. Not hearing anything at the moment, I didn't waste any time. I was at the top of the fence when I heard the S.U.V.s and saw the glow of their headlights trying to penetrate the fog, which had once again shrouded me. There were two of them coming fast - I had to move! The way the engines were racing, they were on a mission. *Someone must have seen me,* I thought, *oh no!* I jumped for it!

There was not any razor nor barbed wire across the top; it just ended in those twisted-off diamonds that are ubiquitous to all chain-link fences. It wasn't that hard to get over, but in my haste my pant legs got caught in them and before they ripped loose my momentum slammed me to the ground like a sledgehammer against a rail spike. I twisted, landing in the road on my shoulder, knocking the wind out of me.

The lights were now coming up fast – I had no time. I sprang to my feet... something was wrong! My right arm felt funny... The trucks were almost on me! I ran across the road with my arm flopping around at my side! *I've got no time for this!* my mind screamed when I realized I was hurt. They would see me at any moment. The lights were there! So were the engines! I dived for cover... just making it into hiding as they roared by.

I wanted to lay there, but I forced myself to get up after I heard the sounds of the S.U.V.s fade into the muffled, humid air. My shoulder was gone and my arm hung from what was normally its pit. It dangled from nothing, but ever increasingly-painful flesh and sinew. The joint was completely dislocated. *God... this was going to hurt when I had time to let it.* However, at that moment – I didn't. Thinking about Mel Gibson in *'Lethal Weapon'* I rammed it against a nearby tree in a desperate attempt to quickly relieve the pain and the complications that this new factor would add. And, just for the record, I advise anyone reading this not to follow my example. Life is *not* like the movies. I should have known better. It really made no sense the way that my arm was hanging, and I knew that *immediately* after the red exploding spots of pain dissipated from my vision.

It didn't fix my shoulder, but it definitely cleared my mind. Everything came into a sharp, clear point of focus; I had to move. I didn't know what those S.U.V.s meant, but they were out there, the dawn was coming and the fog would be lifting soon. My shoulder would just have to wait, but my arm hanging unhinged at my side was far too painful; its weight alone made it agonizing. I grabbed my right hand with my left and lifted my arm up over my head, where my forearm could rest across the top of my skull.

That reduced the weight enough for me to withstand the pain and allow me to cover some ground. I must have looked like quite a sight running across the fields with my left hand holding my right arm over the top of my hairy dome. I couldn't let go even to cross the barbed wire fences I encountered. My arm would flop loose the moment I lost my grip. I'd just slide over them, ripping my pants and my flesh when they snagged on the barbs.

Eventually, after a mile and a half, I came to the last field between me and the turnpike. I slid over the barbed barrier just as I had the others, still holding my arm over my head, digging even deeper grooves in the back of my legs. On the other side, I quickly crouched down against the foliage that grew next to the fence line. I'd found the S.U.V.s that had sped by me earlier. They were sitting at the top of a rise on either side of a big, bushy tree. All I could see was the murky glow of their headlights and, as daylight was starting to filter over the horizon, the bleary shapes of the four-by-fours behind them.

What I faced was an open field a couple of hundred yards wide that swooped down in an open valley from the hill the officers sat on. It didn't appear as if they were actively looking for someone. Maybe this was just standard procedure on a foggy morning. Regardless, they knew that this would be the last open stretch before the turnpike and, under normal circumstances, would be uncrossable without being seen from their vantage point. As fast as the sun was rising and the fog was lifting, I had about ten more minutes before I wouldn't be able to cross undetected either. I could already see the landscape, there would be nowhere to hide when the cover was gone. I would stand out like a smoking turd on a fresh snow bank. I had to cross, *now!*

About three quarters of the way across the field, there was one low, rolling hill. I could hear the cars and trucks moving along the highway right on the other side of it. So close! I was in a valley, the last place to give up its hanging blanket of moist cover. I took off walking, away from the trucks on the ridge, angling slightly for the lower side of the mound so I could walk around and have it block me from their view. Wearing a grey prison coat and blue jeans, I figured my chances of not being seen were reasonable. Still, I felt pins and needles crawling up my back, as if I was in the crosshairs of a rifle scope. One step at a time I came closer to my destination. By then I could literally see the haze of the morning evaporating. Twenty more yards, I thought, eighteen, Jesus Lord – fifteen, ten. Five – holy shit! I don't know how I made it, but by the time I got around the hill there was enough light and visibility that I could clearly see the cars on the turnpike and they could clearly see me. I went over one more barbed wire fence, where I found a few bushes and a small depression in the ground to hide me from the immediate view of the passing motorists. However, I was far from in the clear yet.

My shoulder was now starting to stiffen up and become painful in any position. What was I going to do? This was the first chance I'd had to think about it. I didn't know, but I wasn't turning myself in. First things first, I dug my phone out and punched in Ferret's number. "Yeah, Brother," he said when he answered.

"Damn, I'm glad you're awake. Do you have any gas in your truck?" I asked through clenched teeth.

"Yes, why what's up?"

Between painful gasps, I told him the situation. "I need you right now! Get up and head in this direction! My phone will be off to save the battery, but I'll call you back when I get to a place you can pick me up from."

"Are they after you?" he asked.

"Not that I can tell, but if they get on me I'll call you off. Just hurry! In another couple of hours I'm going to be in so much pain I won't be able to function. I don't want to be stuck out here like that. Come – *now!*" I said, with all the urgent authority I could muster.

"Okay... I'm on my way," Ferret concluded.

With that we hung up. I lay there for a minute. I could see about a mile up where the tree-line and barrier fence jetted out momentarily into the thirty-yard wide, cleared shoulder strip, almost to the highway. I didn't know why it did that, but as clear as the day was already, I'd need as much cover as close to the road as possible. I set my sights on it. I had intended to cross, but I would be seen by dozens of cars before I could get over all eight lanes and the service road on the other side. With it now being fully daylight, nothing was going to be easy.

Not to mention my freaking arm! I realized that even if I made it out of there I would still have to have it fixed. It could not remain like it was and the pain was getting worse by the second. I refused to even consider giving up, but going to the hospital would be tantamount to turning myself in. I would not get out of an E.R. without being checked out by the police as well. I thought about that; a hospital, the doctor, what would they do?

The Doc would give me some pain medicine and then pull it back into the socket, the same thing that he would do if it was a broken bone. The only thing the doctor had that I didn't was experience and morphine. The process was still the same. Now that I was calm and thinking clearly, I could picture how my shoulder went together. I've worked out all of my life and have studied many anatomical diagrams. I thought that if I stretched the tendons, maybe I could pull my arm out enough that it would pop back into place. Really, there was no choice; it had to be done. As much as I didn't want to admit it to myself, as things stood with my shoulder this way, my odds of getting far enough to even be picked up were very slim.

It turned out to be a really beautiful morning. I could hear a crow calling and motorists on the highway. I took a deep breath, locking down my nerve before pulling my wrist with its limp arm and swelling shoulder up around my bent knee. Hooking my right hand on my shin bone, I grabbed the back of it with my left so it wouldn't slip loose from the pressure. My senses acute, I noticed the smell of the red Oklahoma dirt I lay on, tinged with my own sweat. Another breath, my heart pounded. Then... I pressed my legs forward, "Aaaaaaaaaa!" I wanted to yell out loud, but I couldn't afford to let the sound out. Instead, the internal scream just reverberated around the inside of my skull. It wasn't working! Oh no – no, it had too... I pushed harder... Aaaaaa! *God, please!* I thought. I wanted to give up, but I couldn't... I'd never be able to endure this again and I knew it. It had to go now! I breathed out everything I had in my lungs and pushed every ounce of strength I had left into my legs. I could feel the muscles, tendons and flesh stretching... the pain was excruciating! I felt the shift and, all of a sudden, with two little sucking pops, my shoulder joint slid back together! *'Oh yes!.. thank you, thank you, thank you, Lord'*, I said in my head, over and over. I fell over, gasping for breath, flexing my hand, tears that I'd squeezed from my eyes blurring my vision.

I knew then that I would make it!

CHAPTER FORTY-SEVEN
THE GETAWAY

I had already accepted that I was going to have to cowboy-up and make it out of the search area before I could deal with my shoulder. Hurt or not, I was still determined to make it, no matter what the pessimistic side of my brain had been telling me. So, when those bones slipped back together it only multiplied the hopeful and reassuring feelings that came surging up into my heart. I was elated! With that obstacle basically overcome, there was no way I was going to fail; even if it meant hiking all the way out of there on my own, which it didn't look like I was going to have to do.

There wasn't any time to rejoice. Ferret was supposed to be on his way. If he was hurrying, like I assumed that he was, it would take him no more than an hour and a half to get there from his side of town. I needed to be somewhere he could pick me up safely by then.

I flexed my hand and raised my arm. It was weak and painful, but incredibly it worked! Still, it wasn't going to be of any use to me to crawl or lift with for awhile, but it wasn't a derailing disability any more either. *I'll be alright,* I thought, I hoped.

Time to move... I peered over the edge of the little burrow I'd commandeered. *Oh, man...* the sky was crystal clear. I could literally see the people inside their cars as they appeared and drove over the horizon. I sure wanted to be on the other side of the turnpike, but there was only one way to get there and that would be to make a bold run for it and pray for the best. There was far too much risk in that; and after what I had just been through, I wasn't going to be reckless.

That left finding a *safe* place on this side; where the search would be concentrated the most. About fifty yards up on the left was a pond and the start of a wooded tract of land. It swung around to the string of trees stretching toward the road that I'd spotted earlier. That was going to have to do.

The only way out of the shallow hole I was in would blatantly expose me to the motorists for several minutes, and it involved me crossing back over onto prison farm property. However, I obviously couldn't stay there. With no time to waste and no choice in the matter I stood up completely visible to the vehicles traveling up and down the interstate, then half-walked, half-jogged, to the property fence. Climbing over the stranded barbed wire was much easier now that my arm was back in place. On the other side I just crouched and ran. It was only forty more yards or so to the edge of the pond, where the tree-line picked up and quickly turned into a full-blown forest.

I breathed a little easier when I got to the little body of water. I knew that, if I had to, I could submerge myself the way I had when I wrecked my bike outside of Barnsdall. It would be cold, but at least it was an option. I kept moving deeper into the trees. At the other end of the pond I found a small creek feeding it. Following the stream, I discovered why the trees stretched towards the road the way that they did. To my utter delight, the creek ran straight under the turnpike through a concrete culvert all the way to the other side. Maybe God was smiling on this endeavor after all, or maybe he just felt like I deserved a break.

Anyway, the trees almost extended to the tunnel, so without any ado, I ran down into the water and splashed my way under all eight lanes. When I come up I saw a mile marker sitting right on the side of the road – perfect, I thought. I continued on to the other side of the access road and climbed up onto the bank and into the woods there. I looked back over my trail. I could see all the way to where I'd reset my shoulder. Fortune was smiling on me! I would spot a following posse a long way off! Comfortable that I could reasonably protect Ferret from being caught up, I pulled my cellphone out. Four times in a row I called... and got nothing but his voicemail.

No flippin' way! Are you kidding me? This is the guy that's supposed to not only pick me up, but help me get out of town! Rage, disgust and a bit of despair came surging up into my throat like bile, but I swallowed it. I had no time to spend on emotions, nor for figuring out what was going on with him. Moving past it, I called the one person that I knew I could count on and who was also the last person that I wanted to involve. Stephanie answered almost immediately. "What's up, Jimbo?"

"I'm in the fucking woods waiting on Ferret to pick me up and his bitch ass won't answer the phone now. I'm in bad shape and I need help …that's what's up," I blurted out.

"What? I knew your crazy ass was going to pull something! You were supposed to let me come and get you in the first place. I can't believe him!" she complained.

"Well, sweetheart, we don't have time to worry about that now. I fell off of the fence and dislocated my shoulder. I've pulled it back in place, but it's fried and hurting and I need you to come get me. We'll deal with Ferret later."

"John's here. We're on our way!"

"Alright, I only have a little over a quarter on my battery left, so hurry. I'll check back with you in an hour …and thanks," I finished.

"Thanks… are you serious? When we have time, I'm going to curse you out for trying to leave me out of this in the first place! When you call back we'll be almost there. I love you, asshole," she said before hanging up.

To myself I thought: *"I love you too. I'm sorry I had to drag you into this."*

I knew for a fact that Steph was coming. I tried Ferret one more time with the same results. *Grrrr.* I shut my phone off and settled back down to watch and wait; thinking about what to do to him before I left town, and how it was going to mess up my plans for a quick getaway.

About an hour later I called Stephanie and John back. "How close are you?" I asked.

"We're almost there. John's hauling ass," Stephanie chirped. "As a matter of fact, we're coming up on the McDonald's overpass right now!"

They were close. I told them to start watching for a creek that ran under the road and highway marker ninety-seven. I slid back down the bank into the creek and went through the first tunnel under the access road. From inside of it I could watch the cars go across the top of the other tunnel. Steph told me they were in a black Lexus.

I had been holding back from being over-confident about making it too quickly. My relationship with karma is one that seems to delight in putting me in my place whenever I get a little bit too sure of myself. With that in mind, I'd just been holding myself with an expectant hope of success. But now I was starting to think… I might actually make it!

I was on the phone with Stephanie when they went by. I alerted her and they pulled over and backed up. Stephanie was still looking around when I climbed up out of the culvert and ran to the car. I jumped in the back and immediately laid down in the seat. "Did anyone see me?" I asked.

"I don't think so, but stay down anyway." Stephanie swiveled around, scanning the road.

John flipped a u-turn and headed back to Tulsa. My heart was still pounding and I hugged the floorboards as we drove under the McDonald's with its windows looking right down on the motorists passing under them. I'd made it! I couldn't believe it! Relief was a calming nectar running through my veins, getting sweeter with every mile.

About ten miles down the road I felt safe enough to sit up. I told them the whole harrowing tale of my escape, of how I busted my arm and, of course, of the Ferret let-down; the reason that they had to drop everything and fly down the highway at nine o'clock in the morning to get me in the first place. When Stephanie found out the full extent of my shoulder injury, she really got pissed. "That mother fucker is going to get his," she vowed. I told her to call him and ask if he'd heard from me. He told her he hadn't, but he'd call her if he did. When she hung up, she looked over the seat at me with her blue-eyes blazing, "You know he's moving some stuff and has quite a bit of money right now? I want to wear one of those evil clown masks when we rob him," she declared.

I laughed. She could almost read my mind!

We talked and I told them my immediate plans for picking up an I.D. and getting some money together before leaving the State. The things Ferret, as a completely unknown conspirator, was supposed to help me with. Stephanie was mildly irritated with me, to say the least, that I had made all those plans without her.

"Honey, I love you. You're just about to get Jaden back. He's only ten and he needs his mom. You can do without my trouble. Besides, you will be the first place the cops will start looking for me."

She blew an irritated stream of cigarette smoke towards the plush burgundy roof of the Lexus. "Well, you see how much you can count on those other people," she shot back. "Now what are you going to do?"

I looked at John. He was a white, middle-aged, middle-class *'drug dealer'*, with sandy-brown hair and coco-coloured eyes. He was concentrating on the road as he weaved in and out of traffic. "Thanks, John," I said sincerely.

"No problem. Glad I could help," he replied, nodding at me through the rearview mirror.

Turning my attention back to Stephanie, I went on: "I don't know, Pamela, a girl I hooked-up with last year would help me, except she sent in a visiting form once. It was never approved, but it's still somewhere police will stake out." I tried flexing my arm. It was getting stiff.

"You can stay at my apartment until you're ready to leave."

Steph was smiling; excitement oozing out of her pores. She was made for this shit. Not to mention, she really wanted to see me free.

"Honey, I'm sorry. Going to my daughter's house on escape is not a very smart thing to do," I countered.

"Nobody knows where I live. I've only been there a little over a week and the apartment and bills are not in my name."

"Yeah, she keeps people away from there too. That probably wouldn't be that bad of an idea, at least temporarily," John interjected.

"Yeah... well, they'll be looking as hard for her as they will be for me, but, I doubt they'll roll out the whole task force over this. I need a shower, clean clothes and some Tylenol anyway. Let's go," I told him. "I should be good for a couple hours at least."

We finished the trip in silence. I looked up into the blue sky and watched the clouds roll by. It occurred to me that this time next week I may be in L.A. with blond hair or something. I wondered if that girl I used to know was still out there.

Before I knew it, we were pulling into Stephanie's place. It was right off the turnpike; no wonder they had got to me so fast. She had a one-bedroom, upstairs apartment in a small complex. *This should do for the moment*, I thought. I got on the phone and called one of my bros, Jamie Tyler, also known as J.T., at the Walls, via his cellphone. As I said, cellphones had become fairly common in the State prisons while I'd been gone. I told him my situation and he, in turn, got in touch with several other Brothers and friends. Within an hour, he called me back and told me a courier would be coming by later with some money and clothes for me.

With that all handled, I took a long bath. Stephanie laundered the clothes I'd had on, while I lay in the water thinking that I was almost home free and daydreaming about the sandy beaches of California...

While I waited for the courier I made a pizza, almost burning the place down. After I ate and aired the apartment out I lay down, exhausted, and slept as hard as a dead man.

I woke up a few hours later to my phone buzzing. It was lighting up with texts coming in and a couple of missed calls. The first text I saw was from Valerie-Daniel, informing me a task force had just kicked in the doors of Maryjo's house, looking for me. About that time my phone lit up again. It was Jamie. I could see where he had tried several times while I'd been asleep. I answered, but before I could get anything out he yelled into the phone: "Brother, turn the T.V. on!"

"Huh... *why?*" I asked as I put the home-made sling I'd made over my neck to hold my arm in place; trying my best to doctor myself.

"You're all over the News. We've got to get you out of there!" He sounded panicked, as if he was the one standing there instead of me. All I had to do was turn on the set to see what he was talking about. It was a media blitz - every few minutes, every channel: 'James Maxwell, also known as Jimmy Maxwell, was found missing from the Northeastern Correctional Center outside of Vinita, Oklahoma, early this-morning. He has ties to Tulsa and is believed to be headed into the area. Maxwell is dangerous and needs to be apprehended immediately... blah... blah... blah...'

"Fuck, what is wrong with these people?" I grumbled. "Okay, you're right. The clocks ticking. I should have never stopped in this town. Tell your guy to drop what he's doing and get his ass over here!"

"He's on his way, bro," J.T. finished.

I turned to Stephanie. "Your mom watched Jaden for you when you and Ferret drove out to Vinita... right? Who brought her? She doesn't have a car?"

"Dagaila did, but she sat in the car. She didn't come in."

"Teddy's girlfriend? Oh shit!" I cursed, pulling a face.

"She wouldn't talk to the cops," Steph said in defense of the girl.

"No, probably not... but if you don't think she wouldn't have told Teddy you're crazy, and we both know *he* will! At least, they probably don't know the apartment number," I finished, frustrated with my own ignorance.

Fifteen minutes later I guided 'Red', the courier, in; giving him his final destination instructions at the last minute. He showed up with a backpack full of clothes for me and a few grand that a couple of my bros had put together, intending to recoup the money from the guys at Cushing. "You're bigger than I thought," the tall, slender man said. "I don't know if those pants in there are going to fit you, but there's clothes and some other things that you'll probably need. I can get you some more later."

I didn't have time to even look. "I need you to get me out of here right now! I've just been plastered all across the News and the police are looking for me a lot harder than I thought they would," I said. My mind was racing. I had made a terrible error. I'd been laying low for so long that I forgot, *'who'* I was, or who they thought I was, anyway. Stopping in Tulsa, *period*, let-alone Stephanie's, was an amateur mistake. All of a sudden, I thought about that bitch karma. I had been thinking I'd made it... and was daydreaming as if success was already assured and, sure enough, here was karma to remind me that I was still just another fool.

"Okay," Red said, running his hand back across his shortly cropped red hair nervously. "Let me pull my truck around. I'll be waiting for you."

After he left, Stephanie grabbed her purse and a couple of things she would need to help change my appearance and we headed out the door. In the complex parking lot there seemed to be a little bit more activity going on than I would have expected, but what the hell would I know about what was normal around there? I was alert, but nothing stood out. I watched our back trail as we left. I could see a long way behind us and we made several turns before jumping onto the highway. I was sure no-one followed us.

For the first time, I truly relaxed. We were in the clear. Stephanie and me were in an unknown truck with an unknown accomplice. There was no ties to me at that moment and short of getting pulled over for a traffic violation there wasn't any reason for the police to even be looking at us. Red was on the phone, telling someone my clothes size and adding a few other things to a list that we might need. We made a quick detour on the west side whereupon some girl ran out and threw a bag of stuff in the back of the truck, then off we went. Red said he thought he was seeing a lot of tinted windows. Of course he was a tweeker, so it didn't surprise me, nor alarm me. I couldn't see any possible way *'the Man'* could be on to us.

We were headed out of town, to a motel in Sapulpa; close enough where I could still take care of business before I left. Stephanie was going to help me change my look, so I could take the picture for my I.D.. I sat with my arm hanging out of the passenger window of Red's cherry-colored

Chevy; my sling blowing in the wind. I was openly smiling now. *Karma can suck it!* I thought. *I've made it.* I let my guard all the way down. We were just hitting the outskirts of town and the wooded patches we were passing were getting thicker. I was so happy that I had my life back. I was going to live a free, clean and low-key life. *God, thank you...* I was saying in my mind. Without warning, Red hit his brakes. I jerked myself out of my reverie and my head swung around to see *'the courier'* looking in the rearview mirror. "What the fuck is that?" he blurted.

I looked out the back window and *'what the fuck'* was right! There were twenty different vehicles from regular cop cars to blacked-out S.U.V.'s all with red and blue flashes in their grills and on there tops – all coming at us! I looked ahead. There were half as many up there, also blocking off all of the traffic! They fanned out around us as Red came to a stop.

"What the fuck are you doing?" I yelled. "Mash the gas... *run!*" I hadn't asked him if he was riding dirty, or transporting anything illegal, but I was sure that he was, so my words were meant for him as much as for myself! Within seconds, the cops were drawing down on the truck with their guns; demanding that the driver throw his keys out and exit the vehicle. To my utter amazement Red complied without hesitation, apologizing to me as he was climbing out of the truck with his hands in the air. I couldn't really blame him, at this point he was probably more confused than I was. I sat there next to Steph completely dumbfounded... Defeat and rage were slamming their fists against the cage door that had just slammed shut in my brain... how did they find me?

CHAPTER FORTY-EIGHT
THE END OF THE ROAD

"**P**assenger, passenger, put your hands up!" one of the officers from the same Fugitive Task Force that had chased me before yelled. They had rolled out after all. Along with a dozen members from other law enforcement agencies, including the F.B.I.. My shoulder still hurting, I grimaced and growled under my breath; directing my angst toward the men aiming their guns at me from behind the safety of their cars.

"Passenger, comply or we will shoot!" another officer repeated.

Red was laying face down on the roadway where the officers had directed him. Stephanie, sitting beside me in the middle of the seat, begged me through her tears to raise my hands and act in accordance with with the officers' demands before I was killed.

I sat there, angry and disgusted; *stunned* at the sudden change of fortune. I finally shook myself and slammed my phone against the dashboard, not wanting the police to retrieve any incriminating evidence against those who had aided me in the escape. I then stuck my address book in Stephanie's purse and stepped out of the truck. I stood defiantly and challenged the small militia who were gathered and threatening me with their guns, locked and loaded, all aimed in my direction.

I haven't got a death wish, but my life's been one jail and prison cell after another and I have become completely worn out and disabused with crime and prison time. I did not want to be caught. I'd put a lot into this escape. To say that I was extremely angry and disappointed would not even begin to describe how I felt as I faced the men and the open bores of their guns. I flipped them off and yelled at them: "Just shoot me!"

One of the officers, whom I knew from a couple of years before, ran up pointing a shotgun at me. I turned and ran. I heard the '*Boom!*' when the firing pin struck the cap of the shell that was loaded in his shotgun, which caused the load to explode from the barrel as he fired. I was immediately slammed from behind as if I'd been kicked in the back by a mule. I was hit hard enough to knock me to my knees. It surprised me how calm I felt as I realized that the end had come. My mind seemed accepting and almost relieved that my struggles were finally over...

Then I took a deep breath. Amazed that I still could. I then tried to get up, to stand and fight as long as possible... To my surprise, I found my body responding. When I regained my feet, I realized that I hadn't been shot with buckshot. The shell had been loaded with a non-lethal beanbag. I took a few more steps and snarled over my shoulder as another officer ran up and pointed a taser gun at me. I saw him right before I heard the pop of him firing it also. I felt the jolt of electricity as the prongs that were attached to a twenty-foot electric lead embedded themselves into my skin. My muscles locked up, but I was somehow able to function enough to roll around on the ground and dislodge the wires from my back. Next came Draco, the police dog, who was either shocked by one of the loose electric leads or stunned by the under-the-muzzle slap that I'd given him when he ran up on me. Whichever it was, the grey and black German Shepherd stopped in his tracks.

Eventually the small army of officers caught up with me, pulling me off of the highway fence. They took me down, hitting, kicking and electrocuting me with a handheld taser that one of them had... We fought... The mob punched and tased me until they were actually starting to hit and shock one another, all wanting to get their lick in. They were trying to get me handcuffed and I wasn't making it easy for them. Then they wrenched on my shoulder! "Damn it... my shoulder... You're fucking tearing my shoulder out again!"

"What's wrong with your shoulder, Jimmy?" Captain Smith, the one who'd shot me with the beanbag-loaded scatter-gun, asked.

"I dislocated it falling off a fence earlier today. I reset it, but your guys are ripping it out of the socket again." I grimaced as I was speaking.

"Well, let us cuff you," he said. When I complied and was finally pronounced *'apprehended'* the stocky, grey-haired Captain told his squad to get off of me.

"We'll have the E.M.T.s check you out in a minute, Maxwell. Just hang tight," Smith stated as they were rolling me over to pull me to my feet.

It was like old home week. Everyone was there; all the officers from the Violent Crimes Fugitive Task Force that had hunted me two years before. Spradlin and the black detective, who I had received the twelve-year State sentence for assaulting during my last arrest and, coincidentally, the case I was escaping from, were right in the middle of it. With my hands cuffed behind, Spradlin and a short, dark officer I didn't know helped me to my feet. "Come on, Maxwell, you tough son-of-a-bitch. We'll try and get you looked at. Just so you know… I've got no hard feelings for you. You are what you are. Hell, if we were neighbors I could see us being friends," the big, white, bald-headed cop told me.

Not only the State had fallen out, but the Feds as well. Once again, the same agents who had hunted me before; Chad Hunt and a couple of others. What really surprised me was that even the Federal prosecuting attorney showed up.; not to mention an army of News media all out to get a shot of the high-ranking U.A.B. ramrod who had graced the State's Newscasts so many times over the years.

I was surrounded by a small militia as they moved me over to the side of the road past the red pick-up. They were just pulling Stephanie out and starting to search it.

When they patted me down they pulled a big wad of one-hundred dollar bills out of my pocket. "You were planning on getting out of State or maybe even the country this time, weren't you, Maxwell?" one of the officers grinned.

I said nothing.

Another officer came up. "Damn it, Maxwell. I like chasing you. You always give us a good run… and we know we're gonna have a fight at the end of it. Me and the others, we gotta lotta respect for you, Jimmy."

I was sitting there crushed; my heart heavier than it had ever been. My defeat so sudden and so unexpected, my future now looking bleak. I knew that I would not have another opportunity to run again for years to come and by then there would be no point. It was not in the cards for me to be free, it seemed. I nodded. "You guys are pretty good yourselves. How did you find me? This is almost uncanny."

"Good police work," he said.

"More likely someone snitched Stephanie's place out," I countered. "But I was sure that no-one was following us when we left there."

"Well, you should have known better than to go to Stephanie's house. We were looking for her from the start. Once we found out what apartment complex she lived in, with a little detective work it was just a matter of time before we figured out what unit. You split before we could arrive. Actually, our guy lost you because he wasn't sure if it was you and could not leave his post. We spotted the truck's description that he gave us on the Broken Arrow Expressway. In that... we just got lucky," one of the Marshalls admitted.

They held me on the grass shoulder of the highway while the E.M.T. cut off what was left of my shirt. They were looking me over to make sure the pronged taser leads were out of my skin as well as checking my ribs where the beanbag had struck me. Captain Smith made sure that they looked at my shoulder as well. The emergency technician said that it appeared that I'd gotten the bone back in the socket, but recommended that they take me to the hospital before they took me to jail, just to be sure.

While I was on the side of the road I could see that Red was talking to an officer in one of the S.U.V.s. Jamie and my friends had been calling periodically, checking on our status and progress. Apparently, according to police records, which also point towards Red's supposed willingness to cooperate with their investigation, a guy called J.T., a.k.a. Creature, who was a long time friend and Brother of mine, called Red's phone whilst he was in the police car. The report says that a female detective in the vehicle recognized Creature's alias when it came up on Red's phone as Jamie Tylor, and she knew that he was an inmate currently doing time behind the walls of the State Penitentiary. I heard later that J.T. and several more of my bros at the 'Walls' were rounded up and taken to the supermax for their alleged connection to my escape. No phones were ever found.

The police had gotten my daughter out of the truck and were in the process of arresting her. They had searched the truck and found a safe with ten grand and a couple of ounces of meth locked in the tool box. They also found a handgun in one of the bags. When the cops started talking about charging my daughter with it, I told the officers who were attending me that if they would drop the charges on Stephanie and let her go, I would take responsibility for whatever they found in the truck. Honestly, although I couldn't and wouldn't say it then I didn't know about the drugs nor the gun, as I said I hadn't asked. I hadn't been clean that long and I didn't want the temptation. I was drug-free at the time and I wanted to start my run for freedom clean and with a clear head. I had learned my lesson about trying to run with one foot stuck in the drug world the last time. Short of dealing with Ferret, the sole reason that my daughter was involved in this escape and now going to jail, I had no intention of ever committing another crime. I was done. I just wanted to be free, change my name and looks and blend in somewhere to live the life of an average citizen. That was my dream. But it was gone now and they were fixing to take my oldest daughter to jail for harboring a fugitive, possession and whatever else they could throw at her.

"Okay… listen," I told the officer standing beside me. "That shit is mine, just let her go and I'll make this easy on you. I'll plead guilty right here on the side of the road for everything that you find in that truck."

"We would be glad to take your confession, but we don't have the authority to make that call. Stephanie is being arrested now," the officer who was standing in front of me stated. "But before you admit that stuff is yours, I need to read you your rights," he went on.

"I know my rights…" I cut him off. "If you're not going to let her go, then I'll just be wanting an attorney." At that point everything stops, for those of you that don't know. When you are being brow-beaten into a confession, even a false confession sometimes, four words: I… want… an… attorney… guilty or innocent, are the only four words that should come out of your mouth.

Officer Spradlin came back over with the money that that they'd taken out of my pocket and counted it in front of me. "Looks like you were set up pretty good this time, Maxwell. I want you to see me count this in front of you. I'll make sure this gets on your jail account."

I said "thanks", but I knew that money would never make it to my books. The Powers That Be would find a fine or fee that would give them the right to keep it… somehow.

The E.M.T.s finally cleared me medically. The officers finished searching and surveying the area and the tow-truck showed up for Red's vehicle. The sun was going down and so was the temperature. I was glad when they loaded us up. The marshals put me in a cruiser with the cameras following our every move; frantically trying to get what they could up on the evening News bulletin.

I was transported to the Federal Building and chained to a bar in a holding cell. In another room, the police interviewed Red and my daughter.

After a few minutes with Red they realized that they may have a honey-hole of information. He was claiming to work for the Aryan Brotherhood. At least, according to him, pretending to cooperate, so that they would cut him some slack. Regardless, they moved him to another floor, completely out of my earshot. On the other hand, I could hear them with my daughter right outside and around the corner.

Stephanie, as I've said, is a petite little gal with a heart of gold and a sweet, heart-shaped face. But, that's where the sweet stops. From there on down she is a straight little lioness and is as loyal as one too. She takes no shit from anyone, not even from me. The more the police harassed and messed with her, the madder she got. I could hear them in the other room prodding her into a fury. I told the Captain to call his boys off of her. He did out of respect for me and things settled down until they started asking her to tell them that the stuff they had found was mine. Then she blew up all over again.

I could hear her yelling: "...the gun was not my dad's, it was mine!" They argued with her trying to get her to change her story, but she wouldn't back down. She was angry and frustrated to tears by the time they brought her back and threw her in the cage next to me.

"Honey, why are you claiming the gun? I know its not yours. The police said it was in one of the bags. That dude looks like he's down there cutting a deal, so why are you protecting him?" I asked her.

"I'm not protecting him! I'm protecting you! They said that they were going to put it on you! And you're too old to have to do more time." She cried out of frustration at the thought of my failed bid for freedom. She knew how my incarceration suffocated me.

"Stephanie, I would rather they put it on me than on you. You weren't doing anything wrong, just trying to help me. This is my fault."

"Bullshit - you wouldn't live through another fifteen year sentence," she went on, "and you're too good a man to die in prison."

"Well, honey, don't say anything else. Wait and see what this guy Red is doing with the cops. I don't know that it's bad yet, but it doesn't look good. We can't say anything about what was found, but we don't need to help this guy throw us under the bus if he turns out to be working with the marshals."

Sniffling, she agreed. "Yeah, they were talking to him. They separated us and took him downstairs an hour ago." I could hear the desperation in her tears and see it on her face. As devastated as I was about my own circumstances at the moment, it was far worse to hear the anguish in Stephanie's voice. I also hated what the fallout of this whole ordeal could be – for a lot of people – if this guy turned out to be dirty.

Soon they came and got Stephanie, who was still full of anger and spitfire from arguing with the detectives. She found the News media waiting when they took her out to transport her to jail. She blew multiple kisses at the cameras on her way down the hallway. I cant help but smile thinking about the heart in that girl.

The same media circus was waiting on me when I left as well. It must have been a slow news night, because I graced the evening News almost exclusively.

After taking me to the emergency room to find out that I had, in fact, done a good job of resetting my shoulder, the posse loaded up and took me to jail too…

They took me straight to *The Hole* this time.

~ □ □ □ □ □ □ □ □ □ ~

Bringing my thoughts back to the interview, I took the last sip from my bottle of water. Then I struggled in my shackles to set the empty bottle beside me on the floor before looking up at Sara. "That's how I find myself sitting here talking to you guys. My one chance to be free in this decade - blown away like Toto in a tornado in only twelve hours!" I said, shaking my head in total disbelief. I flexed my shoulder against my restraints at the memory of resetting it and the goon squad wrenching on it during the arrest. It had been a long story. I was stiffening up and my hard, plastic chair was becoming uncomfortable.

Brad gave Sara a signal, letting her know that there were only two minutes left of the tape. I looked around and saw everyone else shuffling a bit also, getting just as tired as I was, but still intent on the conversation.

Sara leant forward one more time and, after straightening her hair, she stared at me from behind warm, thoughtful eyes. "We're almost done for the day, but I have to ask… Your nineteen year-old son is on the other end of the hall in a cell just like yours. We're going to try our best to get you guys together, but in case something goes wrong and it doesn't happen, is there anything you'd like to say to him? Look right there in that camera and we'll make sure he sees it?" She nodded at Brad, who nodded back as if to confirm the promise between the two of them.

I turned and shot a fleeting glance at Tracy and the rest of the crew. I could feel the attention of the guards boring into my back. An overwhelming flood of emotions came rushing-up, not just for Brandon, but for all my kids... and for all the families suffering from fatherless tragedies. I looked directly into the big lens that Brad was aiming at me and fighting back tears I said in a cracking voice: "Son, I am so sorry that I wasn't a good father. A father who was there to teach you... and guide you... I love you Brandon, and I am sorry that I failed you..."

So it ends where it began... Well.. maybe not this time....

CHAPTER FORTY-NINE

REMADE

I spent a couple of months with Sara and the film crew. I told them this story and others. There are far better stories and there are far worse ones. This one is just mine, at least this part of it. They prompted me to write this book in the first place and the further I got along in it the more I understood what made me into what I am. The short of it, I was what karma had made me out to be... a damn fool whose foolishness had not only cost me, but every member of my family; in particular my youngest son - not to mention the devastated family of the woman who lost her life in that tragic, drug-induced accident.

Not long after I was back inside, some friends of mine paid Ferret a visit. They took him out in the woods and heated a knife over an open flame... then burnt the U.A.B. patch off of his neck. He is now a Federal informant. He played the sympathy roll with the government, saying that he lost his patch because he refused to sell drugs for the Aryan Brotherhood. Naturally, the prosecutors ran with his version and that's how stories of the evil Aryan empire that forces innocents into doing their bidding get started and blown into what they become. Bottom line, he was just another phony piece of crap who left a friend behind and in need, and subsequently paid the price for it.

Teddy got stabbed, again, and ran back to Tennessee where he'd came from for a time. I think now he's actually doing time himself somewhere. I guess you can't rat your way out of everything.

Mr. Big, my half-pint partner lived out the rest if his days in comfort with my parents, until he finally passed December the 26th, 2013. My mother told me he would still run to the window when he heard a Harley roll by – all the way to the end. Rest in peace my little friend, until I see you again.

Look, I know I may have come across a little heavy handed, maybe even slightly arrogant at times through-out this story, but I wasn't always a nice guy. And frankly, the people for the most part in this book aren't nice either. I did and acted the way I thought I had to, and to be honest you don't walk the paths I've walked without ruffling a few feathers and I'm now paying the price for my pride.

I gave up for a time when I got back to prison. Along with my escape case, I caught a couple of assault charges. I even fell back into drugs momentarily, which derailed me in more ways than one.

I was at Granite, a sinister-looking prison with a thirty-foot tall granite wall around it when I caught my last assault. They brought a guy in who used to be almost as high up in the Brotherhood chain as I was until he got out and molested his fourteen year old stepdaughter. He was a *'badass'* who threatened to take out anyone who confronted him. He had hurt a lot of people and committed much evil, so no sooner than I knocked him off his feet, Mutt and another Brother finished him off with a couple of pipes. Actually, he'd caused so much harm and hate that when he went down the whole yard ran up to put their boots on him as well. The excommunicated brother lived through it and after they sewed and stapled him up they sent him on his way to another facility.

Naturally, they immediately came and locked me up for the assault, while eventually identifying a couple more of the mob from the surveillance tapes. I sat in jail wondering about my life. I didn't think I was a bad man. I didn't want to be a bad man, but I guessed I was. When was I ever going to get it? Would I ever? I asked myself: was this all there was to life… God, I hated the cage I'd built for myself.

Tony Mac got the warden to let him come and see me in the hole. He drove three hundred miles to look his friend in the eye and ask me not to give up. He knew me well enough to know that my failed escape, descent into drugs and the assaults were the signs of a self-destruct sequence counting down. He knew I hated the chain around my neck and that I was ready to try to break free, even if it meant getting shot off of the prison wall. He was my friend; he pleaded with me not to do anything stupid.

He left sad.

On top of that, Brandon was in prison now, incidentally at Cushing. It had been unknown to me that in the process of searching for his prison 'identity' he patched out with the U.A.B.. Next thing I knew, he'd been stabbed. It took a while for me to find out that it was no more than a scratch, but the powers over at the Department of Corrections were scared of what I was going to do, or *have* done. They censored my mail, trying to keep me as clueless as possible. At that moment, it was probably wise. I was ready to tear the throats out of any rival gang member I could get my hands on. I soon found out that my son was fine and was actually laughing about how ridiculously the injury had gotten blown out of proportion.

How... I ask myself again, could I have let my family down this way? Why did I lead them along this path? Where would it end? My oldest son, Eric, was sitting at the walls with a fifteen year sentence. Stephanie was on her way back to prison and now Brandon. I had failed them all!

Sara wrote me to check on the progress of the book... "What progress?" I asked. She pointed out that I never seemed like a quitter to her and wrote: "If you were ever going to make more of your life, then now would be the time for it." Sara and me had remained friends since the filming and every now and then she said something that sank in and made me think.

However, what really brought me around was Karyn. Life is full of disappointments, more than joys it seems, but every now and then it still surprises me. I was sitting in the isolation unit twiddling my thumbs and planning - I don't know what. Almost ready to just give up and beat my head in against the concrete floor – speaking figuratively. Sara had said the 'Lock-up' show had aired, of course it didn't really mean that much to me, buried back in the hole with no T.V., radio or outside communication, other than letters, of which I got very few. I was not expecting anything when I was called up to my cell door and the guard slid an envelope through the crack to me. Even before flipping it over to see who it was from, I felt my pulse quicken and my spirit move in me. Don't ask me why, I don't know... it's like thinking of a song you hadn't heard in ages right before it comes on the radio. But, honestly, somehow, I knew before I saw the return address that it was from Karyn. Even though I sensed it before I saw it was her, I couldn't believe it! Twenty years, almost to the day, of meeting her on that Halloween night! I was almost overwhelmed with memories and emotions that I thought I had long-since put to rest. I was so happy standing there alone in that concrete box, smiling to myself so big that tears were forced from my eyes. I ripped the letter open:

> 'Dear Jimmy,
>
> I thought you had disappeared, I was soooo mad at you. I called everywhere and couldn't find you. Then I just happened to be flipping through the channels and there you were on a Lock-Up episode. I couldn't believe it, you've been in prison all this time! I can't explain it, but my heart started racing and I realized that I still love you... '

I felt the love I still held for her wash over me like a tidal wave. I just sat down on my bed, amazed at how the universe works sometimes; then I grabbed my pencil... I couldn't get her a letter back fast enough.

This amazing reunion reminded me that the forces in the universe are real. God is real... and that *anything* is possible. It's left up to us to be worthy. How can we expect great things, great loves, great miracles, if we do not carry ourselves worthy of them?

I wouldn't count myself a great Christian, but I know that God is real and I talk to him often. This book is not about that. This book is about coming full circle, getting real and finding yourself. Most of us that feel like we've been real all along, even though we may be so in many ways, are always the last to see what we really need to see... it's not a question of being real with who we are, but with who we should be. A real individual has the ability to decide what they want to be and become it, whether bad or good... The trick is to decide that what you want to be is a force for good. Not good at following rules or playing *'the game'*, but good at being a human being.

I have made some bad choices in my life and they have led me to a lifetime of regrets. Thirty years and counting of prison and three of my children currently incarcerated. It's time I started making better choices and be an example to my kids and others. An example of what can be.

One day I was sitting there, still in lock-up, writing the beginning of this book. The Warden, Deputy Director Baker and a couple of other big wigs over at the Oklahoma Department of Corrections were there from the regional office inspecting the prison. They just happened to stop by my cell. "Maxwell, what are we going to do with you?" the Deputy Director asked. "I've checked around the State and nobody wants you in their prison. Of course, McAlester will take you, but we expect you to cause trouble where ever you're at right now."

I stood there looking at them, deciding whether I wanted to expose my feelings or not. "Well… actually, it might surprise you where my head is at."

I went on to tell them that I'd had an epiphany and decided that, whether I was in or out of prison, I was going to do something positive in the world before I left it. We spent almost an hour talking about that. They walked away telling me it would be easier and a lot less risk to just warehouse me in a cell somewhere. However, it would be something to see if I really meant what I was saying. They left me with the notion that I would most likely be sent back to supermax and tucked away in a single cell for the remainder of my time, whether they believed me or not.

I sat in the hole four more months; every transport day expecting, hoping. to go somewhere - *anywhere*. Even back to high max, I could at least have a T.V. and radio in my cell. Where I was, I had nothing. My only bright spot was my letters with Karyn and writing this story of my life, which wasn't all that bad, but limbo is never a good place to be.

Finally… "Maxwell! Wrap up your bedroll, you're pulling chains in an hour."

"What? Hell, yeah!" I yelled. There was no sense in asking the guard where I was going. They wouldn't tell me until I was chained and loaded up on the bus, so I just jumped up and threw my stuff together. The people reading this that have had to wait six months or more to pull chains are probably the only ones that can relate to the happiness of leaving one penitentiary to go to another. Everybody was outside the S.H.U. waiting. They had heard that I was leaving. They waved and hollered their well-wishes to me on my way to the transport bus. As I was boarding, I asked the guard: "Where am I going?"

"Dick Connors… it looks like that warden over there is going to give you one more shot." *I'll be damned,* I thought; that was the same medium security yard where David Phelps had been killed - the yard that the administration there had said I would never be allowed back on.

When I got there, and as I expected, they met me with a committee consisting of the Warden, Deputy Warden, Chief and a couple of Captains, as well as a lieutenant or two. "Maxwell, you've had an interesting couple of years. We've got some good things going on in this yard now and you have enough stroke to either be a positive or negative factor. We know about your son. The whole State does. What are you going to do?"

"Well, Warden, as a father I'm angry with the individuals that my son was fighting with and I can't promise that I wouldn't hurt them given the chance. But, I've been contacted by people on both sides of the battle-lines who want this war ended. My opinion? I am a father who loves his son. He is on one side of that line with a long time to go ahead of him. He really didn't get hurt the last time, but if I don't lend my influence and support to those who want to stop this while I have the chance, and years later he either gets hurt or killed, what kind of father would I be? There's a lot of changes about me that you might be surprised by. Sometimes, giving someone a chance is the right thing to do."

I shook their hands, which was a first for me; not counting when I was getting out of El Reno and did so with Lieutenant Turnbull, which now seemed a whole lifetime ago. I walked out with a new perspective and a new mission.

Since I've been here, me and many of the other high-ranking members of both groups ended the bloody war between the two families. Those same members and me cracked down on the drug usage to help people overcome their addictions and solve some of the problems that come with it.

The Wardens have pulled several leaders, as well as retired leaders like myself, together from gangs of all races. By working together, we've helped reduce prison violence. We even put together a Speak-Out program for the new arrivals; intended to help them avoid the pitfalls of prison.

A group of us, with the help of many of the staff and a great outside volunteer named Rebecca Stowers, as well as Deputy Director Baker himself - yes, the same man who didn't know what to do with me - have piloted a dog rescue and training program. I'm training our first therapy dog - an American Pit named Chloe, who will hopefully be used in Veterans' and Children's Hospitals, due to her own story of trauma and abuse. Talk about turning things around...

I'm still an outlaw at heart. I do and always will follow the code that I'm old enough now to have helped write. I'm still very respected by my peers, so don't get it twisted. But I'm tired of kicking against the bricks. I've learned that, sometimes, instead of pushing the load away, you just need to carry it. Now, I'm working on that *'good human being'* thing that I was talking about. At the end of the day, that's what I want to be. That's what we should all want to be, then everything else will just fall into place.

I wish I could say that Karyn and me had been married by this time, but the marriages were pushed back due to some legislation. However, she did just get back to L.A. from flying down and seeing me for a three-day weekend. It was so good to see her again… She was just as beautiful as always and our emotions were just as strong. She is the love of my life. Our future is a ranch with all the rescue animals that we can save and I have vowed to build her a big, beautiful home to grow old in together, but that's another story.

Karyn and me are now waiting for the supreme justices, hoping for sentencing reform to ease up some of the heavy-handed sentencing that our Federal courts mete out. Whatever happens, I am determined that I'm going to be a positive force *wherever* I am; incarcerated or not.

An old sergeant in the County jail used to say: "Free your mind and your ass will follow."

I'm counting on it.

Yours truly,
Jimmy Maxwell
An American Outlaw

THE END

EDITORIAL NOTE

I will admit that I had my doubts when Jimmy Maxwell's manuscript arrived in my inbox. The thought of editing a manuscript for an author who was seven thousand miles away and without internet and phone access was a challenge that I was not sure I wanted to face.

However, I've been mildly active in prisoner welfare both here in the U.K. as well as in the U.S., so I thought that Jimmy's manuscript was at least worth a glance. I opened the Word document and that was it… I was thrust into the narrative and hungry to read more. Through my volunteer work in a London prison, I could see the verisimilitude in his words. I've also been to the supermax in McAlister, the hell-hole known as H-Unit, in my capacity as an opponent of the Death Penalty, so I was familiar with the Oklahoman penal system and the inside of an Oklahoman supermax.

But getting back to the narrative, I knew that as Jimmy's editor I would have my work cut out for me. His propensity for using anacoluthon sentences in the vernacular would be tough to punctuate to a degree that would be acceptable for publication, whilst his writing a first-hand account shooting from his hip meant that many of the rules of writing narrative that a seasoned author employs when writing fiction, such as characterisation, scene-setting and the architectonic three-act structure were lacking in favour of *'this is who I was with and this is what we said'*. So, what we lost in 'colour' in one hand we gained with immediacy and narrative truth in the other. This wasn't Hemmingway's voice – it was Jimmy's voice, and Jimmy tells it as Jimmy sees it. He judges people on what they say and what they do – not the colour of the clothes they are wearing, nor the décor surrounding them.

So, with that in mind, I decided to leave Jimmy's voice as it is and set to work making sure that Jimmy said whatever he wanted to say, however he said it, in a manner that would still satisfy the tough standards of the publishing industry.

I looked at those anacoluthon sentences and took a deep breath… there was a whole world of punctuation marks, capitalisation rules and other literary sundries that Jimmy needed to knock into his head pretty fast, and I had to show him from quite some distance away using the pigeon post.

I did not need to worry. Jimmy soaked up instruction like a sponge and never needed to be shown anything twice. In no time at all we were talking about prolepsis and analipses, amplification, cadence, dissonance, fabula and syuzhet along with countless other literary terms that most Literature graduates do not have in their personal lexicon. Most of all, Jimmy *understood* them.

As a former college lecturer myself, had Jimmy been a Narratology student of mine I would have been proud of his achievements and his unquenchable thirst for knowledge. Most of all, I was astonished at how swiftly he grasped concepts such as free indirect discourse and put them into action.

When I consider the manner in which Jimmy learned his craft, and the place where he learned it, the outcome truly beggars belief. It is true that he is my star student without ever having set foot in my classroom.

What I can also say is that this is Jimmy's first manuscript, and I know that it was impossible for him to put everything that he has learned about writing into a manuscript that he had already written. So, watch this space – the best of Jimmy Maxwell, author, is yet to come!

Mark Parham
London, England
October, 2015.

ABOUT THE AUTHOR

JIMMY MAXWELL is an author / convict currently incarcerated by the Oklahoma Department of Corrections. Although he retired his patch in 2012, he did so with honor and the blessing of those who love and are loyal to him, and still remains an extremely respected and influential member of the prison community on both State and Federal levels. – Justin Case

"My choices have cost me years of family, friends and freedom on the outside – plus a whole lot more – Let the bad choices I made be a chance for you not to follow my path". - Jimmy Maxwell

More books from this author: visit jimmymaxwell.net

Made in the USA
Middletown, DE
29 November 2018